S0-BBO-604

GREY OF FALLODON

GOSHEN COLLEGE LIBRARY
GOSHEN, INDIANA

FISHING ON THE CASSLEY, SCOTLAND
Taken by Dorothy Grey, 1904

Grey *of* Fallodon

The Life and Letters of Sir Edward Grey, afterwards Viscount Grey of Fallodon

by

GEORGE MACAULAY TREVELYAN, O.M.

Regius Professor of Modern History
in the University of Cambridge

WITH ILLUSTRATIONS

HOUGHTON MIFFLIN COMPANY · BOSTON

The Riverside Press Cambridge

1937

GOSHEN COLLEGE LIBRARY
GOSHEN, INDIANA

COPYRIGHT, 1937, BY GEORGE MACAULAY TREVELYAN

ALL RIGHTS RESERVED INCLUDING THE RIGHT TO REPRODUCE
THIS BOOK OR PARTS THEREOF IN ANY FORM

The Riverside Press
CAMBRIDGE · MASSACHUSETTS
PRINTED IN THE U.S.A.

B
G86t
DA
566.9
G8
T7
18273

INTRODUCTION

ONE day, shortly after the end of the War, Grey asked me to lunch at Queen Anne's Gate, on the ground that he had been reading my Life of his kinsman, that other Lord Grey who passed the Reform Bill. But, as I expected, our conversation ran at once into birds and Wordsworth, and never once escaped from those well-worn channels. No word was spoken of the Reformer until, as my host loomed above me on the door step, he remembered and said: 'Oh, yes, I wanted to talk to you about old Lord Grey. People used to praise him and Lord Althorp because they were such fine fellows and passed such a good Bill. Then they used to say it was such a pity that Grey always wanted to be away in Northumberland, and Althorp in Northamptonshire. But that was just the reason why they did so well whenever they were in London.' We both laughed, and I replied, 'If I live to know your biographer, I will tell him you said so.'

Nevertheless, though they both counted the precious hours that they could spend in Northumberland, there were differences between the former and the latter Grey both in character and in fate. The old patriarch of Howick had forty years of pleasant waiting in opposition, mostly spent in rural and domestic bliss, followed by three years of office with the resounding triumph that made his name immortal at one stroke. Edward Grey, after twenty years of great and quiet happiness, had eleven consecutive years at the head of the Foreign Office — years of agony such as none of his predecessors since Castlereagh had had to face — fighting the long losing battle for European peace, suffering the defeat of

August 1914 that darkened the rest of his life, then sacrificing his eyesight in his war-time service at the same post. When the long-hoped-for hour of release came, he returned to his birds, but he could no longer see them; to his books, but he could no longer read them; domestic catastrophes fell on him with pitiless iteration; and the trend of the world's affairs after the war baffled his hopes for the free and peaceful future of mankind. Yet so balanced was his mind, so serene and strong his nature, so vivid and lasting his powers of memory, that the long years of happiness which he had enjoyed before the death of his first wife in February 1906 were with him to the end, and a few months before he died in 1933, he declared that the happiness of his life had on the whole outbalanced the pain.

He was indeed one whom Fortune loved and hated out of the common measure. All that he enjoyed so intensely and suffered so profoundly, all that he undertook and endured and performed, operating on a mind and body of unusual strength, made him a nobler man every year he lived. His full spiritual stature had not been reached when he reluctantly took office in December 1905. Two months later his wife died, and his nature grew under the pressure of private sorrow and public care. His face, in youth beaked and bright-eyed like a hawk's, became like that of the king of birds. Men spoke of his 'sad eagle eyes.' At the close of his life all who were sensitive to the touch of greatness felt it in his presence.

In Edward Grey the craving for the country life was not merely a desire for happiness. If that had been all, his sense of public duty would have triumphed with more ease. But he was not, like most of us, merely enjoying himself in the country: he was exercising a rare talent, which it had been death in him to hide, a genius, akin to that of his friend Hudson, for the observation of bird life in a manner that combined poetry with science. His books have spread his knowledge and his feeling to thousands, whom he has helped to enjoy the purest and most lasting joys of mind and heart. The author of the *Charm of Birds*, *Fallodon Papers*, and *Fly Fishing* is in the category with Izaak Walton, White of Selborne, Richard Jefferies, and Hudson.

He had, indeed, two careers, as naturalist-author and as statesman of foreign affairs. That he greatly and avowedly preferred the former is charged against him as a fault by some, but not by those who served under him in the Foreign Office; and they, if any, should have the right to complain. But they bear witness that his preference never affected his diligence during the eleven years of hard labour that wrecked his health and his eyesight. After all he was not pinioned, any more than his birds on the Fallodon ponds; he might have flown off. If to be wholly without ambition is a fault in a statesman, he was guilty indeed. But in a man who remained so long at his post, it may be forgiven that he often prayed that the luck of a general election or a Cabinet crisis would restore him to the greenwood tasks he loved. He certainly felt the call of duty. Did he feel nothing else? Surely the exercise of great talents on great affairs gave him more intellectual pleasure during his working hours than he records in his private letters, more perhaps than he was conscious of himself.

His two careers had so little in common that it is not easy to write his Life. The only unity in the two parts of the theme is the character of the man — his strength, integrity, simplicity, his steadfastness in any purpose or policy once formed, and his perfect naturalness in every relation of life.

These qualities made him the notable representative of his country before the world as her Foreign Secretary; helped to give the British Empire and her allies confidence and unity at the supreme crisis of fate, and drew so much of what was best in America to help England; but these qualities flowed from the same well-springs of old English rural life which inspired him as a countryman, a naturalist, and an author.

In *Twenty-five Years* [1] Grey has given to the world his own account of his public career down to his retirement from office. And the publication by Messrs. Gooch and Temperley of *British Documents on the Origins of the War*, besides numerous similar publications abroad, have provided ample and almost complete material for the formation of judgment. Never has so strong a search-light been thrown on the action of any British Foreign Minister, as on Grey's up to August 1914. This biography has therefore few 'revelations' to make, but so far as possible I have printed letters that have not yet appeared in *Twenty-five Years* or in Gooch and Temperley.

For the later period of his Ministry, from August 1914 until his retirement in December 1916, I have been allowed freely to examine and transcribe the Foreign Office documents, including his private papers. The scope of this biography does not permit as full a use of these unpublished documents as will no doubt some day be made by historians, but I am, I believe, keeping back no relative new fact of any importance about his conduct of foreign affairs during the war. His most distinctive personal contribution to our policy during that period was his determination, even at some cost,

[1] Page references to *Twenty-five Years* in my text are to the *People's Library Edition*, 1928, 3 vols. The *Autobiography* frequently quoted in the early chapters of this volume has never been printed and has nothing to do with his *Twenty-five Years*.

not to quarrel with America; not to be wholly unjust to neutrals in contraband policy; and to work, if possible, with America, for the foundation of a League of Nations after the return of peace. To these principles he adhered during the war, as faithfully as he had adhered before the war to the policy of the *Entente*, and to the attempt, within its limits, to be on good terms with Germany. He had the quality of steadfastness.

The object of this volume is to present the man, his character as moulded by circumstance, and his life private and public. In his last days he expressed the desire that his private life, particularly during the twenty years of his first marriage, should be an integral part of any biography of him that was written with the help of his family. For this purpose he desired that his correspondence with his first wife should be at the service of his biographer; and for this purpose his intimate friends have trusted his letters to my discretion, with a generosity for which I cannot be too grateful. I am no less grateful for the assistance I have received from his colleagues and subordinates. So many in all departments of life have helped me for his sake, that I shall not endeavour to set down their names. I can only hope that their confidence will not seem to them to have been misplaced.

LIST OF BOOKS BY VISCOUNT GREY

Fly Fishing (Dent and Sons) (E. P. Dutton & Co.) First published 1899.

Fallodon Papers (Constable and Co.) (Houghton Mifflin Co.) First published 1926.

The Charm of Birds (Hodder and Stoughton) (Frederick A. Stokes Co.) First published 1927.

Twenty-five Years, 1892–1916 (Hodder and Stoughton) (Frederick A. Stokes Co.) First published 1925.

I am indebted to all these publishers for kind permission to quote from the above books. — G. M. T.

CONTENTS

BOOK I

FALLODON — THE COTTAGE — WESTMINSTER

1862–1905

BOOK II

THE FOREIGN OFFICE, December 1905 to December 1916

BOOK III

FALLODON AGAIN, December 1916 to September 1933

APPENDICES

ILLUSTRATIONS

BOOK I

FALLODON

THE COTTAGE

WESTMINSTER

1862–1905

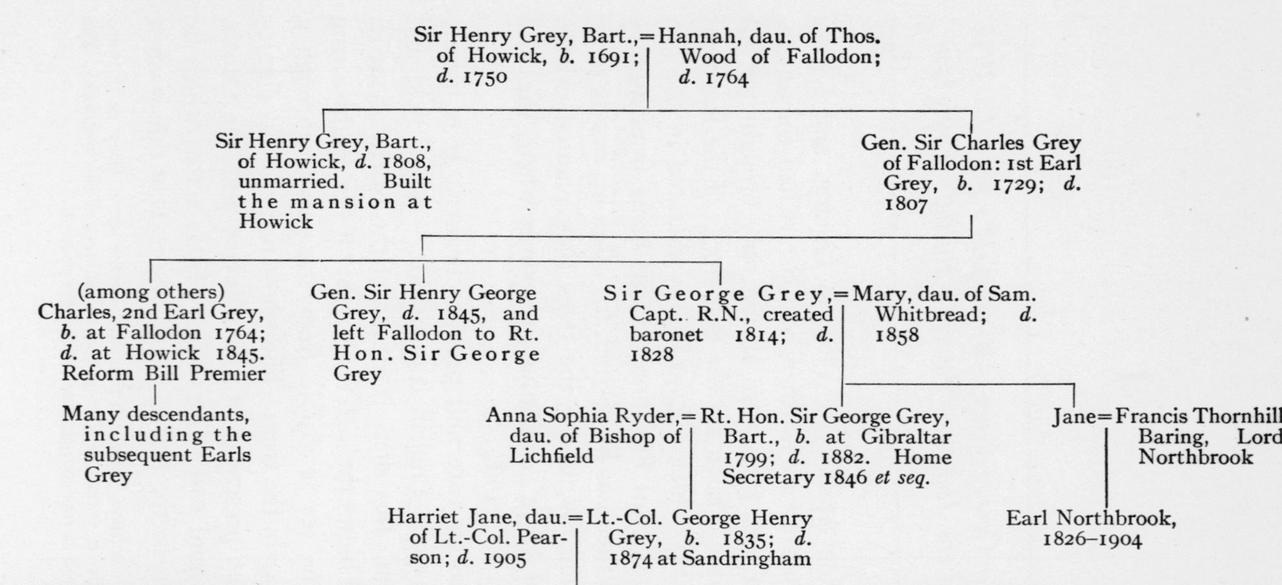

Sir Henry Grey, Bart., of Howick, *b.* 1691; *d.* 1750 = Hannah, dau. of Thos. Wood of Fallodon; *d.* 1764
Sir Henry Grey, Bart., of Howick, *d.* 1808, unmarried. Built the mansion at Howick
Gen. Sir Charles Grey of Fallodon: 1st Earl Grey, *b.* 1729; *d.* 1807
(among others) Charles, 2nd Earl Grey, *b.* at Fallodon 1764; *d.* at Howick 1845. Reform Bill Premier
Many descendants, including the subsequent Earls Grey
Gen. Sir Henry George Grey, *d.* 1845, and left Fallodon to Rt. Hon. Sir George Grey
Sir George Grey, Capt. R.N., created baronet 1814; *d.* 1828 = Mary, dau. of Sam. Whitbread; *d.* 1858
Anna Sophia Ryder, dau. of Bishop of Lichfield = Rt. Hon. Sir George Grey, Bart., *b.* at Gibraltar 1799; *d.* 1882. Home Secretary 1846 *et seq.*
Jane = Francis Thornhill Baring, Lord Northbrook
Earl Northbrook, 1826–1904
Harriet Jane, dau. of Lt.-Col. Pearson; *d.* 1905 = Lt.-Col. George Henry Grey, *b.* 1835; *d.* 1874 at Sandringham
(1) In Oct. 1885, Dorothy, dau. of S. F. Widdrington, of Newton Hall, Northumberland; *d.* Feb. 1906
(2) In 1922, Pamela, dau. of Hon. Percy Wyndham, and widow of 1st Baron Glenconner; *d.* 1928
= (1) *Rt. Hon. Sir Edward Grey, Bart., K.G.* 1912, *created Viscount Grey of Fallodon* 1916; *b.* 1862; *d.* 1933. Left Fallodon to Capt. Cecil Graves, son of (2)
(2) Alice Emma = Charles Graves
(3) George, *b.* 1866; killed in Africa by a lion, 1911
(4) Jane = Rev. C. E. de Coetlogon; *d.* 1926
(5) Rev. Alexander Harry, *b.* 1870; *d.* 1914
(6) Constance Mary = E. B. C. Curtis
(7) Charles, *b.* 1873; killed in Africa by a buffalo, 1928

I

Fallodon—Sir George Grey—Waterfield's School—Winchester and the Itchen—Jowett's Balliol—Creighton

'I WAS born on April 25th, 1862, in London, and I have always felt that my six brothers and sisters had the advantage of me in that they were all not only brought up but born at Fallodon.' Such are the first words of the fragment of *Autobiography* which Edward Grey dictated in the last year of his life.[1] But Fallodon was his home from infancy to death; and there, as he desired, his ashes lie, beside those of his wife Dorothy, under the trees they planted, within the 'fox-proof fence' enclosing the ponds where the wild duck fed from his hand.

Fallodon has no rare and peculiar beauty. It is merely a piece of unspoilt English countryside — wood, field and running stream. But there is a tang of the North about it; the west wind blows through it straight off the neighbouring moors, and the sea is visible from the garden through a much-loved gap in the trees. The whole region gains dignity from the great presences of the Cheviot and the Ocean. Eastward, beyond two miles of level fields across which he so often strode, lie the tufted dunes, the reefs of tide-washed

[1] For the sake of clearness, I never in this book use the terms 'Grey' or 'Edward Grey' without addition, except in reference to the subject of the biography. The *Autobiography* quoted in this chapter has never been printed.

rock and the bays of hard sand; on that lonely shore he would lie, by the hour, watching the oyster-catchers, turnstones, and dunlin, or the woodcock immigrants landing tired from their voyage.

Close at hand to the south, the ruins of Dunstanburgh Castle surround the top of a sea-girt promontory, save where the high basalt cliffs are washed by the tide. Into that ample enclosure the cattle of Fallodon used in old days to be driven for safety in time of Scottish invasion.[1] Eight miles to the north, the keep of Bamburgh rises against the sky, and on the ocean's bosom lie the Farne Islands — still the greatest of British bird sanctuaries, as when Saint Cuthbert lived there alone among the eider duck and tern.

And on the other side of Fallodon, to the west, rise the heather-moors, crowned by Ros Castle Camp, Grey's favourite point of view, closely overlooking Chillingham Park with its white cattle and the castle where his family had borne rule in the old border times. Beyond Chillingham, the green, rounded, Cheviot range hides Scotland and shelters this outpost strip of England between hills and sea. All North Northumberland is visible from Ros Camp, now dedicated as a memorial to Edward Grey.

In no part of the island are the distant views more spacious, nowhere else are the glories of cloudland more constantly unveiled. The sense of freedom and vastness, thus purveyed to the eye, is enhanced to the spirit by the tonic air, to a greater degree than in flatter lands or mountain-girdled dales. Stone farms and cottages, solidly and seemlily built, are scattered over the open country, which is protected from

[1] Grey told me that when, in 1882, he succeeded to the Fallodon estate, he found it still burdened with a payment of half-a-crown a year to the owners of Dunstanburgh in return for this old-world privilege. Dunstanburgh was a favourite place with him, from boyhood to the end.

FALLODON, 1884

the Northumbrian wind by many plantations and strips of beech, ash, and other trees. The denes, hollows and stream-beds hold wild vegetation that luxuriates wherever there is shelter. Outcrops of rock form lines of tall, fantastic cliffs, facing inland, and clad in bracken and wild growth. Such is the land that moulded the character of Grey, consciously ere long, unconsciously during his boyhood of rod and gun.

> The rivers and burns of Northumberland [he wrote to Ella Pease in 1892] go through three stages: first they rise in moors and run in a stony bed; then they go with streams and pools through a rich soil, sometimes between trees; and lastly the soil gets sandy, the bed is mud, there are nothing but fields, and the stream doesn't hurry at all because it has then such a little way to go, before it gets to the sea. It is the third stage you have taken in your picture and it's the sort of place where I used to crawl as a boy amongst burdock leaves to keep out of sight of the trout, and always caught eels and kept on fishing as long as the eels would bite.[1]

The disturbed state of the Border, that only began to improve after the Union of the Crowns under James Sixth and First, caused gentlemen in those parts to continue living in castles and peel towers till the seventeenth century. There are no Plantagenet or Tudor mansions in Northumberland. But in Cromwellian times or thereabouts, a Puritan merchant of Berwick named Salkeld built a small country house at Fallodon. And beside it he and his son after him planted a garden which became famous for its peaches, plums and pears. Already in the reign of William III a bishop wrote that 'the improvements in gardening and fruitery at Falladon are hardly to be equalled, on the north side of Tyne.' The

[1] See also his beautiful account of fishing in burns as a boy, in the last chapter in *Fly Fishing* entitled *Some Memories of Early Days.*

four high brick walls of this garden, built in late Stuart times, remained to shelter the flowers and fruit that Edward Grey so much improved and so greatly enjoyed. 'You can never eat too much fruit,' was one of his cheerful sayings, consonant with his practice in summer time.

The garden walls have stood, while the house has changed more than once. In the year of Blenheim, a certain Thomas Wood bought the small Fallodon estate, and shortly afterwards pulled down the Salkelds' house and began the building of that red-brick mansion with stone facings, which stood, well loved by many successive occupants, till it was destroyed by fire in 1917. After the return of peace, Grey erected the present building on the same site. Close to the house, Thomas Wood dug out, in the fashion of early eighteenth-century improvers, a 'canal' or long rectilinear pond, on the banks of which, two centuries later, Grey used to feed his wild duck.

Thomas Wood's daughter and heiress, Hannah, married Sir Henry Grey, Baronet, of Howick, who in that right became the owner of Fallodon on Wood's death in 1755. At that time Howick was only an old tower by the sea, and Fallodon was already a country house. Thenceforth, through nearly two centuries of change, these two places, five miles apart, were closely connected together, in the annals of the Grey family and of English public life.

Charles, the first Earl Grey, is the common progenitor of the Howick and Fallodon branches of the family. He had fought at Minden, been with Wolfe at Quebec, and earned fame in the long war of George III against Washington. He won the honourable nickname of 'no-flint Grey,' by the order he gave out, on the occasion of a successful night attack on the American lines, that his men should knock the

THE NEW FALLODON, 1932

flints out of their muskets and trust to the bayonet and a noiseless surprise. Fine portraits of him decorate the walls of Fallodon, together with those of other Greys in the red and blue uniforms of the two services during the old French wars.[1]

The general's eldest surviving son was Charles, the second Earl Grey, the Reform Bill Premier. He, like the other Earls after him, inhabited Howick, by this time a fine stone mansion amid its woods of beech stretching down to the sea. But another of the General's numerous children, Sir Henry Grey, lived at Fallodon, and dying in 1845 left it to his nephew, Sir George Grey, the famous Home Secretary of the middle years of Queen Victoria.

This Sir George Grey was Edward Grey's grandfather, and had probably more influence than any one else upon the formation of his character and ways of thought. The memoir of the Home Secretary, written by the family friend, Bishop Creighton, depicts a man in some respects strikingly resembling his grandson. A country gentleman, neither rich nor fashionable, devoted to nature and rural pursuits, popular with his neighbours of all ranks of life, wholly without ambition but constrained by a sense of duty to enter the wider sphere of national public life.

> Sir George Grey [writes Creighton] had a unique knowledge of the House of Commons and a unique influence over it. His influence was founded on the universal respect which his high character inspired and the affection which his genuine kindliness created on all sides. He robbed party politics of their bitterness. No one who heard him speak suspected that he had any personal end to serve, or that he was otherwise than entirely frank in his statements. He provoked no one to attack him, and none dissented from him without an apology.

[1] These portraits and much of the contents of Fallodon were successfully saved out of the house during the fire of 1917.

Sir George Grey resembled in religion and character his sailor father and his mother, a Whitbread born. All three were fine examples of those liberal-minded lay Evangelicals who did so much to found the greatness of nineteenth-century England. Sir George was the most successful Home Secretary of that era of appeasement. His calm, careful handling of the affairs of the Chartist Petition of 1848 allayed the panic of the capital, and helped to save England from any disturbance in a year so fatal to the peace of less free and well governed lands.

Between 1833 and 1874 he sat for several different constituencies. One of his elections was famous: in 1847 he astonished the political world by wresting North Northumberland from the Percy grasp — so popular had he become with the farmers, whom he canvassed assiduously, penetrating on horseback to the remotest homesteads of the Cheviots. But in the following general election of 1852 the region resumed its normal allegiance to Alnwick and the Conservative cause, and remained thenceforth lost to Liberalism, until in 1885, the extension of the franchise to the working-class in the counties enabled Edward Grey to repeat his grandfather's achievement and thenceforth to hold the seat during his whole House of Commons career.

Sir George's last seat was the Borough of Morpeth, in which after the Reform Bill of 1867 the dominant vote was that of the miners,[1] with whose aspirations for laws to better their lot he deeply sympathized. But at the general election of 1874 he retired, rather than stand against Thomas Burt, whom the miners that year put up as one of themselves, and who is remembered as the first and one of the

[1] Before 1885 very few miners had votes because, except at Morpeth, they generally lived outside Borough areas.

noblest of 'labour members.' Thenceforth Sir George lived in retirement at Fallodon.

> My Father [writes Edward Grey] had only one desire as a young man — to go into the army as his profession. This was not at all pleasing to his parents, who had both been brought up in a strictly evangelical atmosphere. My Grandfather [the Home Secretary] felt the Army, as it was before the Crimean War, to be an idle profession which would not make for my father's edification, and would not consent to his going into the Army. When the Crimean War broke out, however, my Grandfather thought it right to tell my Father that now there was opportunity for serving his country, the previous objection to his joining the Army must be put aside. It was a public-spirited decision, for it meant risking the life of an only child, but it was in accordance with what my Grandfather thought to be right, and my Father joined the Rifle Brigade and went to the Crimea; and after that his battalion was sent to India during the Indian Mutiny, and he saw service in both places. He was chosen as one of the first equerries to the Prince of Wales, afterwards King Edward VII.
>
> For convenience in combining his military duties with those of the appointment to the Household of the Prince of Wales, he and my Mother took a small house in London, and were living there at the time of my birth (1862). But as he was an only child, my Father's parents wished him and his wife to make their country home at Fallodon. In a short time my Father sold out from the Army, and having no other occupation except his duties as equerry to the Prince of Wales, he and my Mother lived entirely at Fallodon. As part of his allowance, the Home Farm of about two hundred acres had been handed over to him. He liked country life and all country pursuits. The farming was a perpetual interest to him, and he was fond of hunting, shooting and fishing. He wore a beard, but was one of the handsomest men that I ever remember. He was very good-natured, always in good spirits, and with that sort of manner which made him exceedingly popular with both men and women. He was efficient for all the ordinary purposes of life but had no intellectual interests and did not care for reading or any discussion such as politics.

> My Mother was one of the gentlest of human beings. She shrank even from argument and in order to make life go smoothly was always prepared to efface herself. This made it possible for the arrangement for a joint home between my Grandparents and Parents to work smoothly, and my early recollections are of an uneventful and exceedingly happy home. What we first know in childhood we imagine to be typical and the usual way of the world, and I was brought up assuming that the world was a happy place, in which no grown-up people did anything which was wrong.[1]

At nine years old Grey was sent to a small preparatory school near Northallerton. There were thirty boys, with one 'usher' besides the schoolmaster.

> The school was divided into classes, who stood up while going through a prepared lesson, and took places as they stood on the floor. No regular marks were kept. There was the same want of organization in games. There was a rough field in which we could play, but no organized cricket or football matches.[2]

Two years later, he was sent to a larger and better school, Temple Grove, East Sheen (1873–76), kept by a remarkable man, O. C. Waterfield.

> There were about one hundred and thirty boys, an ample staff of masters, a regular system of marks, and at the beginning of every month a board was hung up in the schoolroom with a full list of all the school and of every boy's place in his class. Now for the first time I could measure myself with other boys and feel the stimulus of competition. This was a spur to which I responded with eagerness.[3]

He rushed up the school and after one year found himself in the first class, which was frequently taken by Waterfield himself, of whom he tells us:

> He had a personality which gave him without effort a complete ascendancy over masters and boys and was one of the

[1] *Autobiography.* [2] *Ibid.* [3] *Ibid.*

AET. 9, 1871

best teachers I ever came under. I preferred home to school, and was homesick when I returned after the holidays, but the school had its own interests. I felt I was part of a going concern. There were organised games of cricket and football, and in my last year I got into the cricket eleven.

During this last year I was sometimes head of the school. My great competitor in this post was Monty James, now Provost of Eton. But he had a real gift for scholarship which I had not. He played no games, but was very popular then for the reasons which have since made him popular, as well as successful, in life. I have a recollection of him sitting on a bench at the side of the cricket field, laughing heartily to himself as he read Aristophanes for his own amusement. I would use my brain to make the best use of whatever was put to me, simply to excel in competition, without having interest in the subject or any natural aptitude for it. Monty James had both and in the last three months he passed me and had the undisputed headship of the school.[1]

Monty James's own recollections, allowing for due modesty, coincide with this account. Of Grey as a smaller boy, before they were rivals for the headship, he writes:

He wore a sort of Norfolk jacket with a belt, and knickerbockers. I remember his being called away by the death of his father and returning in black. I remember also his having a quick temper and I can see him chewing his pocket handkerchief and shedding tears of rage. Later on, some privileged ones, marked by a red cross in the school list, used to go to Richmond on half holidays to get provender, and I can remember going fairly often with Grey. I can also remember applying, with him, to Waterfield for a form of holiday, and being repulsed with severe loss. But I can *not* remember any revelations of youthful ambitions, nor any such cappings of poetical quotation as we find in *Eric* and *St. Winifred's*. In short I was not a close friend of his, but I believed in him and never forgot him.

Arthur Benson, also in the school at the time, recalls Grey as 'a sturdy, cheerful creature,' and the future Provost

[1] *Autobiography*.

'showing me an immense list of Roman Saints with mysterious symbols attached.' [1]

An event of lifelong importance to Grey had occurred, early in his second year at Temple Grove. His father, Colonel George Henry Grey, died.

> One afternoon, while I was there, I was told that a telegram had come saying that my Father was dangerously ill, and I was to go at once to my Mother at Sandringham, whither she had been summoned during my Father's illness. He was Equerry-in-waiting at the time. I travelled to Sandringham that evening. My Father was dying, and actually died in the night. [December 11, 1874.] I imagined his illness to be septic pneumonia. The drains at Fallodon were old brick drains, which had fallen to pieces and become blocked, so that the whole house was in a most insanitary state. My Grandfather was ill with typhoid fever at the time, and it was very doubtful whether he would recover.
>
> My Mother was left alone to face life with seven children. I remember one day of misery at Sandringham. My Mother was in deep grief, and I stunned with that sense of catastrophe which in a child produces continual outbursts of tears. I remember the Princess of Wales coming to see my Mother, and showing a sympathy which was much more than conventional, being a real understanding of my mother's grief and position. My Father's body was taken to Fallodon, and such was my Grandfather's condition at the time that the funeral had to take place without his knowledge of what had happened.[2]

One of Grey's sisters writes of this sad occasion:

> After my father's death, Edward looked on himself as my mother's chief protector, and I well remember when he returned with her to Fallodon from Sandringham his collecting us younger children together and telling us that she was to be our first consideration, that we must be very quiet and thoughtful, and do everything we possibly could to help her and be a

[1] Further details of Waterfield's remarkable school will be found in Arthur Benson's *Memories and Friends*, 1924, and in the Provost's own *Eton and King's*.

[2] *Autobiography*.

comfort to her. He was very stern with us. His thoughtfulness and consideration for my mother were remarkable in so young a boy, and he took his position and responsibility as head of the family very seriously.

Thus at twelve years old Edward Grey passed out of his father's care, and came more than ever under the strong and gentle influence of his grandfather. Sir George had just retired from Parliament, and he devoted much of the last eight years of his life at Fallodon to his seven grandchildren. 'He took my Father's place with us,' wrote Grey.

He was fond of reading aloud, and his reading was one of the pleasantest things I have ever heard. He read Scott's novels as if he were telling them, and his reading was delightful to listen to. He also read Spenser and Shakespeare's plays, and it was always in a natural voice as if he himself were speaking, rather than reading the words of others. He liked children to be with him and would ride with them every morning to favourite places in the neighbourhood and arrange to have something like an hour's reading aloud before lunch. These rides and readings were a great pleasure, and the day's work was always arranged so as to give time for them.

I never cared much for riding, being naturally a bad rider who was never on good terms with a horse, but I had a passion for fishing and shooting. The fishing at home and the shooting did not amount to much, but there were small burns and one little river, the Aln, within reach. There were a few partridges and pheasants, and the sea shore, and these provided the occupation for my holidays, even if the results of my efforts were small. So my holidays were very happy times.

My Grandfather was very religious, but his nature was such that he brought sunshine wherever he was, and was exceedingly popular in consequence. The difference between right and wrong had been his guide through life, and his old age presented one of those spectacles of a nature in which right had become automatic. In any problem he'd ask but one question — what was right — and follow it without hesitation. But he had no pleasure in being censorious. When once he had said,

'That is wrong,' or 'That is not right,' he had no wish to say anything more about it, or anything about the person who did it. We all felt not only his kindness, but his presence as a blessing.

Both he and my Grandmother were very sensible to natural beauty, and I have a vivid recollection of his tall figure and her short one, going round the path that went through the trees in front of the house, with gaps that gave a view as far as the moor at the top of Chillingham Park. They would make a point of doing this at the time of a sunset on a clear, fine evening.[1]

In September 1876 Grey went to Winchester.

I was sent [he tells us] to the House of the Reverend J. T. H. Du Boulay. It was a good house. The head of it when I went there was W. W. Palmer, now Lord Selborne. He was an admirable head of the House, manly and resolute, and with a sense of responsibility. While he was head of the house, nothing really wrong would be tolerated.[2]

I was placed in the highest class to which scholars were admitted at their entrance. My ambition was to press on. I went up the school very quickly, and in a year found myself in the division next below the 'Sixth Book.' Here a great change occurred. I had set myself to get out of this division in one term, as I had done in all the others. It was the rule for boys to stay in this division for one year before being promoted to 'Sixth Book.' I was quite unaware of this and began by going to a high place in the class. The master, 'The Don,' manipulated the class in accordance with the custom of the school, and put me on to construe at the beginning of one lesson. He kept me construing for the whole hour, asking me question after question, till at last, when this ordeal was over, I took my place very near the bottom of the class. I saw the unfairness of the proceeding, but not the reason which lay behind it, and from that moment ceased to do any work in this class. As far as my work was concerned, I was a changed being. Desire to succeed had been my motive for work. I was not to be allowed

[1] *Autobiography.*

[2] Lord Selborne writes to me (1935) that Grey 'was my study fag and our relations were most cordial.'

to succeed, and the motive was gone. The method of keeping me back in this class, which was the neck of the bottle leading to the Sixth, was the worst possible that could have been adopted.

At my third term in the class I was still sitting near the bottom, but the Master arranged that I should go up near the top, for an iambic, in which I afterwards discovered a mistake, and that once up I should remain near the top till the end of term, and so pass on to 'Sixth Book.' But the mischief was done; I had lost the habit of work.

In 'Sixth Book' promotion was mainly by seniority, and I made little effort to excel. 'The Don,' who took the lower division of 'Sixth Book' was Doctor Fearon. He was an admirable class teacher and taught with enthusiasm. He made a little anthology of English verse which, for its size, was as good an anthology as I know. This we learnt gradually by heart, and to some of the things in it I trace the first beginning of liking for literature, of which I then believed myself to be void. In spite of all, Fearon had a liking for me, which I remember with gratitude, and to him I trace some of the first awakenings of my intellect.

So my life at Winchester began with a year of brilliant promise which was then wilted by my experience in the division below 'Sixth Book.' But I was becoming a 'Wykehamist.' All that is conveyed by this word can be understood only by people who are Wykehamists. The ways of the place, its traditions, and the country in which it is set, were all getting a hold upon my heart, though not till afterwards did I realise all that had happened to me. But I had gained something which had become an inseparable part of my affection, which was part of my life's unalterable good, and Winchester, with the exception of my own home, in which I had been brought up and which remained my home through life, was the dearest place on earth to me.

From lower division 'Sixth Book' I proceeded to the higher. This was taken by Doctor Ridding, the Head Master. Ridding was not only a great Head Master but a great man. He was too big a man ever to be irritable; and in teaching he had genius, and I've always regarded the time I spent in Doctor Ridding's class as a great experience.[1]

[1] *Autobiography.*

Such is Grey's characteristically modest account of his own intellectual adventures at Winchester — the check to a purely competitive eagerness, followed by the slow budding of real thought, and of love for books and poetry for their own sakes. It will be well to compare it with the recollections of an admiring junior, Herbert Fisher, now Warden of Wykeham's other great foundation.[1]

> I came [writes Fisher] as a new man to Du Boulay's in September 1878. Edward Grey was head of the house, and on the strength of previous acquaintanceship my father, much to my consternation, for it seemed a most audacious thing for a parent to do, caught hold of a small boy and sent him into toy room to fetch Grey out into the road. A most brilliant and vivid impression he made upon my immature mind. I can see him now standing bare-headed as he talked to my father with the charming unaffected ease which his friends know so well and I remember how handsome and all alive he looked. As our parents had been friends he took me under his protection, made me his fag and was as great a friend to me as one of his eminence in the House and School could be expected to be.
>
> Grey was a 'jig' [clever]. Of that we Juniors were convinced. Though we believed that he did no work, we knew that from time to time he tossed off a copy of Greek or Latin verses which was marked alpha in Senior Division Sixth Book and we were ready to believe that if he had a mind to it, he could sweep the board of School prizes. As with work, so with games, he went his own way. The belief among the Juniors in Du Boulay's was that Grey could have got into Lords [the cricket eleven] as easy as look at you — but there it was, he couldn't be bothered. To us it seemed mysterious, that a man with such a genius for ball games, a man who without a scrap of practice could knock up 60 in a House match by most effective though unconventional methods, should have so little wish to excel in the game of all others which brought renown.
>
> But Grey was like that. He went his own way and thought his own thoughts. His heart was not in School games, much as

[1] From the *Wykehamist*, October 13, 1933, by kind permission.

he enjoyed them, or in building up for himself a School reputation for athletics. His heart was in fishing. So on 'half-rems.' [half-holidays] he would go off by himself to throw his fly on a stream of water in the upper Itchen, nearly always returning with a well-filled basket, some of the contents of which would be judiciously distributed among the Dons. 'Why, Grey, I take it that even a trout can sometimes rise,' observed Doidge Morshead, himself an angler often propitiated by the spoils of these expeditions, on one occasion when Grey came up to books unusually tardy.

He seemed rather solitary. We knew that his father was dead, but that there was a distinguished old grandfather living far away in Northumberland to whom every Sunday he wrote a long letter. Another fact about Grey was a matter of comment among us. It was whispered that he read English poetry for pleasure, and I think also, though here memory may play a trick, that we already knew that his favourite was Wordsworth. There was something in him which made him stand out from other prefects, a self-sufficiency and aloofness, a certain gravity mingled with his boyish high spirits and rich laughter. His tastes seemed to be fully formed, his mind to be constituted not in opinions, but in convictions. The vanities in dress, then much affected, made no appeal to him. So far as I can recollect he showed no interest in politics and never talked in debating societies. All these grave preoccupations came later, when, having gone down from Balliol, he was living at home in Northumberland and there came under the influence of Mandell Creighton; but our House-master always predicted a great political future for him, and we Juniors were certainly of opinion that Grey could do something big if he wanted.

Last spring [1933] when we were both down at Winchester for a meeting of the Warden and Fellows, we went over the old House together. It was an hour when everyone was up to books and we had the place to ourselves. We explored with great thoroughness every nook and cranny, Grey recalling with a minuteness which amazed me how things were in the old days, and I explained, since alas! his power of vision was all but extinct, the position of the studies, the toys [desks], the photographs on the walls and the arrangements in yard for small crockets [a kind of cricket] and fives, a matter as to which his

> curiosity was exacting. It was obvious that his Winchester memories were keen and precious to him and that it was a solace and pleasure to recall them. Indeed my belief is that his visits to Winchester as a Fellow were among the rare enjoyments of his final years.
>
> Save in politics he was a strong conservative. At Winchester the ancient ways were good enough for him. Need I depict his horror at finding that his old house went disguised under the name of Cooks. It was a crime more heinous than lawn tennis. That was bad, for it was among the articles of his philosophy that the hand and eye of a boy should be trained exclusively in hard ball games, but it was worse still that the names of the founders of the houses at Winchester should pass out of memory, when they could so easily be preserved. So, swinging with the strong tides of life, Grey was always at anchor.

Winchester gave also to Grey two things that became imperishable portions of his whole life — the love of the river Itchen and therewith the art of the dry fly. Close by the school playing-fields, between them and green St. Catherine's Hill, those sacred waters flow. The north countryman, accustomed to regard with contempt the sluggish and opaque streams of southern England, when first placed beside the Itchen or Test or any other of the downland streams of the same nature is astonished and enchanted to see a great volume of water, even in time of drought, clear as the becks of the Lake District, and rapid as they or as any peaty burn of Northumberland. On the patches of bright gravel, between the dark masses of weed straining at their roots down the rapid stream, the worshipper descries through the clear water great trout at rest on the bottom, or swimming with their heads against the current in order to remain stationary nearer the surface. These are to be won by the art of the dry fly, cast up-stream over the fish already discerned. But the angler's presence must be unknown to the trout, and the dry fly must seem to it a natural fly, in appearance, position and motion. 'The fly must float as if it were buoyant, cheerful and in the best of spirits,' writes Grey, 'natural flies having the appearance of being very frivolous and light-hearted.' The trout must be got to notice the fly and nothing else, for all the crystal clearness of the water. But I am no fisherman, and is not all set out with authority in chapters II and III of his *Fly Fishing*? [1]

This art Grey learnt as a boy at Winchester and was afterwards the first to introduce into suitable portions of rivers in the North, in the Highlands and in Ireland, where only the wet fly had been used before. His fame as a fisherman is specially connected with the dry fly.

> At the end of my first year, I reached a position in the school in which I was exempt from all fagging and all my spare time was my own, to be spent as I pleased. Fishing was more than a pastime — it was a passion, and one incident which I have not recorded elsewhere has dwelt in my mind ever since. It was a summer holiday, in the afternoon. It was 'names calling,' at which everyone was expected to be present to answer to their names. On a summer afternoon this took place in what was called Lavender Mead. I was on the other side of the river, having a last cast before hurrying round for 'names call.' Unexpectedly I hooked a very large fish. The crowd on the Cricket side of the bank gathered to watch the fish being played. There was a 'foreign' match going on, Winchester in the field, and the Eleven collected with everybody else to watch the fish being played. Fort was Captain of Lords at the time, and I remember hearing his voice saying, 'If the fish is not landed in another minute you must all go back to your places.' How I should have survived the loss of the fish I do not know. Happily all went well, and a large trout of three and a quarter pounds was safely landed. But nearly half of the school had been absent from 'Names Calling' and were, in

[1] And in chapter IV there is much amusing and interesting detail of his fishing at Winchester.

accordance with custom, sent for to explain their absence to Ridding. Ridding, who had seen the whole affair from the distance, received the explanation of the first few boys, and then dismissed the others, saying, 'Yes, yes, Grey caught a fish,' and it was certainly the greatest fishing moment of my life.[1]

But such triumphs in the school meadows were not easily won. That part of the Itchen was not in those days preserved, and owing to constant poaching the fish were shy and few. It was a hard school of patience in which he learnt the art of the dry fly. Fortunately there were other parts of the river sometimes available. His grandfather's nephew, Lord Northbrook, had just returned from his Governor-Generalship of India. He liked Edward Grey, and gave the boy leave to fish in his preserved waters near Itchen Abbas, five miles above Winchester. It is as good fishing of that kind as there is in England, and on 'leave-out' days he was regularly there and never failed to bring back a full basket. 'Those *leave-out* days,' he writes, 'were looked forward to by me as days of Paradise.'

Paradise it was, and still is, beside the river at Itchen Abbas. And there in the splendour of his young manhood, he was to build for himself and his wife 'the Cottage,' where, as will be duly related, not only his fishing but his poetic passion for nature and for the observation and recording of bird life reached their utmost expansion.

Grey's relations to Oxford constitute what would, in the language of our day, be described as a 'record.' After having been sent down for incorrigible idleness in 1884, he was in 1928 elected Chancellor of the University with universal applause. Since Grey, unlike many who have wasted their

[1] *Autobiography.*

time at college, could always work whenever he felt the motive, these fallow years did him no harm beyond opportunity for learning missed.

> The life I led was one of pure pleasure and was one of a kind that I could not have enjoyed at any other time of life. It led to nothing, but it left no scars, nothing to be regretted or effaced. It cleared the way for serious things.[1]

So he speeded the time carelessly, as they did in the golden world. How did he get through the pleasant hours? There was 'real' tennis, in which he played for Oxford. There was mild gambling at Loo, Nap, and a few nibbles at Baccarat, and occasionally boisterous ragging. But most of all the country joys beckoned him, with 'idleness horrid and dog-cart.' At the gaudy in Christ Church Hall, on the evening after the Encaenia of 1929, I heard him tell the great company assembled to do him honour, how idle he had been at Balliol, and how, driving back one day from Eynsham with an equally idle friend, he betted that every other tree by the roadside would be an elm, and won the bet. Alas! he said, how impossible to make any such computation from the modern motor-car on its rush through space, and how much better and more wholesome was the dog-cart as a method of idleness, although, as he told us, Cumnor was then the furthest common limit of undergraduate range. He knew those slopes, 'And what sedged brooks are Thames's tributaries.'

It was during this Oxford period that he came under the influence of two great men, Jowett at Balliol, and Mandell Creighton at home in Northumberland. Grey writes:

> The living of the Parish of Embleton, in which Fallodon is situated, is in the gift of Merton College, Oxford, and a very

[1] *Autobiography.*

remarkable man had come there as Vicar in 1875. This was Mandell Creighton, afterwards Bishop of London. He took certain specially recommended pupils in history. He had a great admiration for my Grandfather, and my Grandfather found the greatest delight in his society. There sprang up between them a peculiarly close friendship and my Grandfather asked Creighton in my first long vacation if he would take me as a pupil in Classical Moderations. Creighton replied that I needed no coaching for Classical Moderations, but he could provide the atmosphere of work only if I would come and live in his house. This was arranged, and I spent a month or two at the vicarage.

Creighton had wonderful power of concentration. He was at the time writing his history of the Papacy. In his study there were two pupils reading history, and Creighton would break off his writing in order to take them out one by one, in summer weather, to walk up and down the garden path and talk to them about the period of history of which they were reading, and then return to his writing again. I meanwhile was left alone in the drawing-room, to read books which were required for Moderations.[1] In this way I did read a certain amount during the hours which were set apart in the vicarage for work, and to this no doubt it was due that eventually, in the autumn of 1881, about one year after I went up to Oxford, I got a second in 'Mods.' More than this I certainly did not deserve by the amount of reading I had done.

I was now supposed to read for the Greats School, but the time for it was not due till May 1884. I had more than two years before me. The time passed pleasantly, but as far as work was concerned, quite unprofitably, until at last I found myself in October 1883 with only a few months to prepare for the School of Greats. I felt that it was impossible to do justice to such an examination on a few months' work, and I went and

[1] In July 1908 Grey wrote to Katharine Lady Lyttelton: 'So you read *The Times* hungrily from cover to cover! You are so much more suited to be a Cabinet Minister than I am. I am now as I was when I read for some Oxford examination in the Vicarage garden at Embleton, and got restless when I saw the gardener wheeling the wheelbarrow outside, and wanted to change my work for his, having "all my young affections out of doors." Some day when there is a storm and you are all hugging your houses and reading your Timeses, I shall take the road and be no more seen, and wander till I cease upon the midnight somewhere in the open air.'

explained the situation to Jowett. He was naturally enough annoyed and thought it incredible that I should have wasted so much time. I told him that in my opinion I could make nothing of Greats School in so little time as remained, but that I could do something by cramming Law. Jowett sent me to see Sir William Markby, whose special subject was the Law School. Sir William Markby naturally did not receive my opinion of the Law School favourably, but the matter was arranged as I wished and I switched on to Law. Another term passed, and I was still found to have done no work at Balliol. Jowett then sent for me and told me I must try if I could read at home. I went home and lived there alone for about two months. My grandfather having died in 1882 was spared the knowledge of how ingloriously my Oxford career ended.

When I was sent down from Oxford I lived the months of February and March entirely alone, but I was never dull. I bought my first five pairs of waterfowl, which afterwards became a great interest in life, and I remember finding extraordinary the opinion of one of my Oxford friends that I should have been bored at home, when on the contrary I had not been conscious of one dull moment. This fact was the first thing that gave me some idea that I was different from other people in this respect.[1]

And to this period belongs a story which shows Jowett in a light peculiar to himself. Though I was sent down he asked me to stay with him in one of his customary week-end parties and I had to leave the breakfast-table to catch the early morning train. Jowett in those days sat with his back to the entrance. I shook hands and explained why I had to go. To my surprise I heard Jowett's feet following me out after I had said 'goodbye.' In the passage he took me by the arm and said in a

[1] In 1917 he wrote to Miss Constance Herbert. 'I never remember, even in earliest years, being bored when alone.' The Naturalist, Mr. Seton Gordon, writes of Grey (*Nineteenth Century*, May 1934), 'In the year 1884 he was at Oxford, and as he was doing no work he was sent down for February and March. During those two months he founded the bird sanctuary at Fallodon. I wondered whether anyone else, sent down from Oxford or Cambridge, ever achieved so much during his period of banishment.' By May 1885 Grey notes that he had already collected seventeen different kinds of waterfowl on his ponds. He himself would never use the term 'bird sanctuary' for the enclosure at Fallodon, because it was for the use of mankind also.

> pleading voice: 'You will read, won't you? Please do!' then hurried back into the breakfast-room. That was the only reference he had made to my present predicament and the reason why I had been sent down. I have told this story because it happened to myself and bears no trace of the ordinary pungency of Jowett stories.
>
> Jowett was not a great talker, in fact he said very little, but what he did say was like the result of distilled thought with a sort of finality about it, as if it was an opinion arrived at after all excrescences of language and fancy and imagery had been cleared away, and only the real truth about the matter remained. It was as if he made thought visual. Many of the stories about him are misleading because they do not give the impression of the real kindness which was part of his nature. To merit which had real need he was really kind, but merit by itself did not necessarily appeal to him.[1]

The record in the Balliol minute-book, signed by Jowett is as follows (January 19, 1884):

> Sir Edward Grey, having been repeatedly admonished for idleness, and having shown himself entirely ignorant of the work set him in vacation as a condition of residence, was sent down, but allowed to come up to pass his examination in June.

He did return in June and took a Third in Jurisprudence, which, together with his Second in Classical Moderations of three years before, entitled him to a B.A. degree. But he neglected to take it and his first Oxford degree was his Honorary D.C.L. in 1907.

Grey had been idle at Oxford. He was never idle again. He was sent down from Balliol in January 1884. Yet that year and the next may be called the formative years of his life, both in intellectual development and in power of action. The moment he had left the University he proceeded to discover, by characteristically amateurish and unpretentious experiment, his genius for bird-observation in general

[1] *Autobiography.*

and for wild-duck culture in particular. He put himself, as his note-books show, through a systematic course of reading in history, thought and poetry by the best English authors. He entered official life in London and political life in Northumberland, winning at the age of twenty-three a resounding electoral triumph. And at the end of 1885 he married Dorothy Widdrington.

This sudden blossoming out of all his powers, this quick, serious, voluntary response to the call of duty at an unusually early age, may be ascribed in part to the influence of Creighton, and in part to the fact that his grandfather's death had left him the head of a family of young brothers and sisters, a Baronet and owner of a small estate of two thousand acres with an honourable name and tradition to maintain; his new and responsible position was brought home to him as soon as he had finally left Oxford for Northumberland. But, most of all, the ripening in due season was the result of his own intrinsic nature and quality of mind.

II

Entry into Official and Political Life — The Member for North Berwick — Journal of 1885: On Gladstone and Others — Dorothy Widdrington — Marriage — Politics to 1892

Up to the moment of leaving Oxford, Grey had never made a public speech — no, not even at the Union — and he had taken scant interest in politics. He had been brought up in a Liberal atmosphere but was not yet specifically a Liberal. When Lord Frederick Cavendish was murdered in 1882, he sympathized with the popular outcry for martial law for Ireland, but was brought up short when his grandfather, the old Home Secretary, said 'martial law is the suspension of all law' — one of those unargued, casual rebukes which, when uttered by a man of character and experience, sometimes impinge on the waxen mind of youth and leave a lasting impress.

But when in 1884 he found himself back at Fallodon as his grandfather's successor, the family sense of public duty was aroused. That summer, of his own initiative, he asked his friendly kinsman, Lord Northbrook, then First Lord of the Admiralty in Gladstone's Cabinet, to get him some 'serious and unpaid employment.' And so, at the age of twenty-two, he began public work as private secretary to Sir Evelyn Baring [1] at a conference in July, and in October as private secretary to Childers, Chancellor of the Exchequer. That autumn he resided with his mother and sisters in London, to perform his duties at the Treasury, which brought him into personal contact with political and governmental life, and with the famous men of the party from Gladstone downwards.

But already, before he began service under Childers, he had been drawn into party and platform politics in Northumberland by his sudden interest in a great public question. In July 1884 the Lords refused to pass the government's Bill to enfranchise the working classes in county constituencies, on the ground that it ought to be accompanied by an agreed Redistribution Bill. An agitation against the Lords broke out all over England. Liberal squires were not common in North Northumberland, and the young, untried Baronet of Fallodon was asked to take the chair at a demonstration in Alnwick. 'A common sense of fairness, and a feeling that the people among whom I had been brought up, and my own neighbours in the country, ought to have what had been given in the towns in 1867, made me accept.' [2]

A first public speech is a serious matter for a lad of twenty-two, especially when the eyes of all men in his own countryside are fixed on him at a moment of high political excitement. But a sage counsellor was at his elbow. Creighton was at that time an active Liberal — not a usual activity for a parson in a rural district in those days. I remember that a few years later one such was known as 'the blue priest' *par excellence* — blue being the Liberal colour in Northumberland. But Creighton came over from the Vicarage to Fallo-

[1] Afterwards Lord Cromer. It was then, he tells us, that he formed his lifelong admiration for that great man.

[2] *Autobiography*.

don, and there in the library Grey rehearsed his first speech with no audience save the historian of the Papacy. 'He said it was exactly the right thing for me to say.' The dog-cart was again brought into requisition, not this time for the mere counting of elms, and as Grey wrote to Mrs. Creighton, 'We drove into Alnwick together from Fallodon; he spoke at the meeting also and pleased the people very much.' [1] But the young Chairman's speech had been the success of the evening. Thus was Grey stamped and sealed a Liberal.

So favourable was the impression made by this first public appearance, that a movement was set on foot to put up 'Sir Edward' as the Liberal candidate. Since his grandfather's defeat in 1852, North Northumberland had remained Conservative, but the new franchise would put a new face on matters there as in so many other county seats. Why should not Grey beat Percy again? There were rivals for the Liberal candidature and the party's choice dragged on undecided for many weary months. Grey's diaries for 1885 show that the person who principally persuaded him to stand and principally urged the desirability of selecting him on other Northumbrian Liberals was my grandfather, Sir Charles Trevelyan of Wallington. His activity in this matter may be called his last act of public service. He died in 1886. He had been a friend of Sir George Grey and a frequent visitor at Fallodon.

Edward Grey refused all offers of seats elsewhere, and in the summer of 1885 he was at length selected as candidate. Then began the round of nightly meetings in far separated hamlets, and visits to remote farms and cottages, which in the pre-motor age kept him constantly on the road. He usu-

[1] Letter to Mrs. Creighton, April 25, 1902. The letter goes on to deny the absurd story that was put about in the election campaign of 1885 that Creighton wrote his speeches! In fact Grey's politics became that year too Radical for Creighton.

ally managed to get back in the dog-cart to Fallodon late at night, often soaked to the skin. In his later elections, he covered much ground on the machine now designated as a 'push-bike,' which he used for pleasure and business on the long roads of Northumberland.

The strong Presbyterian element in the Border region was on his side. The fishermen, hinds and shepherds were grateful to the Liberals who had given them the vote, and they liked the young man, and understood and trusted what he said.

Indeed his method of speaking, destined to win the confidence of greater audiences on more fateful occasions, was admirably suited to the country folk of Northumberland. Though carefully prepared, his speaking was in its method of delivery like the very good conversation of a friend and neighbour telling one what he really thinks. To some kinds of people such speaking is more persuasive than oratory with its flinging about of arms and epithets and appeals to the Almighty as umpire of our unhappy politics. Oratory depends for its effectiveness on the spice of temper, real or assumed, that makes it dangerous. But Grey's speaking was discussion, that never blazed into anger, and only sometimes warmed into eloquence.

> During much of the summer and autumn of 1885 I was engaged in making speeches in village after village. I had no difficulty in making a speech when I had anything to say: then speaking was merely a matter of arranging one's material. But to find new material for speeches was a most wearisome matter, and I soon became nauseated by it. I expressed this opinion once to Professor Bryce (afterwards Lord Bryce). He replied, 'Oh, you need not be disturbed as long as you feel like that. The time to become alarmed is when you find that you can speak quite easily without having anything to say.' [1]

[1] *Autobiography*.

When Grey won the seat from Lord Percy at the general election of November 1885, it was the end of an epoch for political Northumberland. Some of the landowners could not submit with a good grace to the loss of power that they had exercised at elections since time immemorial, and on some great estates cottagers suspected of having used their newly acquired votes for Grey were turned out of their homes. But he had won the lasting affection of a strong-hearted folk not easily dragooned, slow indeed to accept new friends, but, once they gave their confidence, not quick to change. The feeling for him in the Berwick Division, as North Northumberland was now officially called, was personal as well as political, and increased year by year. In the local language, 'they thought that tarrable of Sir Edward.' He never lost the seat, not even during the long years of Liberal depression that followed the adoption of Home Rule. Grey, who 'revered the permanencies of Nature and life,' found in the ever-lengthening political connection between himself and his rural neighbours a bond not lightly to be broken. He would have had fewer affinities with a city population, or with the 'Celtic fringe' that has so often given refuge to Liberal statesmen in distress. But these North-English children of the soil, accustomed to think and act each for himself, had many of those qualities that endeared democracy in the person of the Lakeland shepherds to the youthful Wordsworth. Grey, in his first election campaign, wrote to his fiancée Dorothy Widdrington, 'Really the people of the Cornhill district, farmers and labourers alike, are excellent specimens; it is quite a pleasure to meet them, good-humoured, shrewd and honest almost to a man.'

His response to the faithfulness of such a people to himself, and his knowledge that 'the local organization was kept alive practically without pay, by the enthusiasm of our Liberal workers,' helped to restrain the promptings of half his nature to be done with politics. At every fresh election from 1886 to 1905 he and his wife indulged what they called 'the coward hope' that defeat would set them free. He would gladly have accepted such manumission, nor sought to creep back any other way into Parliament. But he could not refuse to represent his neighbours; he had not the heart to wound the love and reject the services that were so freely offered him at each successive contest. 'It was the constituency that kept us in public life,' he wrote.

From January to June 1885 Grey kept a private journal in which he recorded from day to day the books he read, the feelings he experienced and the opinions he formed. Some quotations from this intimate diary of the boy turning into the man throw light on his rapid growth at this period. One of the earliest entries, in January 1885, records his progress during the previous half year:

> When I came to Fallodon last June I looked forward to idleness till February. Instead of that I have had much political experience and work as a Private Secretary to Sir E. Baring at the Conference in July (1884) and to Mr. Childers since October. Official life has given me business habits, and I have got some idea of the wheels of the political machine and how they work. I have made five speeches but only two political ones: [1] before August I had never opened my lips in public or private in a speech. Last June I had hardly formed one political idea: now ideas have formed and are forming daily. Then I knew no Political Economy: now I have even got glimmerings of original ideas on it. In June I cared little for Music, and not at all for Poetry, Nature or Art: now I have strong feelings about them all. I have dipped into Ruskin with

[1] He had not yet been chosen candidate for the Berwick Division.

great pleasure, and I have read and even committed to memory a good deal of poetry. I have enjoyed a good deal of sport but it has become a recreation, and the consuming interest I felt in it is now employed in carving my way into Politics, Social Problems, moral philosophy and culture. Oh! if I could only progress every year by such strides as this! But the baby which puts on fourteen pounds of weight its first year may only put on seven pounds its second year, and will certainly not manage the fourteen pounds its third year.

January 8, 1885. Enjoyed my three days' shoot immensely: but all sport leaves a kind of dust and ashes taste behind it. Political, Literary and Aesthetic pleasures never seem to leave off, but sport comes to an end each day. When I look back on one 'hot corner,' it merely makes me impatient for another tomorrow. On the other hand when I read a charming book I enjoy as I read, a more soothing and less fiery enjoyment certainly, but yet more complete and more all-pervading than that afforded by sport. When I leave off reading, passages and ideas remain with me, which seem to spring to life in my mind, and so enjoyment of this kind is an ever abiding companion with me.

The young hedonist had not yet realised that in the observation of nature and bird-life he would find pleasures as pure and lasting as those to be drawn from books, yet with the advantage of being as 'out-of-doors' as sport itself. But the diary of 1885 is full of instances of his intense feeling for the beauty and the vitality of Nature.

If he cared less for shooting than for fishing, he cared least of all for hunting; but during this winter he met his future wife, Dorothy Widdrington, in the field, and was at once drawn towards her. She, however, had still a high disdain for all young men, and said to one of her girl friends that he was the sort of man the Swiss would call *l'héritier Anglais*. Dorothy, no doubt, is the secret of the following entry in Grey's journal:

January 23, 1885. I was to have hunted at the Kennels, but frost stopped me: very provoking and I was much annoyed: perhaps in my heart of hearts more at the loss of the company I hoped to meet out hunting than of the sport itself.

Meanwhile the tale of books read continues daily: Vergil, Tennyson, Wordsworth, Mill's *Political Economy*, Milton, More's *Utopia*, George Eliot's Life, *Progress and Poverty*, Seeley's *Expansion of England*.

A little of Charles Lamb's *Essays of Elia*. A very idle day indeed and went to sleep at 9.30.

March 24, 1885. Albert [Grey, of Howick] came to see me at the Treasury: says my chances for North Northumberland are ruined by my unsound Radical views as to fixity of tenure and fair rents. Everyone [including Creighton] is down upon me for this and I should like to throw up the whole game. Am feeling low in health and depressed and so inclined to distrust my own views. In fact I am doubtful whether, if land had a fair start, my views would be absolutely right in theory, but considering past legislation, such as Irish Land Bill, Agricultural Holdings Act, Hares and Rabbits Bill, and considering the temper of the mass of the people, and the accumulation of evil of hundreds of years of bad land system, I believe I am, if not literally right, at any rate on the right tack.

April 6. The Bank holiday seemed most successful today. I saw crowds of people, especially children, in St. James's Park, and not one unhappy face amongst them. But for how few hours in each year are most of them as I saw them today! Surely it would be possible to secure that it should be so to more of them more often, say a few hours in each day. And if so it is a fit object to which to devote a man's energies. Moral progress, social progress and better distribution of wealth, these are the objects to keep in view, which ought to rouse men in my position to labour.

Yet the great Radical champion of the day did not wholly please him:

April 28. Chamberlain spoke at Eighty Club Dinner. A powerful speech and immensely clever. But it was unfair. He

> criticized Goschen keenly and admirably, but he made no allowance for his sincerity, his unselfish labour and his individual character. He apparently understands nothing of the motives and disposition of the men who are less advanced than himself, and a man of really large sympathy could hardly be so unfair, so harsh and so one sided as he is. I seconded the vote of thanks.

This criticism, strange in a very young politician listening to a fine fighting speech on his own side, throws more light on the man who made it than on the leader whom he censured — who was what he was, and that not all hardness.

Grey, always primarily interested in the perfection of character and personality, was never contented either with himself or others, and was not given to hero-worship; among public men his own intimate friend, Haldane, ere long came nearest to his ideal. Of Gladstone he has much to say. 'I have no doubt,' he wrote at the end of his life, 'taking force of character, energy and intellectual power combined, that Gladstone was the greatest man in whose presence I have ever been.' But he never passed uncritically beneath the spell.

> *February* 19, 1885. I think Gladstone's manner and speech last night shows up one of the great flaws of his character most painfully. His great eloquence has generated a certain egotism in him and this has become a sore point. With all his enthusiasm for a principle and a cause, he has come to identify himself with that cause. He is angry with the cause or principle if it fails, because he can't bear to allow himself to fail. So now he is half angry with himself for having let Gordon go out, half angry with Gordon's fanatical chivalry for so putting his plans about by staying at Khartoum and getting killed. He won't confess to the first feeling and he daren't utter the second. Yet he had to say something, and the result was a sullen and embarrassed refusal to apologise for himself or even to give credit to the merits of Gordon, our Army and the Colonies. He began with a defiant assertion that, spite of all

facts to the contrary, circumstances in Egypt and the Soudan hadn't modified his policy one jot from what it was two years ago. And then left all the eulogy of Gordon, troops and Colonies, one bright spot amid the awful gloom, to be set forth by Sir Stafford Northcote, his opponent.

April 19. Gladstone is no foreign politician, but his faults in that direction are negative rather than positive. He is absolute in Home Policy, and expects to be so, but he looks to his Cabinet for Foreign Policy, while his Cabinet, accustomed as it is to worship his Home Policy, is incapable of taking the strong initiative which he, unconsciously perhaps, desiderates in Foreign Policy.

The last entry in young Grey's journal records 'an hour's conversation with Mr. Gladstone after dinner.'

He quite fascinated me, not by his cordiality or condescension or manner or ability, but simply by his immense personal character. Such an opportunity was of course not to be lost, and I put my own case from a young man's point of view, particularly dwelling on the disturbing effect of the first plunge in politics — finding that everyone attributed to everyone else some secret and low motive other than appeared on the surface. He quoted Lord Aberdeen, who, he said, never did so, and then asserted that a belief in other persons' honesty (except where actually proved to the contrary) combined with honesty in oneself would tell, and end in success. Many reflections occur to me on this, but I leave the sentiment, coming from such a man, to stand untouched. In after years I may, perhaps, weigh it and judge its truth.

Mr. Gladstone also strongly advised an early entrance into Parliament. I stated my difficulty as having to declare my own individual opinions at twenty-three, against those of other candidates; this he recognised. He strongly advised political life, yet only today I was saying how much nobler a being, how much more exalted in the everlasting sense of the word Mr. Gladstone would have been if he had not been subjected to the influence of politics. And I think so still.

That entry was made under the date June 5, 1885, and it is the last. For on the same day he notes: 'Went to Sir J.

Pease's for Lawn Tennis, only young people there: Dolly Widdrington amongst others!' A brief courtship followed, too breathless for notification in a diary, and in July they were engaged. *L'héritier Anglais* had revealed unexpected qualities of mind and soul, not perceived at the covert side. Henceforth he had no further use for a note-book as confidant, but his biographer finds a fair equivalent for the journal in the letters that for twenty years he wrote to Dorothy, on every day that they suffered separation.

> It was during this period that the greatest change of my life occurred; my engagement and marriage to Dorothy Widdrington. The Widdrington home was at Newton, south of Alnwick, about sixteen miles from Fallodon. In those days of horses it was practically out of reach. We were in the habit of going to Alnwick a distance of sixteen miles there and back; but houses on the other side of Alnwick which involved a drive of over twenty miles to get there and back, were outside driving distance. But the Creightons had been in the habit of going to stay at the Widdringtons, and of having the Widdringtons to stay with them, and they spoke frequently of the uncommonness and character of Dorothy Widdrington. Her parents had taken her up to London already once to give her a London season, and had thrown her in the way of young men. None of these had interested her, and she had kept them all at arms' length. Stirred by what I had heard of her, and by what I saw, I made advances when we met in the hunting field: but to her I seemed like any one of the other young men she had met, and I was kept at the same distance. But in 1885 when I was in London we met under circumstances which enabled us to talk and to get to know each other.[1]

They were married at her home at Newton-on-the-Moor, on October 20, 1885. He was in the last stage of his first electoral campaign, into which she threw herself with eager sympathy. Her father was a moderate Conservative, but the chief influence upon her mind had been that of Creighton.

[1] *Autobiography.*

One of Grey's letters to her, a month before their marriage, will help to give a picture of him as he then was.

September 7, 1885. I drove to Belford to meet the Liberal Association and thank them for having chosen me as their candidate. On the way a wasp flew into my collar and stung me in the neck, which was untoward. I do hate wasps with a bitter hatred; they eat up all one's wall fruit, they come buzzing round one for no earthly reason whatever, they play the fool by getting into one's boots and shoes or flying stupidly against one's neck, and then sting one, as a fool, when irritated at his own folly, sometimes turns and rails at someone else rather than own himself a fool as he is. Whether it was the wasp or not I don't know, but I was thoroughly bored with my meeting. To be sure the people drivelled badly about Disestablishment and the opening of museums on Sundays, etc., but I ought to have done better than I did. I drove one of the carriage horses in the dog-cart back to Fallodon and at times we simply flew along; the wheels hardly seemed to touch the ground and I did the ten miles home in an hour easily.

This evening I had the blue devils badly: dinner had been altered to 7.30 and I sat reading till I found dinner announced and the room full of girls in evening dress. I bundled them in to dinner, went up to put on the costume of the universal waiter and came down grumpy and late. Afterwards however they gave me some ravishing music, the blue devils fled and I enjoyed the music more than anything without you since we first confessed that we were necessary to each other. I am a little annoyed with myself when I think how fearfully subject I am to moods: how dependent I am on external influences to affect my mood. I have to fly humbly to the help of Nature, music, books or fellow-creatures to ensure my being in the mood I wish.

I have been reading *Othello* tonight. Relentless Shakespeare! When once the plot begins to thicken, he makes all the characters proceed steadily to their tragic end, without one relieving check, till one almost cries out to him to give at least one scene's breathing space. But it makes one feel big as one reads, and is conscious what great emotions one can contain. And if it is so wonderful to receive such conceptions second-

> hand, what must the man have felt who actually conceived and worked them out. I should like to have watched Shakespeare writing one of his most powerful passages.
>
> Don't you feel for Othello when he says of Desdemona
>
> 'There, where I have garnered up my heart,
> Where either I must live or bear no life'?
>
> I believe however busy, however active, however flustered a man may be with the battle of life, he is always looking for some place, where he may lay his inner heart, his soft and tender nature in safety; else there is danger that he may lose it altogether or find it injured in the rough struggle. Such a place he finds in a woman, and when he really loves, he confides it all to her freely without reserve.

His union with Dorothy had so great an influence on the growth of his mind and character and in particular on his relation to Nature and bird-life, that it will be best to treat the subject in a separate chapter, and to be content here to record the external events of his political career up to the moment of his first taking office in 1892.

In 1886 Gladstone proposed Home Rule and broke up the Liberal Party. Grey, already a member of Parliament, chose the Home Rule side, less, as he tells us, on the authority of Gladstone than by convictions derived from John Morley's articles in the *Pall Mall Gazette*: that 'coercion was not, under modern conditions, possible as a permanent system of governing Ireland,' and that 'the only alternative was Home Rule.' During the next few years Morley's clear-cut and limpid intellect had a great fascination for young Grey, not on political questions alone. His letters to Dorothy reveal a moral admiration for the Morley of those early days, whose writings on the French philosophers and *Compromise* became a part, but only a part, of Grey's spiritual being.

Grey never spoke in the first Parliament to which he was

H. S. Mendelssohn

AET. 23, 1885

elected, though he rose in vain several times during the debate on the Home Rule Bill. His maiden speech on February 8, 1887, was a quiet exposition of Liberal principles in relation to Ireland.

In the following year Grey and Haldane took an honourable and independent line by speaking and voting for Balfour's scheme of land purchase in Ireland, in spite of the fact that the rest of the Liberal Party opposed it on the ground that it was not coupled with Home Rule, as Gladstone's land-purchase scheme had been two years before. Next year Grey spoke in favour of payment of Members, in order to enable more working men to enter the House of Commons; he knew Burt and Fenwick.

During his period of Liberal Opposition between 1886 and 1892 the great political alliances of his life were founded in personal friendship.

> I worked closely in the House of Commons with Asquith and Arthur Acland and Haldane. We were distrustful of Mr. Gladstone's absorption in Home Rule, and anxious for a strong Liberal Government which should be radical in Home Affairs. My private understanding with Asquith and Acland was that I would not enter the Government unless Asquith was in the Cabinet and Arthur Acland included in the government. On the fall of the Conservative government in 1892 my wife and I had been down to our cottage for the week end. On returning on Monday morning I went to Arthur Acland's rooms. I found Asquith with him, and as I entered Acland said: 'You see two Cabinet Ministers,' thus telling me that he and Asquith were both in the Cabinet. That of course settled the question, and when I received the offer of the Parliamentary Under-Secretaryship for Foreign Affairs, I of course accepted it.[1]

But he took it all with his accustomed calm. Indeed the letter that he wrote to his wife in August 1892, at the crisis of

[1] *Autobiography.*

the government-making, is certainly not that of an ambitious man eager to get his foot on the first rung of the ladder:

> I dined with Haldane and Asquith last night, but didn't discuss my own position with Asquith — that is reserved for tonight. Mr. G. is very imperious and inclined to chuck us all about by the scruff of our necks, but I can see that Asquith means to go in, and I fear we are doomed to be immolated on the altar of office. Oh! great God Pan, that hatest London and hearest the voice of Under Secretaries when they cry unto thee, what wilt thou think of me? Meanwhile I read all the way up to London, finished the Ice Age and have quite come over to Miss Austen. 'They sympathized with each other in the insipid propriety of their demeanour and their general want of understanding.' Can't you see the two women and isn't it beautifully put? 'She was not a woman of many words, for, unlike people in general, she proportioned them to the number of her ideas.' Oh! it's a beautiful simple pen, but what sharp little digs it gives. And then the idea, which these women have, that any girl who reads must be 'satirical.' They don't know what the word means, or what the girl reads, but nothing will convince them that the word is not appropriate, and that they are not justified in disliking 'satirical' people.

And again he writes to Dorothy:

> It's a terrible plunge, but I am inclined to make it and at any rate purge my soul of the possibility of regret before I go into private life. The change made by office is very great. Pleasure is to take a back seat, and get through the four seasons of each year on the scraps which work may throw it at long and uncertain intervals. It is a new life with my back turned to the country.

Until August 1892 Grey had been more interested in home affairs and social reform than in foreign politics, in which he had received no previous training. Lord Rosebery's choice of him as his lieutenant to answer for foreign policy in the Commons decided the destiny of his life.

III

Dorothy Grey — Nature and Bird-Observation — W. H. Hudson — Fishing — Tennis — Fallodon Ducks — The Cottage on the Itchen — Grey's Thoughts on Nature and God — Politics or Private Life? — Haldane

Dorothy Widdrington [1] came of the same family as that stubborn hero of the Chevy Chase ballad:

> For Witherington my heart was woe
> That ever he slain should be:
> For when both his legs were hewn in two
> Yet he kneel'd and fought on his knee.

Her parents' home was at Newton-on-the-Moor, on the wooded edge of highlands overlooking the plain through which Coquet winds to Warkworth and the sea, and commanding as spacious a view of earth and sky and ocean as can be found even in Northumberland. Here she grew up, more in harmony with Nature than with any human being, a proud, silent girl, critical of herself and others, disdainful of ordinary society and its conventions which in those days were more obtrusive than now, aspiring secretly after a life of the spirit that she did not yet know how to realize. Her mind was an unopened bud until it expanded under Creigh-

[1] The Memoir of her written by Mrs. Creighton at Grey's request, entitled *Dorothy Grey*, was privately printed in 1907.

ton's deft and sympathetic touch; he taught her to look more serenely and fairly at the world.[1] At the same time she began to make close friends like Miss Ella Pease of Alnmouth and Miss Constance Herbert, and shortly afterwards the Francis and the Sydney Buxtons. Indeed after her marriage she developed a true gift for friendship, though to the end those who were not in her close circle often thought her cold. But she had warmth of heart and a desire to share life, that only demanded a type of sincerity answering to her own, a condition not always easy to fulfil. One of her friends, Herbert Paul, said, 'She had the best sort of cleverness, the cleverness of the heart.' It certainly required no ordinary 'cleverness' to win the admiring attachment of three such different judges of mankind as Bishop Creighton, W. H. Hudson and Lord Rosebery.

> She was [wrote another friend] by hereditary instinct a Conservative, but her large and active mind had liberated her from all preconceived ideas, and every question that came up was treated by her on its own merits, in the clear cold light of reason. Regardless of anything so petty as 'party,' she always desired to get at the absolute truth of every question, and was an outspoken opponent of any kind of indirect answer or *ad captandum* argument. Her downright question 'Why?' often startled and almost terrified a careless talker, but was in truth to those who knew her the best proof of her keen attention and interest.

All those friends who lived within the pale of her toleration and love, bear witness to the 'uncommonness' of her personality, and the high interest of conversation with her on

[1] When Mrs. Creighton after her husband's death was beginning to prepare his biography, Dorothy wrote to her about those early days, 'It was extraordinarily comforting that he understood how much I wanted to be good. I had been in a perpetual state of self-defence, and was hostile and superior because I was in such a fright of people. Then I was filled with gratitude to him and began to understand that I had better be kind too to other people.'

any subject, small or great, owing to the first-hand character of all her opinions. Most of us take three-quarters of our opinions from the great world, or from some small world in which we live: Dorothy always thought and felt for herself.

These admirable characteristics are not in all ways suitable to a politician's wife. She became active as a 'Liberal Woman' both in Grey's constituency and outside it, but she could not, in doing these services, be other than what she was. She often gave offence to 'great ladies,' but won the heart of the wives of humbler Liberals, for she took everyone at their intrinsic value as it appeared to her. She was adored in Northumberland, but more by the commonalty than by the 'neighbours' — her close friends excepted. If she had lived to be the hostess of the Foreign Office, it would have been 'as good as a play' to see what happened, but one can hardly imagine it going on for eleven years — certainly not without incidents. For she hated ceremony and was less able than her husband to endure what she disliked. And most of all she felt

> sadness at the long heart-wasting show
> Wherein earth's great ones are disquieted.

At the time of her marriage, 'her beauty, so uncommon in its stateliness, in its expression of radiant health and strength,' was a match for the good looks of her husband; it took people's breath away when they entered a room side by side. But it was characteristic of her that she indignantly denied that she was beautiful, perceiving some irregularity of feature.

Towards young men she had always been ultra-virginal, and it is unlikely she would ever have been married had she not come across Grey, whose likeness to her in tastes, thought and temper was a marvel. In most happy marriages, husband and wife have some interests separate and some in common; and as a general rule for the world this ordering shows the wisdom of Providence. But Edward and Dorothy Grey had common tastes and interests, and scarcely any others of importance. Their friends used laughingly to say that the only difference they could see was that Dorothy liked Meredith rather better than Wordsworth, and Edward liked Wordsworth rather better than Meredith. The difference typified her greater subtlety and rapidity of mind, against his simpler and more central judgment. Each had something to give and to receive.

But the most important outcome of their close alliance was their daily partnership in developing those powers and habits of bird-observation that played in the end so great a part in Grey's life and achievement. 'In our early married life,' he tells us, 'we had no great knowledge of birds'; but even in 1885 this was only relatively true of the breeder of the Fallodon wild-duck, and it soon ceased to be true at all. The observation of the life habits of wild birds of the woodland and the shore, scientific in its accuracy, poetic in its motive and feeling, became to both man and wife, the principal expression of their intense oneness with nature, which their friend, W. H. Hudson, the greatest perhaps of all our writers on natural history, thus described in his obituary of Dorothy Grey.[1]

> I remember my first meeting with her distinctly as if it had been yesterday, though it is now over a dozen years ago. It

[1] From *The Speaker*, March 3, 1906. It was on Grey's advice that Arthur Balfour as Prime Minister gave a pension from the Civil List to Hudson, to enable him to live in the country and write his books, with the happiest consequences for English literature and natural history. When his circumstances became a little easier, he insisted on giving up the pension.

was a rare pleasure, a surprise, to find one in her world who did not use the customary phrases, who was of so original a mind, so transparently honest, as to make it a mental refreshment to converse with her. But my chief pleasure was in the discovery that she herself was a native, so to speak, of my world — one which may seem to most people a strangely silent and solitary world where I am at home with my non-human fellow-creatures.

We are all in some degree nature-lovers. In Lady Grey the feeling had that in it which appeared to make it essentially different from the common regard and pleasure which others have. It was not a feeling or a state of mind to be put off and on with a change from town to country, a spirit for the place and occasion as in most persons, but was always alive in her, a flame and secret source of contentment and happiness, all the sweeter because it was shared by another who was one in soul with her. She was conscious of this, which made her different from others, but reticent about it. The common expressions of delight in nature and terms of endearment lavished so freely on the lower animals she did not use and they did not suit her. But the feeling was there and could be divined. . . . Her love of all creatures and of all visible nature in all seasons and all weathers had its reward, since it made her happier even during illness than most persons are when in perfect health.

At the Cottage on the Itchen when her husband could not come down, she would dismiss the one servant and spend the night out of sight and sound of any other human habitation until the following morning. There are few persons who can endure solitude; she was able to love it, because of that feeling that was in her, as it was in Thoreau, which he described as a sense of an infinite and unaccountable friendliness in nature, like an atmosphere sustaining him. Notwithstanding her devotion to Wordsworth, who was her acknowledged spiritual guide and master, it always seemed to me that she was really nearer in spirit to Thoreau. The clear vision and courage to look steadily at the problems from which most of us veil our eyes, the impatience of all disguises and the desire for realities and simplicity of life — her whole philosophy of life in fact was like his; but the resemblance was most striking in that beautiful sense of the friendliness of nature.

GOSHEN COLLEGE LIBRARY
GOSHEN, INDIANA

These words may be taken, with hardly a change, and applied to her husband. That is the secret of their joint lives, and of his life after he was left alone. It caused Hudson to write to him in 1910 at the Foreign Office:

> It is a stormy period you are in; but I think that if there is anyone living who possesses that which your favourite poet finds in everything in the outside cosmos, a 'central peace subsisting at the heart of endless agitation,' it is yourself.

That quotation from the Fourth Book of the *Excursion* became very dear to Grey, who strove to feel it sometimes even during the War. The memories he amassed in the first half of his life, with Dorothy among the woods and the birds or alone with his rod by the waters, were the capital on which he lived during the long years of his widowhood, his grim struggle to guide the brute forces of Europe into the paths of peace, and the blindness that mocked his final escape from office. His memory was unusually strong and he always exercised it, calling up scenes as Wordsworth did the dance of the daffodils, and getting by heart long pieces from his favourite poets. His accurate recollection of bird adventures long ago, enabled him, as an old blind man, to write *The Charm of Birds* and *Fallodon Papers*, in which he coined the thought, feeling and observation of half his life as currency to circulate among all lovers of nature. But as early as 1899, in the prime of life and happiness, he published the first of his books on natural history, his *Fly Fishing*, which has won its place as a classic of our literature and a storehouse of technical advice, second only to Izaak Walton's book.

The fisherman penetrates into the most beautiful recesses of the land, and closely observes their most lovely detail in pursuit of his craft: that was one half the attraction for

Grey. The other half was the primaeval thrill derived from our hunting ancestors, in his case increased by his amazing skill in cast and play. Not only the Itchen and the English streams knew him well, but the Highland Cassley and Spean. Dorothy used herself to fish, more in the great Scottish salmon rivers than on the Itchen. Mrs. Francis Buxton reports how 'Dorothy always fished with Edward, generally taking out a book and reading at odd moments, but preferring as a rule to watch him when she was not fishing. She was very strong, and remained erect and graceful as ever while wading in deep water and casting the heavy salmon line, even at the end of a long day.'

The climax of his Highland fishing came in 1905, in the wild precipitous gorges of the lower Findhorn, seemingly less suited to the angler than to the cragsman. It was during that last summer of his happiness that he took Relugas House, where the gorge of the Divie joins that of the Findhorn: it seemed, he wrote, a 'dream place, a world of two enchanted rivers, which you are permitted to see by walking in woods. If the woods weren't there and you approached in the open, the rivers would stop and change their course.' Here, during her last summer on earth, Dorothy wrote to a friend, 'In his few intervals indoors he sits by a window which overlooks a good pool, and murmurs, "What a nice word *river* is." The keener he gets the smaller is the rod he uses, and it may be heard making a sharp, whistling sound up and down the banks, quite different to the usual sound of casting.'

Although the Highlands never became a home to him, they had a strong influence on his imagination. In 1898 he writes to Dorothy from Glenmure:

> The weather has been extraordinarily bad for fishing. But there are other things. Last night I walked up above the lodge

and lay down on the top of a little hill out of sight, and listened to the sound of the streams from everywhere. I never felt the great impersonal personality of inanimate nature so before, nor understood so well before why Wordsworth lived in this sort of country and went out so much at night.

One of the oldest and most beloved of his many fishing friends was the Liberal statesman, Sydney Buxton, who, when death parted them after half a century, wrote a description of Grey fishing on the Itchen:

> Fisherman, rod, line, cast and fly were all in unison. Without apparent effort, the line went out as straight as an arrow, as light as thistledown, or the drag would be overcome by the exact amount of slack — it all looked so simple and so easy. He fished with a stiffish rod, the better to control the hooked fish in a stream abounding in weed beds. He confined himself mainly to four flies plus the Mayfly. Curiously enough he could not fish with his left hand, but made up with greater dexterity with the right.

Another of his fishing friends, Mr. Samuel Whitbread, writes:

> Edward's fishing, as everything he did, was a model of good style, and his back-hand cast under bushes was a joy to watch.

The last page of Grey's *Fly Fishing*, in the revised edition of 1929, contains his final word, written in that year:

> Thus, as the angler looks back, he thinks less of individual captures and days than of the scenes in which he fished. The luxuriance of water meadows, animated by insect and bird and trout life, tender with the green and gay with the blossoms of early spring: the nobleness and volume of great salmon rivers: the exhilaration of looking at any salmon pool, great or small: the rich brownness of Highland water: the wild openness of the treeless, trackless spaces which he has traversed in an explorer's spirit of adventure to search likely water for sea trout: now on one now on another of these scenes an angler's mind will dwell, as he thinks of fishing. Special days and successes

he will no doubt recall, but always with the remembrance and the mind's vision of the scenes and the world in which he fished. For indeed this does seem a separate world, a world of beauty and enjoyment. The time must come to all of us, who live long, when memory is more than prospect. An angler who has reached this stage and reviews the pleasure of life will be grateful and glad that he has been an angler, for he will look back upon days radiant with happiness, peaks and peaks of enjoyment that are not less bright because they are lit in memory by the light of a setting sun.

The house and small estate of Stocks, below the beech-clad hills of Ashridge in Hertfordshire, became in 1891 the property of Grey's mother with reversion to himself. But as Stocks had no water to fish he never thought of living there, and it was sold to the Humphry Wards. It was on the banks of the Itchen that he and Dorothy found their week-end refuge from London.

But before describing the Cottage at Itchen Abbas, or resuming the questions of fish and birds, we must take a glance at an athletic accomplishment that was a feather in Grey's cap of youth, his prowess as champion at tennis — the 'real' tennis of the resounding court. He had played for Oxford against Cambridge, and was afterwards for many years Alfred Lyttelton's chief rival for the Gold Racket of the amateur championship played for at Lord's, often beaten by him, but finally beating him in 1896. Then, if not before, Grey was for one year Amateur Champion.[1] But next year he was beaten by Eustace Miles, and tells the story of his defeat in a characteristic letter to Dorothy.

[1] There was another amateur championship played for at Queen's, which Grey won five times, in 1889, 1891, 1895, 1896 and 1898. Alfred Lyttelton did not compete for this. I am indebted for information on this complicated subject of the two championship contests to the Honourable R. H. Lyttelton and to Mr. Alfred Cochrane.

> *July* 21, 1897. I am going to tell you about my match: it has been full of experience and all that followed it in my spirit has been interesting and satisfactory. One or two little buds seem to have opened in me under the influence of defeat and I am rather pleased with them. It was a good match, but Miles was too strong for me. [He then describes the match in detail.]
>
> Then came the interesting time. All my tennis so far has been improvement and increasing success. This is the first step, and a very marked one, downhill. I was really pleased to find that it didn't affect my spirits at all. I walked about the garden this morning thinking it over, remembering how keen I had been some years ago, and the recollection of that made me realize how much more pleasure Miles must now be feeling than I should have had in beating him, and it seemed as if it would have been wasteful and not in the fitness of things for me to have won. Years, which bring defeat, bring also 'the philosophic mind.' And just a word on behalf of philosophy, 'the good horse in the stable, but an arrant jade on a journey'; — you can bring philosophy to bear upon defeat in a game, but you can't well go down on your knees and seek for the consolations of religion: it would be too much to expect God to be interested in a tennis match.

Grey's splendid physique enabled him to scour the country to his heart's delight as cross-country walker and on his bicycle, often with his wife beside him in the trailer. Lord Shuttleworth once took him to Francis Galton's 'Anthropometric Laboratory,' where men were measured for their physical characteristics. 'Being the older man,' writes Lord Shuttleworth, 'my measurements were taken first, and I was complimented on my lung capacity; but when Edward Grey's turn came they said, "Hallo, this beats all records." His was the largest lung capacity that had been recorded up to that time. This had an amusing sequel when his friend, Bromley-Davenport, wrote to him saying, "I hear you are the greatest wind-bag out!"'

It was not till 1890 that the Greys built their Cottage on the Itchen. During the previous four years, their first four together, their chief interest had been Fallodon, though there was a journey to India in 1887, almost the only pleasure-tour across the sea that they ever took. In these first years they planted many trees, some of rare kinds, which Grey lived to see thick and high, and which he used to show to visitors with pride.[1]

But their very first act, in 1886, was to make another pond for the further reception of wild duck, a little above the old one, and to plant it round with suitable bushes to make it an attractive home for the birds. The 'fox-proof fence' was extended round the whole area. Every year more species of English and foreign wild-duck were acquired, some of them very rare, and with infinite pains and skill induced to accept unpinioned their new home, to nest, to breed, and finally to feed out of the hand. 'In the enclosure you must have quiet,' he writes in *Fallodon Papers*, 'because waterfowl spend, in the early spring, when they are in pairs, some weeks looking about for nesting places, cautiously and quietly by themselves, and if they find that they are watched, or should you come suddenly upon them, and they are disturbed, they will not select that nesting place and will not nest at all. So even in the case of one's self or the gardener, care must be taken not to walk at random in the nesting season.... There must be someone who gives daily attention to the birds and takes an interest in them, and at Fallodon that has been done by my gardener, Mr. Henderson.'

[1] Apropos of his love for trees, he writes to his friend Captain F. R. Barton, after a visit to the National Gallery, 'I sat down for a long time in front of the Crome oak. I got to dislike the people bathing because they didn't seem to be caring for the oak as I was. *Oakiest of oaks* is a good phrase for it. I wish they would put that sort of thing in the Catalogue instead of their banal descriptions.' Crome's 'Mouth of Yare by Moonlight' was another of his favourite pictures.

Under these conditions, year after year, fresh species, imported from all over the world, or come of their own free will from the neighbouring coast, were induced to breed on the ponds. An eighteenth-century note-book, stoutly bound in green leather, with old-world Fallodon accounts at one end, was used at the other end by Grey to record the duck-breeding from 1886 to 1905, together with observation of other wild birds and natural life at Fallodon. There are some one hundred and fifty large pages covered closely with his handwriting. It may be of interest to some to read a few quotations from this Fallodon green book in the First Appendix below.[1] For the rest, the world knows the story of the ducks, inimitably told by Grey himself in chapter V of *Fallodon Papers* and in the concluding chapters of *The Charm of Birds*.

At Fallodon Dorothy and he tamed other shy friends beside the ducks — at one time a covey of partridges! The famous squirrels were daily visitants in his writing room, that came to be called the 'squirrel room.' The little red fellows continued to comfort him all his life long. At Christmas 1911, after the Agadir crisis, he writes to Captain Barton:

> I have just succeeded in getting to Fallodon and am alone here for a few days. I like to be alone at first after a strenuous time. I can rest and sleep when I please and think of past years. There is also a good deal of work every day sent from the F.O. My squirrels come on to my writing table and take nuts from my hand as if I had never been away. There is something restful in the unconsciousness of animals — unconscious that is of all the things that matter so much to us and do not matter at all to them.

[1] Pages 419–26 below. I have printed on pages 393–94 his friend Sydney (Lord) Buxton's account of his successes and methods with the duck.

But another spot of English earth became as dear to Grey as Fallodon itself, and is as much associated with his observation and love of birds.

The Cottage on the Itchen was really a 'bungalow' as he once called it, which he built with brick foundations and chimney, wooden walls and trellises, and corrugated iron roof, ere long completely buried in roses and creepers. It was only a 'lodge' in a 'wilderness' of delight. In the first year of his Parliamentary life, a week-end refuge from London was needed nearer at hand than Fallodon, and his thoughts turned at once to the clear rushing waters of the Itchen, which ever since his boyhood at Winchester held a high place in his affections as fisherman and as lover of nature.[1]

Mrs. Creighton, one of a few friends besides Hudson who were privileged to have occasional use of the Cottage when the Greys were away, thus describes it in her Memoir of Dorothy:

> The happiest part of her happy life was spent in the Itchen valley. The first year they stayed at the Plough, the little inn in the tiny village of Itchen Abbas. Then for some years they stayed in a fishing cottage belonging to Lord Northbrook. At last in 1890 they made a home of their own on the Itchen, so dear as to become in truth to them a sacred place, where they felt 'hidden and safe,' sure of the joy and peace that each day would bring without fail, for each day was like the living waters of the Itchen, a never-failing spring of peace and pure delight.
>
> An avenue of tall limes leads across a gently sloping field to the half-acre of land on which the Cottage stands. Here the avenue abruptly ends, the last three great trees standing in the little garden and sheltering the Cottage. These limes seem alive with long-tailed tits who build their nests high up among

[1] See pages 18–20 above. For Hudson's description of the Cottage see his *Hampshire Days*, chapter XII.

the thick foliage. Below the Cottage, the field slopes abruptly to the water meadow, where the Itchen and all the little streams which flow from and into it wind swiftly and silently amongst great masses of flowering reeds and yellow flags, marsh agrimony and purple loosestrife. On the other side of the water meadow [three hundred yards across] the deep woods of Avingdon Park slope gently upwards. The air is full of the song of birds, the cries and splashing of the water fowl, and the hum of bees among the limes. The scents of the Cottage are as characteristic as its sounds.[1] A hedge of sweet briar encloses the garden, and in the little square behind the Cottage which is given up to flowers, there is room for a wealth of sweet-scented things. This little garden is all light and colour; open towards the West, it seems in the evening to catch and hold amongst the flowers the last glory of the sun. In front of the Cottage is a little lawn with a border of roses, where the birds, sure of a loving welcome, come daily to be fed. There is no path anywhere, not even through the lime-avenue, nothing to point the way to the Cottage to the passer-by along the Winchester road. It lies safe and secluded, hidden amongst its trees from all curious eyes, and yet a walk of five minutes across the field brings one either to the station or to the little village.[2]

Next to the garden lies an old chalk-pit, full of trees and bramble bushes, the haunt of many birds. Here kingfishers, red-backed shrikes and nightingales have been observed to breed. The cows used to get in from the field and disturb the peace of this refuge for the birds, and it was a great joy to the Greys when, in 1902, they were able to rent the chalk pit. They railed it in to keep out the cows, and planted bulbs and flowering shrubs without disturbing the brambles and wild roses.

[1] Grey was as much interested in the scents as in the sights and sounds of Nature. He writes to Captain Barton about the 'clumsy' smell of the hawthorn. 'I love the smell, but it is very nearly a nasty smell, and it is now clear to me that the hawthorn, being in nature pure and innocent and full of good intentions, has all but stumbled into a horrible mistake and made a mess of its smell. But it just hasn't.'

[2] Grey writes to Captain Barton. 'Thank goodness, with all their inventions, anyone who wishes to reach this cottage on wheels can still do it only in a wheelbarrow; and I don't notice much change in the fashion of wheelbarrows. The type seems persistent — all honour and respect be to it.'

THE HAMPSHIRE COTTAGE

Dorothy Grey in the doorway. Taken by Edward Grey. A few years later the cottage was overgrown by creepers and roses

The Cottage itself was simple enough, 'a tin cottage' as Dorothy always called it, with its roof painted red, its wall covered with trellis so that it is buried in creepers, honeysuckle, roses, clematis, amongst which many birds build their nests. It was meant only to serve as a necessary shelter, for all real life was lived out of doors, but like everything else that Dorothy touched, it has a dainty charm of its own. No servant lived at the Cottage: but a woman, the same faithful Susan Drover all the time, came across the fields from the village to cook and clean.

So here the two lived at week-ends and holidays, close to mankind but absolutely alone among their 'non-human friends.' Grey divided the time between fishing and long hours of watching the birds and listening to their songs, which he could distinguish with the nicest ear. Dorothy watched the birds all day, alone or in his company.

We intended it only as a fishing cottage [writes Grey in his *Autobiography*], but it became much more and we made a special life there. It was to both of us a lovely refuge. I refused ever to make a political speech within miles of it. We spent every weekend there, refusing invitations which might interfere with it. What the life was may be understood from a little diary called *Cottage Book*, which I had privately printed after my wife's death. It began from a desire to leave on Monday something which would tell us what to look for on the following Saturday, and the first entries are written solely for this purpose. But it became in time much more than that. It was a record of our stay there and of our feelings and enjoyment. It was always left open so that either of us might write in it when we felt moved to do so. The entries made by my wife I marked with the letter D.; my own are similarly marked with the letter E.

We rented a house in Grosvenor Road, and when we were in Office from 1892 to 1894, and unable to get away from London until the Saturday morning, we used to call ourselves by an alarum clock and walk over Lambeth Bridge, not without thought of Wordsworth's sonnet on Westminster Bridge, pass St. Thomas's Hospital, along a street whose name I never knew but which we called Wood Street, because there was always a thrush singing in a cage as described in Wordsworth's Wood Street;[1] up to Waterloo Station and down by the 6 o'clock train to Itchen-Abbas Station, whence it was but a few steps to the old lime avenue which led down to our cottage.

Trout fishing in that part of the river was excellent. At the time when I first joined the club,[2] it was not the custom to fish on Sunday, and even when fishing on Sunday became usual, I still kept my old habit of not fishing on Sunday, but spending it by bicycling about the country, and revisiting particular spots that had some particular merit at a certain time of the year. In this way the Cottage at Itchen became to us even dearer than Fallodon itself. It was something special and sacred, outside the ordinary stream of life.

The quotations from the Cottage Book in Appendix II will enable the reader to realize the occupations of the day; and I am kindly allowed to quote the two following passages from Grey's *Charm of Birds*.

In one mile of the Itchen Valley that had much rough tussocky ground, too rough and coarse to be mown, there used always to be two, and sometimes three, pairs of grasshopper-warblers; and just when the even-song of birds had ceased in the warm dusk of June and July evenings, the grasshopper warblers would begin to sing. Thus to me the song became associated with failing light and the end of a day's fishing. The territory of each bird became familiar to me, the presence of each was greeted every year and noted evening after evening on the way home in the quiet twilight: my waders, brushing through the lush, soft growth on the river bank, made a sound not out of keeping with that of the bird. Apart from the act of singing, the grasshopper-warbler is not seen: its small dark

[1] Humour was never far below the surface with Grey, either about Wordsworth or anything else. In 1915 he writes to Frank Pember: 'There is always Wordsworth's never to be forgotten "*solemn* bleat" of a single sheep in the hills. Who but an undaunted downright daddy Wordsworth would ever have dared to give that epithet to the bleat of a sheep? I say "Bravo, Daddy!" when I think of it.'

[2] The fishing club that rented some three miles of this part of the Itchen, as good fishing as any in England, consisted usually of three persons. Of the six 'rods' Grey had two. The club employed a watcher, the excellent Collins.

form is as unobtrusive in its ways as a mouse in the thick rough herbage, where the bird nests. The sound it makes suggests dryness; as if there were no moisture in the palate. Its manner is very quiet, but the length of time for which the song is sustained gives the impression that the bird takes exceeding pleasure in it.

. . . .

At the Hampshire cottage the destruction of the nests in the little garden and the thickets of the adjoining chalk-pit was heartbreaking. The nests that were known to be destroyed were, of course, nests that we had found and were watching: otherwise we should not have known of their fate. The proportion of those that came to grief was so large that in some years it seemed that the breeding season must be a failure. It never was so: there was always a good output of young birds from nests that we had not found. There was no reason to think that human mischief was to blame for the robbing of nests in this particular spot. There were stoats, weasels, rats, field-mice and jackdaws, and these were enough to account for all the damage: but why did the particular nests that we found appear to suffer so heavily, while others, of which we did not know, prospered? It is probable that when a human being finds and examines a nest he leaves some track or trace that betrays the treasure. A bent twig or a misplaced leaf may catch the keen eye of a hungry jackdaw looking down from above. The thought thus suggested discouraged me from nest-finding at the Cottage, and in later years I was content to be assured by ear that the birds were there.

After Dorothy's death the record of the Cottage Book was no longer kept, but the place remained for many years a consolation to Grey. In March 1914 he writes to Captain Barton:

This is the first Sunday of the year at my Cottage, full of pleasure because of the number of well known things that greet me again, varied also by disappointment because I don't see everything at once. For instance only seven out of the twelve sorts of birds that ought to come to my bread have been seen so far. I feel as offended as a Sovereign whose levee has been badly attended, and as anxious as a parent whose children have stayed out too late.

After the war, when he was too blind to fish with the dry fly, he went less to the Cottage, but it was still very dear to him. In February 1923 befell one of the many blows that rained on him in his later years. He received a pathetic letter from Susan Drover's sister and successor, who then looked after the Cottage:

> My Lord. What can I say to you? I am sore vexed but your pretty cottage is burnt to the ground. What will you say my Lord?

The Cottage and the occupants have gone, but the spirit of the valley remains. The place has not yet been developed and brutalized. Houses have grown up along the road from Winchester to Itchen Abbas, but have approached no nearer to the edge of the water-meadow. The lime avenue is still intact; aloft in its branches the bees still hum and the long-tailed tits still nest. The chalk pit is still safe within its fence. The birds flit freely as of old on their busy errands.

> Cows flap a slow tail knee-deep in the river.

The strong clear current still bends the anchored weeds and water grasses, pointing their heads down towards Winchester. Below on the gravel the big trout lie, and one can still watch them from 'Grey's bridge,' still in its old rustic simplicity. Only in place of the little garden and cottage there is a tangle of sweet-smelling wilderness; the kitchen chimney alone stands erect, so completely overgrown that with those who do not know the Cottage-history it passes for an ivy-clad tree. All is well. A man and what he loves and builds have but a day and then disappear; nature cares not — and renews the annual round untired. It is the old law, sad but

GREY WATCHING FISH FROM 'GREY'S BRIDGE,' OVER THE ITCHEN, BELOW THE COTTAGE

not bitter. Only when man destroys the life and beauty of nature, there is the outrage.

Grey loved all the outdoor world — the shapes of cloud and the colours of sunset, the sleeping strength of the great mountain forms in the Highlands, the force of rivers swift and slow, the greenwood trees each after their kind, the gnarled Scotch firs 'patiently waiting for winter to come and show them off,' the little four-footed inhabitants of field and hedgerow. But most of all he loved the birds, because by their notes and flight and every gesture they express joy, better than any other part of the creation except occasionally man; and even man, as the poets have often said, cannot express joy in its purity like the skylark soaring in song. 'The winter is rather depressing to me,' he wrote in his sad December of 1906, 'I feel it would be better if the birds would sing, that gives me more conviction of the existence of joy than anything.'

As his own poet had said:

> The birds around me hopped and played,
> Their thoughts I cannot measure,
> But the least motion that they made
> It seemed a thrill of pleasure.

Near the end of his life Grey wrote:

> To all this must be added the full song of woodland birds; the long vibrating notes of curlews, the first fresh green of deciduous trees. Year after year all this loveliness for eye and ear recurs: in early days, in youth, it was anticipated with confidence; in later years, as the season approaches, experience and age qualify the confidence with apprehension lest clouds of war or civil strife, or some emergency of work, or declining health, or some form of human ill may destroy the pleasure or even the sight of it: and when once again it has been enjoyed we have a sense of gratitude greater than in the days of confident and

> thoughtless youth. Perhaps the memory of those days, having become part of our being, helps us in later life to enjoy each passing season. In every May, with the same beauty of sight and sound, 'we do beget that golden time again.' [1]

The passionate feeling of his life, which in his last years he cast into such fine literary form, was that in the enjoyment of nature lay the greatest good of man. It grieved him that most men are blind to their opportunities of joy, and that they are destroying the heritage of future generations by turning the good world of nature and God into a man-made world of machinery, great cities, and a vulgarized countryside. Modern war, the ultimate horror to him, was the logical outcome of the machine mind.

Thus, like Wordsworth, he saw God through nature, and praised him in the words of the English poets. He had no consistent scheme of philosophy or religion; but he fed his spirit on the pantheism — if that is the true word — of the early Wordsworth,[2] with a strong Christian tinge, that like Wordsworth's increased as life went on. He believed in a future life and after Dorothy's death was sustained by a confident hope of reunion. But dogma, whether orthodox or agnostic, was repellent to his intellect and to his character. Dorothy shared his general outlook but had a touch of greater hostility to the orthodox, particularly to the Church of England because she had been brought up in it, whereas to Grey, old association was no reason for disliking anything.

[1] *The Charm of Birds*, end of chapter IV.

[2] On December 17, 1927, he wrote to the Reverend T. F. Royds: 'In *Tintern Abbey* the divine element is described as pervading all nature, as well as "the mind of man." It goes further in this respect than the passage in the *Excursion*, and it is more beautiful as poetry. But there is four-square solid strength in that passage in the *Excursion*, which has always gripped me.' Possibly the passage referred to is Book IV of the *Excursion*, the end of the Sage's exhortation, especially lines 1132–87.

In 1888 he wrote to her, after a talk with her father: 'He told me all his views about Christianity, and they are exactly the same as yours and mine; i.e. no doctrine, but taking Christ's teaching as the best platform of morality that has been laid down.' In another letter of the same year, after a very sympathetic account of Condorcet's life, culled from John Morley, he adds:

> He at any rate couldn't have felt the want of any other religion to keep him up to the mark, but then just before the Revolution the state of France was fearful. Government, Priests, Kings, landowners, everyone who had to do with Christianity, was out and out bad. Now at the present time Christianity is not all bad, it isn't even all dead, and amongst the sparks of good which are flitting about the world, it strikes out not a few itself, and some of those real large ones for everyone to see.

In 1904 he and Dorothy read Miss Caroline Stephen's *Quaker Strongholds* with great sympathy and even emotion.

> Edward is reading *Quaker Strongholds* aloud [she wrote to Miss Pease]. I feel as if we had really always been Quakers, and I believe we shall join definitely some day. One would even be able to be kind about the Church of England if one didn't belong to it perhaps.

Grey, always somewhat more 'kind about the Church of England,' wrote to Dorothy about *Quaker Strongholds*:

> It is natural to pray in that silent spirit, looking into oneself and spreading out what one is made of, not hiding the bad but not minimizing the good, and I got strength by it. We must go on with it together. It isn't a question of creed but of feeling.

To some of his more orthodox friends he seemed always 'a religious man,' nearer to Quakerism than to anything else. He attended the Church of England service at Embleton, the

Fallodon Parish Church, where Creighton had ministered. In 1907 he writes to Katharine Lyttelton:

> I had a comforting contrast in Church here on Sunday. They struck up the Athanasian Creed, which always offends me; it starts me analyzing its smug dialectic, its cocksureness and its damnatory intentions, till the unchristianness of it seems to start up and hit me in the face. So to avoid it I opened a Bible and went on with the Lesson which was in Revelations and I came upon this — 'and I will give him the morning star' — it is a verse all to itself. Isn't it nice and doesn't it make the Athanasian creed faint? I do believe if I had been a clergyman I could have been a very good one, but Hugh Cecil would have turned me out of the Church.

After the War the Vicar of Embleton was Mr. Dawson, with whom Grey in his last years made friends. He attended his ministrations every Sunday he was at Fallodon, waited at the church porch to discuss the sermon, and 'always stayed for Holy Communion on the Festivals and occasionally at other times,' which had not been his custom in earlier days. Mr. Dawson writes to me:

> He often touched on religious questions in conversation with me when we were walking in the woods, or by the quarry-pool. He said it was comfort to him to realize that God sees all things — all nature, all life; it is one complete whole to Him. And that thought, he said, answered many difficulties he felt about life. I remember several occasions when he spoke of the appreciation of what is beautiful in life, and the growing knowledge of the life of nature, as a preparation for life to come, when a man will find his true place if he has learnt to love beauty here. That seemed to be a strong article in his creed. He loved the Bible, especially the Psalms. He was interested in parallels between a thought of any of the Bible writers and that of any classical writer. The parallel, for instance, between Saint Paul's picture of the Glass in which we now see life reversed and 'darkly,' and the well-known passage from Plato, where the men in the Cave see shadows on

> the wall as they sit with their backs to the light. He appreciated the Scottish Presbyterian divines, and said he thought they 'belonged to a good type.' He was fond of quoting any example he remembered where such an old fashioned divine would use homely language in illustration. When I was sitting beside him one day on the grass, by the quarry pool, tying a fly for him which he could no longer see to tie himself, he quoted for me the saying of the minister of a rustic Scottish parish: 'God sees us, and our ways. He is like a moos [mouse] keekin' at us frae a dry-stane-dyke.'

One thing Grey unconsciously shared with some of the older forms of religion. He was constantly concerned to save his own soul — though not by believing the Athanasian or any other creed. His interest in the right development of his character, the attainment of the right 'moods' as he calls them, holds a prominent place in his intimate letters. It has been truly said of him, by his great but discriminating admirer Lord Cecil, that Grey's interest in his own 'moods' helped to make him a disciple of Wordsworth, who felt interest in nature less for her own sake than for her effects upon himself.

In seeking thus carefully to spend his life to the best spiritual advantage, he was confronted with a choice of Hercules. On the one hand he believed that the best life possible to men lay in contemplation of God's world of nature, a life for which he himself had opportunities and qualifications of a rare kind. On the other side was his sense of duty to the world of men, of which his Whig ancestry and tradition made him unwillingly aware. He obeyed the sterner call, but he never ceased to murmur and look back. He was one who said 'I go not,' and went. From the point of view of perfecting his own character he chose right: there was danger of hedonism in the naturalist's life lived under the pleasant conditions of Fallodon and the Cottage, and if he had not shouldered the public burden he would never have become the noble character that his countrymen felt him to be in his later years.

The alternative was never wholly absent from his mind at any period between 1887 and 1916, although actually he never left public life till he was too blind and too ill to continue there. After Dorothy's death in February 1906, practically coincident in time with his own elevation to the charge of our Foreign Affairs, he had less motive for seeking retirement and more for continuing to serve the public. But in the previous twenty years he had often been very near retirement. The following letter written to him by Dorothy, while he was first in office in the summer of 1893, shows how their minds worked on the matter, and what was the nature of their friendship with Haldane. This letter, unlike her others, was copied out in Grey's own hand, eight months after her death. He notes that she wrote it in their London house, and sent it down to him at the House of Commons.

> I want to write to you: first about the Hudson book. I have read a good deal: it touches very fine notes of feeling for nature. I felt first sad because it was such a long way off from what we are doing: then the feeling stole over me of being very faithful to the holy things and very firmly separated from towns. I read on and on and old Haldane came in in the middle. After the usual commonplaces I sort of let out, and we talked from five to eight and the result is that he has gone away saying 'I understand at last. You must not stay in politics. It is hurting your lives. It is bad.' I piled up my feeling to hurl at him and among other things said that if we went on crushing our natural sympathies we should probably end by destroying our married life, because the basis and atmosphere of its beauty would be taken away and it would die. This seemed to strike him in an extraordinary way. He said he had felt in himself how much your unhappiness in office made it difficult to talk to

you or be intimate, and that he had been feeling there was no spring or heart in either of us.[1] Then he said many nice Haldanesque things and reproached himself for not having understood before our passion for the country. Then we talked for a long time, he arguing in favour of giving up politics and I against it, and I believe he had the best of it. I was quite touched by him; we must be nice to our Haldane. He thinks now that it would be quite reasonable if you resigned at once, though I told him we had no idea of that. I wonder if you will see him in the House tonight and what he will say to you. He told me he had had a talk with you today which had been nicer than of late. It's funny to write and tell you all this but I may be gone to bed when you come. I shall read more Hudson tonight and store it up for you like honey.

Haldane had clearly been carried off his feet by the suddenness of Dorothy's onslaught, for he soon recovered himself, and in October of the following year he writes to her in the opposite sense:

The one blow that I should feel a heavy and even crushing one would be that Edward should leave politics. For me it would rob the outlook of much of its hope and meaning. I think his presence is of the last importance to the Liberal party. And how much I believe in that Liberal party and in the work we have to do, you know. All I ask is that you should not come to any decision just now, and that I do ask on personal as well as general grounds. If only Edward was in Rosebery's place [Prime Minister], I should feel sure of what I only hope for now. We are all soldiers in a great struggle, and cost what it may to our feelings let us storm the breaches, that have been made visibly in the opposing barriers. It is a religious question with us.

The intimacy of the Greys with Haldane was very close. They were a great comfort to him in his own troubles and

[1] In 1912 Grey wrote to Katharine Lyttelton, 'It is one of my bitter memories that in 1892–95 my unhappiness and groaning in office made Dorothy sometimes unhappy. And I am afraid I should have been doing the same now, for of course I am harder driven now than then.'

disappointments, and but for comradeship with him Grey would almost certainly have left politics during the long discouraging period of Liberal divisions and impotence. As far back as 1890 Grey had written to Haldane:

> Your influence will always be greatly indirect, and it will be your privilege never to be able to measure it. If it were not for you I do not think I should have even the hold on public life which I have now. There are others too more worth influencing. I should say, for instance, that Asquith owed some of the very best of himself to you; in knowing you both I feel as if it was so.

IV

Parliamentary Under-Secretary at the Foreign Office, 1892-95 — Opposition Again — Question of Foreign Travel and Foreign Languages — West Indian Commission

THE Liberal Government of 1892–95, with its bare majority of forty, counting British and Irish Home Rulers together, exceeded expectations by staying in office for almost three years. The first year was occupied, under the heroic leadership of Gladstone at the age of eighty-four, in passing through the Commons, amid fierce opposition, the Home Rule Bill that everyone knew the Lords would with impunity reject. After that had been done, Gladstone retired in March 1894, and Rosebery took his place as Prime Minister — Lord Kimberley succeeding Rosebery at the Foreign Office. Grey was Parliamentary Under-Secretary to the two peers in succession. His post gave him little share in the highest counsels of the Office, but he had the important task of explaining and defending the Government's foreign policy in the Commons. It was this apprenticeship that first drew his mind away from domestic to foreign affairs, while his manner of speaking in the Commons won him a national reputation that rendered his intended return to private life more difficult. For in spite of his subordinate position he spoke with authority and not as the scribes.

While Rosebery remained at the Foreign Office, Grey saw much of his chief, and a personal friendship began which lasted for many years, and in which Dorothy came to play no small part. At this time Grey shared Rosebery's views on foreign and imperial policy, as for instance in the question of Uganda. We had of recent years partially occupied it, and our missionaries had converted many of the tribes. Opinion was divided as to whether Uganda should now be abandoned or more effectively occupied. Rosebery and Grey were strongly against evacuation, but Asquith and Haldane were doubtful. In October 1892, Grey writes to Dorothy:

> Haldane is in great form and has been acting as a go-between from Sidney Webb to Asquith with great success. He is quite convinced that the Home Office [Asquith], the Local Government Board [Fowler] and the Education Department [Acland] could by administration only, not legislation, put new life into Liberalism all over the country. I went for him about Uganda: he is very Haldanian about it. 'I admit that it must be done but it is not to our credit.' However that is enough if the Cabinet would only say so much. Asquith hates it, but public opinion and Rosebery together are apparently convincing him that some 'compromise' must be come to. It is an abominable word and has been at the bottom of all Mr. G.'s troubles in Egypt, the Soudan and Africa. If we 'compromise' it will only be by great luck that we escape disaster. Haldane thinks public opinion will be down on us, if we give Uganda up, but this in his mind doesn't touch the merits of the question.

We remained in Uganda.

But Grey, from the very first, was not unaware of Rosebery's weakness as a national leader. When he became Prime Minister, not without murmurs from the Irish and Radicals under Labouchere, not to mention some of his Cabinet colleagues, Grey writes to Dorothy:

> Rosebery is, I think, rather angry with the Irish and the Labbyites: I had suspected the latter from his having protested

> so much about the disabilities of a Peer. He will have a very rough time, and he seems to be facing it, but I wish he was a little more buoyant and would ride over all but the biggest waves instead of plunging through them and getting the brine in his eyes. Haldane tells me that George Meredith and Rosebery met some time ago and took a mutual dislike to each other: Rosebery would naturally resent being explored by Meredith's critical faculty and Meredith would be huffed at his resenting it. Meredith is said to be very keen on politics just now: he was too lame to go to the great anti-Lords demonstration in the Park on Sunday, but he sent his gardener to represent him. Haldane has been in here for a talk. We discussed how to make Rosebery *great*, which is rather funny when you come to think of it, and could not be discussed except with Haldane. (March 21, 1894.)
>
> I dined with Rosebery last night to meet Rhodes. Rhodes is not exactly what you call a Liberal: he has a new version of 'one man, one vote' for South Africa, viz. that he, Rhodes, should have a vote, but nobody else should. (November 2, 1892.)

On March 28, 1895, the Under-Secretary made in the House of Commons a pronouncement on Anglo-Egyptian claims to the upper waters of the Nile in view of possible French encroachments. It became known in history as the 'Grey Declaration' and had importance at the time of the Fashoda incident a few years later.[1]

The essential parts of the speech were as follows:

> I stated the other day that in consequence of these claims of ours and in consequence of the claims of Egypt in the Nile valley, the British and Egyptian spheres covered the whole

[1] Grey in his *Twenty-five Years* (chapter II) says that he spoke without previous preparation, because he had not expected that the question would be raised in the House that night. On the other hand, Lord Kimberley had seen Baron de Courcel that morning with regard to 'the rumours of a French expedition towards the basin of the Nile. I said that they had caused some disquiet here, as his Excellency would have seen from the remarks on the subject in the public press, and it was probable that they would be referred to in the House of Commons tonight.' (F.O. 27, 3229, No. 111, Africa, March 28.)

> Nile water way.... *I cannot think it possible these rumours* [of a French expedition to the Upper Nile] *deserve credence, because the advance of a French expedition under secret instructions right from the other side of Africa, into a territory over which our claims have been known for so long, would be not merely an inconsistent and unexpected act, but it must be perfectly well known to the French Government that it would be an unfriendly act, and would be so viewed by England....* During the whole of the debate no foreign power has been alluded to except the French Government. Why has that been so? I think it has been so because events in Siam and Africa have created an unfriendly effect on public opinion.... During the last two years no provocation whatever as regards the French has come from our side. But something else besides our own effort is necessary, and that is the co-operation of the French Government and the French public. We rely now, as we have relied not unsuccessfully hitherto, on the sense of justice and fairness of the French Government and the French people, to reconcile what conflicting interests there may be in different parts of the world with the maintenance of close and good relations between the two countries.

Such was the 'Grey declaration.' Joseph Chamberlain at once rose from the Opposition Bench and emphasized the importance of what the House had heard, as being 'the fullest and clearest statement of the policy of the Government with regard to this subject that we have yet had from a responsible Minister.'

Next day, writes Grey, 'there was a row in Paris, and (so I understood) in Downing Street. Some members of the Cabinet [particularly Harcourt] disapproved of my speech; others, including, I gathered, Lord Rosebery the Prime Minister, and Lord Kimberley, maintained that what I had said was defensible and salutary.' And salutary it proved in the event. For if France had not had full warning, the Fashoda affair, when it occurred, would have been more likely to have led to a war, fatal alike to England and to France.

In connection with the Grey declaration, there is interest in the following letter that he wrote to his friend Munro Ferguson (afterwards Lord Novar) in January 1897, when Kitchener's advance on Khartoum was being prepared under the auspices of Lord Salisbury's government:

> MY DEAR RONALD. The pivot of the whole question of a movement into the Soudan has always seemed to me to be the condition of the Mahdi's or Khalifa's power. When that power broke up the reoccupation would be easy and therefore opportune. That is the first point.
>
> The second point is that when the Khalifa's power breaks up anarchy must ensue. This anarchy produces such disorder and weakness on the Egyptian frontier that you are almost bound to interfere: but it does more than this, it creates a standing temptation and provocation for other powers, be they Belgians or French, or some devilry working through Abyssinian intrigue, to interfere, to occupy and to establish claims for themselves. If we do not push Egypt forward, we leave interests on the Upper Nile open to others: indeed by standing deliberately aloof now, we almost invite others to go in, to our prejudice and to the prejudice of Egypt for whom we are trustee: for while our interest in the matter is important, that of Egypt is vital.
>
> Having occupied Uganda, we ought to see that our frontier is co-terminous with that of Egypt. As long as the Khalifa was strong it did not so much matter: he stopped development and progress, but he was an enemy of all the world and the mischief to us and Egypt was negative and stationary. The expedition to Dongola has shown that the Khalifa is rotten: that is the beginning and end of my opinion that a forward movement is right. It is right (1) because it is opportune and practical; (2) because it is necessary to prevent new developments, which were not on the cards as long as the Khalifa's power was not known to invite attack.

During the three years when Grey as Under-Secretary was learning the grim facts of the international situation from inside the Foreign Office, our chief difficulties arose from the hostile attitude of France and of Russia, perpetually breaking out in those many quarters of the globe where their territory or interests touched our own. But behind these more patent preoccupations of those in charge of the Empire's peace, there was growing up in their minds a secret uneasiness as to the attitude of the other great power that might so well, in the circumstances, have seen its own interest in securing our friendship. The way in which Germany took advantage of our difficulties with France and Russia made a strong impression on the mind of the young Under-Secretary, ten years before the time when, as England's Foreign Minister, he implemented Lord Lansdowne's entente with France, and negotiated a better understanding with Russia.

The following letter, which he wrote to Sir E. Goschen in 1910, recalls how these impressions were thus early made upon his mind:

> In 1892, Lord Rosebery began his term of office by informing the Ambassadors of the Triple Alliance that he meant to continue the policy of Lord Salisbury: a policy which included an attitude so benevolent towards the Triple Alliance that the French Press sometimes wrote about the 'Quadruple Alliance.' The German Government, and I suppose the other two also, expressed great satisfaction.
>
> What was the result as far as our relations with Germany were concerned? The Germans worried us about Witu: they showed no consideration for our interests anywhere in Africa, though we asked for it at least once when they were themselves negociating a boundary arrangement with the French in the region of Nigeria; and the general impression left on my mind was that we were expected to give way whenever British interests conflicted with German interests, and that we got no diplomatic support from Germany anywhere and continual friction. It is true that the Germans did support us in Egypt, but I remember once at any rate a threat to withdraw that support if we did not clear the way for German railway concessions in Turkey. In the meantime, we were always on bad terms with

France and Russia, and the German Emperor openly expressed his satisfaction in conversation when it seemed that we were on the brink of war with France about Siam.

I am telling you all this from my own recollection of my time in the Foreign Office as Under-Secretary from 1892–95. I have not attempted to verify from papers the instances which I have given, but I remember most clearly that the position was anything but comfortable, and that we appeared destined to be for ever on bad terms with France and Russia, with Germany as a 'tertius gaudens.'

After 1895, when I left Office, I followed Foreign Affairs only to the extent which was necessary to enable me from time to time to take the part which was expected from me in the House of Commons. Naturally I welcomed the settlement of our differences with France and with Russia: had they not been settled, they must sooner or later have led to war with one country or the other. My impression is that Lord Salisbury and Lord Lansdowne always desired friendship with Germany, but that they were worried into a more distant attitude by finding that ostensible friendship with Germany meant no return from Germany, and constant trouble with Russia and France.[1]

Grey, therefore, when he left the Foreign Office for the first time, carried away a much graver impression of the dangers to European peace and of the isolated position of England than anything that disturbed the minds of the ordinary Liberal politician. Hence he sympathized on the whole with Lord Rosebery when in 1896 the ex-Premier resigned the leadership of the Liberal Party as a protest against isolated action by England in the Armenian question, which Gladstone had returned to advocate on the platform. Grey, both at this time in opposition and as Foreign Secretary in later and yet more dangerous years, deeply sympathized with the oppressed Christian subjects of Turkey, but

[1] Gooch and Temperley, editors, *British Documents on the Origin of the War*, VI, 538. Cited herein as *G. and T.*

believed that only through the Concert of Europe could England safely and effectively do anything on their behalf. The other great powers unfortunately cared little about Turkish misgovernment; yet only by dragging them after her could England effect anything at all. Such was Grey's belief, consonant with the line of thought that made him in 1915 one of the earliest advocates of a League of Nations — that better Concert of Europe which he hoped would emerge from the Great War.

Thus in May 1897 he wrote to Munro Ferguson, on the Cretan question:

> My own opinion hitherto has been that Salisbury could do nothing by standing outside the Concert: and that, miserable as the Concert is, he may do some good inside it, if he insists upon the liberation of Crete from Turkish officials and Turkish administration. If he makes this an essential condition of all he does and brings it off, I really don't see why we should strike attitudes about whether Crete is annexed to Greece or not.

His speeches in the House in 1897 and 1898 are in this line; he supports action through the Concert of Europe, but complains of its miserable slowness to save the Christians of Armenia and Crete, and urges that Salisbury should show more energy in dragging the Concert forward.

The General Election of 1895, though it relegated the Liberals to opposition for another decade, saw Grey returned by an increased majority by his faithful Northumbrians. He was touched, and felt grateful to his neighbours for this unexpected result; but he was not altogether glad in his heart.

> *To Ella Pease, July* 31, 1895. It is nice of you to be pleased that I won my contest, but this increased majority is more

H. W. Barnett

AET. 38, 1897

than I bargained for and has embarrassed me very much. It was really touching to see how the people worked and cared and upset all the influence of landowners, clergy and licensed victuallers. Of course I did my part too as well as I could: it would have been shameful not to have done it, but all the same a glorious opportunity of being set free has failed to come off. I should have gone out, dying a natural political death, regretted by my own side and praised by the other: now I shall have to commit political suicide some time.

He did not enjoy electioneering, even in Northumberland. A fortnight before, at the beginning of the campaign which he expected to lose, he had written from Fallodon to Ella Pease:

There is a good time and great relief coming afterwards; it is like having my last tooth out, but having the process last a fortnight. All sorts of childish expedients occur to me to help me through. I have marked all the days down on paper and am crossing them off: sometimes I feel tempted to go into the garden and eat so many strawberries that I must be very ill, but am keeping that in reserve at present.

During his first period of office Grey had been able to supply Dorothy at Fallodon with occasional 'bird news' about the inhabitants of the St. James's Park water, which he so often passed on his way to the Foreign Office, and once he saw a 'rare bird' in Piccadilly itself!

I have some bird news: it is very ridiculous that it should be so, but I can't help that. As I was walking down Piccadilly a flock of sparrows flew down to a cabstand and one cock had white wings: I put him up once or twice and there was no mistake and it was very conspicuous, but no crowd collected, and I thought poorly of the Piccadilly people for not noticing.... I wish I could sit under the trees and feel pure, but somehow, though the feeling is well remembered, I feel too grimy: as if my lungs were black and air could not be pure.... Yesterday two people sitting at the table next to me at dinner talked the usual thing about the country. One of them (call him A) told B that he had a friend with a very nice place in the country. B said he didn't think he would care to live at a country place. 'Oh! of course,' said A, 'you have to be very fond of shooting.' B then confessed that when he retired from the bar, driven by what he called 'that fell disease Anno Domini,' he had to think of something to do, as if it was quite difficult to find anything! He fell back upon London clubs and moving from place to place. Don't you see how easy it is for people to work who have to think hard to find something else to do? . . . You must cling to the knowledge that office is only temporary: even Pitt was out of office sometimes. . . . Some future day when we have a good summer, quite free, in prospect, we will walk through those old streets right up to the F.O. door: I think we will say nothing as we walk, but look and smile about once a street: then when we get to the F.O. door I will feel for my key and shan't find it and so not be able to go in, and go off with you instead.

There is little wonder that Gladstone said of Grey, 'I never knew in a man such aptitude for political life and such disinclination for it.'

Once, by a rare reversal of parts, Dorothy is in London and he is at the Cottage, whence he writes to chaff her:

I hope things are all right in London: are the cabmen feeding their horses nicely? The blackbirds are feeding their young very well here. And are you appreciating the smell of the streets? The smells here are all right, and the proper sounds are all round me, light wind in the leaves and wren and several goldfinches and a new cuckoo. I hope London is keeping up its own noises too and that you are not missing any of the things which you prefer so much to your dull Cottage. (June 12, 1903.)

And once he writes from London:

A great deal of rain is being sent and I like to think of the great Hampshire downs spread wide to receive it, and of the springs under them, which do not see the rain fall, but will presently find their life and vigour being mysteriously re-

H. W. Barnett

DOROTHY GREY, 1897

newed and will rise up in such volume at the sources of the Itchen that the river will wonder at the strength of its own stream. (February 20, 1900.)

He loved rain. In 1900 he writes from the Cottage to Katharine Lyttelton:

> As soon as I was thoroughly wet through on the way home, I became one with the weather and would not have changed the day. It is only while one is dry that one is out of sympathy with rain; when one is wet through, one minds it no more than the trees do, having become part of the day itself.

In 1902 he writes from Novar to Dorothy:

> I feel Scotch hills in every muscle already. The Alness comes out of a most wild mountain loch — a long one amongst mountains. I began to fish where it leaves the lake and as I put up my rod there came from birch trees opposite a well known and much loved voice, or rather two voices known to belong to one thing. Nothing (except your whistle) could have so surprised me with tenderness. It was a wood wren; both song and plaintive notes; so strange in far north mountains.

There are some, including not a few of Grey's admirers, who think that during the period of opposition between 1895 and 1905 he should have travelled on the Continent, made the acquaintance of French and German statesmen, and perfected himself in their tongues. However this may be, the reason why he did not will already be clear to readers of this book. He did not regard himself as the destined successor of Salisbury and Lansdowne. He hoped, and on the whole expected, ere long to be free of politics and to live a life which he regarded not only as more pleasant, but as higher in the scale of human activity, at any rate in his own case. Whether in fact his conduct of foreign policy would have gained by a more personal contact with Europe is a question on which opposite opinions can reasonably be held. A little knowledge is a dangerous thing, and personal acquaintance with a few patches in the vast field of Europe often breeds one-sided views which would be peculiarly undesirable in a Foreign Minister, who above all must keep his proportions right and his sympathies impartial. Moreover, the methods of the Old Diplomacy were not those of the present day. The custom was for the English Foreign Secretary — Salisbury, Lansdowne, or Grey — to sit at home, to be informed about the various foreign countries by specialists, and to transact business by letters and telegrams to our Ambassadors abroad and by interviews with foreign Ambassadors in London. Geneva was not; and the days had not yet come of constant rushing through the air to concert measures with foreign Prime Ministers through the medium of personal talk.[1]

But in any case censure on this subject comes strangely from Mr. Lloyd George. He has written in his *Memoirs*:

> Grey was the most insular of our statesmen, and knew less of foreigners through contact with them than any Minister in the Government. He rarely, if ever, crossed the seas. Northumberland was good enough for him, and if he could not get there and needed a change, there was his fishing lodge in Hampshire.

Well! Wales was 'good enough' for Mr. Lloyd George, and we all like him the better for that. But his own very insular training did not prevent him, when Prime Minister, from usurping the charge of Foreign Affairs from that most widely travelled and instructed of Foreign Secretaries, Lord Curzon. He might have been right in relegating Curzon to the background, but if so it undermines his criticism of Grey.

In fact Grey was not as ignorant of the French language as

[1] Lady Oxford writes to me that her husband, when Prime Minister, said to her several times that no Minister for Foreign Affairs should leave this country.

is often supposed, though his accent was decidedly British. In an account of a visit of British Cabinet Ministers to Paris in 1916 he writes:

> Asquith would not, Lloyd George could not, and I had to speak French. In French I know my vocabulary to be limited, my grammar to be imperfect and my genders to be at the mercy of chance; further, I am told that my accent is atrocious. But with my back really against a wall, something relevant could always be forthcoming. When the Council was over, and we three British Ministers were safely outside, Lloyd George said to me: 'You know *your* French was the only French that I could understand.' [1]

Let us leave it at that!

The extent and limitations of Grey's French scholarship can be amusingly illustrated by letters in French which he often wrote to his friends, partly as a serious exercise and partly for fun. In April 1901, just after the 'Khaki Election' during the Boer War, he writes to Munro Ferguson describing a talk with John Morley:

> Le Ministre de Finance [Hicks Beach] vient de frapper d'un taux d'un 'shilling' tout le charbon envoyé du Royaume Uni en étranger. Une très grande orage s'élève; nous poussons tous des cris terribles à pleins poumons, et le Nord Est d'Angleterre se crêve d'indignation et de rage. M. John Morley cependant donne raison au gouvernement; il dit qu'il veut faire souffrir le Nord Est d'Angleterre en revanche de son *Jingoism*. Je lui ai dit 'C'est injuste; le Nord Est a élu MM. Burt, Fenwick, et Cameron, *pro-Boers* tous les trois.' 'N'importe,' a repondu le nommé J. M., 'ils ont amoindris la majorité de M. Atherley Jones!' 'Je crois,' lui ai-je dit, 'que vous voulez donner de coups de fouet à la première personne qui passe, n'importe qui que ce soit.' J.M. sourit amèrement; c'est un mouton enragé et on ne sait jamais à quoi s'en tenir a son égard, mais je l'aime toujours néanmoins.

[1] *Twenty-five Years.*

And to Munro Ferguson's wife, Lady Helen, he writes:

> You ask about French. I have just read the first six pages of *Anna Karénine* out in the heather. But what a poor language it is! The first sentence that met me was '"Je me suis réservé la vengeance," dit le Seigneur.' How can one recognise this as the equivalent of '"Vengeance is mine," saith the Lord.' I translated it '"I have reserved my vengeance," said the Count,' and shouldn't to this moment have known any better if my wife hadn't been there. (August 19, 1898.)
>
> *To Ella Pease, June* 16, 1904. I like Montie's joke about the motor going faster than he could sit: it's good. In return let me tell you that I hear there is a splendid misprint in Herbert Spencer's Autobiography. He quotes the French proverb 'Pour connaître l'amour il faut sortir de soi,' which is true and moral. But it is printed 'Pour connaître l'amour il faut sortir le soir,' which is less true and less moral.

Once indeed, during the long gap that divided his two periods of office, he did cross the seas for a considerable period, not indeed to Europe but to the British West Indian Colonies, on a Royal Commission to enquire into their economic difficulties. It was in 1897 and Dorothy came with him for a small part of the prolonged and intricate voyage among the islands. His reasons for accepting the invitation of Chamberlain, then Colonial Minister, that he should go on this mission are explained in a letter to Munro Ferguson:

> I went to London on Sunday night and saw Asquith and John Morley and found a letter from Rosebery. All the opinions were rather against my going to the West Indies, on the ground chiefly that I might be let in for something such as differential duties, which could not be justified on the wide ground of British and Imperial interests, though it might be the only remedy for the sugar producing Colonies. However I went to the Colonial Office and there I found that the condition of the Colonies is getting desperate, but that the alternative remedies are more than I supposed, and the whole question more complicated and interesting than I knew before.

> So I decided to accept. I am not sanguine as to the result of the Commission, but the job is one which it is worth putting one's back into and I don't think I should have been justified in refusing. I dined with Haldane to have a final talk over it and he agreed, but there is nothing on which I find it so difficult to take advice as on a personal question. (December 16, 1896.)

The next few months showed him much of the tropical colonies of the Empire. In the intervals of hard work, he delighted in the scenery and the vegetation, and above all the birds. He writes to Dorothy from British Guiana:

> I used English birds as little pegs in my head on which to arrange and sort the birds I saw. There were distinct pied flycatchers, very like the pictures of British ones and behaving in the usual way. There were cousins of sedge warblers, a wren of sorts for certain, the song of a lesser whitethroat too hidden to get at. There were other birds, one of very bright colours, which I could not join on to any species I know. The commonest bird here has a bright sulphur breast and is like a large shrike.... Yesterday I read [Richardson's] *Pamela* and wondered whether it is really possible for any two people to have their fill of the extremes both of passion and of sympathy of interest and thought. Passion is attractive, but there is a love which is larger and stronger and has a fuller life. Why didn't you see that I read *Pamela* before? I read at it by the hour together and have now got them well married. Really this book is very wonderful: it has more absurdities than ever I thought could be invented, but Pamela is bewitching in spite of them, and makes me jealous of Mr. B. in spite of his egotism which one otherwise would only hate and despise.

The Commission in its Report pointed out the danger which threatened those British Colonies where sugar was practically the only interest, and suggested various remedies, some of which were adopted. At its recommendation an Imperial Department of Agriculture was set up in 1898, with headquarters at Barbados; it has done much to help the establishment of new industries and to relieve many islands from dependence on sugar alone. The Chairman of the Commission, Sir Henry Norman, also recommended countervailing duties on bounty-aided foreign sugar, but Grey and the third Commissioner, Sir David Barbour, refused assent.

In 1898–99 Dorothy was seriously and even dangerously ill of Graves' disease. 'We have looked over the edge of a precipice,' Grey wrote to Katharine Lyttelton. For some years she was much of an invalid. He used to take her about in a trailer attached to his bicycle. But in the first years of the new century she gradually recovered health and they began once more to look forward to many years of unbroken happiness.

To Dorothy.

September 11, 1899. I feel quite depressed by this Dreyfus verdict: it is horribly unjust. Doesn't it make you feel that the French army is an evil thing? There are a lot of fine spirits too amongst the French, for the Revisionists are really fine men, who are standing against a storm of obloquy from sheer love of justice. The two officers on the Court Martial who voted against the verdict must be fine men and I honour them.

March 5, 1903. All the Louis XIV time seems to have been a mockery of greatness. The whole time wore a mask painted to represent greatness and success and trailed its robes to hide the stilts on which it walked, and was never found out till its secret history came to be known and its skeleton was examined. My thought always pursues Louis XIV as the man who died most in debt to the world; having taken everything and suffered nothing; having deserved ill and got a great reputation. The need for justice to be done to Louis XIV would alone make a future state necessary. I hate him.

February 9, 1896. *Mentmore* [Lord Rosebery's country house in Bucks]. I am in a large house and my room looks out on a courtyard with four walls and a huge iron gate. I heard the birds singing this morning, but the sound came faintly from beyond the outer walls and I felt they were freer than I. Very large houses have their grounds so constituted as to keep birds at a respectful distance. There are many large glass doors, but some are locked, others open with difficulty — and egress and regress are more or less formal; you may go out or in but not slip out or in.

July 31, 1900. I saw Rosebery off to Durdans. I drove with him to Waterloo, where the platform with the train starting for Winchester made me very Cottage sick. I have now been returned to Brooks's alone in R.'s brougham. The obsequiousness of the station officials to R. was wonderful; his neat little man in black had gone ahead, bought a ticket, engaged a compartment and put the whole station on the alert, and the head station-master condoled obsequiously with R. upon the death of Prince Alfred of Coburg, which is just announced by telegram. It seemed as if the train would hardly be able to start, so great was the occasion, but the engine driver, with great nerve and presence of mind, kept his head and started the train at the usual time in the usual way, just as he does when it is only me going down to my cottage with my bicycle in the Cloak room at Winchester.

V

The South African War — Education and Protection Controversies — Liberal Recovery and Reunion — The N.E.R. Chairmanship—Grey's 'City Speech'—Rosebery — Crisis of Cabinet Formation, December 1905 — The Death of Lady Grey, February 4, 1906

For some time after the resignation of Rosebery from the leadership in 1896 the Liberal Party had no recognized chief; Harcourt and Morley were as much given to retiring in a huff as Rosebery himself. Campbell-Bannerman, more resistant and reliable, was, in his capacity of leader in the House of Commons, the nearest approach to leader of the party that the party could then endure. But his performance on the Opposition bench was, as his biographer allows, by no means so spirited or successful as his leadership of the House proved when he was Prime Minister in later years. Grey was not the only Liberal who considered 'C.-B.' incompetent in those early days. The return of Rosebery was regarded as possible, though Grey did not think it likely because he knew him well. Rosebery had had enough of the contests of the arena; moreover his opinions were changing over to Unionism on the Irish question, thereby disqualifying him for leadership of the party in the future. Neither Grey nor Haldane ever shared this retrograde tendency, though, like Asquith and eventually Campbell-Bannerman himself, they saw the necessity of approaching Home Rule step by step in view of English opinion.

On a party thus distracted fell in October 1899 the South African War, calculated to give it the *coup de grâce* by accentuating to the utmost the latent differences between 'Little Englanders' and 'Imperialists.'

The refusal of Kruger, the President of the Transvaal Republic, to enfranchise the English and cosmopolitan population of the mining districts, and the creation of formidable Boer armaments on the borders of British South Africa, were the occasion of the war. Behind lay a long chain of blunders perpetrated by successive Liberal and Conservative Cabinets in relation to South Africa.

In October 1899 the war had become a work of necessity, which the Crimean War never was, but the destruction of the two Boer Republics was more devoid of all pretence to moral beauty than the Crimean or any other war in which modern England has been engaged. It was smeared by the trail of capitalism in one of its least attractive forms. And the Jameson Raid, followed by an imperfect enquiry, had bred suspicion of British good faith in every quarter of the globe.

About such an affair the Liberal Party was certain to be divided. The Liberal Imperialists rightly felt the duty to support a war that, when once begun, must be carried through if either South Africa or the Empire was to have a safe and peaceful future. The other and larger group, stigmatized as 'Pro-Boers,' were equally right in their view that the Boers, all of whom either were already our fellow-subjects or were about to become so at the end of the war, must be reconciled if ever there was to be peace in South Africa. It is easy at this distance of time to see that each section of the

Opposition had a useful function to perform, and it is to their credit that they managed so to play their opposing parts that they did not shatter the fabric of the Liberal Party, though the strain put upon its cohesion was for three years hardly to be endured.

The smaller, Imperialist section of the Liberals had Rosebery for their silent chief in the background, and Asquith, Haldane and Grey for their champions in the House and on the platform. In the course of the heated recriminations of a party at strife with itself, Grey went further in his approval of the war than Rosebery, who sat, godlike, above the mêlée till he descended in a fortunate hour at Chesterfield. Grey, indeed, went further in his applause of Milner than was consistent with his own Liberal views. For he always said and meant that Boers and Britons must be given full self-government when the war was over, whereas Milner objected violently to that course when the Liberals took it in 1906. Grey found out ere long that he had been mistaken in two personal judgments which had largely affected his action at this period — in his belief that Campbell-Bannerman would always be hopelessly incompetent as a Parliamentarian, and in his belief that Milner was not only a great administrator and a devoted servant of the public (as he certainly was), but a wise and liberal-minded statesman. There is no doubt that Grey's conduct during the Boer War was one reason why the more advanced sections of the Liberal Party in later years regarded his foreign policy with constant distrust. He made his mistakes and he paid his penalty.

Grey's private letters during this unhappy time will make his opinions and motives clear:

> *To Munro Ferguson, October* 1, 1899. Kruger has put himself altogether in the wrong by refusing the five years franchise

proposal made to him on Sept. 8 by the Government. I suppose he will have another chance this week of accepting something moderate, and if he still refuses we must either enforce our demands or drop them. We cannot drop them, and the demands are admitted even by Morley to be reasonable. In July I was afraid we might be hurried into war, before we believed war to be inevitable: since then the situation has changed and I really don't see what more the Government can do to avoid war, if Kruger persists in refusing the five years franchise. I fear the younger Boers think they can beat us, and if so they won't give way.

October 5, 1899. It is most annoying that such a bad face has been put upon our case against the Transvaal by that criminal raid, and some hot-headed diplomacy. But when Parliament meets, if the last chance of peace is over, we must brush aside what is superficial and go straight for the great serious issues upon which the future of South Africa depends. And after all Kruger had so fair a chance last month of settling on reasonable terms, that if the Boers had been prepared to concede any real reform, he would have done it then.

To Katharine Lyttelton,[1] *October* 17, 1899. I am depressed about this war: I admit the necessity of it and that it must be carried through but it has no business to be popular, and the cry of 'Revenge Majuba' dishonours us and destroys our reputation for good faith. I should like to break the heads of all the Music Halls first and then go out and teach the Boers gravely and sternly the things which they do not know.

To Haldane, November 10, 1899. Last Sunday I spent at Dalmeny and walked in the park with Rosebery for three hours. We had very good talk: he pointed out of course that my speech at Glasgow went beyond the line that he takes. I said it was so, but that though his speech at Bath struck a full and fine note, it was hardly possible for us, who have several speeches to make and to wrestle with constituents, to keep within the same limits: we had to argue and to say whether we were in the right or the wrong in this war with the Boers.

December 4, 1899. It looks to me as if we shall have trouble next session: we shall not get fair play — witness the attempt

[1] Wife of General Sir Neville Lyttelton. Both were Grey's lifelong friends.

to distinguish between us and Asquith — and if so I shall show my teeth.

The Government can hardly propose anything but a liberal settlement on equal lines for both races after the war, but Harcourt is sure to fake up some new kind of amendment to whatever is proposed, in order to keep the division in the party open. These are one set of difficulties ahead of us.

On the other hand, there are other difficulties: Jo's speech about the German alliance (unless it was expressly dictated beforehand by the German Emperor, which I can't believe) was disastrous. I never read anything which struck me as being more of a mess. He really must be kept out of foreign politics or he will make everything impossible, even friendship with America.[1]

At the same time Grey wrote to Munro Ferguson:

Jo seems to have made a most extraordinary speech about a German alliance: unless what he says has been sanctioned by the German Emperor, it seems to me most unwise to speak as he has done, in face of the fact that German public opinion is all against us.

The main points of Grey's speeches in the House and in the country were a defence of the justice and necessity of the war against the Boers; an attack on the Government as incompetent, and responsible by its oversight for the military disasters with which operations began; and a definition of the objects of the war as twofold, first to secure equal rights for all white men in a self-governing South Africa, into whatever districts it might be divided; and secondly to prevent for the future the creation of armaments in South Africa under any but British control.[2]

After the occupation of the Boer capital by the British

[1] Chamberlain had declared that 'the most natural Alliance is that between us and the German Empire,' and had invited the United States to join in the new triple alliance. These public proposals were ill received.

[2] For instance, his speech on February 1, 1900, *Hansard*, 78, pages 374–90.

army, the 'Khaki Election' was held in the autumn of 1900, on the plea that the war was already over, though it did not come to an end for nearly two more years. In this election campaign Chamberlain attacked all sections of the Opposition as unpatriotic, much to Grey's indignation. On the whole it is remarkable how little the Liberals lost at the polls considering their divisions and the fact of the war; 2,105,518 electors voted for Liberals and 2,428,000 for the Government. Probably if there had not been a section that supported the war, the Opposition would have suffered still heavier defeat. Both sections came back with a fair representation in the new Parliament.

> *To Haldane, May* 28, 1901. I went to meet Milner. I gave him your message and added something about your having been a very staunch friend to him, and he responded very warmly, saying, 'yes, I know that; one gets to find out in these times who one's best friends are.' I told him we were much exasperated by Jo's electioneering, and disbelieved in the general efficiency of the Government, and therefore voted freely against it on everything which did not compromise the issue in South Africa. But that we were quite firm on four points. (1) The prosecution of the war to a successful end. (2) Annexation. (3) An interval of direct Imperial administration leading eventually to representative government when the new territories had filled up and settled down. (4) That he was to be the administrator.
>
> I told him I believed these points to be absolutely secure, and that the personal attacks upon him (which Jo makes so much of) did not matter. They might divide the Liberal Party if carried far enough, but would have no influence on the course of affairs.

It will be well to contrast this letter with one that he wrote in March 1908 to Lady Helen Munro Ferguson, in reply to her request that he would speak about the Empire for the Victoria League:

> Well, I am ready to come. Only I don't think I can talk about the Colonies with Milner. He always says such rasping things, and he cannot keep attacks upon the Government's South African policy [of self-government] out of his speeches — a policy which he says the people of England should have 'spat out of their mouths.' Couldn't the Victoria League get Cromer to represent the Unionist side? May I come and see you about this?

Grey had by that time discovered that Milner and he had never 'meant the same thing' about South Africa. Milner had always intended British racial supremacy; Grey had meant equal rights for Boer and Briton.

As the war went on, Grey's disappointment was growing with Rosebery, who would not take the field. Grey looked to him in vain to erect a standard to which the country could rally.

> *To Munro Ferguson, October* 18, 1900. I think my word to R. will be that if he doesn't come out into the open in the next two years his chance will be gone anyhow, and that he may at any time get an ultimatum from some of us that we are not going on any more without him. If C.-B. goes on as leader, the only choice will be either to go full steam ahead on one's own line, or else to chuck it; and one's own line if C.-B. remains nominal leader and there is a resurrection of Harcourt, will be towards the Government, where I am neither wanted nor want to be. I don't care to fight for my own hand; there is nothing in C.-B. to fight for; and a good deal in Harcourt to fight against.
>
> *To Dorothy, August* 16, 1901. To be an ally of a man of genius, you have either to pay the price which he asks (sometimes an impossible one), or serve him for nothing. I sometimes think that the reason why Rosebery attracts so much attention is that the genius in him lifts him up so that he is conspicuous in the crowd, a head taller than it; people keep looking and admiring, no one else can stand so tall, but those who are quite close see that his feet aren't upon the ground. It's as if God dangled him amongst us by an invisible thread.

> *January* 28, 1902. Things seem pretty quiet. I hear nothing from R., and what I hear of him is rather tiresome and petty. He has a habit of hiding his light, and making it seem as if the light that was in him was darkness. I am all for letting him go his own way, but I don't think I can help him much to play his game at present. It is an *underground* game, which is all right for him; but for us, who are in the House here, it is difficult to take part in it without playing the *underhand* game. We are in contact with much from which he is free.

Once only during the Boer War did Rosebery descend to earth with trumpets and with pomp at Chesterfield, and then indeed with great effect. In December 1901 the much advertised meeting took place to hear his pronouncement. Chesterfield had been chosen as the navel or central point of England. The speech was indeed worthy even of such elaborate staging. It struck a note to which the country responded and to which the Government was soon fain to respond. Rosebery showed the futility of refusing terms to the Boers and demanding unconditional surrender; he repudiated indeed much of Campbell-Bannerman's criticism of our methods of warfare, but he demanded a display of that generosity to our future fellow-subjects which was being refused by the rigidity of Milner and the helplessness of the Government at home. The speech created a new atmosphere in which peace became possible. Six months later, largely through the good offices of Methuen and Kitchener, the Peace of Vereeniging closed the war on terms which brave men could accept. Chesterfield was the last great action of Rosebery's life, which thenceforward was lost in shallows and in miseries, like a river turning to swamp as it reaches the plains near the sea.

But though, by hastening peace, Chesterfield eventually solved the difficulties of the Liberal Party, for the moment it seemed to aggravate the intestine feud. Tempers were getting on edge with the long strain. The appearance of Rosebery as a rival leader, though only for a moment, incensed the followers of Campbell-Bannerman, and an interview between the two only made matters worse.

Grey's comments on Chesterfield were not very helpful. 'I agreed with the whole of Rosebery's speech,' he wrote to Sydney Buxton. 'His attack upon the government is the true line of attack but it is utterly spoilt by C. B. and the "pro-Boers."' The year 1902 was a year of rival leagues and dinners — 'war to the knife and fork' — within the Liberal ranks. Already, before Chesterfield, a Liberal Imperial Council had been founded with Grey as President; after Chesterfield the Liberal League took its place with Rosebery as President, and Asquith, Grey and Fowler as Vice-Presidents.[1]

What was the relation of Rosebery's League to the Party and to Campbell-Bannerman? It was a vexed question, to which different men gave different answers, and which only time would solve. If Rosebery had gone on with frequent speeches and active leadership, the split might have become complete and permanent. Fortunately he did not. He sank back after the Chesterfield effort, as Grey had foretold.

With the return of peace the chief cause of Liberal dissensions was removed. And there followed in quick succession Balfour's Education Bill of 1902 and Chamberlain's Protectionist campaign, which united Leaguers and former

[1] 'Campbell-Bannerman always distinguished between Asquith and other members of the Liberal League. He had the pleasant little habit of applying the term "master" to men whom he suspected of being up to mischief. It was "Master Haldane," and even "Master Grey," but it was never "Master Asquith."' (*Life of Lord Oxford and Asquith*, I, 145.)

'Pro-Boers' in hearty opposition. Asquith took the lead as protagonist in the country against Protection. Grey was active and enthusiastic; as was every Liberal of every hue, while the Unionist party was split from top to bottom. In this new and joyous excitement the very existence of the Liberal League was almost forgotten by its Vice-Presidents and by all men — except by its remote and lordly President, who thought it a force in politics long after it had ceased to be so.

Grey, from the beginning to the end of his life, was a convinced free trader. He regarded Chamberlain's proposals not only as ruinous for English commerce but as more likely to disrupt than to unite the Empire. As to Balfour's Education Bill, he spoke often and effectively in the House and country against its injustice to Nonconformists, while approving of the principle that the Counties and County Boroughs should become the Education Authorities. 'I would have no small School Boards in country districts, but I would have the Parish Councils partners in the management of education — subordinate but partners. Two members should represent the Parish Council, two the Local Authority and the Denomination should appoint the other two.' Throughout the debates on the Bill he took an active part in amendments and details, inspired by his belief that the country people whom he knew and represented should have a share in the control of their village schools, but subject to the Education Authority of the County as a whole.[1]

Throughout the years 1902–05 Grey took his full part as a speaker in the House and on platforms for the great causes in which he believed. The complaint made by Mr. Lloyd George in his *Memoirs* that Grey shunned the hard work and

[1] *Hansard* for 1902 *passim*, *e.g.* 107, pages 822–35.

blows of party warfare is not true of this period of his freedom, and is only so far true that during his subsequent eleven years as Foreign Secretary he had not the time or the physical energy to take as great a part as some Cabinet Ministers in the Budget and other campaigns. After 1905 his first duty was to Foreign Affairs, and in that he spent himself, breaking his health and losing his eyesight.

It may be noted that as early as January 22, 1902, he spoke in the House in favour of an agreement with Russia on Asian questions, especially on Persia. He deprecated, as equally wrong, perpetual quarrelling with Russia at all points, and a policy of drift. The first would lead to war, the second to Russia gaining all the points; so an agreement ought to be made.[1] It is clear then that he had come to this opinion on his own account when in Opposition, and did not merely imbibe it from his Foreign Office advisers after 1905. Nor is this wonderful, for peace with Russia was part of the old Gladstonian Liberal tradition.

In June 1904 he spoke in the House welcoming the agreement that Lansdowne had made with France about Morocco and Egypt. The word 'Germany' does not appear in the speech, but he said:

> Europe was some time ago divided into two, I will not say hostile, but certainly not friendly, camps, the Triple Alliance and the Dual Alliance. There has been a tendency to obliteration of the hard and fast lines between those two camps. Italy has made her arrangements with France directly. Austria has made her own arrangements with Russia directly. And we in our turn have now taken part in making a sort of arrangement with a view to creating greater frankness and friendliness between ourselves and France. Some time ago the atmosphere between ourselves and France may be said to have

[1] *Hansard* 1902, 101, pages 609–10.

WINSTON CHURCHILL, HALDANE, EDWARD AND DOROTHY GREY
At Lady Tweedmouth's Highland home, Guisachan, 1901

> been a glacial epoch. It has happily been changed to a genial epoch. . . . I welcome the agreement and hope that the government will lose no opportunity of making it a working model for other cases where it is possible to do so.

On this subject, that proved ere long of such grave import, Grey differed from Lord Rosebery. And it was one of the things that led to a more 'genial epoch' as between himself and that loving friend of France, Campbell-Bannerman.

> *To Dorothy, July* 12, 1905. At dinner at Rosebery's last night Lady Fisher made a lot of corking remarks, which corked everybody but Fisher. Fisher was talking with zeal of Togo, and Lady Fisher said 'Had Togo been a Christian he would not have sunk the Kowshing.' Fisher demurred. Whereupon Lady F. said to him across the table, 'You would not have done it.' 'Yes, I should,' said Fisher, 'but then I am not a Christian,' at which we all looked surprised and shocked. Rosebery was striking high notes about the French alliance. 'You are leaning on an aspen,' he said in tragic tones, 'and the German Emperor has four millions of soldiers and the second best navy in the world.'

This argument of Rosebery against making friends with France was based on the presumption that we should seek the strongest ally; but the Entente policy was based on the opposite idea, that neither we nor France were strong enough to afford to go on quarrelling in presence of the lord of four million soldiers and the second navy in the world. Would not Rosebery's line of policy have helped to set up a German hegemony which must have been fatal to us in the end, by destroying French independence? But Rosebery thought that Lansdowne had plunged too light-heartedly into the European maelstrom.

> *August* 13, 1905. *To Munro Ferguson.* I think more and more that Rosebery is wrong about Germany, and I feel it so strongly that if any government drags us back into the Ger-

man net I will oppose it openly at all costs. But it is a pity, now that we are free from German entanglements, to keep up an anti-German campaign in our press.

The distance now dividing Grey from Rosebery was great and was constantly increasing. He knew him to be unreliable as a leader and a party colleague because he would shroud himself in retirement and mystery; and the two men differed on the most fundamental question of foreign affairs. Dorothy alone still clung to the image of the Rosebery of the past. In October 1905 Grey writes: 'My wife is much against my going into office; she is one of the few out-and-out Roseberians that I know.'

During these years of waiting for the final demise of the Conservative Government, dying of old age and of Protection, Grey saw the possibility, but not more than the possibility, of being asked to take office on terms that would oblige him to accept. He still hung suspended between private and public life. In 1895 he had characteristically refused a Privy Councillorship, so as not to feel himself conscripted to politics. Eight years later his mind was made up only on one point: he would not after the next General Election perform any longer the futile antics of Opposition, in which he had spent nearly two decades. It should be either office or retirement to private life.

To Katharine Lyttelton, *April* 1903. I hate politics as much as ever and can't write about them: I think this Government [Balfour's] will flicker out in a year or two and a Ministry will be reformed under Chamberlain. I see no prospect of Liberals coming in before 1910, and have no more thoughts of office than for the last several years; but I have a Railway Board and other business, which is definite work, at which one can sit with one's feet on the ground, instead of standing on one's head hurraying with one's heels, which is almost all one can do in Opposition, while one goes on mouthing about public affairs. Fallodon is let again this year — that is another of the delights of politics.

Ever since 1898 he had been a director of the North-Eastern Railway, with a modest salary of three hundred pounds — not enough to save him from the dire need of letting Fallodon during the summer months of 1902–05, for he was never a rich man. The work was congenial and so was the company of his brother Directors, men like Sir Matthew Ridley and Sir Hugh Bell. Twice a month they met at York, dining pleasantly together overnight and transacting their business next morning. The Station Hotel, York, which he liked, played a large part in his life.[1] In 1904 he was chosen Chairman, on Ridley's death, with more work and a salary of two thousand pounds a year, which would have enabled him to live exactly as he wished. 'I am in for what may be my life's job,' he wrote to Dorothy.

> The year 1905 was one of the happiest of my life; the work of Chairman of the Railway was agreeable and interesting, but it left in those days plenty of leisure. There were many days spent at home, in the Itchen valley or in Scotland. If only I could be free from politics, there was a prospect of permanent and interesting work, with income sufficient for all we needed, and a more constant home and country life than we had yet enjoyed. Life, which had been very pleasant since 1895, promised to become more pleasant still. It was not to be.[2]

[1] In March 1899 he writes to Dorothy from the Station Hotel, of a walk after a Board meeting: 'I have had a walk alone in a fine March wind and sun up the Ouse, and watched the ripples and wondered whether I could have put a salmon fly as far as the opposite bank, and at last I came to quite open country, larger than Battersea Park, with no people, and felt as if having seen the wide fields and free sky I had looked God in the face and been refreshed, and I thought I would write and tell you.'

[2] *Twenty-five Years*, chapter IV.

In September 1904 he wrote to his friend Barton:

> We are now in a state of suspense. I have one foot in business and one in politics; if the Liberals win the next election and come into office, and I with them, I should put both feet in politics. If not I shall probably after the next election put both feet into business. I can't go on any more with half and half, and politics in Opposition perpetually are wearisome and useless.

In a letter to a friend connected with another railway line he describes one aspect of the North-Eastern Railway policy:

> I think your Directors are wrong in not recognising the Union to the extent of letting the men be represented by the man or men of their choice. The N.E.R. always met the officials of the Union. No doubt the Union kept putting forward demands on the N.E.R., but the Union was strong, and did what other Unions do, and the trouble would have been worse between Directors and men, if the N.E.R. had not recognised the Union. I suppose the other Lines think they can smash the Union or prevent its being formed in their systems, but I believe that Unions will form anyhow and that in the long run you can deal better with organised than unorganised labour.

Grey retired from the Chairmanship and from the Board of the Railway when he became Foreign Secretary in December 1905, and was re-elected to the Board in January 1917, the moment he recovered his freedom.[1] The railway indeed was no inconsiderable part of his life and of his connection with his northern neighbours of all classes, many of whom came to feel for him, as years went by, the deepest reverence and affection.

The unpopularity of Balfour's government in its last years was completed by the introduction of Chinese indentured

[1] After the amalgamation he became a director of the London and North-Eastern.

labour into the South African mines, which seemed to the average elector a poor outcome

> For all this waste of wealth and loss of blood

in the war. Grey shared the Liberal feeling on the subject, though he expressed it with his usual temperance of language. But the differences inside the party were not yet over.

> *To Dorothy, February* 23, 1904. There is a horrid set being made at Haldane because he abstained from the vote against Chinese Labour. The Massingham people now count on excluding him from the next government, and they are so elated by things generally that they think they can exclude us all, including Asquith, and have a real Radical government of their own. What a futile thing it would be — all froth! Isn't Haldane curious? He has so often differed from the party by rising into idealism above it, and now on Chinese Labour he has thrown ideals aside, and followed the narrow practical point that without Chinese Labour there will be a deficit in the Transvaal Revenue. But he is the same dear old Haldane still.

Before leaving the subject of South Africa, it will be well here to print a letter which Grey wrote to his old Winchester fag-master, Lord Selborne, whom the Balfour Government made High Commissioner in South Africa in 1905 and who retained that post under the Liberals until 1910. The letter is dated December 22, 1905, a few days after Grey took Cabinet office. It shows that he was then, as he always had been, in favour of unequivocal equality between Boers and British; that he wanted responsible self-government set up at once in place of the 'Lyttelton Constitution,' and that he did not need to be persuaded to this course in the following February by Campbell-Bannerman's famous appeal to the Cabinet. He always spoke in the highest terms of Campbell-Bannerman's conduct of South Africa as Prime Minister, and it was one of several things that led him, when in office, to feel a real admiration and personal loyalty to his chief, whom in opposition he had so often misunderstood.

FOREIGN OFFICE,
December 22, 1905.

MY DEAR SELBORNE,

Your letter is not specially directed to what was the one practical point in my speeches in the autumn, namely, that the experiment of Chinese labour was already on such a large scale that it ought to be arrested at the point it has now reached, and that if it was to be continued in the future it should be done after longer experience by a representative and responsible Government in the Transvaal and not by the Imperial Government at home.

As to the general question of Chinese labour, with which your letter does deal, I cannot but feel strongly that it is a bad foundation on which to build up an industry; that the less of the mining industry there is that rests on the foundation of Chinese labour the better; and that it would be much better for the mining industry to develop slowly on a healthier foundation than to develop rapidly with the help of Chinese. I was not much in love with the system of Indian apprenticeship in the West Indies; it is open to abuse. But there, at any rate, the imported Indians live a normal life with their wives and families in open villages. There are not restrictions on their movements in holiday time, nor upon the sort of labour in which they may be employed, and at the end of their term of apprenticeship they are encouraged to settle in the country, to take up land, and to engage in any occupation which they please. All these conditions are absent in the case of the Chinese in the Transvaal, and that, to my mind, makes a world of difference.

I realise the risk of introducing responsible government immediately, and am impressed by what you say about it, but are not the risks greater on the other side? Will not the Representative Assembly, when it has been elected without responsibility, at once, or very soon, pass a Resolution demanding responsible government? The grant of responsible government will then have the appearance of being extorted by force from a Government at home which was reluctant to give it. If there be a British majority at the time, the Boers will say that we held our hand till we had made sure that there would be a British majority to keep them down. If, on the other hand, there be a Boer majority, it will no doubt be said that a Liberal Government is betraying the British to the Boers. Would it not be better, even if the elections have to be postponed for a few months, that representation and responsibility should be simultaneous, and that the first elections which take place in the Transvaal should be with a full knowledge on the part of the electors that they are voting not merely for representation, but for responsibility?...

I can write to you only as a friend and not as a Member of the Government, so please take all I have said as my private and unofficial opinions, which don't necessarily represent anybody but myself.

As the autumn of 1905 drew on towards winter, there was a general feeling that Balfour's Ministry must presently come to an end. A Liberal Government of some kind, strong or weak, brief or long-lived, appeared certain. And expectation pointed to Grey as Foreign Minister. At the same time Germany was threatening France, on the question of Morocco; Delcassé had resigned to avert the worst consequences of German indignation. 'Your friends the French are trembling like an aspen,' said Rosebery to Grey. What would England do? Would she implement her undertakings about Morocco or would the Anglo-French understanding melt away in the beams of the Kaiser's wrath? A good deal that was written in the English Liberal press seemed to augur that a new Ministry would revert to splendid isolation rather than run the risk of a quarrel with Germany. There was grave alarm in Paris. For the two extremes of the Liberal body, Rosebery and the Radicals, appeared to agree in dislike of the policy of Lansdowne. In these circumstances the speech that Grey made at a meeting of Free Trade electors in the City on October 21, 1905, was of great importance at the time, in checking this movement in England and abating these fears in France. And it remains today of real biographical interest, because it puts on record the views on our future relations with Japan, France, Russia and Germany which he had formed for himself in opposition, before he came in contact with the magnates of the Foreign Office as his official advisers. The part of his famous 'City Speech' that referred to Foreign Affairs was as follows:

> I observe in some quarters that there is being industriously circulated an idea that a change of Government in this country would bring some new and unwelcome change in foreign policy.... In my opinion there is no foundation whatever for such a suspicion. There are three cardinal features at the present moment of British policy, not one of which does the Liberal Party wish to see changed. The first is the growing friendship and good feeling between ourselves and the United States, a matter of common ground and common congratulation to all parties in this country.
>
> Another feature is the alliance between Great Britain and Japan. Now it is quite true that, looking at the question of alliances not in the particular but in the abstract, there is a good deal which might be said. People do say, with perfect truth, that any question of entering into a definite alliance with regard to future contingencies with any power whatever is one which should be carefully guarded and watched. Were the policy of alliances rashly entered upon, I quite admit that there would be a danger that this country might be led into undesirable entanglements. That, I think, is perfectly true; and all that should be borne in mind whenever it is a question of contracting any new alliance with a foreign Power. But the question as regards us and Japan has not been the making of a new alliance but the renewing of an old existing alliance — a very different question to which these general considerations do not apply. I am convinced of this — that the next House of Commons will not be one which will support a Government

which weakens with regard to the Japanese Alliance. I say that with confidence, because it is in its essence a defensive alliance. It has regard to the *status quo* in the Far East as recognised now by the whole world after the war; it has regard to the policy of the maintenance of the integrity of China and of the open door in China, about which, I believe, also, the world is agreed. It has also regard to our Indian Empire....

Another cardinal point in our foreign policy has been our French Agreement. I am aware that the details of that agreement have, in some quarters, been the subject of criticism. I do not think that the spirit of the agreement has been the subject of criticism in any quarter, and I have always said, and I think subsequent events have confirmed the truth of the observation, that the spirit of the agreement is more important than the letter of the agreement. It is true that, since the agreement has been made, there has been some diplomatic trouble. I think the causes of that trouble are not to be sought in the agreement, but in other, deeper, and further-reaching causes. But if anyone is disturbed by the diplomatic trouble which has taken place, I would advise him to ask himself, whether, if there had been no agreement between us and France, it is not probable that there would have been trouble more serious for France and possibly for ourselves. I hold to the opinion I first expressed with regard to that agreement — that it is a matter of cordial congratulation to all of us that we are now on terms of such friendship with our brilliant neighbour on the other side of the Channel.

But you may fairly ask, Is there no room for improvement in some other respects? With most powers our relations I believe, at the present moment, to be perfectly satisfactory. In one or two respects, no doubt, they might be improved. We are perfectly ready to enter into new friendships bearing in mind that you can never make a new friendship which is worth having by backing out of an old one. That is the condition of further pacific advances on the part of British diplomacy today.

Those who are anxious for further advances, I think, have in their minds especially Russia and Germany.... If Russia accepts, cordially and whole-heartedly, our intention to preserve the peaceable possession of our existing Asiatic possessions, then I am quite sure that in this country no Government will make it its business to thwart or obstruct Russia's policy in Europe. On the contrary, it is urgently desirable that Russia's influence should be re-established in the councils of Europe. The estrangement between us and Russia has, in my opinion, its roots not in the present but solely in the past. It may be, perhaps it must be, that confidence between the two countries must be a plant of slow growth; but the conditions should be favourable to its growth, and it should be the business of both Governments to foster and encourage those conditions.

I cannot mention Russia without saying a word on a more delicate matter, and that is our relations with Germany.... I am sure of this that if there is a desire for the improvement of our relations with Germany — I do not mean in the relations of the British and German Governments, because so far as I know, those are quite correct, but an improvement between the Press and public opinion of the two countries — if there be a desire for that in Germany, it will meet with no obstacle in this country provided it be clearly understood that nothing we do in our relations with Germany is in any way to impair our existing good relations with France. In other words it must be, in my opinion, a condition of any improvement in the public relations between Germany and ourselves that the relations of Germany with France on all matters which come under the French Agreement should be fair and good also.

I think it is important at the present moment to emphasise the need for continuity of foreign policy.... There is an impression in some quarters that free governments owing to the changes of party, cannot have the same trustworthy and reliable foreign policy as autocratic governments. I believe that to be wrong — as regards ourselves certainly wrong; and I wish at the present moment to emphasise the fact that the friendship of the people of this country is as sure and as well worth having as that of any monarch or autocratic government in the world.

Two months later, in his Albert Hall speech, Campbell-Bannerman announced the continuation of the entente with

France as an integral part of the policy of the new government.

Two other letters of Grey's this same autumn show that he did not think the Foreign Office always right:

> *To Munro Ferguson, October* 31, 1905. I think our people are getting a little afraid that the officials in the F.O. are too anti-German. The Madeira port might be construed as showing too great anxiety to take points against Germany in advance. Haldane is now the recipient of the woes and lamentations of the German Ambassador. We have long lived in dread of hearing that he has received the Victorian Order, and we now fear that it may be accompanied by the Red Eagle. But he seems quite sound about foreign policy nevertheless.
>
> *November* 23, 1905. I am not clear as to why we blocked the Germans at Madeira.[1] It is always a mistake to erect a small question into a big one. Let us be stiff on the things that matter to us, not on the things that don't.

The principle here laid down is highly characteristic of Grey and underlies all his subsequent handling of Foreign Affairs.

Late in November 1905 it was known that Balfour was on the point of resignation. The Liberal ship seemed coming into port before a favouring breeze, but even then there were shoals that almost caused a wreck. The first was Rosebery's revival of the Irish question. The Free Trade vote, that was to sweep the Liberals into power at the coming election, was composed of elements by no means agreed on Home Rule. But to abandon Home Rule was impossible to the Liberal leaders, for reasons both of expediency and of conviction. They must not alienate Redmond, though he could not in the next Parliament be satisfied: and Home Rule was still in

[1] The Madeira question here referred to is mentioned in *G. and T.* III, 61, and VIII, 51. It never came up in an acute or even in a definite form, nor did Grey's policy when he came into office differ from Lansdowne's in the matter.

their belief the only ultimate solution of the Irish question. After consulting with Asquith, Campbell-Bannerman made a careful statement in a speech at Stirling, in which he announced the 'step-by-step' policy for Ireland, indicating that a Home Rule Bill could not be introduced into the next Parliament, and that British opinion must have time to ripen before the Irish question could be finally settled. Rosebery, quite out of touch in his self-chosen isolation, did not know that Asquith had agreed to this policy, and at Bodmin on November 25 he attacked Campbell-Bannerman as having 'raised the banner of Home Rule'; he declared, 'I cannot serve under that banner.' The supporters of the falling Government read Rosebery's speech as men read an unexpected reprieve from a sentence of death; Free Traders were proportionately dismayed. For it was already known that Balfour would resign office in a few days, and if a split among the Liberal chiefs coincided in time with their call to office, the country might reject them in disgust at the polls. But Asquith and Grey, unlike Rosebery, were Home Rulers and agreed with the principle of the Stirling announcement. Grey at once made a speech to say so, and received sheaves of letters from Liberals of all colours thanking him for having saved the situation. Rosebery complained that his Vice-Presidents in the Liberal League had not informed him of their previous concurrence with Campbell-Bannerman and of the interpretation that they placed upon the Stirling speech. Asquith and Grey complained in return that Rosebery had spoken at Bodmin before consulting them. The fact was that the Liberal League and the loyalty to Rosebery which it implied had become a thing of the past to almost everyone except Rosebery himself, who had tried for too long to be both in and out of politics. To a common friend he spoke of Grey's attitude to his Bodmin speech as 'the greatest blow I ever had in my political life'; but he kept his temper. The personal friendship was not broken, but the political separation was complete. The following private letters throw light on Grey's part in the affair:

Rosebery to Grey, November 28, 1905. I was delighted to see your speech and that you read C.-B.'s speech quite differently from me. I wish with all my heart that yours is the right reading, and can scarcely doubt that it is so after what you tell me of Asquith's conference with C.-B. But how could I guess that conference? How could I divine it? Is it not a pity that I should be kept entirely in the dark with regard to a matter of such supreme importance, particularly when I was on a speaking tour? All I can say is that I was in a house full of people who all took the same view as I did. What is more important is that the Irish press did the same. I am not the least infallible, but the case for my interpretation (without the secret interpretation of the conference with C.-B.) seems to me overwhelming. Anyhow I hope C.-B. will openly confirm your view tonight.

Grey to Munro Ferguson, December 1, 1905. I was in a bad corner when I spoke on Monday. I knew that C.-B. had told Asquith before his Stirling speech that he didn't disagree with A.'s declaration on Ireland in October and meant not to dissent from it. I didn't construe the Stirling speech as a departure from that, nor did Asquith, who telegraphed to me on Monday just before the meeting.[1] About the same time as A.'s telegram, arrived Allard with letters and views from Cornwall (not from R. but from those who were with him) urging me to back up R. without qualification. Of course Asquith and I ought to have bethought ourselves to warn R. not to take C.-B.'s speech as he did; but to speak frankly I don't think C.-B.'s speech should have given the Cornwall party quite the impression it did.... I cannot say that my aphorism 'In politics great men are always troublesome, especially to each other' was suggested solely by Balfour and Chamberlain.

[1] The telegram ran: 'Hope you will repudiate R.'s interpretation of Stirling speech which is perfectly innocuous sense Asquith.'

Rosebery to Grey, December 1, 1905. Twice has C.-B. raised voice and said nothing. This is significant. He could put an end to the present situation in a sentence by saying that you and Asquith rightly interpreted his utterance and that I interpreted it wrongly. The responsibility rests with him and his silence, and not with — your A. R.

Grey to Rosebery, December 2, 1905. Of course C.-B. must be responsible for the consequences of his own silence. Meanwhile, with the possible exception of Bob Reid, everyone who has spoken this week has deciphered C.-B.'s Stirling speech as I did; and everybody knows what the limit of Irish policy must be in the next Parliament. This being so I think it is a pity to make more of the Irish question than need be; it is not really the test issue for next election.

Rosebery being thus disposed of by his own deed, it might have been hoped that the decks were now cleared for the Liberal action. Balfour resigned on December 4 and Campbell-Bannerman proceeded to form his Cabinet. He was prepared to treat the Liberal Imperialist 'Triumvirate' as handsomely as their great abilities and influence required. Asquith would be Chancellor of the Exchequer and Grey Foreign Secretary; Haldane would not indeed hold the post of Lord Chancellor which he coveted, but which the Prime Minister reserved for his own tried and faithful friend Bob Reid; but Haldane was of far more use to the country as War Minister. These arrangements were eventually carried out, but at the eleventh hour they were almost thwarted by a crisis in Cabinet-making, for which all three members of the 'Triumvirate' must bear a certain share of blame.

In order to understand what happened in those foggy December days in Campbell-Bannerman's house in Belgrave Square, it is necessary to go back to bright September at Relugas, the fishing lodge above the wooded gorge of the Findhorn, where Grey was flinging his salmon line from the steep rocks. While he was so employed, Haldane brought Asquith over to Relugas, and on their joint initiative persuaded the more passive Grey to enter into the 'Relugas Compact,' as Haldane called it, to the effect that unless Campbell-Bannerman would take a Peerage and leave the leadership of the Commons to Asquith, they would none of them take office. Thus the initiative in this affair was taken by Haldane and Asquith, though it was Grey who persisted longest in trying to carry out his part of the agreement.[1]

The wish that Campbell-Bannerman should take a Peerage and leave the leadership of the Commons to Asquith may have been a mistake, but it was a very natural mistake at the time. The view was shared by some colleagues who were not of the Imperialist section.[2] And Campbell-Bannerman's confidential medical man warned him, a week too late, that he was not in a fit state of health to lead the Commons in

[1] Haldane's story in his *Autobiography* (page 159) is quite definite: 'We resolved to take some step. Here Asquith and I were more practical than Grey, who hated to have to make any move. I went to Asquith at a country house he and his wife had taken at Glen of Rothes in the north-east of Scotland. Grey had a fishing at Relugas, only about fifteen miles off. After consultation, Asquith and I decided to go over to confer with Grey. This was at the beginning of September, 1905. We talked the situation over with him. It was decided that it was of great importance that the King, who would soon have to summon a Prime Minister, should be cognizant of the situation. Asquith thought that as I had been much in contact with the King over London University, I would be a natural channel of communication. Grey did not dissent, but he thought that Asquith should also see Campbell-Bannerman as early as possible and tell him our difficulties. What we agreed on was as stated above, that if Campbell-Bannerman became Prime Minister he should take a Peerage, and that Asquith should lead in the Commons as Chancellor of the Exchequer. Unless our scheme were in substance carried out we resolved that we could not join Campbell-Bannerman's government. What we thus resolved on we used afterwards at times to speak of among ourselves as the "Relugas Compact."'

[2] *Grey to Dorothy, February* 13, 1905. 'I had rather a good talk with Morley; we lunched together at the Athenaeum, and while we were talking Joe and Buckle coming in, no doubt for the same purpose, stumbled upon us, which amused us all. I really think I got John M. to see that it is vital to have Asquith in at once as leader of the H. of C., if we form a Government.' In later years Morley wrote of this as 'a truly unhappy suggestion,' but he had not apparently so regarded it in February 1905.

addition to his duties as Prime Minister: in fact he hastened his own death by undertaking the double charge. But for the 'Triumvirate' to try to impose their arrangement on Campbell-Bannerman by refusing to join the Government on any other terms was a grave error. Particularly was it wrong to risk a split in the party on the eve of a General Election. The 'Relugas Compact' had been made in September on the assumption that the new government would be formed after the election, not before it as proved to be the case. Asquith in December saw this and withdrew from his agreement with Haldane and Grey, after sounding Campbell-Bannerman — and finding him unwilling to promise to go to the Lords. Haldane stood by the Compact a few days longer than Asquith, and Grey for a few hours longer than Haldane. He had no wish for office for himself, and considered that though Asquith was necessary for the success of a Liberal Government, he himself was not.

Grey was misled by two beliefs, both of which he afterwards admitted to have been wrong: first the belief that Campbell-Bannerman could not effectively lead the House — a mistake not unnatural to those who had watched him there as leader of the Opposition;[1] and secondly the belief that there might still be differences in policy between the friends of Campbell-Bannerman and the former 'Imperialist' section of the party. Such a possible divergence rendered it necessary, in Grey's eyes, that the Government spokesman either in the House of Commons or in the House of Lords should be one of his old allies — either Asquith in the Com-

[1] Mr. J. A. Spender writes: 'On his *form* in Opposition it was by no means unreasonable to suggest that he might be unequal to the double burden of conducting the Government and leading the House of Commons in the new Parliament. There never was in fact a more miraculous change in the *form* of a public man than from Campbell-Bannerman as leader of Opposition to Campbell-Bannerman as Prime Minister.' (*Life of Campbell-Bannerman*, II, 404–05.)

mons, or Haldane in the Lords, since Rosebery was now out of the question.

On December 4, 1905, the day Balfour resigned, Asquith and Grey saw Campbell-Bannerman and found themselves in complete agreement on Irish policy and all seemed most amicable. But that night at ten o'clock Grey went back alone to the Prime Minister elect and told him that he could not serve under him unless he transferred his own leadership from the Commons to the Lords. It was a strange interview. Campbell-Bannerman was much hurt, and complained that Grey had come 'all buttoned up and never undoing one button.'

It emerged that Asquith no longer supported Grey in issuing the ultimatum, but Haldane still stood by the Relugas Compact. For three days the whole political world was in confusion, and the formation of the Ministry was held up by Grey's refusal to serve. Campbell-Bannerman, who never lost his temper under very trying circumstances, consented to keep the Foreign Secretaryship vacant while the peacemakers went to work. There was indeed no one else whom he wished to appoint to the post — neither Morley nor another. Among many mediators, Arthur Acland and Mr. J. A. Spender were the most active and influential in making the two recusants see reason. Grey was living at Haldane's house. Dorothy was at Fallodon during these critical days, and her letters show that her influence was not strongly used in either direction; she hoped her husband would remain in private life, she cared for politics even less than before since Rosebery had quitted the scene; but she was aware that her husband had a duty to the party, and above all to his Northumbrian constituents, and this last consideration weighed heavily with them both.

On December 6 Grey proposed as a compromise that Campbell-Bannerman should continue to lead in the Commons, and Haldane become Lord Chancellor and answer for the Government in the Lords. But the Prime Minister stood firm by his promise of the Chancellorship to his friend Bob Reid. Late in the afternoon of December 7, Haldane was persuaded that he ought to surrender for fear of splitting the party on the eve of the polls, but he would not go into office without his friend. That evening he and Acland besieged Grey, who at last yielded to the united voices of all his political allies.

His fear of injuring Asquith's career by deserting him was one motive for his surrender. Another, and the most potent, was the fear strongly felt by all whom he consulted that a split among the Liberal leaders would mean disaster for the Free Trade cause at the coming General Election. His comment in retrospect is that these fears about the election, which led him to take the right course, were themselves erroneous, for the event showed that nothing could have prevented the country from voting Liberal. But he also admits that the reasons which made him wish to refuse office were no less mistaken, for he found that Campbell-Bannerman led the Commons excellently (though it cost him his life), and there proved to be no divergences of policy. 'I had made difficulties, as I now think unnecessarily, about going into office, but when in it I made none.... From the moment his Cabinet was formed Campbell-Bannerman made no distinction in personal relations, in intimacy and sympathy between those who had helped him and those who had made difficulties for him when the party was in opposition.' [1]

[1] *Twenty-five Years*, chapter V.

A year later Grey wrote to Campbell-Bannerman:

> All my forecast before the elections was wrong, and your presence in the House of Commons has been not only desirable but essential to manage this party, and keep it together; and so it continues to be; and I most sincerely wish you health and strength for the coming year.

The story of this curious affair, which so nearly gave another management to Britain's foreign policy and army in the fateful years that ensued, has been told at full in Mr. Spender's *Life of Campbell-Bannerman* and in Haldane's *Autobiography*. The following letters will throw further light on Grey's motives in his prolonged obstinacy and final surrender.

> *Grey* (from London) *to Dorothy* (at Fallodon), *December* 5, 1905. All is going splendidly so far. I told C.-B. that I could take no office unless he went to the Lords and Asquith led in the Commons. He said there would be no question of his going to the Lords at any rate at first. I said then I must stand out; we parted quite cordially; he took my really outrageous (from me to him) proposal in perfect temper and said very nice things. I left him; told Asquith, and wrote a letter at midnight to C.-B. saying I should not change. So I am in the position of having definitely refused. Of course the situation may change and C.-B. give way. I devoutly hope not.

The first and the last sentence of this intimate letter prove that his desire to be able to remain in private life gave strength to his political doubts; the letters that follow show how these wishes and doubts were at length outweighed by consideration for Asquith and for the Free Trade cause.

> *Asquith to Grey*, *December* 5, 1905. I saw C.-B. again this afternoon, but too late to come to see you afterwards. I gathered from what he said that he was rather smarting from the way in which you had presented the case to him, and that he would therefore regard it as a 'humiliation' now to recede.

But the impression left on me was that he would not be indisposed to yield, if something in the nature of a golden bridge could be constructed for him. Do you think you could do anything in that direction?

Grey to Dorothy, *December* 6. It is harassing beyond all experience: I held out all yesterday against pressure on some points, which were peculiarly difficult, especially this that I was wrecking Asquith (not urged by Asquith himself). This morning I offered an alternative, viz. that Haldane should go to the Woolsack and lead the Lords, C.-B. remaining in the Commons. I cannot possibly carry both points; if I don't carry one in the next twenty-four hours I stay out altogether; but if either is conceded I must go in. Don't think I have been very weak. You can't realize till I tell you how the matter has been complicated by Asquith's difficult position. R. B. H. is sublime, but of course he isn't in the fighting line yet.[1] Asquith's position is the more difficult and painful; but it seems to C.-B. and the rest as if, had it not been for me, there would have been no difficulty. I am afraid they must think me a beast; in a way I feel one, but I am a beast in the right. Now don't form any opinion on all this till you see me. It has put me on short rations of sleep for two nights. If I go in, you mustn't judge me, till you have heard. If I carry neither point, I stay out and no explanations to you will be necessary. If I stay out, Asquith will have to decide what he does; if he goes in without me his position will be horrid and people will say he has abandoned me in order to have office. If he stays out with me it is considered that the Liberal Party will smash and Free Trade may be beaten at the Election. Do you see what it will be for him if he has to decide alone? Your very much harassed and highly wrought E.

December 7. C.-B. has refused either to go to the Lords or to put Haldane on the Woolsack. Asquith has been to tell me so, and to say that he cannot take the responsibility of staying outside the Government and splitting the party. So he goes in.

R. B. H., dear man, stays with me. Don't blame Asquith; it was hard for him, cruelly hard. I have written a letter to C.-B. giving my reason, to make sure there is no misunder-

[1] Haldane had not yet been offered a post and had not yet therefore refused one. But it was known that he stood with Grey.

> standing as to why I stay out. I have promised Asquith to stay in town till tomorrow morning so I shall not get to you till Saturday evening.

Actually Grey changed his mind late that night and accepted office next day.

> *December* 8. *Grey to Munro Ferguson.* All four Vice-Presidents of the Liberal League are going to join the Government. Rosebery's outburst about Home Rule has had a bad effect on our prospects for the Election, and we cannot stand them being made any worse by any of us standing out. That is the deciding factor as I know it.

Rosebery wrote a letter handsomely congratulating Grey on taking office, and was present at a Liberal League party on December 11, which the Greys attended. Rosebery was delightful, and on the whole the party was a gay one, but Dorothy, who had come south at last, was sad: 'This is separation,' she said. Three years later Grey wrote to Munro Ferguson, 'I never forget Dorothy's saying *This is separation* when I went in, but for all that there isn't one of the issues on which we were working together in the League, which I can fairly be said to have sacrificed.'

Dorothy accepted her fate with a meek resignation and the resolve to do her duty. On December 21 she wrote to Ella Pease:

> This last fortnight has been quite the most horrid we have ever had and it is a great grief to both of us that E. is in a government without Rosebery. But I am very glad he should have work that interests him so much. There is a lot of flummery about the Foreign Office, and I try not to think about how badly I shall do my small part of the work. But I shall try very hard.

And to another friend she wrote:

> I have got spoilt by living in a small way and being rather ill and just seeing either people I liked very much or nobody

> at all. And now I've just got to come out of that and we have properly to try and like it. It won't last long though, and I shall go back.

It lasted eleven years for him, but only a few weeks for her. There is little doubt that if she had lived, the mere fact that she was there, even if not her direct advice, would always have been a pull to draw him back out of office; whereas the misery and vacancy caused by her death made him, year after year, welcome the most exacting work as the surest relief.

The last weeks of their married life were strange indeed. Fate was weaving its net around him, never to be loosed again. The loud roar of the Liberal landslide at the General Election penetrated into the large cold room at the Foreign Office; but it brought only a little joy to the heart of the new Foreign Secretary, who found himself face to face with a crisis that might mean war in a few weeks, and did mean war in eight years. He had exchanged Hudson and the birds for Cambon and the Sphinx riddle of the modern world, little realized as yet by his countrymen. His action as Foreign Secretary during that first December and January will be discussed in later chapters.

Meanwhile here are his brief notes to Dorothy at Fallodon:

> *F.O. January* 1, 1906. I am up to my eyes in work and have a settled sadness at being in office. I think of it every morning when I wake and feel just as I did about being at school. The electric light has gone out suddenly and I have nothing but two quiet candles to work on with in this large room. It is very cold.
>
> *January* 15. The polls today are overwhelming. Happy and brilliant Winston! I still can't believe that everything will go like this. Do you see that a man named Jowett has been elected? Do you think he can be at all like our Jowett?
>
> *January* 16. Things are better and have for the time a better

appearance in Foreign Affairs. I had another talk with Cambon yesterday and feel just a little as if I was seeing my way and had my hand on things. I dined at Brooks's last night: there was a crowd in the hall watching the tape. I left when about twelve Liberal gains had been announced, and after I came home I heard the Liberal Club crowd cheering at intervals, so I knew other Liberal gains were appearing. This morning I see there were even more than on Saturday. I am very sorry that Hugh Cecil is out; but Robert Cecil is in and will add to the interest of the H. of C.

February 1, 1906. I had tremendous difficult talks and work yesterday and very important [the famous interview with Cambon, see page 148 below]. I do not know that I did well but I did honestly. But I don't think it can have been harder to face than your talk with [a servant from whom Dorothy was parting at Fallodon].

That was his last letter to her, and she never read it. She was alone at Fallodon, waiting for Grey to join her for the Sunday. On the first of February she took out the dog-cart and drove north along the lanes. The horse shied; she was thrown out on her head and stunned. They took her into the little schoolhouse at Ellingham, where the Vicar, her friend Mr. McGonigle, took charge, but she never recovered consciousness. Her husband, fetched from London, stayed in the village till she died on the early morning of February 4, 1906. Mrs. Creighton, the intimate friend of both Edward and Dorothy, wrote in the *Memoir* of her:

> They carried her body back to Fallodon that afternoon. It lay in the library, beautiful in death, with a smile of perfect peace. The sun streamed in through the open windows and the squirrel came in as usual to fetch its nuts from the box. The first snowdrops from the garden were laid upon her breast.

According to her desire, she was cremated at Darlington, in the presence of her husband, Mrs. Creighton and two or three other friends.

> In 1886 [writes Mrs. Creighton] a cousin of Dorothy's, meeting her for the first time after her marriage at a ball, said to her, 'I wish you a long and happy life.' 'No, not long,' Dorothy answered, 'only twenty years.' She had had her twenty years, twenty years of happiness which had made others happy, of a happiness which was like a blessing. I do not think she would have asked why it was cut short. She had too clear a sense of the bigness of things to imagine one can either understand or explain. She was very reverent where she could not understand. We, too, would be very reverent when we think of the mystery of her swift passing, of the pure wonder of her noble life.

Those who have read the third chapter of this book will understand that his wife's death meant to Grey even more than the tragic end of a happy marriage usually means to the survivor. He had shared with her all his mind, all his happiness, all his pursuits. He had no life but their common life. All had now to be rebuilt, on the basis of solitude — and remembrance of things past. Now would be seen how great was his strength, never before tested to the full. That his character gained by this ordeal of suffering is certain. He was a nobler man in the latter part of his life than he had been in the days of his perfect happiness.

He did what was right and wise in this crisis of his soul: he shouldered his work and he opened his heart to his friends. There were only four days during which the Foreign Office pouches did not come; he started on them again the day after her funeral, and a few days later was back in London. His letters to Mrs. Creighton and some others, and his talk to Haldane, had no concealments, now and for years to come, as to his sufferings and his fight to master them. For he was too close to nature to be reserved where there was no occasion, though he had in a supreme degree a natural dignity, impressive without offence.

He had been awakened from his dream of happiness with Dorothy amid the woods and birds, a dream as beautiful as their friend Hudson's imaginings in *Green Mansions*. Yet it had not been a dream; for long it had been a reality on earth and it lived in his retentive and practised memory. On these terms he was left alone, to face for eleven years a task as grim as any British statesman has ever had to face. His eyes were grave to sadness, as men saw who looked on him, but the well-springs within were not dry.

NOTE

In a letter to Mr. Spender of May 10, 1923, Grey writes:

> On the afternoon of February 1, 1906, I remember that John Morley lunched with me in my room at the F.O. Later I went to the Committee of Defence: while I was there Louis Mallet came over with a telegram saying that my wife had been thrown out of a carriage and was dangerously hurt and unconscious. I caught the evening train north from King's Cross and after that my mind is a blank for some days as regards Foreign Affairs. My wife remained unconscious and died in the night of February 3 to 4. I began to have F.O. papers sent me again after the funeral on the 7th.

BOOK II

THE FOREIGN OFFICE

DECEMBER 1905 — DECEMBER 1916

Introduction

Grey's Principles of Policy

For eleven years, from December 1905 to December 1916, Grey was the mouthpiece of England to foreign nations. Every year he loomed larger in the eyes of Europe and America, at least until the guns spoke and diplomacy became the handmaid of war. His increasing prominence in the world's counsels was due in part to the unusual length of his tenure of the same office; in part to his personal character, its weight, steadfastness and moderation; and in part to the unchanging nature of the policy he pursued.

Even in wartime, though the desperate needs of the doubtful struggle for national existence overrode some of the principles of his peacetime diplomacy, such as his objection to making secret treaties, yet the aim and temper of his previous policy of peace still survived in some important respects: as for instance, his desire, so far as national safety permitted, to be just to neutral needs and rights in matters of 'blockade'; his determination in particular to keep the friendship of America, which alike in peace and war he always regarded as England's most vital interest of all; and his preparation of the ground, in co-operation with American statesmen, for a League of Nations to preserve peace, when it should return, by a system of collective security. Such a League as he was dreaming of in 1915 was to be a new and much improved substitute for that Concert of Europe which he had struggled to galvanize into life under the old regime, with occasional success, as when in 1913 he used the Concert to avert a general war from arising out of Balkan questions that year.

But if even in wartime he did not forget to apply his principles so far as they could any longer be applied, he had in time of peace pursued a most unwavering course. From December 1905 to August 1914 he struggled to preserve the peace of Europe; and at the same time to provide that, if war came, England should not be without friends to stand by her in the storm. In the first object he failed, in the second he succeeded. The principles by which he pursued this double objective remained the same throughout the nine years of his tenure of office before the war. It is therefore possible to state what those principles were. Foreign affairs, he believed, could not be safely conducted by a series of unrelated opportunist experiments, successively adopted as sudden waves of emotion or electioneering needs seemed at each moment to dictate. British peace policy remained steady under his guidance, actuated always throughout the crises of nine stormy years by the principles which he had adopted during his first weeks in charge of the Foreign Office, and which indeed he had already stated in public in his City Speech when still in Opposition.[1] Those principles, reaffirmed by Campbell-Bannerman as Prime Minister, were the policy of the whole Cabinet. Grey never foisted them on his colleagues. They were never challenged or even questioned in the Cabinet at all events until 1912.

[1] See pages 101–05.

The first and most important aspect of this policy was the implementing of the agreement with France made in 1904 by his predecessor Lord Lansdowne; and the extension of the system by a somewhat similar agreement that he himself made with Russia in 1907. The condition which he attached to these settlements of our old quarrels with our two ancient rivals was that the agreements should not be turned into alliances, and that Britain should continue to pursue friendly relations with Germany, provided Germany would acquiesce in our friendly relations with France and Russia. This system failed to avert war, or rather it failed to avert it for longer than nine years; but it did provide that when war came it came in a form less disastrous than the destruction by Germany either of a friendless France or of a friendless Britain.

Nevertheless since Grey's system did not avert war, it is often criticized in retrospect, as it was criticized at the time, by two opposite schools of thought, the one maintaining that we ought not to have made agreements with France and Russia, the other that these agreements ought to have been converted into alliances. These two opposite lines of criticism cannot both have been right; I believe they were both wrong.

The first line of criticism was commonest in the North of England, in Labour circles and among Liberal supporters of the Government, some of whom feared lest the agreements with France and Russia would involve us in war with Germany, and hankered after a return to the 'splendid isolation' that our country had enjoyed in the nineteenth century. But that splendid isolation had been a luxury dependent on our complete and unchallenged command of the sea. Under Twentieth Century conditions such complete command is no longer possible — even if we leave the United States out of account as a conceivable enemy, as Grey always did. In the Far East our alliance with Japan, which Grey inherited and continued, alone gave us the safety in those seas which stood us in such good stead during the war.[1] Nearer home the Germans were building a fleet that in the event proved dangerously near a match for our own at Jutland. We should have lost the war if there had been no other navies on our side, or if we had not in the previous years kept up the ship-building programme of which Grey was the most constant protagonist in a divided Cabinet.

It was an axiom of Grey that 'What really determines foreign policy in this country is the question of sea power.' Britain's need for safety at sea would no longer permit her to regard with indifference either the crushing of France by Germany, or the drawing of France and Russia into the orbit of German diplomacy.[2] Yet if, in pursuit of isolation, we had returned to our former bad relations with France,

[1] See page 102 above; see also Grey's speech in the House of Commons, July 10, 1912, *Hansard*, 40, pages 1991–94, where he defends the continuance of the Anglo-Japanese alliance as a local substitute for great naval expenditure in the Far East.

[2] See his speech to the Dominion Delegates at the Committee of Imperial Defence, 1911 (*G. and T.* VI, 782–84). 'What really determines the foreign policy of this country is the question of sea power. It is the naval question which underlies the whole of our European foreign policy....There is no danger, no appreciable danger, of our being involved in any considerable trouble in Europe unless there is some Power or group of Powers in Europe which has the ambition of achieving what I call the Napoleonic policy. That would be a policy on the part of the strongest Power in Europe, or of the strongest group of Powers in Europe, of first of all separating the other Powers outside their own group from each other, taking them in detail, crushing them if need be, and *forcing each into the orbit of the policy of the strongest Power or the strongest group of Powers.... The result would be one great combination in Europe, outside which we would be left without a friend.* If that was the result, then the naval situation would be this, that if we meant to keep the command of the sea, we should have to estimate a probable combination against us of fleets in Europe not of two Powers but five Powers.'

or had continued on bad terms with Russia, one or both would have become the vassals of Germany, either after a war of conquest, or by arrangement made to prevent such a war. The Czar of Russia had actually signed a treaty with the Kaiser at Björkö in July 1905, five months before Grey took office: by its terms Russia entered the orbit of German diplomacy. After the signing of that treaty, the Kaiser wrote to the Czar in high spirits that it was directed against England, and that France would be obliged to join. The treaty was not indeed ratified; it was still-born, but the incident proves the gross reality of the danger of such a European combination. In Russia there was always, right down to the war, a strong pro-German party, particularly at Court, though the Czar did not long remain at its head. As to France, if she found that we were not ready, in face of the Kaiser's wrath, to stand by the promises of the Lansdowne agreement to support her in Morocco, she would conclude that our friendship was of no value in the realist terms of armed Europe, and she would seek safety by agreement with Germany. For what else could she have done if we had failed her? How little she could stand by herself against Germany was demonstrated in 1914–18, when even the armed help of England would not have sufficed, without that of America, to save France from destruction.

German hegemony in Europe was an extremely probable event, and if we permitted it to be realized by a return to the policy of British isolation, we should not long be able to hold the sea against the force of an united Europe, organized in a warlike system far more formidable than that of Napoleon. This danger, envisaged by diplomatists who knew Europe, would have continued to seem incredible to the easy-going and ill-informed people of England, had not the premature naval development of Germany in obvious competition with our home fleet warned Grey's countrymen in time.

Nor must it be forgotten that the agreements with France and Russia were undertaken in order to remove the constant threat of war. Again and again during the previous generation we had been on the verge of hostilities with one or other of those two countries on some clash in outlying parts of the globe — Siam, Newfoundland, the Upper Nile, Afghanistan, the Baltic — in Gladstone's time no less than in Salisbury's and Lansdowne's; and in Grey's own time war with Russia in Persia could only have been averted either by the much abused arrangement that he made, or by abandoning the Persians wholly to the Russian power, together with our own great interests in Persia, and the approaches to Afghanistan and India. To allow these constant disputes with France and Russia to continue to arise as before, was to risk war with one or both; and to drift into such a conflict in the presence of the German power would have been suicide.

The opposite line of attack on Grey's policy of the *via media*, is to argue that the ententes with France and with Russia should have been converted into military alliances. It is argued that if Germany had known for certain that we should be on the French side in arms in all events, she would never have hazarded war. This retrospective criticism is sometimes heard today; and before the war the policy of alliance instead of entente was urged upon Grey by Sir Arthur Nicolson, on the somewhat different ground that there was grave danger first of Russia, and then of France, going over to Germany unless we gave them the security of positive alliance.[1] But Lord Hardinge was always opposed to the policy of alliance, and so was Grey's Private Secretary in the Foreign Office, William Tyrrell. Grey had no hesitations; he always steadily refused to convert the entente into alliance for two reasons.

The first reason why he would not was the excellent reason that he could not. He was neither Czar nor Kaiser nor Fascist Dictator, but Foreign Minister of a constitutional country, who could do nothing on the big scale without consent of Cabinet colleagues and of the House of Commons. Neither colleagues nor Commons would have agreed to turn the entente into an alliance. Liberals were divided and uneasy even about the entente and would have revolted unanimously against alliance. If Grey had wished to be more closely bound to France and Russia, his only way to demand it would have been to go out of office and preach an alarmist crusade against the German menace, with or without the aid of the Conservative Opposition as might be. Such an anti-German campaign in the country would have been more likely to precipitate war than anything else.[2]

[1] Nicolson was Ambassador in Russia 1906–10, and Permanent Under-Secretary in the Foreign Office, 1910–16, in succession to Hardinge.

Sir A. Nicolson to Sir Edward Grey, St. Petersburg, March 24, 1909. 'When we have passed through the present *Sturm und Drang* period, I should not be surprised if we were to find both France and Russia gravitating rapidly towards the Central Powers, as neither of the former, distrustful of each other, feels that she can stand alone against the power of the central combination. Our entente, I much fear, will languish, and possibly die. If it were possible to extend and strengthen it by bringing it nearer to the nature of an alliance, it would then be possible to deter Russia from moving towards Berlin.' (*G. and T.* v, 736.)

The student of the British documents must bear in mind that letters and minutes by Nicolson, Eyre Crowe, Lord Hardinge and others are statements of their own views, not statements of British policy. As Grey wrote, 'I did not regard anything except my own letters and official papers as deciding policy.' (*G. and T.* VI, ix.)

[2] Grey's answer to the letter of Sir A. Nicolson quoted from in the last note contains these words: 'I do not think that it is practicable to change our agreements into alliances: the feeling here about definite commitment to a Continental war on

Secondly Grey would not have turned the agreements into alliances, even if the state of British opinion had left him the choice. He had not sufficient confidence that the pacific intentions of France and Russia would survive the positive assurance of British support in every possible case. Lansdowne had bound us to support France over Morocco, but on other questions we were not bound. Russia certainly and France not impossibly would have been emboldened by an actual alliance to adopt more aggressive courses, which might have led to war under circumstances where our side would have been much less 'in the right' than in the case of August 1914. It seemed therefore to Grey a lesser evil that Britain should maintain the atmosphere of uncertainty with regard to her ultimate action, as conditional on the merits of a *casus belli*. As he said to the House of Commons, at the time of the Agadir crisis:

> Our friendship with France and Russia is in itself a guaranty that neither of them will pursue a provocative or aggressive policy to Germany. Any support we would give France or Russia in times of trouble would depend entirely on the feeling of Parliament and public feeling here when the trouble came, and both France and Russia know perfectly well that British opinion would not give support to provocative or aggressive action against Germany.[1]

The very uncertainty of the position, in spite of its undeniable disadvantages, acted as a restraint on the conduct of France and Russia, with which it would have been most

unforeseeable conditions would be too dubious to permit us to make an alliance. Russia too must make her internal government less reactionary — till she does, liberal sentiment here will remain cool, and even those who are not sentimental will not believe that Russia can purge her administration sufficiently to become a strong and reliable power. Meanwhile, let us keep an entente with Russia, in the sense of keeping in touch so that our diplomatic action may be in accord and in mutual support.' (*G. and T.* v, 772.)

[1] *Hansard*, 1911, November 27, volume 32, page 59.

dangerous to dispense; nor would British opinion consent to be absolutely bound to fight till it knew how the particular quarrel would arise.

It was impossible to induce England to make up her mind beforehand. And one of the immense difficulties of the situation was that to discuss its real dangers in public and so educate and arouse the nation, as many critics now say the Government should have done, would have made it far more likely that Germany would precipitate the war.

Grey found it easy to open his heart to the representatives of America with whom he had to deal — first Theodore Roosevelt, then Colonel House and Walter Page. Wilson did not desire confidences or he too might have had them. But in order to know what Grey was feeling in his inmost heart, it is no bad plan to read what he said to his great American friends. In December 1906, when he had been a year in office, he gave this account of his policy in a confidential letter to President Roosevelt; first he thanks him for the support America had recently given to France and England in the Algeciras Conference.

> Now, a word as to our policy. It is not anti-German. But it must be independent of Germany. We wish to keep and strengthen the Entente with France, who is now very peaceful, and neither aggressive nor restless. She also plays the game fairly, and as long as she trusts one she is a good friend. The weak point is that she might some day have a scare that we intended to change. I think Germany has already tried more than once to make her imagine this.
>
> In our view, the Entente with France means good and easy relations for both of us with Italy and Spain. This means that peace and quietness are assured among the four Western Powers of Europe. To complete this foundation, we wish to make an arrangement with Russia that will remove the old

traditions of enmity, and ensure that, if we are not close friends, at any rate we do not quarrel.

If all this can be done, we shall take care that it is not used to provoke Germany, or to score off her, if she will only accept it, and not try to make mischief.

If, on the other hand, by some misfortune or blunder our Entente with France were to be broken up, France will have to make her own terms with Germany. And Germany will again be in a position to keep us on bad terms with France and Russia, and to make herself predominant upon the Continent. Then, sooner or later, there will be war between us and Germany, in which much else may be involved.

It is in German diplomacy alone that one now meets with deliberate attempts to make mischief between other countries by saying poisoned things to one about another. It is the lees left by Bismarck that still foul the cup. The economic rivalry (and all that) with Germany do not give much offence to our people, and they admire her steady industry and genius for organization. But they do resent mischief-making. They suspect the Emperor of aggressive plans of Weltpolitik, and they see or think they see that Germany is forcing the pace in armaments in order to dominate Europe, and is thereby laying a horrible burden of wasteful expenditure upon all the other Powers.

The long and the short of the matter is that, to secure peace, we must maintain the Entente with France, and attempts from outside to shake it will only make it stronger.

Austria, at present, is no danger and no problem except to herself. What questions may arise if she cannot settle her internal difficulties is another story.

I can give you no forecast of Japanese policy. They have been quite satisfactory allies; cautious and not exacting. But they are very reserved, and I do not feel that I know the working of their minds on questions outside the alliance itself.

As for ourselves.

We should detest war anywhere. This is not because we have grown weak or cowardly, but because we have had enough war for one generation. Before the Boer war, we were spoiling for a fight. We were ready to fight France about Siam, Germany about the Kruger telegram, and Russia about any thing. Any

Government here, during the last ten years of last century, could have had war by lifting a finger. The people would have shouted for it. They had a craving for excitement and a rush of blood to the head. Now, this generation has had enough excitement, and has lost a little blood, and is sane and normal. Its instincts are, I think, healthy.

We are really well disposed (though there are perhaps too many sentimentalists), and there is a real friendly feeling towards the United States. Some people call it Anglo-Saxon race feeling. But it is not really that as between us and you. Your Continent is making a new race and a new type, drawn from many sources, just as in old times the race in these Islands was evolved from many sources. So I do not dwell upon race feeling. But common language helps to draw us together, and religion also, for I think religious feeling in this Country is in degree and kind much like the American. But, more than all this, I should say that some generations of freedom on both sides have evolved a type of man and mind that looks at things from a kindred point of view, and a majority that has a hatred for what is not just or free.[1]

For the reasons given above, the main principles of Grey's policy were these — entente but not alliance with France and Russia, accompanied by constant efforts to achieve more friendly relations with Germany. The policy was right, but this does not prove that he was wise in every step that he took to give it effect: such will not be the contention of this book. There has, however, been a tendency, even in England, to minimize the general rightness of his policy, by laying continual stress on certain important details in which he is said to have erred. In retrospective criticism, people forget the appalling danger of the situation with which he had to deal from 1906 onwards, though the actual course of the war surely made it manifest in the event; they forget the limitations on his action due to conditions

[1] *F. O. Grey Papers*, 71, pages 123 and 167.

at home; and they fail to make allowance for the great difficulties of an English Minister, called on to answer publicly for his actions in Parliament, dealing with despotic governments that could keep their own secrets. House of Commons conditions render it impossible for even so honest and frank a Foreign Minister as Grey to be always frank and always therefore completely honest.

In particular it is said that he committed the country more deeply than it was aware. The two leading cases cited are the Military Conversations with the French army chiefs which he allowed to take place in January 1906 and the naval arrangement with France in 1912. These will be discussed more fully in their place; here it is enough to say that they were both dictated by the urgent needs of our national survival in view of the immense German strength on land and subsequently at sea. Had it not been for the policy of the Military Conversations of 1906 and the Haldane Army Reforms that were built upon them, Paris would have fallen within a few weeks of the outbreak of war, before a British expeditionary force had crossed the Channel by routes previously arranged. The only thing that was wrong with the Military Conversations was that the Cabinet was not told of them at once. Grey erred in thinking that all others would regard the Conversations as he himself regarded them — as a technical affair of experts without any political implications. But those who blame Grey most for this, seldom mention the equal responsibility of the Prime Minister, Campbell-Bannerman, who knew of the Conversations but did not bring them before the Cabinet.

At any rate the Military Conversations did not commit us to fight for France. There was more 'commitment' in the Admiralty's disposal of our naval force in 1912 which the

Foreign Office regarded with alarm. Yet there was only a choice of evils, and the lesser one was chosen. For by that time the building of the great German fleet had created a situation in which, as Mr. Churchill wrote to Grey, 'if France did not exist, we should make no other disposition of our forces' than concentration in the North Sea and partial withdrawal from the Mediterranean. The 'naval arrangement' with France was therefore in 1912 a necessity to our existence, unless indeed we built a fleet colossal beyond the dreams of Jingoism, at the price of the abandonment of 'social services' at home. Such a course could not have been adopted by any British government, let alone by a Liberal government, many of whose followers, led by Mr. Lloyd George, were in a constant state of mutiny against the existing naval expenditure.

It was indeed the building of the German fleet in rivalry to ours that ruined Grey's effort for peace in more ways than one. It prevented the friendship of the German and British peoples, which he desired as a pledge of peace, bridging the Triple Alliance and the Triple Entente. Germany would only have friendship with us on terms of our deserting the Entente. And she thought to frighten us into this change of policy by building a fleet which we should be afraid to encounter. It was a fatal miscalculation of the British temperament. When the greatest military power sought to become also a naval power in the same category as Britain, the entente of the countries whom she threatened was drawn closer by the very means which were intended to dissolve it. Thus the building of the German fleet ruined one-half of Grey's policy, the attempt to pacify Europe. But it enabled him to attain his second object, the union of England, France and Russia in case war could not be avoided.

The other fact that ruined his policy of peace was the 'irrepressible conflict' of Slav and Teuton in the Balkans, and more particularly the rivalry of Austria-Hungary with Russia in that region. Grey successfully averted the war that threatened to arise from that source in 1913 by evoking the Concert of Europe with the help of Germany; he failed in 1914. It is unlikely that any action by England could for long have prevented the clash of irreconcilable ambitions of Russia and Serbia on the one hand and Austria-Hungary on the other, or that the racial problems of the Dual Monarchy could possibly have been settled without war.

The charge that Grey fostered a policy of 'encirclement' of Germany, though often repeated in that country, does not stand any test of truth. Grey, in the earnest pursuit of better relations, offered Germany outlets into Asia and Africa, by the Bagdad railway agreement and the agreement that Germany should have her share in case of Portugal's sale of Colonies. Was that 'encirclement'? Moreover in the part that Grey so often played as disinterested mediator in the Balkan troubles, he carefully discouraged the creation of a Balkan or a Slav bloc against Austria-Hungary, and he declined to oppose the dominating influence that Germany herself acquired at Constantinople.

Politically, therefore, there was no encirclement. And militarily it was precisely Germany's central position that gave her such immense and almost decisive advantage when war came. The encirclement, such as it was, was of Germany's own making. She had encircled herself by alienating France over Alsace-Lorraine, Russia by her support of Austria-Hungary's anti-Slav policy in the Balkans, England by building her rival fleet. She had created with Austria-Hungary a military bloc in the heart of Europe, so powerful and yet so restless that her neighbours on each side had no choice but either to become her vassals or to stand together for protection. The accident that the Teutons lay between the French and the Slavs put the Germans by the nature of geography in the centre of a 'circle,' thereby rendering their military power all the more formidable. They used their central position to create fear on all sides, in order to gain their diplomatic ends. And then they complained that on all sides they had been encircled. When Bismarck, in evil hour, made the Alliance with Austria-Hungary, he began a system that ere long caused the Franco-Russian Alliance to follow. Germany thus began the fatal system of Alliances which prevented the 'localization' of any future quarrel between two great European powers, and in the end dragged more than half the world into a war begun on a Balkan issue.

A fierce searchlight has been thrown on Grey's every act, by the unreserved publication of all relative documents, in volumes that have been ransacked by thousands all the world over, some seeking truth, others seeking material for propaganda or revenge. No British statesman has ever before been subjected to such a test, and few indeed could have borne it. The wonder is, not that faults have been found, but that his reputation has been so little scathed. The principles which were the pillars of his policy still challenge refutation. They failed indeed to keep the peace in the end; but they kept it for nine years, and they secured that Britain entered the war with powerful allies and with a fair name among neutrals on both sides of the Atlantic. Where he failed no one could have succeeded; where he succeeded many would have failed.

I

The Testing of the Entente, Morocco, 1906
The Military Conversations — Algeciras

WITH the exception of July 1914, the most important month in Grey's long tenure of the Foreign Secretaryship was January 1906. He succeeded Lord Lansdowne in the middle of December 1905, at a moment of acute crisis, which if mishandled would have led either to war or the collapse of the Entente; and he met it by laying down the lines of policy to which he afterwards always adhered. It was well that the new Foreign Minister was a man of firm will and cool judgment, who had already before taking office clearly conceived the line and the limits of our action, who had not therefore to improvise a policy with distracted colleagues during a General Election, and who was not afraid to let both the German and French Ambassadors learn at once what their respective countries could look for in the action of England.

It was well, too, that the death of Lady Grey did not occur till the beginning of February, when the decisive interviews with Metternich and Cambon had already taken place. Even as it was, that wild January might have distracted a less calm and well-equipped newcomer to the Foreign Office. A General Election campaign — which is now a matter of days, but was then a matter of weeks — had scattered the Cabinet Ministers over the Island, haranguing for their political lives on Free Trade and Chinese Labour, to audiences for whom the continent of Europe had temporarily ceased to exist, except as a place where, Liberal candidates assured them, men ate horseflesh because they suffered under Protection. Grey himself had to take his share of speaking, and that month his voice was heard in one village schoolroom after another in farthest Northumberland. But during the intervening days that he spent in London, he sat in the big room over St. James's Park, dealing with a position little realized by his countrymen.

A danger had arisen over the Morocco crisis of an armed attack on France by Germany, or at the very least of the threat of such an attack carried to a point calculated to break up Lansdowne's Anglo-French Entente. Bismarck had declared, after a long experience, that England was liable to change her foreign policy with every change of government, and Holstein and Bülow hoped that the Liberal Ministry would be ready to retreat from the engagements upon which the Conservatives had entered. If Rosebery had been Prime Minister or Foreign Secretary, such a retreat would presumably have been made. But Campbell-Bannerman was firm for France, and so was his confidant, the veteran Liberal, Lord Ripon, who had sat in Gladstone's first and last Cabinets, had been the most 'liberal' of all the Viceroys of India, and who had stood by Campbell-Bannerman against Grey during the Boer War. In the heat of the General Election it was impossible to hold a Cabinet, but Grey consulted not only the Prime Minister himself, but Ripon as elder statesman and as Government leader in the Lords. They both supported his view that the Entente must be maintained in the face of German threats. And to this view they remained constant to the end of their lives. In December 1906 Campbell-Bannerman, writing to Grey to suggest some friendly concession to Germany, ends the letter with these words: 'But France is another matter. We must stand by France.'

There is a tradition that dies hard in some quarters that Grey, Haldane and Asquith, being Liberal Imperialists and old followers of Rosebery, smuggled through the Entente policy against the will or without the knowledge of the more pacifist colleagues of Campbell-Bannerman. The theory is in stark contradiction to the facts. Rosebery was against the Entente, and it was precisely Campbell-Bannerman and Ripon whom Grey consulted during those fateful weeks in January when no Cabinet could be held.[1] Not only were those two old 'pro-Boers' strong to continue Lansdowne's agreement with France, but in the following year they joined with John Morley in giving valuable aid to Grey in carrying through the agreement with Russia. If in making friends with our two ancient rivals Grey betrayed Liberal principles, Campbell-Bannerman, Ripon and Morley were his allies in the betrayal.

[1] Grey in January submitted to Campbell-Bannerman and Ripon the draft of his despatches to Sir F. Bertie in Paris and wrote full explanations of his policy to Campbell-Bannerman, who approved. See *G. and T.* III, 176, E. G.'s minute; *Life of Campbell-Bannerman*, II, 245–59; *Twenty-five Years*, ed. 1928, I, 131–36 (chapter VI); and chapter VII, pages 196–98, Grey's Letter to C.-B. of January 9, 1906. Wolf's *Life of Lord Ripon*, II, 291, tells us that:

'With the exception of the Foreign Secretary, Lord Grey, he [Ripon] was the only member of the Cabinet who endeavoured to secure adequate consideration for these portentous questions. The result was a close alliance between the two men, in which also Fitzmaurice, then Foreign Under-Secretary, participated. Ripon had learnt during his tenure of the Colonial Office to appreciate the danger of German ambitions, and more especially the unstable character of the German Emperor.' On retiring in October 1908, Ripon wrote to Grey: 'It has been most agreeable to me to have been able ever since the formation of C.-B.'s government to give a constant and unhesitating support to your management of foreign affairs.' (*Ripon*, II, 302.)

Grey inherited the Entente with France from Lansdowne; it lay with him to implement it or to let it languish and die. The Lansdowne-Cambon agreement of 1904 had removed the old and bitter causes of quarrel between France and England as regards Siam, Madagascar, the Newfoundland fisheries and Egypt. In return for the friendly acknowledgment of our position in Egypt, France obtained the promise of our diplomatic support in Morocco.[1] Lansdowne had also signed secret articles: these did not, as some have alleged, provide for a partition of Morocco between France and Spain, but they did provide for the respective spheres of influence of France and Spain in case the Sultan's Government of Morocco should at any future time disintegrate. Grey never consented to secret treaties or clauses, except during the war, when many rules of good behaviour had to be sacrificed to the stern needs of national survival. So long as peace lasted, he introduced and adhered to the principle that secret treaties were not to be made; he insisted on this, for instance, in the negotiations with Germany about the future sale of the Portuguese Colonies. But he inherited the secret clauses of Lord Lansdowne's agreement, which he has described, perhaps too optimistically, as 'a clause or two of no

[1] The terms of the 1904 agreement will be found in *G. and T.* II, 374–98. The leading clauses as regards Morocco are as follows:

Article II. 'The Government of the French Republic declare that they have no intention of altering the political status of Morocco. His Britannic Majesty's Government, for their part, recognise that it appertains to France, more particularly as a power whose dominions are conterminous for a great distance with those of Morocco, to preserve order in that country and to provide assistance for the purpose of all administrative, economic, financial and military reforms which it may require. They declare that they will not obstruct the action taken by France for this purpose, provided that such action shall leave intact the rights which Great Britain, in virtue of Treaties, convention and usage, enjoys in Morocco, including the right of coasting trade, etc.'

Article IX. '*The two governments agree to afford to one another their diplomatic support in order to obtain the execution of the clauses of the present Declaration regarding Egypt and Morocco.*'

importance, which were not published at the time owing to regard, as I suppose, for the susceptibilities of the Sultan of Morocco: even these were published a few years later,'[1] in 1911.

French Algiers bordered on the primitive and loosely governed territories of the Sultan of Morocco. Such a situation has led in case after case, all the world over, to the gradual penetration and eventual absorption of the more disorderly land by its Europeanized neighbour. Whether the familiar process be right or wrong, it was the way by which the Pax Britannica had already been extended over all India and a quarter of Africa. It was inevitable that France as ruler of Algiers would so act in the case of Morocco, when anarchy next broke loose. It was inevitable that other countries of Europe should look with anxiety and suspicion at the first steps taken by France along this well-known road, and ask how their own economic opportunities in Morocco might suffer in the end. If Germany had been content to voice that anxiety and to insist on her own rights by ordinary methods of diplomacy, no one could have rightly complained of her action. She had a case in 1905, and again in 1911. But she used Morocco as a means to break up the Anglo-French Entente, in order to establish her own predominance in Europe. And her methods of diplomacy, beginning with the Kaiser's melodramatic landing at Tangier in March 1905, were clumsy to a degree.

For some time, however, these methods seemed to succeed. In the summer of 1905 Germany had pressed for an International Conference on Morocco, and the Kaiser had enlisted the services of President Theodore Roosevelt as 'honest broker.' Roosevelt had helped to induce the French,

[1] *Twenty-five Years*, I, 106.

by friendly persuasion and advice, to consent to a Conference on Morocco to be held in 1906 — afterwards known as the Algeciras Conference with which Grey had to deal. Fear of German invasion, which the French armies were in no position to resist while Russia was still engaged in the Far East, was the major reason why the French Cabinet accepted the Conference called for by Germany. Delcassé, who had signalized his long tenure of the Foreign Office by winning for France the friendship both of Italy and of England, resigned rather than agree to the very necessary act of prudence on which his colleagues insisted. His resignation was regarded by his countrymen generally as a humiliating sacrifice made to avoid German invasion. 'The result,' wrote Lord Lansdowne on June 12, 1905, 'is that the Entente is quoted at a much lower price than it was a fortnight ago.'

In that same summer of Delcassé's resignation, the Kaiser, on the yacht at Björkö, had signed a treaty with the Czar which would either put an end to the Franco-Russian Alliance, or convert it into a pan-European Alliance with Germany against Japan and England. The Treaty of Björkö had indeed been torn up as soon as made. But the German effort to disrupt the Russo-French Alliance and the Anglo-French Entente was not abandoned. The coming Morocco Conference would be the testing of the Entente. And if it broke, Russia and France without England were at Germany's mercy. Russia, still staggering from the blows of the recent Japanese war, and rent by internal trouble, could not by herself save France from conquest.

Such was the situation when the Liberal Government took over the reins in December 1905. Two events of the past summer, the resignation of Delcassé, to avert German wrath, and the Treaty of Björkö, suggest that both France and Russia were so hard pressed that another successful push would have put an end to their resistance. If, at the coming Conference on Morocco, the 'diplomatic support,' which England was pledged to give by the Lansdowne Treaty, proved insufficient, if Germany again made her will prevail, both Russia and France would conclude that our platonic friendship was of no use in the iron age, and would make their terms with the conqueror of Europe. They would be shepherded into the German orbit, and Britain would be left exposed, without a friend, save far Japan, to an armed and hostile Continent. Under such conditions she could not long have maintained herself in the coming age of submarines, aircraft and long-distance guns.

It was in these circumstances that Paul Cambon, the French Ambassador in London, began to enquire on behalf of his Government whether the 'diplomatic support' promised over Lansdowne's signature would be forthcoming at the Morocco Conference, and whether that 'diplomatic support' implied a readiness on Britain's part to stand by her friend in arms, if Germany pushed the matter to war. It was easy for Grey to answer 'yes' to the first question. What really mattered was the reply he would give to the second.

Grey answered both questions at once in his two famous interviews with the French Ambassador, on January 10 and 31, 1906. He promised our diplomatic support at the coming Morocco Conference; as to military support he replied that he could not pledge the country, but that in his opinion all would depend on the circumstances that led to war; that in case of frank German aggression he believed that the country would consent to defend France in arms, but even of that he could give no definite promise.

This did not wholly content the French statesmen, and that had the good effect of making them act with caution. But to hold out to France even this much hope of military aid in case of war, while concealing it from Germany, would have been a gross mistake. Grey always realized that he must raise at least as much fear in the mind of the German Government as he raised hope in the French. And therefore on January 3, a week before his interview with Cambon, he warned the German Ambassador, Count Metternich, who duly passed it on to Berlin. Early in January the Kaiser and his advisers were aware that the new Foreign Secretary believed that Britain would defend France in arms if she were wantonly attacked. And this knowledge must have greatly conduced to the successful outcome of the Morocco Conference in the spring. France could not count on England's intervention as certain, but Germany feared it as probable. Both countries therefore were on their good behaviour. Such was Grey's policy in January 1906, and such it remained at all junctures till August 1914.

The warning that Metternich sent to his Government as early as January 3 ran as follows:

> Today I had an important conversation about Morocco with Sir Edward Grey. Since my recent conversation with him I had been careful not to mention it to him; but today he began upon it himself. I will first say that Sir Edward Grey gives me the impression of being a frank, straightforward man, that one knows where one is with him.
>
> He said that . . . the Entente with France and the removal of the old quarrels were very greatly welcomed in England, and that they wished to keep to it and run no risks with it. The feeling was general here that England must not leave the French Government in the lurch in a question arising out of the Anglo-French agreement. This was the standpoint of the British Government, whether Liberal or Conservative. . . .

GOSHEN COLLEGE LIBRARY
GOSHEN, INDIANA

> Later in the conversation Sir Edward Grey said he had found among his predecessor's memoranda a conversation with me in the previous summer, in which Lord Lansdowne indicated that, if there was war between Germany and France on account of Morocco, public feeling would force the Government to fight for France. He, Grey, believed that the British people would not stand France being involved in war with Germany on account of the Anglo-French agreement, and that, if it happened, any British Government, whether Conservative or Liberal, would be forced to help France.[1]

Grey's account of this interview which he sent to Sir Frank Lascelles, our Ambassador in Berlin, confirms this part of Metternich's report. And Grey further represents himself as having said:

> We did not intend to make trouble at the Morocco Conference. We wanted to avoid trouble between Germany and France, because I really thought that if there was trouble we should be involved in it. Public feeling here would be exceedingly strong, not from hostility to Germany, but rather because it had been a great relief and satisfaction to the English public to find themselves on good terms with France, and if France got into difficulties arising out of the very document which had been the foundation of the good feeling between us and France, sympathy with the French would be exceedingly strong.

And to Campbell-Bannerman he wrote:

> To the German Ambassador I have given it as a personal opinion that feeling in England and sympathy for France, if she got into trouble over the document which originated our friendship with her, would be so strong that it would be impossible for any government to remain neutral. (Lansdowne I find had also said as much.)[2]

Such was the warning to Germany. It was at least as strong as the hope held out to France in the interview with

[1] *German Diplomatic Documents*, E. T. S. Dugdale, III, 234–36, *Gr. Pol.* XXI, 45.

[2] This statement about Lansdowne's warning to Germany is borne out by Sanderson. See *Life of Lansdowne*, page 488.

Cambon a week later. Grey's full report of that interview has been so often printed [1] and is so well known, that I will here print instead an abbreviated version of the interview, also by Grey, that I found in the Foreign Office papers:

> The French Ambassador asked me today [January 10] whether, in the event of an attack (*une aggression brutale*) by Germany upon France arising out of the Morocco difficulty, France could rely upon the armed support of England.
>
> I said I could not answer this question: I could not even consult the Prime Minister or the Cabinet during the elections. I was sure that there would be a strong sentiment and sympathy on the part of the English public; more than that I could not say and all I could promise was diplomatic support now. M. Cambon said he did not believe that there would be war, but that there would be no danger of war, if the German Emperor knew that we should fight to help France.
>
> I said that I thought the German Emperor probably did expect this; but that it was one thing to let it be supposed in Germany that we should join in a war; it was a different thing to take an engagement to France to do it; it would be a very grave mistake to make a promise of that kind till one was absolutely certain it would be fulfilled.
>
> M. Cambon mentioned the word neutrality and I said at once that neutrality — benevolent neutrality, if there was such a thing, I would promise but that was all.
>
> Our great desire was to see the Morocco Conference have an issue favourable to the Anglo-French Entente, but a pacific issue; if that failed, I could not say what England would do; much might depend upon the manner in which war broke out.
>
> Monsieur Cambon said he would again ask me after the elections were over.

It is possible that, whether Grey suspected it or not, the effect of this interview was rather less damping to the French Government than it would otherwise have been, because at the end of it Grey told Cambon that he had no objection to Military and Naval Conversations proceeding between pro-

[1] For example, in *G. and T.* III, 170–71, and Grey's *Twenty-five Years*, I, 133–36.

perly authorized experts, to provide for the possible contingency of the outbreak of a war in which England was involved on the side of France. I shall presently deal with this subject at greater length.

Grey was returned to the new Parliament on January 25; on January 31, the famous second interview with Cambon took place, immediately after a Cabinet held that morning at which Grey had 'informed the Cabinet as to the progress of affairs at Algeciras.' How much he discussed his policy with that Cabinet is not on record, but he had by this time fully discussed it with the Prime Minister and with Ripon, who saw nothing to object to in the line he was taking, as it was merely fulfilling the pledges made in the name of the country by Lansdowne. In these circumstances Grey saw Cambon on January 31, the day before Lady Grey's accident.

Often as this report of his famous interview has been printed, I will print it here once more, because, as he himself wrote:

> It defines the position that was maintained up to the very outbreak of war. From time to time the same question was raised, but never did we go a hair's breadth beyond the position taken up in the conversation with Cambon on January 31, 1906.

Sir Edward Grey to Sir F. Bertie

FOREIGN OFFICE,
January 31, 1906.

SIR — The French Ambassador asked me again today whether France would be able to count upon the assistance of England in the event of an attack upon her by Germany.

I said that I had spoken on the subject to the Prime Minister and discussed it with him, and that I had three observations to submit.

In the first place, since the Ambassador had spoken to me a good deal of progress has been made. Our military and naval authorities had been in communication with the French, and I assumed that all preparations were ready, so that, if a crisis arose, no time would have been lost for want of a formal engagement.

In the second place, a week or more before Monsieur Cambon had spoken to me, I had taken an opportunity of expressing to Count Metternich my personal opinion which I understood Lord Lansdowne had also expressed to him as a personal opinion, that, in the event of an attack upon France by Germany arising out of our Morocco Agreement, public feeling in England would be so strong that no British Government could remain neutral. I urged upon Monsieur Cambon that this, which I had reason to know had been correctly reported at Berlin, had produced there the moral effect which Monsieur Cambon had urged upon me as being one of the great securities of peace and the main reason for a formal engagement between England and France with regard to armed co-operation.

In the third place, I pointed out to Monsieur Cambon that at present French policy in Morocco, within the four corners of the Declaration exchanged between us, was absolutely free, that we did not question it, that we suggested no concessions and no alterations in it, that we left France a free hand and gave unreservedly our diplomatic support on which she could count; but that, should our promise extend beyond diplomatic support, and should we make an engagement which might involve us in a war, I was sure my colleagues would say that we must from that time be consulted with regard to French policy in Morocco, and, if need be, be free to press upon the French Government concessions or alterations of their policy which might seem to us desirable to avoid a war.

I asked Monsieur Cambon to weigh these considerations in his mind, and to consider whether the present situation as regards ourselves and France was not so satisfactory that it was unnecessary to alter it by a formal declaration as he desired.

Monsieur Cambon said that in Morocco, if the Conference broke up without favourable result, Germany might place herself behind the Sultan and acquire more and more influence, that trouble might be stirred up on the Algerian frontier, that France might be obliged to take measures to deal with it as she had done before, and that Germany might announce to France, as she had already once done, that an aggression on Morocco would be an attack upon her, and would be replied to accordingly. In such an event war might arise so suddenly that the need for action would be a question not of days, but of minutes, and that, if it was necessary for the British Government to consult, and to wait for manifestations of English public opinion, it might be too late to be of use. He eventually repeated his request for some form of assurance which might be given in conversation. I said that an assurance of that kind could be nothing short of a solemn undertaking. It was one which I could not give without submitting it to the Cabinet and getting their authority, and that were I to submit the question to the Cabinet I was sure that they would say that this was too serious a matter to be dealt with by a verbal engagement but must be put in writing. As far as their good disposition towards France was concerned, I should have no hesitation in submitting such a question to the present Cabinet. Some of those in the Cabinet who were most attached to peace were those also who were the best friends of France; but, though I had no doubt about the good disposition of the Cabinet, I did think there would be difficulties in putting such an undertaking in writing.[1] It could not be given unconditionally, and it would be difficult to describe the conditions. It amounted, in fact, to this: that, if any change was made, it must be to change the 'Entente' into a defensive alliance. That was a great and formal change, and I again submitted to Monsieur Cambon as to whether the force of circumstances bringing England and France together was not stronger than any assurance in words which could be given at this moment. I said that it might be that the pressure of circumstances —

[1] Lord Sanderson was just retiring from the position of Permanent Under-Secretary for Foreign Affairs. Two days after Grey's interview with Cambon, at Grey's instructions, this wise veteran of the public service called on the French Ambassador to discuss the situation, and said to him, 'It was a maxim that had been impressed on me by several statesmen of great eminence that it was not wise to bring before a Cabinet the question of the course to be pursued in hypothetical cases which had not arisen. A discussion on the subject invariably gave rise to divergences of opinion on questions of principle, whereas in a concrete case unanimity would very likely be secured. M. Cambon observed that this view was a perfectly just one.' Grey's comment is: 'I am glad this point was so well pointed out to M. Cambon.' (*G. and T.* III, 184.)

the activity of Germany, for instance — might eventually transform the 'Entente' into a defensive alliance between ourselves and France, but I did not think that the pressure of circumstances was so great as to demonstrate the necessity of such a change yet. I told him also that, should such a defensive alliance be formed, it was too serious a matter to be kept secret from Parliament. The Government could conclude it without the assent of Parliament, but it would have to be published afterwards. No British Government could commit the country to such a serious thing and keep the engagement secret.

Monsieur Cambon, in summing up what I had said, dwelt upon the fact that I had expressed my personal opinion that, in the event of an attack by Germany upon France, no British Government could remain neutral. I said that I had used this expression to Count Metternich first, and not to him, because, supposing it appeared that I had over-estimated the strength of feeling of my countrymen, there could be no disappointment in Germany; but I could not express so decidedly my personal opinion to France, because a personal opinion was not a thing upon which, in so serious a matter, a policy could be founded. In speaking to him, therefore, I must keep well within the mark. Much would depend as to the manner in which the war broke out between Germany and France. I did not think people in England would be prepared to fight in order to put France in possession of Morocco. They would say that France should wait for opportunities and be content to take time, and that it was unreasonable to hurry matters to the point of war. But if, on the other hand, it appeared that the war was forced upon France by Germany to break up the Anglo-French 'Entente,' public opinion would undoubtedly be very strong on the side of France. At the same time, Monsieur Cambon must remember that England at the present moment would be most reluctant to find herself engaged in a great war, and I hesitated to express a decided opinion as to whether the strong feeling of the Press and of public opinion on the side of France would be strong enough to overcome the great reluctance which existed amongst us now to find ourselves involved in war. I asked Monsieur Cambon, however, to bear in mind that, if the French Government desired it, it would be possible at any time to re-open the conversation. Events might change, but, as things were at present, I did not think it was necessary to press the question of a defensive alliance.

Monsieur Cambon said the question was very grave and serious, because the German Emperor had given the French Government to understand that they could not rely upon us, and it was very important to them to feel that they could.

I am, with great truth and respect, sir,

Your Excellency's most obedient, humble servant,

E. GREY

Such was the diplomatic position taken up by Grey in January 1906, to which he adhered till the end, eight and a half years later. And in that same January he authorized the continuance of Conversations already begun between the French and British experts, naval and military, to which he gave a somewhat more definite official sanction than they had already received under Lansdowne. Grey appears to have underestimated the diplomatic significance which France and Germany were likely to attach to those Conversations, and, as he himself later admitted, the Cabinet ought to have been informed of them at once. But Campbell-Bannerman as Prime Minister, was even more responsible than Grey for the neglect to bring the Conversations before the Cabinet of which he was Chairman, a fact which some of Grey's critics studiously ignore.

But to make these admissions is by no means to condemn the Conversations themselves. They were absolutely necessary as a part of the policy which we had adopted in 1904, and confirmed in January 1906. Since we contemplated as possible that we might have to defend France against a sudden German attack on the Moroccan issue, it would have been lunacy to allow Paris to fall from sheer neglect to make war plans in advance. Yet such might well have been the outcome. Cambon said to Grey, 'War might arise so suddenly that the need for action would be a question not of days but of minutes'; and without any exaggeration it would have been a question not of weeks but of days. Already the German war plan was formed of the lightning stroke through Belgium on Paris. When at length it took effect in 1914, Belgium fell and Paris was within an ace of falling. Yet by that time plans for Anglo-French co-operation had been elaborated over a number of years, and Haldane's Reforms had been built up on their basis to supply a British expeditionary force and a detailed scheme for its immediate transport overseas by agreed routes, to join the left wing of the French army. In 1906 the position of France and Belgium in face of the German armies would have been worse; Russia, just emerging from defeat at the hands of Japan, was then in no condition to launch such a formidable diversion as she was able to make in 1914. The Military Conversations and the Haldane Reforms based on them only just saved the situation in the end. And in 1906, with Russia in her then condition,[1] it would have been foolhardy in the extreme not to have allowed plans to be formed for a defensive war that might be forced on France and Britain at any moment.

The Military Conversations had, as I have said, a greater diplomatic effect abroad than Grey supposed; but that effect was to the good, for German knowledge that our soldiers were in consultation with those of France and Belgium was probably one of the reasons why the Algeciras Conference of 1906 reached a peaceful conclusion.

It was indeed high time that England should have a war plan in case the need arose. In December 1905 she had none;

[1] As Professor Temperley has written (*Cambridge Review*, February 1, 1935): 'Japan's victory permanently weakened Russia and was the dominant event in international relations until 1909. It explains Germany's sudden raising of the question of Morocco and the crises of 1905–06.'

what was worse, her naval and military men hovered between two strategies, diametrically opposed. Admiral Fisher was against an expeditionary force to France, and favoured an attack on the German coast, which the soldiers knew to be hopeless.

The principle of Conversations was not introduced by Grey. Already under Lansdowne 'the French Naval Attaché had been unofficially and in a non-committal way in communication with Fisher, as to what help he could give in a war between Germany and France,' with the cognizance of Cambon.[1] And in the first days of January 1906, Repington, the Military Correspondent of *The Times*, after consulting Lord Esher, and Sir George Clarke, the Secretary of the Defence Committee, sounded the French Government through Major Huguet, the French Military Attaché in London. In this way Repington obtained some important replies from Monsieur Rouvier, the Prime Minister, on questions of cooperation in case of attack on France by Germany, which it was thought might break out soon and with very little warning.[2] Grey was informed by Repington, and at the same time in the interview of January 10 Cambon begged him to allow these Conversations to continue. He had either to stop them and leave England without a war plan in a moment when she might not impossibly be involved in war; or else he must regularize the Conversations, taking them out of the hands of *The Times* correspondent and placing them in

[1] *G. and T.* III, 171, Minute by Lord Sanderson, and page 203, Grey to Tweedmouth, January 16, 1906: these passages bear out Grey's statement in *Twenty-five Years*, I, 139. 'Plans for naval and military co-operation, had, I found, begun to be made under Lord Lansdowne in 1905, when the German pressure was menacing. The naval conversations had already been direct; the military conversations had hitherto been through an intermediary [Colonel Repington]: they, too, were henceforth to be direct.'

[2] *The First World War*, by Col. Repington, 1921, chapter I.

those of the British Military Authorities. He chose the latter course.

Campbell-Bannerman was consulted, and agreed that the Conversations should proceed, although he had misgivings. 'I do not like the stress laid upon joint preparations,' he wrote to Ripon on February 2. 'It comes very close to an honourable understanding, and it will be known on both sides of the Rhine.' But he did not stop the Conversations, and he did not bring the question before the Cabinet.

Asquith apparently did not know of the Conversations in 1906, though of course he knew and approved of them when he became Prime Minister in 1908.[1] But immediately after his interview with Cambon on January 10, Grey informed Haldane as War Minister. The two friends were speaking together at Berwick, in Grey's constituency, and 'I found,' writes Haldane, 'that he had ordered a carriage to take us after the meeting for a long drive and private talk. He told me that the French were concerned about the possibility of a German movement against them in the summer. Had we compared ideas about preparation with the French Generals?'

> I went at once to London [writes Haldane] and summoned the heads of the General Staff and saw the French military attaché, Colonel Huguet, a man of sense and ability. I became

[1] *Life of Asquith*, I, 179, 348–49. See also Grey's letter to Asquith in 1911 recording what happened in 1906. 'The French then urged that the military authorities should be allowed to exchange views.... Up to this point C.-B., R. B. H., and I were cognizant of what took place — the rest of you were scattered in the election. The military experts then conversed. What they settled I never knew — the position being that the government was quite free, but the military people knew what to do if the word was given.' (*Twenty-five Years*, I, 164.) From this letter, printed by Grey in his reminiscences, I conclude that Grey's memory failed him in detail when on August 3, 1914, he told the House of Commons that Asquith knew of the Conversations in 1906. Grey had much else to think of that day. But the point is perhaps not quite certain, for Haldane in his *Before the War*, page 30, says that Asquith knew.

> aware at once that there was a new army problem. It was how to mobilize and concentrate at a place of assembly to be opposite to the Belgian frontier, a force calculated as adequate (with the assistance of Russian pressure in the East) to make up for the inadequacy of the French armies.[1]

Thus the Military Conversations of January 1906 led to the Haldane Army Reforms and the formation of the Expeditionary Force. The Colonel Repington era of the Conversations came to an end, and General Grierson, Haldane and the General Staff took charge.

'Without the guidance we derived through the Conversations, we could not have been ready in July 1914. The Expeditionary Force was shaped to meet the demands so defined,' writes Haldane in his *Autobiography* (page 191). In short the Conversations, which are by some put at the head of the charges made against Grey, saved England and Europe, thanks to the sequel given to them by the initiative of his friend Haldane. It was certainly as well that the two friends had not carried out their 'Relugas Compact,' and refused office in the previous month.[2]

[1] Haldane's *Before the War*, pages 30–31; *Autobiography*, page 189; Grey's *Twenty-five Years*, I, 138, bears out Haldane's account of their meeting: 'We met on one of my election platforms at Berwick.'

[2] A few days before the interview at Berwick, and before his interview with Cambon of January 10, Grey had written as follows to Haldane:

FOREIGN OFFICE,
January 8, 1906.

MY DEAR RICHARD:

Persistent reports and little indications keep reaching me that Germany means to attack France in the spring. I don't think these are more than precautions and flourishes which Germany would naturally make à propos of the Morocco Conference. But they are not altogether to be disregarded. A situation might arise presently in which popular feeling might compel the Government to go to the help of France, and you might suddenly be asked what you could do. Fisher says he is ready, by which I take it he means that his ships are so placed that he can drive the German fleet off the seas and into shelter any time. I don't ask you to give a definite answer in a hurry, but I think you should be preparing one.

On January 13, after his interview with Haldane, Grey appended a minute to Cambon's account of their interview of January 10:

> This agrees with my own record in substance; except that I did not go so far as to approve of the communications by intermediaries [Repington] referred to at the end. I did not dissent, but I reserved my opinion, because I did not know what they were. I do however approve of their being continued in a proper manner, i.e. with the cognizance of the official heads of the Admiralty and War Office. In the case of the Admiralty I gather that whatever is being done is known to Sir J. Fisher. I have now spoken to Mr. Haldane as regards the War Office and he is willing that the French Military Attaché should communicate with General Grierson. The communications must be solely provisional and non-committal.
>
> E. G.
>
> 13.1.06.

By Grey's permission, the Conversations with the French were at the same time extended to the formation of similar plans with the Belgian military authorities for the defence of their country's neutrality, under the same safeguards that the consultations were not diplomatic promises of help, but 'solely provisional and non-committal.' [1] The French were warned that they must on no account enter Belgium 'unless compelled to do so by previous violation of Belgian territory by Germany' — indeed Repington had already had the good sense to emphasize this point on January 5.

Although there is no reason to suppose that Fisher's Conversations with the French Naval Attaché had been mentioned to the Cabinet in Lansdowne's time, it is to be regretted that neither Campbell-Bannerman nor Grey brought the fact of the Conversations before the Cabinet at the first

[1] *G. and T.* III, 179, Grierson's letter of January 16, 1906, and pages 187–203. A few years later uncertainty arose as to whether Belgium would defend herself against German aggression, and this uncertainty continued till August 1914.

meeting after the election on January 31, the day when Grey saw Cambon. At that meeting, as the Prime Minister wrote to the King, 'Sir E. Grey informed the Cabinet as to the progress of affairs at Algeciras,' [1] but neither he nor Campbell-Bannerman appears to have mentioned the Conversations. Their silence cannot be attributed to Lady Grey's accident, which only took place the next day. Campbell-Bannerman was uneasy about the Conversations, but he did not think it worth while to bring the question before his colleagues. Both he and Grey regarded the Conversations as a departmental matter that need not be referred to the Cabinet any more than the Naval Conversations in Lansdowne's time had been so referred. The Prime Minister, as head of the Government, with his former experience of Cabinets and of the Secretaryship of State for War, was surely more responsible for this decision than Grey, who had never sat in a Cabinet before.

In the following years those Cabinet Ministers who sat on the Committee of Imperial Defence, including Morley and Harcourt, were present when plans concerted with the French generals were discussed. Morley afterwards forgot this, but Haldane proved it to him.[2] Finally in 1912, on questions being asked after the Agadir crisis, the system of Military Conversations was explained to the whole Cabinet. Not all Grey's colleagues shared his view that the making of provisional war plans in common with the French did not in any degree commit us because we so declared. They demanded that it should be put in writing that the Military Conversa-

[1] Windsor MSS. R. 27.16. Letter of January 31, 1906. I take this opportunity of expressing my gratitude for gracious permission to use the Windsor and Buckingham Palace MSS. Grey in his *Twenty-five Years*, I, 153, seems to have forgotten that there was a Cabinet on the thirty-first.

[2] Haldane, *Autobiography*, pages 228–29.

tions were politically non-committal. Grey had put it in writing years before, but he now did so again in a yet more formal manner, in a document transmitted to the French Government:

Sir Edward Grey to M. Cambon, French Ambassador in London

FOREIGN OFFICE,
November 22, 1912.

MY DEAR AMBASSADOR:

From time to time in recent years the French and British naval and military experts have consulted together. It has always been understood that such consultation does not restrict the freedom of either Government to decide at any future time whether or not to assist the other by armed force. We have agreed that consultation between experts is not, and ought not to be, regarded as an engagement that commits either Government to action in a contingency that has not arisen and may never arise. The disposition, for instance, of the French and British fleets respectively at the present moment is not based upon an engagement to co-operate in war.

You have, however, pointed out that if either Government had grave reason to expect an unprovoked attack by a third Power, it might become essential to know whether it could, in that event, depend upon the armed assistance of the other.

I agree that, if either Government had grave reason to expect an unprovoked attack by a third Power, or something that threatened the general peace, it should immediately discuss with the other whether both Governments should act together to prevent aggression and to preserve peace, and, if so, what measures they would be prepared to take in common. If these measures involved action, the plans of the general staffs would at once be taken into consideration, and the Governments would then decide what effect should be given to them.

Yours, etc.,

E. GREY

Neither in Grey's mind nor in that of the French Government was the situation altered by this restatement. But at least it now had the full authority of the Cabinet. Thenceforward, as Grey wrote on May 4, 1912, 'The Cabinet has now the same knowledge of what has taken place that the Prime Minister and I have: the understanding is that the First Lord of the Admiralty and the Secretary of State for War will keep in touch with the Cabinet from time to time and act in accordance with its decisions.' Contrary to the intention of those who had demanded it, the exchange of letters was widely interpreted as having confirmed and extended the Entente.

On February 1, 1906, Lady Grey met with her accident. Grey's own account of the immediate effect of her death upon his work, officially considered, is as follows:

> I wrote to Campbell-Bannerman saying I was very much shaken, and suggesting that I should resign. He encouraged me to go on, and after a week the Foreign Office work was sent to me at Fallodon. The mechanism of the brain began to digest work as that of the body digests food; that is how life continues in such an ordeal for a time, but personality seems stunned and work is done mechanically. It does not, however, appear, nor do I remember, that any important decision was taken or required in the interval before I returned to London at the opening of Parliament and again took my place at the Foreign Office and in the Cabinet.[1]

By the time the long-expected Morocco Conference came to grips with its problems at Algeciras, Grey was again able to give the powers of his mind to each successive crisis, though his heart was dead within his breast. He had need of all his faculties, for the Conference was beset with dangers. Actualities in Morocco had their importance, but their chief value on the card table at Algeciras was as counters in the deadly game of European 'prestige.' The Germans were bent on another diplomatic victory. The French could not afford to allow it, and if they were again defeated there would be an

[1] *Twenty-five Years*, I, 174.

end of the Entente with England. They were suspicious of the degree and honesty of English support, and the Germans worked secretly to foster these suspicions by false rumour. 'It seems almost a miracle that the Entente survived,' wrote Grey, looking back. 'I was at any rate more alive to the delicacy of the situation at the end of the Conference than I had been at the beginning.'

The crisis came in March. It had been agreed that the State Bank in Morocco should be under the control of France, England, Germany and Spain. But it had also been agreed, much to Germany's chagrin, that the police in the Moroccan ports should be under Franco-Spanish officers. Germany put up Austria-Hungary to propose that the port of Casablanca should be an exception. France saw behind the proposal the intention to introduce German influence into Morocco through that port, and stir up the Sultan against France. It became the test question, upon which hung peace — and the Entente.

That Germany gave way over Casablanca was due to the resistance not only of Great Britain, but of the other Powers, with the rather lukewarm exception of Austria-Hungary. The powers could not regard Germany as the champion of their own rights in Morocco, and they reacted against her methods of violence, which had caused general alarm for a year past. Spain, the other Power besides France directly concerned in Morocco, was in agreement with France and England, and her interests had been provided for. Italy supported them, for Italy had already qualified her adhesion to the Triple Alliance by a quasi-agreement with France, out of which she hoped some day to get Tripoli; and it was a principle of her policy not to quarrel with England. Russia played her part as ally of France, when she saw the line taken by England. But perhaps the make-weight that tipped the balance for peace was the action of America. President Roosevelt, a friend both to France and Germany, had in the previous summer persuaded France to agree to the Conference which Germany demanded. But when the Conference had met, Roosevelt thought that the Germans were overbearing, and since in his opinion 'the interests of France and Spain in Morocco were far greater than those of other Powers,' he supported France with his usual directness. It was a fine instance of the influence that America can exert for European peace, whenever she deigns to emerge from her policy of isolation.[1] Roosevelt's action partly took the form of private appeals and warnings to the Kaiser. His intervention had not been prompted by Grey, who was not yet personally acquainted with him. But in the course of the year a friendly and even intimate correspondence began between the two men. Roosevelt told the whole story of his relations with the Kaiser to Grey, who replied in answer to his confidences on December 2, 1906:

> Your own relations with the German Emperor have been immensely interesting and a revelation. It was felt all through the Algeciras Conference that American influence was not being used against France and us. We *had* feared you might be an ally of the Emperor there, but in the event I felt it was not so, even before I knew the story. If you asked why we feared, I should say your telegram to the German Emperor after the Portsmouth Peace had given an impression of a 'parti pris' on the side of the Emperor. The explanation of that telegram has given a different and a very amusing light on it to me.

Grey would not have written in this familiar and 'unbuttoned' style to a European statesman whom he knew as

[1] See what Grey says about Roosevelt's action, *Twenty-five Years*, I, 202–03, note at end of Chapter VII. See also J. B. Bishop's *Roosevelt*, I, chapters XXXVI–VII, for the documents.

little as he then knew Roosevelt. But the two men had a natural affinity, and Grey's first principle of Foreign Policy was Anglo-American friendship, based on a fundamental oneness of outlook which he believed to exist.

The success of the Algeciras Conference, in preserving both peace and the Anglo-French entente, subserved, in Grey's mind, the additional purpose of preparing the way for an understanding between Britain and Russia, which should put an end to their perpetual clash of interests in Asia. Russia had been watching Algeciras to see how much English friendship was worth in the case of France. It stood the test. As early as February 19, 1906, Grey had written to his friend Cecil Spring Rice, at that moment in charge of the Embassy at St. Petersburg, explaining our Moroccan policy, and adding:

> Meanwhile I am impatient to see Russia re-established as a factor in European politics. Whether we shall get an arrangement with her about Asiatic questions remains to be seen: I will try when she desires it and is ready.

And on April 12, Spring Rice wrote a private letter to congratulate Grey on the issue of the Conference:

> May I (although it isn't quite the correct thing to do) express the very warmest admiration for your conduct of affairs in the last few weeks? Your absolutely straight unwavering and frank declaration of your intention to stick to Lord Lansdowne's engagement, has made the deepest impression both here [St. Petersburg] and at Paris. I don't believe the Russian Government would have quite come up to the mark without your example. The ally couldn't do less than the friend.... There were certainly very many in Paris who doubted and told the French that there was reason to doubt. One breath of truth blew the whole fabric away.

The action of Germany in using the Morocco question as a weapon to break the Anglo-French Entente had rebounded to her own injury and also, alas, to the injury of the peace of Europe. Under the hammer-blows of Germany, a treaty of friendship originated to remove differences between two ancient enemies was being welded into an understanding against an outside aggressor. It only needed that Germany should build a fleet in rivalry to England to turn the Entente into 'an alliance in all but name.' Nothing that Grey could have done or left undone could have averted the issue: Germany had refused our friendship when it had been offered, and now she would not allow us to be friends with France unpunished.[1]

With the exception of the Military Conversations of 1906, which Campbell-Bannerman and Grey had both regarded as a technical affair of soldiers not concerning the statesmen of the Cabinet, Grey in all other matters of Foreign Policy gave his colleagues full and detailed information. And he regularly circulated to them important Foreign Office papers which some of them sometimes very humanly neglected to read, and afterwards very humanly complained of never having seen. Most of all he consulted Asquith (after Campbell-Bannerman's death), Crewe, Haldane and John Morley; Morley several times took over the Foreign Office work during Grey's brief holidays. The accusation subsequently made that there was a 'Liberal Imperialist' conspiracy to keep the rest of the Cabinet in the dark is entirely untrue.

[1] In March 1906 the following humorous (or semi-humorous?) notes were exchanged between Morley and Grey during a Cabinet:

(J. M.) 'After my stupefying exhibition of diplomatic gifts at Calcutta, I'm astonished you don't beg me to go to Algeciras. Asquith would give me a "personal allowance."'

(E. G.) 'I haven't had a chance yet of congratulating you on the settlement in India. I thought you handled the affair and the big man excellently. But what I would suggest is that you should go to Berlin (where the real difficulty is) and see if you can master the German Emperor as you have done Kitchener.'

II

Letters and Friends, 1906–14 — Fallodon Station — Roosevelt's Visit — Balmoral

THE loss of his wife changed everything for Grey, for he had shared with her his daily thoughts and feelings in unusually close and constant communion. Her death was as shattering a blow to his private happiness as the war afterwards was to his public work and hopes, or his blindness to the consolations of his later years. These, and many other misfortunes that marked the course of his remaining life like milestones, he endured without despair or even bitterness. Endurance tested and ennobled his character, and he grew in moral stature as the married happiness he had so ardently cherished receded into the past, and as the pursuits of the nature-lover were cut down to a fraction, first by the duties of office, and after his retirement by the failure of his eyes.

After 1906, his powerful memory enabled him to live on the capital of the happiness he had already amassed, and to watch the birds beside the Itchen as he walked the London streets. The quiet humour that flavoured his outlook on everyday things and enriched his talk and letters, helped to bring him back to normal feelings and to some enjoyment of life, though henceforth under a sunset sky.

The letters in this chapter show him in the first stage of his long struggle with adverse fate, from Dorothy's death to the outbreak of war. They were mostly written from Fallodon or the Hampshire Cottage, during precious days snatched from the Foreign Office and Parliament, when the pouches followed him down to the country to occupy his morning, leaving a part at least of the day to watch the birds and write to his friends. It was by those half-holidays that he lived, and preserved the balance and sweetness of his mind.

The letter that he wrote to Haldane on the very day of his wife's death shows how quick and instinctive was his salutary double decision to open his heart to his friends and to stick grimly to his work.

FALLODON,
February 4, 1906.

DEAR RICHARD:

It is over, and we are companions in sorrow now until life ends. I shall feel the need of friends, a thing I have never felt while I had her love every day and could give all mine to her. If I could realise at once all that this means I could not live, but I suppose nature will dole out to me just the suffering every day which I can bear. My best chance is to begin work again at once, and I have told them to begin sending F.O. work to me tomorrow. Will you have me in your flat if I come to London next week and have all my things moved down from the flat above?

So the two friends lived close together during their London life, and had no reserves.[1] Indeed, it would be difficult to overestimate what Haldane did for Grey at this crisis. As they lived close together during the Sessions of Parliament, few letters passed between them, but during Grey's visits to

[1] Grey's letter of February 4 refers to the flat in Whitehall Court which the Greys were sharing with Haldane. But Dorothy had already taken a house, 3 Queen Anne's Gate, into which Grey soon moved, while Haldane moved into Number 28 in the same street.

Fallodon and the Hampshire Cottage he wrote frequent and intimate letters to his other friends, most often and most intimately to Mrs. Creighton and to Katharine Lyttelton, the wife of his friend General Sir Neville Lyttelton.

His friendship with Mrs. Creighton was deeply and doubly rooted in the past. Her husband, as has been already told, was the beloved mentor of Edward Grey's youth after his grandfather's death, and had been an even greater help to Dorothy in her girlhood. In all that Creighton had been to them both, Mrs. Creighton had had a full share. Then the Bishop's death in 1901 had drawn her closer than ever to the Greys. They were, in fact, united by many memories and many ties. She had been one of the very few people who sometimes occupied the Hampshire Cottage. When, therefore, Dorothy died, Grey had no reserves from her and leant strongly upon her help. Very soon he asked her to undertake the private Memoir of Dorothy, which she wrote as admirably as she had already written the Life of her own husband. This first letter to her is dated not a fortnight after Dorothy's death.

> *To Mrs. Creighton. February* 17, 1906. Your letter is very good. I am having a hard struggle. Every day I grasp a little more of all that it means. Just when I have got my spirit abreast of life, I feel and understand more sorrow and sink again. Sometimes it is like a living death; and the perpetual heartache, which has set in, wears me down. I have gained time by work; I did it all this week and did it well and could give my mind to it. But sorrow keeps pace with time; it gets fuller and makes itself more felt and realized. If a memoir is done at all I should like it to be done by you.
>
> *February* 22. *House of Commons.* Sorrow there is always, sometimes it is cold and dark and heavy, but sometimes it is still and pure. My plan is to go on working in the belief that some life and spirit will come back in time. Meanwhile I do

the work and the days pass slowly, but they do pass. I shall be away for Sunday; I shall go a long country walk.

April 17. *Fallodon.* (To Mrs. Creighton at his Hampshire Cottage.) I liked very much hearing from you. We always knew from the first that you cared for that country and the peculiar spirit of the place in the same way that we did; that was why we liked you to go there, and enjoyed your letters written from the Cottage. The days of peace, innocence, joy, beauty and love that we had there were like days not belonging to this world. Nothing here can last; that condition we must accept and recognise as limiting all our happiness in this world; but there is enough beauty and pure joy possible to fill us with hope and promise.

I go out a good deal at Fallodon; I took my bicycle over the moorland road from North Charlton and went to the top of Ross Camp one day; a year ago I trailed Dorothy over that road and round by Chillingham and Bellshill. This year too it was a beautiful day and I heard wonderful bird sounds, the spring notes of golden plovers and above all of curlews, as different from their autumn notes as the song of birds is from their chirp, and the sun was glorious and the whole view full of light. I was sad all day, seeing and listening to it all, but thinking and longing. Then in the evening after supper, when I was lying on the sofa in the library, the whole beauty of the day, of all I had seen and heard, seemed to find a way to me unawares and I became very peaceful.

Politics seem very remote, and except that I do the F.O. work directly after breakfast and get it over, I don't think of them. But I won't give them up, because that would be trying to anticipate another world in this one, and I know that can't be done, certainly not now.

To Katharine Lyttelton. April 15, 1906. *Fallodon.* It is very touching that you should have thought of me in this way, and I will tell you about myself. There need be no fear of my being alone here. It is true that I am alone, but in that way I learn what sorrow teaches and that is to the good. For instance, I ask if Dorothy joined me again should I be more or less loving now? And the answer is 'more loving.' I had learnt all that happiness could teach me and now I have learnt more, for sorrow and happiness both teach love, only each leaves so much untaught, which only the other can give. And so if I am learning and growing, my spirit is becoming more fit to meet hers or to go, when the time comes, wherever hers has gone.

These thoughts come to me in solitude. We both had an unusual gift of solitude, the power to enjoy being alone, but she had used it more than I had done, and in the last ten years she had grown more than I had, partly by illness, partly by being many days alone, partly by strong friendships; while I had been always more hustled and bustled by public life and work and business, so that I was getting left behind. Now in a time like this, when I am constantly thinking and longing, love goes on growing and I would not have it disturbed by anyone else with me just now. Much of each day is very sad. But I am used to that and before each day is over there come thoughts, which turn to peace, and at the worst I am never angry or impatient or in despair.

I am glad you are having a happy time. You ought to if you have got a nice cottage, because there is extraordinary joy and health in such weather at this time of year; warmth and the great singing time of birds don't last for long together nor are there many days of them, very often, in April, nor many in May, and early in June the songs begin to cease. So make the most of them, and try to teach the daughters to enjoy them, so that next winter they may still be thinking of them, and begin months before to wonder whether next April will bring such days again.

In August he was again at Fallodon, and the process of recovery is marked by his humorous enjoyment of a visit from the lively and earnest Cecil Spring Rice.

To Lady Helen Munro Ferguson. August 26, 1906. *Fallodon.* Springy talks to me of some sort of death which comes unexpectedly from overwork and can only be guarded against by constant watching. But as it seems to be quick and painless I have been explaining to him that I do not intend to take any precautions against being taken that way. He then talks in a very proper 'duty to the country' style, to which I listen with the respect that is due to it. He insists on mistaking all my china for pieces of great value; advises that jars which have stood forty years on a mantelpiece should be removed without delay to a place of safety; assumes an air of horror at seeing other jars used for electric light lamps, etc.; I have told him that next time he comes everything will have been put in the cellar for safety and he will find the house bare. This morning he has walked off to church with my nephew who has a passion for cricket, but he will no doubt be equal to this and every other occasion. He is however not equal to Bridge, which he does not play, any more than Haldane, who came at tea time on Friday. It is a pity that one should love Bridge and then find that one has collected for friends the only people in the world who dislike it, though I agree generally in disliking the people who like it; which suggests a doubt whether if one likes Bridge one is really fit to be the friend of anyone who dislikes it. Happily I play it badly.

To Mrs. Creighton. August 14, 1906. *Fallodon.* I am glad to be here. There is something of the parent about one's home; and how few people can have a home in which they have been brought up as children and which remains their own and their home. It strikes me as a very rare thing. At first I was very low on coming back here. Now I am better than I have yet been. A feeling has come over me that love is going on unimpaired.

September 1. *Fallodon.* I haven't brought myself yet to look into Dorothy's letters [for the Memoir which Mrs. Creighton was to write]; but I must do it. The best hours of the day have to be given to the F.O. work; then I go out and when the evening comes and I have any time I shrink from taking out the letters. I am used to thinking; I can do that now without distress, but there is growing on me a sense of the awfulness of living on alone. I feel as if I could take it and get to the heart of it if it wasn't for the outside work; but if I don't begin the day with the work it isn't done properly, and when it is done I shrink from the ordeal of reading the letters. But I will begin soon.

To Katharine Lyttelton. August 6, 1906. *Fallodon.* When I saw such a fat envelope from you I was afraid it couldn't be all you and that there must be an enclosure. Then I was pleased to find that it was all you, but the paper was rather thick and I found I was at the end, when I thought there was another sheet to come, and that gave me a little twinge of disappointment.

I have been very low. The Session left me tired and out of sorts. My first day here I felt as if I was hanging over an abyss and ready to drop. As long as one's body and mind are vigorous, one has strength to learn what sorrow teaches, and then one feels that one is being fitted for still more perfect love and to be used for God's purposes. But when one is tired one feels as if one could not learn and could not be used, and as if one's suffering was purposeless. If only there were not so long to wait! I could manage a few years bravely, but there may be so many and it seems impossible to keep up for 30 or perhaps more. And yet it is not wise in these things to worry about what may be.

The anniversary of the days of Dorothy's accident and death (February 1–4) he always passed, as far as possible, in solitude.

To Mrs. Creighton. February 2, 1907. *Fallodon.* I have been in London all this week and had to stay for a Cabinet yesterday. This morning I got home at sunrise. There were many of these winter morning home comings and I always used to go straight to Dorothy's room and she had a fire lit and we sat by it and had a little tea, while I told her all my news. I have the tea and the fire put ready for me now and go to sit there first. There I found your letter this morning and I am very grateful for it; it gave me comfort. What you have learnt by your own sorrow is a priceless gift to your friends, when they have to tread the same path. My great prayer and struggle now is for strength; I cannot feel interest in politics at all, nor in my work as I should; it continues to die away and that makes things very hard for there is so much work and it is so incessant. However the struggle goes on. It is hard to put energy into oneself, when one is overworked and physically low, and I trust that, where there is perfect knowledge, all this is known and taken into account. I long to follow Dorothy quickly, but whether it be soon or later I must be able to say that I have gained and not lost since we parted.

April 22, 1907. *3 Queen Anne's Gate.* I had to go to a Colonial Premier's dinner on Saturday, so half a Sunday and

Sunday night was all I had at the Cottage. It rained and I walked over Itchen down to Abbotstone and enjoyed the rain. But to keep you in touch with the Cottage, I send you a little news. The long-tailed tits' nest is safe, but whether eggs or birds are in it I do not know; it has a ruddy cock pheasant's feather in the mouth of it. The cock chaffinch still drags a wing but is in good spirits; both it and the rival are very tame. The wag-tails have gone. A willow wren has come, but no nightingale yet. This morning was beautiful, blue sky and warm sun on moist earth; it was heartrending to leave it. I see no signs that any of the Colonial Premiers care for these things, and a Japanese Mission is being sent all the way from Japan on purpose to destroy by another official dinner my beech Sunday in May. There are no less than four official dinners in that one week.

May 12. The long-tailed tits' nest is still safe and two little heads were resting their chins on the sill of the opening and basking in the heat; sometimes the opening is full of heads.

To Haldane. Fallodon. September 3, 1906. I want to preserve the entente with France, but it isn't easy, and if it is broken up I must go.

Fallodon. September 4, 1907. I am satisfied about the Russian agreement. But I am not very comfortable about other things; there are signs that the Morocco trouble is reacting unfavourably upon our relations with France, and I hear of a tendency in the press to whittle away our obligations to France about Morocco; to say that it is our business to let Germany put pressure on France in the interests of the open door; and to emphasise the troubles France is having. This will be a very mischievous line.

Also I am not altogether without apprehension about the German Emperor's visit. There is an idea that he will bring Bülow as well as von Einem; no other sovereign comes with two ministers; the King only took one to Kiel, and the Emperor has a habit of turning visits into demonstrations which is tiresome. All the other sovereigns are so much quieter. I hope you admired his last speech — the one in Tuesday's *Times*.

I have been rather sad here; the contrast of what my home is now with what it was is very sharp.

To Mrs. Creighton. December 1, 1907. *Forest Park Hotel, Brockenhurst, Hants.* It seems so cruel that one should by one's work be depriving oneself of the power to perceive. Really I suppose one is by the discipline of work storing power for future use. I have had a good walk from 11 till 6.30, the last part in the dark. The German Emperor is perilously near, but I know he can't find me in the forest — people with motor cars are chained to the roads and there is no freedom like the freedom of one's own feet.

To Mrs. Pember. Fallodon. December 29, 1907. I am so glad you have found what you tell me in Mrs. Creighton's Memoir of Dorothy, and your reading is a very true one. I hoped the book might help friends who knew enough of Dorothy to see what a true account it is, and might encourage them to keep free spaces in their lives in which they could find for themselves things which cannot be found in work or in society.

To Katharine Lyttelton. 3 *Queen Anne's Gate. February* 4, 1908. (*The anniversary again.*) I never said that I was going to Fallodon, only that I should spend Sunday alone. I went to the hotel which Dorothy found for me in the New Forest and was out in the Forest for many hours on a beautiful day and came back by star-light. That is the sort of thing I am really made for — not politics. Sometimes as I walked I felt full of the things that Dorothy liked best in me, and thoughts came to me which I knew she would have liked me to say to her. These last two years have taken a lot out of me and I am now perpetually tired, except physically — I can walk and all that. So it is no good goading me to take more politics upon me than I have. You will be enthusiastic and high spirited to the end, and I see that you and Winston have been talking a lot of nonsense together. I know that he knows nothing about the F.O. work, and thinks that because a Parliamentary Under-secretary can travel and pick and choose and gallop about the field and toss his head and sniff what breeze he pleases, therefore a Foreign Secretary can do the same. And I am sorry to see that you know no more about the F.O. work than he does.

What I might do would be to do my railway work again, and live mostly in the country and be nice to a few friends when I saw them or wrote to them, if they would remember that I was on the ebb tide. Would you like to lunch or tea on Saturday?

I would make you very welcome and tell you something of what Dorothy really did expect of me in office.

To K. L. Post Office, Rosehall, Scotland. April 18, 1908. This isn't a good place for writing in. I go out after breakfast and when I come in, in the afternoon a huge pouch of papers has arrived from the F.O. and they last me more or less till bedtime. Of course your Charlie Masterman [married to Lady Lyttelton's daughter Lucy] is right to take office. There are two common ways of failing in politics. One is to be an idealist, not in touch with the practical side, always advocating the impossible, never getting anything done — like an overkeen soldier firing all his ammunition at something out of range. Another way is to lose all ideas, to be an opportunist, a place hunter out of office and a drudge in office. Your C. M. runs no risk of the second failure, but he might of the first, and office will help him to avoid it. What is wanted in politics is an idealist who can estimate rightly the limits of what is possible in his own generation. C. M. has got a gift of speech and writing with which he can educate and stir the public; a few years of office will give him an education and insight and correct judgment, which can be got in no other way. It won't impair his gift but it will add to his wisdom. So I am sure he is right to take it. All this is on the assumption that C. M. wants to continue in the H. of C. and not be a Ruskin or a Carlyle outside it, a great writer who preaches and tells mankind what they should feel. That is another and a different career. The H. of C. is mainly a place for settling what should be done.

To Lady Helen Munro Ferguson. Rosehall, April 19, 1908. I will come like a lamb on the 20th of May [to speak at the Victoria League]. If I spoke my mind it would appear something like this. 'Ladies and gentlemen of the Victoria League, I think there is too much tendency here to slobber over the Colonies, and they are too much given to spit at us; I except Canada from this criticism, but for Australia it might be put even stronger, etc. etc.' I fear this wouldn't do.

To Katharine Lyttelton. F.O. July 3, 1908. Last week I went to the Horticultural Garden at Wisley with Mildred Buxton and Pamela Tennant. We went to see flowers and incidentally found a Great Spotted Woodpecker's nest, and saw both the old birds and heard the clamour of the young. There has been no such surprise since Saul went out to look for his father's asses and found a kingdom.

I don't much believe in your A.D.C. being fond of birds and I expect you were a little premature in showing him the bird bits in the Memoir. You always have to discount 85 per cent of the interest, which any man appears to take in the subject on which he finds a woman sympathetic, at any rate if she is one on whom he wishes to make a good impression; and I suppose every A.D.C. wishes to make a good impression on the wife of his commanding officer. It isn't very nice of me to have written this, but it is too much to scratch out, and I really wrote it because I was amused and not displeased.

I fear I am grumbling too much just now. I infer it because I got a sort of reproof from dear Birrell in his good-humoured breezy way the other day. But one does one's work better if one can blow off a little steam; otherwise one might burst.

September 8, 1908. *Fallodon.* I have just come back from London. I spent two nights and Sunday with John Morley at Wimbledon. He had a very light tweed suit; I told him it was the most holiday-making suit I ever saw: it was a very nice soft suit, much better than my stiff dark thing, and he looked very light-hearted in it. He said it was made by Pool. It was very good to be with a mind which has voyaged so far and long through seas of thought, and I enjoyed it, fearing however the while that I could not be an adequate companion. We talked about the many clouds in the political sky, and he was sometimes thoughtful, sometimes grim, but often breaking into those gleams of humour, when his expression is so delightful; his wreathed expression I call it, if you know what I mean by that. I feel quite proud whenever I tell him anything which makes him light up and laugh. We talked of books and got taking down volumes to show each other passages, so that by the evening the great library was littered with loose volumes lying about, which is always a good sign.

To John Morley (*note passed across the Cabinet Table: no date*). I have heard a story that someone once said to Tennyson, 'Browning has no music in him,' and Tennyson growled out, 'You're wrong, he's got plenty of music in him, but he can't get it out.'

To Ella Pease. Cottage, Itchen Abbas. November 8, 1908.

The German Emperor is ageing me; he is like a battleship with steam up and screws going, but with no rudder, and he will run into something some day and cause a catastrophe. He has made a fool of Germany. [Referring to the Kaiser's famous interview published in the *Daily Telegraph*.] And all the world is laughing at him, and he has the strongest army in the world, and the Germans don't like being laughed at and are looking for somebody on whom to vent their temper and use their strength. After a big war a nation doesn't want another for a generation or more, but after forty years of peace, if a nation is strong it begins spoiling for a fight. It was so with us between forty and fifty years after the Crimean War, and it was so with Russia; and it was so with the United States nearly forty years after her Civil War. And now it is thirty-eight years since Germany had her last war, and she is very strong and very restless, like a person whose boots are too small for him. I don't think there will be war at present, but it will be difficult to keep the peace of Europe for another five years.

To Mrs. Creighton (*at the Hampshire Cottage*). *F.O. September* 14, 1909. The spirit of the Cottage is very peculiar and unfailing. I wish I didn't have it for such short periods. There isn't time in the two or three days of a week end to sink down into it: it is after two days that one is thoroughly in tune. And for these last four years there has been disturbing work to do at the Cottage and that must be so as long as I am in office. Foreign Office things are always in a mess: they are not as if one was doing constructive work, or writing a book or a lecture, or reading up a subject, and they can never be put aside for a day. Nevertheless Cottage is a refuge always and there is quiet.

September 5, 1909. *Hatfield House*. I am reading *Forgotten Tales*, a selection of cautionary and improving stories of the end of the eighteenth and early nineteenth century; E. V. Lucas has dug them up and they have many delightful expressions. 'The boy's father, *though* a labouring man, had a generous heart.' And two little boys writing to their little sister say 'Our rabbit has kindled,' which apparently means that it has had young.

I like what you say of the unchangingness of Ella Pease and her mother: there is something spiritually antiseptic in good Quakerism.

August 26, 1908. *Fallodon.* I was thinking the other day what a secure possession the past is. The happiness and beauty that it had cannot now be spoilt or impaired: having had it one cannot be pessimistic either about this life or another.

To Katharine Lyttelton. April 9, 1909. *Fallodon.* I came here with a heavy cold which however has been beaten by two days of sun and open air. It took away my sense of smell. It is sad to put one's nose against a Daphne Mezereum and smell no more than if it was a Begonia. Nevertheless these two days have been very splendid. I went over the moor to Ross Camp today and lunched and read and slept a little in the heather. I see the wonderful beauty of the world as it still is, and I think of the happiness I have had and I do from my heart say 'Oh! that men would therefore praise the Lord for his goodness!' For I have had that which is worth being born for or dying for or waiting for; and others may have it all too. The beauty of the world at any rate is for all who have eyes to see and hearts to feel. I shall die grateful for what I have had, whether I die soon or late, and whatever happens to me between now and then.

And this sentiment he repeated in the last year of his life, after much had happened to him that was exceedingly painful.

To K. L. April 25, 1909. *Fallodon.* There has never been a day of complete holiday now for nearly three and one half years, and I am not the sort that *likes* work — all my affections are out of doors. I am forty-seven today and I wish I was seventy-seven.

October 24, *Fallodon.* Today I went to church unintentionally, by which I mean that I put aside the church-going clothes when I got up, and put on the others intending not to go. Then after breakfast I changed my mind, though not my clothes, and went and enjoyed it. It seemed to be harvest thanksgiving when I got there: the Church was decorated with chrysanthemums and oats, and an occasional beetroot or carrot; and we had four harvest hymns. Do you remember the touching simplicity of harvest hymns? They make me wriggle and purr with enjoyment.

'And keep us in His grace
And guide us when perplexed
And save us from all ills
In this world and the next.'

The simplicity gave me such a *douce attendrissement* that I felt as if I could kiss the whole choir for singing it. But they missed out one verse of 'We plough the fields and scatter,' and I nearly made a fuss and interrupted the service then. We had too the 118th Psalm and a fine chant for it: do you know that psalm? It is splendid and buoyant and says things two or three or four times over because it is so glad.

I go on with the *Adventures of Philip*. It is very early Victorian, and oh! the difference between Thackeray's women and Meredith's. You cannot think of any of Meredith's women in a crinoline, nor of any of Thackeray's out of one. If it wasn't for the fact that they had children I should be sure they slept in their crinolines. Nevertheless there is in Thackeray what belongs to all times and all ages of both sexes.

I also continue with Gibbon. He has a naughtiness which amuses me, as when he speaks of the 'pious obstinacy' of the early Christians when persecuted. But he has a respect for Athanasius, which I hadn't before but I have now. I leave these books here, Gibbon and Thackeray, when I go to London. And when I come back, I find Gibbon with my mark in it and Thackeray open where I left off on the reading stand by the bed. That is homey.

It is strange how as long as one's body keeps well one can enjoy life and yet want to die. I should have said it was impossible, but it isn't. Death now seems like going home. If I was dying and found my friends sorry, I feel as if I should say 'Never mind, you will die, too,' as if it was a thing to be desired. In 1904 I was making speeches and doing railway work and Dorothy was at Cottage and writing me such dear letters about it. I read them as the days come round again.

To Lady Helen Munro Ferguson. April 1910. What a horridly dull dream about me! What did you think of me in your dream when I gave you Harrods Store List? And does the dream reflect most upon me or upon you? For instance did you dream this dream because I am the sort of person who suggests Harrods Stores, or because you habitually think of Harrods Stores? Your letter came at tea time and I went out afterwards and caught a salmon, which I am sending to you to make up for my share in the dream.

January 1914. I like the stock of coarseness and impropriety that I acquired in youth in the pages of Fielding, Benvenuto Cellini, Boccaccio, and Sterne; but I take little pleasure in adding anything more to this stock; though I hugely enjoy an improper story, when it is really witty, as for instance the story about Lady . . ., which Ronald always asks leave to tell in your presence, which you always forbid him to tell and which he then tells before you with éclat. Have you read the *Crock of Gold* by James Stephens? He is not always intelligible, but he has genius and huge fun and much beauty in his writing.

It was a great convenience to Grey during his eleven years at the Foreign Office that he was able to stop trains by request at the little Fallodon station, a few hundred yards from his door. It was an ancient right of his family, acquired at the time the railway was made through the Grey land. In this way he was able to secure more week-ends at home than he could otherwise have had in full session. After the Walter Runcimans had, to his great joy, established themselves at Doxford, a mile beyond Fallodon, he often took his friend up with him to their little wayside station after Cabinet meetings. And all guests staying at Fallodon could, with his authority, stop the trains there.

He never complained of the beloved N.E.R. as being too near; the sound of the trains close at hand through the wood was one of the old 'Fallodon noises' and as such 'homey' and 'liked.' Where the road crosses the railway line there is a signal box, behind which it was his roguish pleasure to take his stand with a guest close up against the gate, when the Scotch Express was due, to see the guest 'jump' as the giant in his speed rushed out from behind the signal box, scarcely a yard away. He never tired of this game: in one of the last years of Grey's life, a distinguished visitor was astonished at being hurried away from a visit to Bamborough Castle and motored back in haste to Fallodon, in his host's anxiety not 'to miss the Scotch Express'! The schoolboy was one element in Grey's nature to the end. His nephews adored him and he delighted in them: his letters describe games of cricket played with them on the sands, half in and half out of the water, the stumps being periodically washed away by the encroaching tide. He liked boys: in June 1916 two of them from Winchester, wandering up the Itchen but with no idea of finding him, met the hooded figure of the half blind statesman on the riverside in front of his Cottage. They were complete strangers, but they spent half an hour with him in such talk of birds and fishing as one of them has never forgotten; before they left they were made to eat an immense dish of strawberries on the steps of the Cottage.

Grey was devoted to German music: not to Wagner, whose assault on the emotions he found intemperate, but to Handel and Beethoven and Bach. On the evening of July 28, 1914, after a day when his peace efforts were crumbling in his hand, he sought composure at a musical party at Lady Glenconner's, when Mr. Campbell McInnes sang some Handel songs which at his request were repeated. The singer, who had noticed the ashen misery of his face, went home and impulsively wrote to him:

> DEAR SIR EDWARD:
> I am so glad you liked the music, and if the world is going to become a howling wilderness, won't you let me sing to you again?

For some days the letter was unanswered. But early in the morning of August 5, a few hours after the outbreak of war, Grey wrote the following note which he sent round by a Foreign Office messenger:

> DEAR MR. MCINNES:
> I am touched by your letter and will keep it by me in case there is a time when I can come. I love Handel music and it does me good. Europe is in the most terrible trouble it has ever known in civilized times, and no one can say what will be left at the end. But Handel's music will survive.

And several times during the war Grey went to Mr. McInnes, who sang to him Handel and Bach and old Italian songs.

In June 1910 ex-President Theodore Roosevelt paid his long-expected visit to England, after his tour round the world. The visit for once brought the two parts of Grey's life together, for it was marked by two characteristic performances of Roosevelt, a speech at the Guildhall in praise of what he had seen of British work in Africa and particularly in Egypt, and his famous 'bird-walk' in the New Forest with our Foreign Secretary.[1] Both are described in the following letter to Bryce, then our Ambassador at Washington:

> 17 *June*, 1910. My dear Bryce, I have waited till Roosevelt's visit had concluded before telling you about it. He came to me as soon as he had arrived, and told me what he wished to say in the Guildhall. It struck me at once as being a very great compliment to our work in Africa. I felt also that it would be sure to give great satisfaction to our officials in East Africa, Uganda, and the Soudan, who had taken a great deal of trouble over Roosevelt's journey and who, I had heard from independent sources, had been very much pleased with him. I knew

[1] In November 1908 Bryce had written to Grey while Roosevelt was still in office: 'The President, with whom I had a long talk yesterday, is anticipating three things with that fiery interest which belongs to him — his time among the lions and rhinoceroses in East Africa, his Romanes lecture at Oxford, and the woodland walk with you to observe the English birds in Spring. I told him of your proposal and he was enraptured.'

there would be a row about what he proposed to say with regard to Egypt, and I told him so, adding that I supposed he was prepared for that, both in the United States and in our own press. He replied characteristically by a most vigorous improvised sketch of a leading article which would appear in the United States press, denouncing him.

He dwelt on the point that he did not wish to say anything which would embarrass me, and he asked whether I would like to see a manuscript of the speech. I answered that I did not wish to see one. I thought it better that I should be quite free, after he had made his speech, to say that he had stated things in his own way. He said that I was not to be committed in any way by this interview, and as far as he was concerned he was content that the fact of his having consulted me should not be known.

After the speech in the Guildhall, he asked whether what he had said was in accordance with what he had told me beforehand. I replied that it was, and that if there was trouble about it I would say that it agreed with my views, and that I regarded it as a compliment to our work in Africa, the more so as it was true and came from an impartial observer. But it was understood that no mention of his having consulted me was contemplated, and this understanding continued until he left England.

Last Monday, however, there was a debate in the House; Roosevelt was criticised; and I decided, while the discussion was in progress, that it would not be fair to him to let it be supposed that he had been discourteous in not giving me an opportunity of objecting to anything which he proposed to say. When I spoke I had to steer between the extremes of, on the one hand, representing him as having had his speech inspired or dictated by me, and, on the other hand, of leaving it to be supposed that he had been brusque and wanting in taste. I endeavoured to make my account of what passed between us cover all he had done, without giving the impression that I had tried to make use of him, or that the speech was anything but his own. I think the situation is now clear. I am very glad the speech has been made, not only because it will encourage our people in Africa, but also because it is a tribute to our work there which it is good to have on record.

The walk which Roosevelt and I planned long ago through you took place as proposed. We could not leave London very early, but by train and motor car combined we reached our starting point at the head of the Itchen valley soon after one o'clock. There we began to walk.

I found that he must have spent a good deal of time in his life over birds, for he has an ear trained to catch their songs, and to pick them up extraordinarily quickly. He knew all about the birds, so we did not trouble to get sight of them. He would ask me to what bird a particular song belonged, and then tell me whether the bird had any relations in America, and if so how the song compared.

We walked down the valley of the Itchen to the village of King's Worthy, near Winchester, to which I had sent the motor car. We motored from there to Stoney Cross, in the New Forest, whence I sent the car on to the hotel outside Brockenhurst at which we were to spend the night. We had tea at Stoney Cross, and then plunged into the Forest and walked through the heart of it till we reached the Brockenhurst hotel at about a quarter to nine. It was a most delightful day: I enjoyed it immensely and so did Roosevelt.

I liked very much everything I saw of him while he was here, and found him most attractive and stimulating. It amused and delighted me to think of the difference between giving an official luncheon or dinner at the Foreign Office, as we usually do when a distinguished foreigner comes to see us, and the spending of a day in the country like this one with Roosevelt. As far as I can judge, the whole of his visit here was a great success. He gave me the impression of having felt at home and of having liked us. People criticised his public utterances; but everyone who met him personally delighted in him, even though some approached him with a good deal of prejudice.

To Mrs. Creighton Grey wrote:

I have liked Roosevelt immensely and really enjoyed the walk and whole day. We saw forty different species of birds and heard the songs of twenty of them, and his knowledge of and interest in birds is that of a real lover of birds. We had good talk too about politics and books including poetry, of

> which I found he knew by heart several of the things I have learnt. He has a peculiar faculty with it all of imparting healthy courage and vigour. I have loved him.

After the Agadir crisis in 1911 Grey wrote to his friend Roosevelt from Fallodon:

> The Germans, or rather the Prussians — for the south Germans are of different ideals and temperament — are very difficult people. Their way of beginning a conversation is to stamp upon your foot to attract your attention when you aren't looking, and then they are surprised and very annoyed when the conversation doesn't go smoothly afterwards. Nevertheless I wish we could get on better with them: it may be easier, if they have really settled the Morocco question as far as they are concerned. But to get on well one must feel that one is dealing with someone who can be trusted not to take some untoward turn.
>
> I shall always follow with interest all that I hear of your part in public affairs. But as you said in a letter that you wrote me in March it is the private things concerning a man's home that count most in life: I should like very much to see you there as you said in the same letter you would like me to do, but my spell of office must come to an end first. Pending that I wish you could come here, preferably in the time of the singing of birds: I wish the hours of our walk had been days instead of hours. I did at various times — on Sundays mostly — go all over that ground again this year. It was a hot dry year and the birds ceased their songs sooner in consequence — owing probably to difficulty of food supply that made it harder to feed their young and made them less well fed themselves. I noticed this year that, at the time corresponding to that of our walk the year before, there was much less singing.
>
> It is the habit of the wild squirrels here to come into my library for nuts and it was very refreshing after I had been away for weeks to sit at my writing table and find them come on to it as usual, with a most convincing unconsciousness of Morocco and all foreign affairs. Their complete unconsciousness of all the things that worry mankind is very soothing.

Readers will by this time be aware that it was part of

Grey's nature, enhanced by the memory of Dorothy's similar distaste, to dislike all formal society and all functions of State.

Two years after they had taken Cabinet office together, he wrote to John Morley:

> I am glad to have the description of the levée to recollect and smile about secretly, when I stand to watch the Corps Diplomatique go by and Cabinet Ministers ranged in a row against the wall. In time, as mechanical ingenuity proceeds apace, perhaps all of us 'persons of high position' will be allowed to order with our uniforms mechanical dummies, which will wear the uniforms and pass the throne and bow and stand at levées to represent us, and the only live persons there will be the Monarch of the day and the Bobby Spencer of the day, who will press the buttons necessary to make the figures work. 'The middle classes' can continue to come in the flesh as long as they continue to enjoy levées.

So there was groaning whenever he had to go to Balmoral. But it was observed with amusement that when there he always enjoyed himself, and that he always came away under King Edward's charm. Balmoral indeed was very different from a levée. Other evidences of this, lying under my hand, convince me that the two following letters represent his real feeling:

> *To Lord Knollys. October* 11, 1907. I was very much touched by the King's kindness to me at Balmoral, and by the kind way in which he recalled memories of days when my father had been with him in Scotland, and showed places to me.
>
> *To the King. October* 1, 1908. Sir Edward Grey presents his humble duty and begs to thank Your Majesty for the kindness shown him during his stay at Balmoral. He very much enjoyed the days spent there, the more so as he was most graciously made to feel that it was Your Majesty's wish that they should be enjoyed. Sir Edward Grey would venture again to take the opportunity of saying how much he has been touched by Your Majesty's kindness, which has made his official at-

tendance a real pleasure to him and has increased the satisfaction of serving Your Majesty and the desire to do that service well to the best of his power.

Lord Knollys to Sir Edward Grey. Balmoral. October 3, 1908. Haldane is delighted with himself, as the day before yesterday he went out to fish with worms in a burn and caught 14. On enquiring however as to their size, I was told they were no bigger than Sardines!

Grey to Miss Haldane. August 2, 1910. I am amused with the suggestion that Richard should be taught to fish with fly: but I am sure he won't consent. He was so proud of his success at Balmoral with worm that he will never risk a loss of reputation by any other method.

In February 1912, when King George was graciously pleased to confer the Garter upon Sir Edward Grey, Asquith wrote to his old friend: 'I only send you a line to assure you that, after nearly four years of what is called *power*, this is the one thing which, in a personal sense, has given me deep and abiding pleasure.'

On the same occasion Grey wrote to Katharine Lyttelton:

> I suppose my real feeling about the Garter was that I was very pleased at being offered it, but shrank from having it. It will make life a little more conspicuous and more complicated: and it gives me a feeling of being still deeper in. I do long to be in the country and free to go and look at the sun and be out for the day without having to work early before I go out and late after I come in, to make up for having spent a day out of doors. It is more than six years since I have done that, for even when John Morley has taken my work I have kept in touch with some things, and he has only had charge for a fortnight — one fortnight in six years. However women are always in office in their own houses, so you may not sympathize.

The Walter Runcimans had established themselves at Doxford, a country house only half an hour's walk from Fallodon. Such close rural propinquity, and like-mindedness in Cabinet counsel, led to a friendship between the two statesmen that was never afterwards cooled. In April 1914, when Walter Runciman and his wife were touring in Greece, Grey wrote them an account of his invasion of their grounds:

MY DEAR WALTER:

On Friday I went to your lake, partly to fish it, partly to eat my lunch there, and partly to see how Doxford looked in your absence. I ate my lunch on the seat of the embankment of the lake. The breeze and ripple came towards me and an April sun soon made all the ripple sparkle: the air was rich with thrush and blackbird songs and several willow-wrens were singing in the young wood. They only arrive this month and I heard them on Friday for the first time this year. Do you know their song? It has a sort of pleading lingering cadence, and made me get very fond of it. But the bird is badly named, being neither a wren nor a frequenter of willows in general. Some swallows skimmed the water and I heard a pair of sandpipers. There was a sort of bright spring happiness that makes me feel not only the prospect of summer, but the possibility of heaven in some other planet not so very unlike the earth, but with no cities and no influenza and where the foxes are not carnivorous (for my collection of water fowl that I began thirty years ago is being destroyed and broken up by a fox). However I lunched in the sun with content and after lunch fished from the embankment. In about an hour I had landed nineteen trout: I returned all but five, because I didn't want to deplete your stock. The lake really is first-rate trout fishing now.

The children seemed happy but I thought it right to condole with them on the absence of their parents, and they received the condolences in a proper and filial spirit. After what I have written I can't say that inanimate objects were mourning for you, unless perhaps the exceeding lowness of the burn is a sign of grief; if so I may adapt the lines applied to the Tweed on an analogous occasion and say

'The burn, best pleased in chanting a blithe strain,
Saddens his voice again and yet again.'

The country is in truth very dry and the springs are very low.

III

Grey and the Foreign Office Staff—Home Politics, 1909–14—Relations with Mr. Lloyd George—Death of George Grey.

IT WOULD be a mistake to suppose that Grey felt little interest in public life, although when he was longing for country joys he often wrote as if nothing else on earth had value. Politics made his chief bond with his most intimate friend Haldane; they were always talking about them; for Hegel was a tiresome mystery to Grey, and Haldane could scarcely tell a robin from a sparrow. Grey, as others of his friends bear witness, delighted in the small change of political gossip, and was besides deeply interested in great affairs. During his long working hours he was utterly absorbed in the Foreign Office work. He could not indeed bring to the Sphinx riddle of the European tragedy the high spirits of a Palmerston; he wrote no 'rhyming despatches' like Canning; but he was not, like the greatest of his predecessors, reduced to cutting his own throat. The craftsmanship of his official letters, memoranda and speeches show that his whole mind was given to their composition. But the reaction was strong when the tired man left off, and during these hours of repose it relieved him to objurgate his bondage in his private talk and letters, often to the amusement and sometimes to the irritation of his colleagues. Some were known to scoff when he spoke of an interview with an Ambassador as of less importance than an appointment with a wild duck. Birrell could be breezy on the subject. What Grey said and wrote in that vein, of which plenty will be found in this volume, may have been partly humour and partly habit. It was true but not the whole truth, any more than Carlyle's explosions on the miseries of authorship can be taken as a complete account of the psychological genesis of *Sartor* and *The French Revolution*. If Grey had not been profoundly interested in his task during the working hours, he could not have carried on for eleven years. There was little joy, but there was intellectual absorption so long as the matter was in hand.

I found among his papers a loose half-sheet of notepaper on which he had written the following words: 'Living for the week-end. Work done conscientiously, but not living in thought. Advantages of detachment — nothing done to keep office. On the other hand to desire to keep office causes concentration.' This self-questioning arose when he reviewed his past life at the time he wrote his memoirs. He had, in fact, no need to reproach himself, because, if he had thought about Foreign Affairs all the week-end and not at all about birds, his work would have lost its freshness and he would soon have broken down. It was the Sundays when he got his 'eight hours in the air and sun' that saved him. But even those days had their allotted round of work. 'In this room,' he wrote to Morley from Fallodon, 'my Sunday task used to be to repeat the Collect for the day to my Grandfather, now it is writing foreign telegrams.'

Though Grey never pretended to like the heavy burden of work, he bore the whole load. In 1924, when these things had passed into history, Sir William Tyrrell, who best knew, wrote to him of 'the exaggerated notion people have of your week-end passion, never realizing that you never neglected for it anything worth doing.' The Foreign Office had no complaint to make of him as a Chief, assiduous at his task and considerate to his subordinates. Indeed he won the hearts of the men who served under him. One of them, Sir Algernon Law, writes to me:

> The most striking feature in Edward Grey's nature was the nobility of his character: simple, frank and cordial, he struck me at once as being an old friend. There was something so easy in his manners and movements, so pleasant in his smile, that I was always glad to be summoned to his room to explain a case and to discuss it with him. Some Ministers are prone to be very impatient of views which run counter to their own. Grey was always most tolerant of opposition. He liked to hear and to weigh arguments against a line of conduct which he was inclined to favour. His was the fairest of minds.

And Mr. Alwyn Parker, who was in the Foreign Office during the whole of Grey's Secretaryship, writes:

> Sir Edward Grey's assumption of office in 1905 almost coincided with a thorough reorganisation of the Foreign Office, for which Eyre Crowe was responsible. It aimed at developing the sense of responsibility and initiative amongst members of the staff and at promoting necessary devolution of work. That such devolution was becoming a growing need is apparent if it is noted that only 44,041 papers had been received at the Foreign Office during the year 1895, when Sir Edward was Parliamentary Under-Secretary, and the corresponding total for the year 1916, when he finally resigned office, was 298,460.[1]
>
> During the formative period of transition and reorganisation, and in the following years which were critical in foreign affairs, Sir Edward Grey was supported by a team of lieutenants whose merits were very happily combined. The Permanent Under-Secretary was Hardinge, then in his prime,

[1] For the organization of the Office, see *The Foreign Office*, 1933, by Sir Stephen Gaselee and Sir John Tilley.

always maintaining a balance and proportion, restraining, discerning, and directing, for his great knowledge and experience had made his judgment mature; there was Crowe with a zeal and fidelity beyond all praise, his state papers a model for posterity; and Tyrrell was so skilful and circumspect that he brought men to work together, allayed those stubborn jealousies which constantly impede the course of peaceful negotiation, and often overcame apparently insoluble problems.

It was indeed no small thing that Sir Edward was seconded by such collaborators as these and others, at home and abroad. But the asset was of value mainly because the Secretary of State was able to bring out the best there was of accomplishment and character in his officers around him. We all knew that we had a leader who could be induced by no earthly motive to commit a dishonourable act, one whose qualities were unalloyed by the slightest shade of self-seeking. His style was always terse, luminous, simple, pregnant with meaning; the student of history will scarcely find a superfluous sentence or an ambiguous term in his minutes and despatches. In every department of the Service the influence of his mind, the embodiment of a robust common sense, was felt. His intellectual horizons were large, and he had ideas of policy that were coherent and his own, but he had also the talent of the fine learner and never failed to make the necessary adjustments to growing knowledge, and he was only impatient if men overworked secondary points. Thus while he never slurred over difficulties he had nothing in common with that desperate type of counsellor who takes all the small points and raises objections instead of helping to contrive expedients. He was ever ready to be moderate and conciliatory where concession was indicated and did not sacrifice the root of the matter. This was indeed the guiding principle which underlay every effort he made, and all the negotiations he conducted so patiently, to reach a settlement with Germany in the years before the War. His French accent was deplorable, but on one of the few occasions when he sent for me he quoted a saying of Napoleon which well illustrates the analytical bent of his own mind: *'Pourquoi' et 'comment' sont des questions si utiles qu'on ne saurait trop se les faire.*

Though Grey listened well to everyone who had a right to advise him, and was admirably served by several great public servants, he was master in his own house; he was not the mouthpiece of Foreign Office opinion. The general lines of the policy he pursued had been thought out by him and announced in public before he became Foreign Secretary. He did not follow Nicolson in his demand for Alliances, or Eyre Crowe in his emphatic anti-Germanism. To these men, as to Lords Hardinge and Tyrrell, he was always most grateful and faithful, but he had a high Whig notion of the position he occupied as the political chief, and he laid it down that 'I did not regard anything except my own letters and official papers as deciding policy.' Historians must read the *British Documents* in the light of those words.

For eleven years Grey worked and interviewed his diplomatic visitors in the large first-floor room, with the double outlook westward over the pelicans and water-birds in the Park, and northwards over the Horse Guards Parade. Thanks to Palmerston's refusal to have Whitehall rebuilt in the 'Gothic style,' there is ample air and light, but the classical spaciousness of the room is too palatial for comfort and was in contrast to Grey's domestic surroundings whether in town or in his country homes.

Arthur Balfour once described Grey as 'a curious combination of the old-fashioned Whig and the Socialist.' Perhaps the blend makes the perfect Liberal. At any rate Grey's sympathies with the aspirations of the working class to greater control of industry and better conditions of life made him a strong supporter of the great programme of social reform, which his colleagues were carrying out during the years when he was engrossed in the Foreign Office work. Both the

Whig and the Socialist in him were aroused to fighting pitch when the Lords in 1909 threw out the Budget in utter disregard for the custom of the constitution. Yet even in the heat of that conflict he disliked the shrill Limehouse note. He said to a friend that Mr. Lloyd George's speeches were unfair 'and the real root of Liberalism is fairness' — an interesting definition. But the attacks on the famous Budget and its author seemed to him even more unfair, and he defended both with great effect on the platform. To a correspondent who had written to him abusing Mr. Lloyd George, Grey replied:

> I cannot agree with what you say. Mr. Lloyd George is a colleague with whom I have always been on the best of terms personally, and the Budget raises the money required in a way which presses much less, I believe, upon the poorer classes than any alternative that could be devised.

After the election of January 1910, which returned the Liberals with a reduced majority of over one hundred, dependent on the Irish, the question arose how to tackle the problem of the Lords. All were agreed that the power of the Peers to reject money bills must be abolished. But Grey differed from the majority of the Cabinet and the party in desiring to abolish the hereditary House of Lords altogether and substitute an elective chamber; he wished to fight the next election on that issue and not on the proposal to limit its powers according to the 'C.-B. plan' advocated by the late Prime Minister, which afterwards took effect in the Parliament Act of 1911. Whether he was right or wrong as to the desirability of two elective Houses, there is no doubt his policy could not have been carried into effect. After a quarter of a century's further experience, we now realize the immense difficulty of getting people to agree on House of

Lords reform, even when they have plenty of time and are encouraged and commanded to try by the Preamble of the Parliament Act. To make the attempt in 1910 instead of pushing on the limitation of the Lords' powers would have lost the Irish vote and split the Liberal Party, for the supporters of the Government would not brook the delay that would ensue: they wanted their Bills passed into law.

Grey's difference with the party on this matter was not due to deficiency in democratic Radicalism on his part, but rather the opposite, for he desired to abolish, root and branch, the historic House of Lords, which still flourishes in spite of him under the Parliament Act, with diminished powers indeed but with undiminished splendour of ancientry. The following extract from a draft of his letter to Asquith before the newly elected Parliament met in February 1910, explains what he wished:

> The great issue has been forced upon us. That issue is the contest with the House of Lords. If we shrink from that, we shall disgust and alienate our party. If we attempt to deal with it by comparatively small expedients we shall fail with the electors. If we fail, a seat in the House of Commons will cease to be worth having for any Liberal. I do not believe that we can win with the so called C.-B. plan. The principle involved in it is overlaid by details, which are dull and unattractive and confusing. It is open to the charge of being in effect a single Chamber plan, and from a single Chamber Constitution I believe the country would recoil.
>
> I should advocate a much larger scheme and propose to abolish altogether the political privilege of Peers, and substitute for the House of Lords a new Second Chamber, much smaller in size than the House of Commons, based upon the elective principle, with if desired a minority of distinguished life-members.
>
> This would be a real challenge to the Opposition on principle. We should eventually appeal to the country upon it and the

Opposition would have to fight as the defenders of privilege and hereditary right against the principle of election. We must in any case stake everything upon the next appeal to the country, and the bold course of submitting outright the true issue is in my opinion that which will be the most honourable and the most successful.

An attack upon the principle of the constitution of the House of Peers which is vicious and antiquated according to modern ideas, will succeed: an attack upon its Powers (apart from Finance) will fail, for it will involve us in a controversy about Second and Single Chamber systems in which we shall appear to be on the wrong and losing side. It is the constitution of the House of Lords and not its Powers which are an anomaly.

If it is objected that an elective Second Chamber would have more influence than the House of Lords, I should reply that if so it would have influence by its merits, and this would not be a public evil. As much superiority as is due to the House of Commons might be secured by a provision that in case of deadlock then both Chambers should sit and debate and vote together. The numerical majority of the House of Commons would thus finally prevail if its opinion was strong and settled.

For some time Grey was very obstinate on this issue and caused much commotion in the party. On March 14 he made a speech in which he declared that 'to confine ourselves to a single-chamber issue and to leave the policy of Reform of the Second Chamber for the other side, would result for us, politically speaking, in disaster, death and damnation.' But in spite of this language, unusually strong in his mouth, he was already on the way to be persuaded by events that his plan was impossible for the actual moment. The great majority of the Liberals did not agree with it, and the Irish refused to let the Budget pass on any such terms. One of the steps of his gradual surrender is indicated in the following letter, suggesting in effect the Preamble that introduces the Parliament Act:

To Lord Crewe. March 15, 1910. I see no way out of the veto difficulty, unless it is announced that the limitation of the veto (in C.-B. form) is proposed and will be used only to secure the passage of a Bill to establish a new Second Chamber. Unless this is said we steer straight on the Single Chamber Rock.

After a tentative offer of resignation, not strongly pressed, he accepted the position and fell into line. Then followed the death of King Edward, the Conference of certain leaders of the two parties to seek an agreed solution of the Constitutional crisis, their failure, and the end of the truce, followed by the second election of 1910 just before Christmas. Grey took his share in the battle, now supporting the 'C.-B. resolutions' to reduce the powers of the existing House of Lords, subject to the promise of a future reform of its constitution 'on a popular instead of hereditary basis.' In the middle of the election he wrote to Katharine Lyttelton from Fallodon:

My brother George is here with me, having never seen an election since 1880. He thinks my speeches sensible on the whole. But they are getting very stale speeches and I feel inclined to stop in the middle and say to him, 'Is that the 6th or only the 5th time you have heard me compare the referendum to a Pig in a Poke?' The gardener would insist on sending me a Sunday paper into the house this afternoon, a thing which I never countenance, and I see that Charles [Masterman] is well in, at which I am pleased.

December 26. I have been through the furnace of an election once more. It was a short nightmare this time. I heard one or two of my colleagues; one only this time, I think, shrieked rather loudly while he was suffering from it, but I hope we shall all meet with our nerves steadied by the Christmas holidays and our tempers soothed by plum pudding. Arthur Balfour looks as if he didn't eat enough plum pudding. I thought he got rather wild in the Election. Elections consist of saying that the proposals of the other fellow mean something which he says they do not mean. I am weary at the thought of another spell of office. All last year I kept loosening the straps, thinking I might soon put the burden down. Now I have to buckle it closer without having put it down at all. But one must take life as it comes.

To K. L. August 5, 1911. What a state people have worked themselves into over the Parliament Bill! Two years hence the Bill will be detested by the Liberal party and be the sheet anchor of the Tories.

On December 16, 1910, he wrote to Henry Newbolt, who ten days before had published a letter in *The Times* distinguishing between him and his colleagues in the Cabinet to their disadvantage:

My dear Newbolt,

As you have invited comment on your letter to *The Times*, I hope you will not mind if I tell you exactly what I feel. Of course, I recognise the high-minded intention of the letter, and am grateful for its kindness about myself, but I wish you had acted otherwise.

I will not argue the main point: if a man feels as you do, he had better vote Conservative, and I understand his position. I myself cannot vote Conservative, because I see as much selfish motive on one side as on the other, and the selfishness of the rich and the appeals to their selfishness are much more hateful to me than the selfishness of the poor and the appeals to them, much as I deprecate both.

Now, for the personal side. There was once a man named Aristides. There were no newspapers in his day, and therefore no people could write to them. But I think that some of his friends, with the best intentions, must have spoken of him in the same way as you have written of me. The result was that, instead of his influence being increased, he was expelled as a public nuisance.

I think it very unfair to my colleagues to put me on a separate pinnacle. Asquith, Crewe, Morley, Loreburn, Haldane — to mention only a few — are just as well entitled to your praise as I am. What you have said about me, ignoring them, cannot but tend, if it influences them at all, to separate me from them. Some of them are not only my colleagues, but my intimate friends. You could hardly wish to make a breach between them and me, even if you might desire to do so between one or two of my other colleagues and me.

The upshot of it all is, I think, this: You are perfectly entitled to take the line which you have taken. Your decision to vote on the other side is quite intelligible, though in my opinion mistaken. My politics, now as always, remain entirely detached from my private life, my private thoughts, my pleasures, and my friendships. Amongst the latter, my friendship with you is one of those I shall always value most.

Grey was a strong supporter of Woman Suffrage and played an active part in endeavouring to secure it during the complicated negotiations and manœuvres of 1911–13; their failure was in his opinion due to the campaign of Suffragette outrage. He particularly admired Mr. Lloyd George's speeches in favour of the enfranchisement of women.

He was also a strong Home Ruler, and the Curragh crisis in the spring of 1914, when a section of the army in Ireland appeared to him to be used by the Opposition to dictate to the Government, roused him nearer to rage than any other political happening of his lifetime. On April 3 he wrote to Katharine Lyttelton, the soldier's wife:

Would you and Neville be able to lunch on Saturday. I would like to see Neville and hear what he thinks about the army. I am inwardly boiling with indignation at this stupid prejudiced attempt to dictate policy to us and break us, for that is what it is really; and if it goes on I shall be for taking the hottest election, upon who is to govern the country, that has ever been in our time. I haven't made this sort of speech yet, but I've got it in me and I don't know whether even Neville could soothe me. French is a trump and I love him, and some of the other officers are splendid, but the political lot make me ready to sound the tocsin.

When things had come to such a pass that Grey was ready to 'sound the tocsin,' one wonders if anyone except his friend the German Emperor could have saved these devoted islands from civil war, though Asquith's firm and quiet hand averted that particular crisis.

The 'socialist' side of Grey came out over the Miners' Strike of 1912, when he said to Lord Riddell, 'One cannot help feeling that the men employed in a big business have as great an interest in it as the proprietors, or shareholders, as the case may be.' His sympathy with the miners was so strong that on a sudden wave of emotion he startled Asquith one day by proposing to resign.[1] But in fact the Government dealt with the situation by passing a Minimum Wage Bill, which helped to bring the strike to an end. Grey had taken, with Mr. Lloyd George, an active part in the previous negotiations with the miners' and owners' representatives, and he spoke last for the Ministers on the Second Reading division on the Bill. The quiet appeal to good will and good sense, coming from him, helped the Bill to pass by rather more than the usual Government majority.

Next month Masterman said to Mr. Lloyd George's friend, Riddell, 'L. G. and Edward Grey have now joined hands. That is the new alliance. It dates from the coal strike. They are in sympathy regarding the Labour question and foreign policy.' Riddell agreed. Next year Mr. Lloyd George said to Riddell, 'Grey is with me. He is a kind fellow, the only man I would serve under except Asquith. I would serve under Grey.'[2]

[1] Information from Lady Violet Bonham-Carter. What was the total number of resignations and quasi-resignations Asquith warded off during his Premiership? A list might be composed, however imperfect. Morley's resignations would easily head it.

[2] *Riddell's Diaries*, July 19, 1913.

To Katharine Lyttelton. April 8, 1912. This coal strike is the beginning of a revolution. We shall, I suppose, make it an orderly and gradual revolution, but labour intends to have a larger share and has laid hold of power. Power has passed from the King to the nobles, from the nobles to the middle classes and through them to the House of Commons, and now it is passing from the House of Commons to the Trades Unions. It will have to be recognised that the millions of men employed in great industries have a stake in those industries and must share in the control of them. The days when the owners said 'this industry is mine; I alone must control it and be master in my own house' are passing away. The owners still say that, but it has ceased to be real because they cannot act upon it. The Unions may of course like blind Samson with his arms round the pillars, pull down the house on themselves and everyone else, if they push things too far; or if the owners are too unyielding, there will be civil war. But I do think the good temper and spirit of compromise that is inherent in English character will save us from catastrophe. Mistakes will be made and suffering will result, but we shall all learn by experience. There are unpleasant years before us; we shall work through to something better, though we who have been used to more than five hundred pounds a year may not think it better.

The only thing that I doubt, is whether, if I were God, I should not say: 'This boasted civilization that has defiled beautiful country, made hideous cities, been built up and is being maintained by ghastly competition and pressure, makes men swarm together and multiply horribly, is so abominable that I will sweep it all away.' If God does think that, then the great industrial countries will perish in catastrophe, because they have made the country hideous and life impossible. And I can't say that this would seem unreasonable to me, for I see nine hundred and ninety-nine people out of a thousand living a life that I should hate. Only they don't seem to hate it, but I am not sure that God does not hate it.

So the Foreign Secretary and the Chancellor of the Exchequer still continued on good terms in spite of some mutual irritation with one another's methods. Mr. Lloyd

George wrote a letter of generous congratulation to Grey on one of the occasions when he effected a temporary appeasement in the Balkans: '... your brilliant achievement, for it is entirely yours, ... the greatest triumph yet scored for the government. I shudder to think what would have happened in Europe had you not taken the lead.'

And on June 19, 1913, Grey defended the Chancellor of the Exchequer and the Attorney-General in the House of Commons from exaggerated interpretations of their confessedly unwise action in the Marconi affair. Next day both Mr. Lloyd George and Rufus Isaacs wrote him warmly expressed letters of thanks for his defence of them, which had certainly been most influential. Some have thought that on this occasion Grey's motive was only to get his party out of a scrape; but I am certain that he would not have made the speech if he had not also been convinced that his two colleagues were in some quarters getting less than fair play.

Edward Grey was devoted to his brothers George and Charles, especially at this time to George. But they were seldom in England. George was by fortune and nature a colonist, a native administrator, a lion hunter and an explorer of the waste places of the earth, as much at home in the African desert as Edward in the English woodland.[1] But George's visits home were becoming more frequent, and the hope that, since he was unmarried, he would soon settle at Fallodon for good gave a prospect of a new home life on

[1] Lord Selborne wrote of him: 'I doubt if in the whole history of the Empire any Englishman has ever performed a more tiresome and intricate piece of administrative work than the disentanglement of European and native rights in Swaziland by George Grey.' An interesting account of his remarkable career and attractive character can be found in *Some Account of George Grey and his Work in Africa*, privately printed by the Chiswick Press, 1914.

which Edward had begun confidently to build. In December 1910 he wrote to Katharine Lyttelton from Fallodon:

> George and I are having a placid Christmas here. We play draw-bridge with each other from dinner to midnight. Shall we still be doing that when he is eighty and I am eighty-four? And will you come to stay with us then? I shall have three bath chairs so that we can all go out together.

But George went back to Africa for another bout of native administration, and never came home again. One day he was pursuing a lion, as he had often done before; it turned and charged on him downhill, his shot failed to stop the rush and it leapt on him and mauled him so that he died in a few days.

> *To Mrs. Creighton. February* 4, 1911. Your letters always have a steadying power of comfort, which helps me. I am suffering more than I thought any new grief could make me suffer. George had been very tender to me; I think he liked making a home with me, and I had come to make one with him. I feel as if I couldn't stand up against this, after bearing the greater struggle against the other. And the contentions of politics suit ill with grief: if it were some other work it would be easier.
>
> *February* 9. George, especially in the last year, had been so touching and endearing. He had become a very strong character, but with the strength had grown gentleness, tenderness and sympathy to a wonderful degree. He didn't say much of this directly, but he made it felt. And in this last year he had enjoyed life more: he had taken an interest in Fallodon more than ever before and made me feel that he was enjoying it with me. I had begun to feel that he was really making his home with me and that it was a joint home. Last year is full of little incidents of life together, which were exceedingly pleasant. Even at Cottage it was so. And now suddenly there is to be no more. Charlie has been telling me quietly and gradually of George's extraordinary influence in Africa over men of all sorts. To the roughest people there he was a man to be admired without criticism. What he did was accepted by them all.

> *To Munro Ferguson. February* 7, 1911. I am so glad you knew enough of George to feel as you do about him. He had the great qualities, and also those which made him endearing and lovable. I feel as if the loss of him must finish what was left of me: but he wouldn't have liked that and I must try to be worth something. He judged me so generously.

As the years went on, it became a part of Edward Grey's heavy fate that every person with whom he desired to make a home for life was doomed to die, and that every habitation in which he loved to dwell was burnt to the ground.

IV

The Anglo-Russian Agreement — Persia — Congo — Grey and the Press

GREY was the principal author of the Anglo-Russian Agreement of August 1907, though he acted with the warm approval of Campbell-Bannerman as Prime Minister, and of John Morley, who as Indian Secretary gave him active official assistance and public support.

There were two motives in Grey's mind for this logical extension of Lansdowne's policy into a new sphere.[1] First, that an Anglo-Russian understanding would be a work of liberalism and peace: it would put an end to the traditional hostility which had again and again brought us to the verge of war, and might still at any moment plunge us into that catastrophe either on the Persian border of India and Afghanistan, or in the heart of Persia itself. The Disraelian hostility to Russia in the Balkans had been long ago brought to an end by Gladstone and Salisbury, largely for humanitarian reasons connected with Turkish misrule. But the advance of Russia towards India remained as threatening as ever, and the conflict of Russian and English interests in Persia was acute. Our recent alliance with Japan had not

[1] How far such an extension had been contemplated by King Edward and by Lansdowne in 1904 can be studied in *G. and T.* IV, 188–90.

improved Anglo-Russian relations. The interests of the two Empires touched at so many sore points — not only in Persia but in Tibet and Afghanistan — that Grey believed only a friendly agreement, directly negotiated by the two governments, could avert a clash. This essentially liberal and pacific desire to improve our relations with Russia by an agreed demarcation, was regarded as visionary and dangerous by the older school of Anglo-Indian tradition and by the Jingo elements at home. But Grey had held the view for some time past, and had expressed it publicly in his City speech two months before taking office.[1]

A second reason for this change of policy was brought strongly home to him during his first months in office by the Moroccan crisis between Germany and France. What would be the consequence to us and to Europe of a war between Britain and Russia, with such a power as Germany on the flank? And how was it possible to be friends with France while remaining at enmity with her ally? Friction with England in Asia might at any moment push the Czar back into the policy of Björkö, where only the year before he had come to terms with the Kaiser in a pact that was intended to operate to the disadvantage of England.

On February 12, 1906, Grey wrote to Sir Arthur Nicolson, then representing us in the critical Algeciras Conference:

> I am in hopes when Russia recovers we may get and keep on good terms with her; if so this also will count on the side of France.

And in a memorandum that he wrote on Morocco on February 20 we read:

> If there is war between France and Germany it will be very difficult for us to keep out of it. . . . There would I think be a

[1] See pages 103–04.

general feeling in every country that we had behaved meanly and left France in the lurch. The United States would despise us, Russia would not think it worth while to make a friendly arrangement with us about Asia, Japan would prepare to re-insure herself elsewhere, we should be left without a friend and without the power of making a friend.... On the other hand the prospect of a European War and of our being involved in it is horrible. I propose therefore, if unpleasant symptoms develop after the Conference is over, to tell the French Ambassador that a great effort and if need be some sacrifice should in our opinion be made to avoid war....

I have also a further point in view. The door is being kept open by us for a *rapprochement* with Russia; there is at least a prospect that when Russia is re-established we shall find ourselves on good terms with her. An entente between Russia, France and ourselves would be absolutely secure. If it is necessary to check Germany, it could then be done. The present is the most unfavourable moment for attempting to check her. Is it not a grave mistake, if there must be a quarrel with Germany, for France or ourselves to let Germany choose the moment which best suits her?[1]

To Spring Rice he had written the day before:

Meanwhile I am impatient to see Russia re-established as a factor in European politics. Whether we shall get an arrangement with her about Asiatic questions remains to be seen. I will try when she desires and is ready, and till she is ready we do not wish to change the situation in Persia or elsewhere.

Both the need and the difficulty of an agreement about Persia were very great. The desire of the forward party in Russia to absorb all Persia could certainly not be resisted with success by the Persians themselves, and unless we came to an agreed compromise with Russia, the alternatives were war to defend Persia, or else the surrender of our large commercial interests in Southern Persia and the Gulf to Russia,

[1] *G. and T.* III, 249, 266–67.

and the arrival of the Russians at Seistan on the Afghan and Indian frontier. Those critics who blame Grey's Agreement with Russia have never said which of these two agreeable alternatives — war or the abandonment of all Persia — they would have preferred.

As is so often the case, large sections of English opinion, especially among the Labour men and among the Radicals in Grey's own party, clamoured for a policy which must have meant war, and at the same time called for disarmament. The generous but impracticable wish that we should save even Northern Persia from Russian encroachment was increased by a very natural antipathy to the character of the Czar's domestic government. The fierce triangular duel between Red Revolution, Duma Liberalism and Black Reaction that was raging in Russia during all the years of Grey's Secretariate immensely increased his difficulties. He knew that British interests in Russia were allied to the Liberal element in the conflict, and that the last thing the poor Russian Liberals desired was the end of the entente between their country and England. Under a constant fire of criticism from those who did not understand the real impossibilities of the situation either in Persia or in Russia, Grey stuck to his ungrateful task of keeping friends with the untrustworthy government of Russia and making the bad best of a dreadful situation. I shall leave his letters to reveal his mind.[1]

> *Grey to Lord Knollys.* (*The King's Secretary.*) *March* 28, 1906. We have had more than one intimation that the Czar feels that his visit to England has never been returned and that he very much wants the King to visit him. Witte and Lamsdorff have both made it clear to us that with every disposition on their part to improve relations with England no

[1] Besides those here printed, others will be found in his *Twenty-five Years* and in *Gooch and Temperley*. So far as possible I am printing letters not yet published.

real progress will be made unless the Czar puts his hand to it. And this he will not do as long as he remains unvisited.

An entente with Russia is now possible, and it is the thing most to be desired in our foreign policy. It will complete and strengthen the entente with France and add very much to the comfort and strength of our position. But it all depends upon the Czar and he depends upon the King.

This is one side of the question — the bright side — now for the other.

Even if the state of Russia gets no worse, I do not think the King could pay a visit inland. It is not only the question of risk — that might be less for him than for anyone, but still he ought not to go, if there is any risk; apart from that Russia in its disturbed state is not suitable territory in which to hold a social gathering.

The utmost that could happen would be a meeting on yachts in a cruise in the Baltic, which would be a personal visit to the Czar — not a national affair. The Czar has already referred to the suggested meeting with the Emperor in the Mediterranean and might be pleased with a meeting of the same kind in the Baltic. I hope this may be kept in mind as a possibility. But a decision about it would have to be deferred till later.

If revolution breaks out again in Russia and massacres take place no one could expect the King to make such a visit; it would not be welcome to public opinion; and anything like a public entente between the Governments would be repugnant. All therefore that I want to do for the moment is to point out what is to be desired as an object of foreign policy and how entirely it will in the long run depend upon the King, but for the present it is impossible to come to any decision and we must wait upon events.

In July 1906 occurred the famous visit of the delegation from the Duma to London, which was overtaken by the shattering news that the Czar had suspended the Duma in their absence. Campbell-Bannerman's cry, '*La Douma est morte, Vive la Douma*,' was a 'calculated indiscretion' that won the approval of Grey and of Cambon and did more good than harm in Russia.

From June 1906 to August 1907 the negotiations for an understanding with Russia were carried on. Though Sir Arthur Nicolson was now our Ambassador at St. Petersburg, the task was almost beyond the power of the ablest diplomacy. The rival interests in Persia were diametrically opposed.

Spring Rice wrote to Grey from Teheran in November:

> Hartwig is very friendly indeed and sincerely anxious for an agreement mainly on European grounds. But of course he is under no illusions as to what one section of his government desires. That is — the whole of Persia under Russian influence.

Against this, the Indian Government demanded as the British sphere of influence the whole of Southern Persia, including its whole coast line on the Gulf.[1] Such a clash of opposing ambitions could only be settled by war or by some such compromise as that which Grey, supported by Morley, eventually carried through. 'Without Morley,' wrote Grey to Campbell-Bannerman, 'we should have made no progress at all, for the government of India would have blocked every point, and Morley has removed mountains in the way of negociations.' And to Morley he wrote on the completion of the Russian Agreement:

> If you had not taken the strong and clear line which you did, we should have had to go to the Cabinet time after time to get authority to overrule the objections of the Indian Government to point after point in the course of the negociations.

[1] *Grey to the King. September* 24, 1906. 'The desire of the Indian Government, as contained in the telegram from the Viceroy of India, is to secure for ourselves a line from North of Birgand to Khanikin. Such a line could not, Sir Edward Grey feels sure, be obtained by diplomacy, and if it were to be adopted as the object of British Policy, it would have to be secured by independent action and eventually by occupation of the whole of Southern Persia, a very serious addition to Imperial responsibilities.' (*G. and T.* IV, 395.)

> The result would have been that progress would have been very slow and difficult and the whole thing might have come to nought.

The letters that passed between Grey and Morley during the period of these negotiations and for years afterwards are couched in terms of cordial intimacy and co-operation. The two men were always in close touch on Foreign Affairs, and there was nothing Morley liked better than to take on the work of the Office when the Foreign Secretary went for a short holiday. His expressed differences with Grey's policy were, for the most part, afterthoughts.[1]

The accompanying map shows the lines of demarcation between the Russian and British Spheres of Influence in Persia and the Neutral Sphere, as assigned by the Treaty. Russia and England, with very different degrees of sincerity, bound themselves to maintain the 'independence and integrity' of Persia, which Russia had already violated and continued to violate in the Northern Sphere. On our part there was no military occupation of the British Sphere of Influence, not even round Seistan: the promise now obtained from Russia

[1] General Morgan writes in his *Viscount Morley* (page 42) that on September 13, 1914, Morley said to him: 'I was always opposed to the Russian agreement.' This is so flagrantly inaccurate that either General Morgan misunderstood him, or else Morley's memory must temporarily have given way. I say 'temporarily,' because in his *Recollections* (1917) he makes true report of his activities on behalf of the Agreement, printing such documents as his letter to Minto (II, 177–79). The evidence of his active support is abundant, *e.g.* his letters to Grey, Minto and Nicolson, and his speech in the H. of C. on February 17, 1908, defending the Agreement as 'an Agreement that this country may not only be contented with but proud of.' See also his despatch of March 20, 1908, printed in the official *Record of Lord Kitchener's Administration in India*, pages 193–96. As late as July 12, 1912, Morley writes to Grey a letter showing that he was still in cordial agreement with Grey's Anglo-Russian policy especially as regards Persia, and says that the *Manchester Guardian* has 'a bee in its bonnet about Foreign Policy.' Morley may have changed his mind about the Russian Agreement after the outbreak of war in 1914, but there is no shadow of doubt as to what his mind had been at the time when the Agreement was being made.

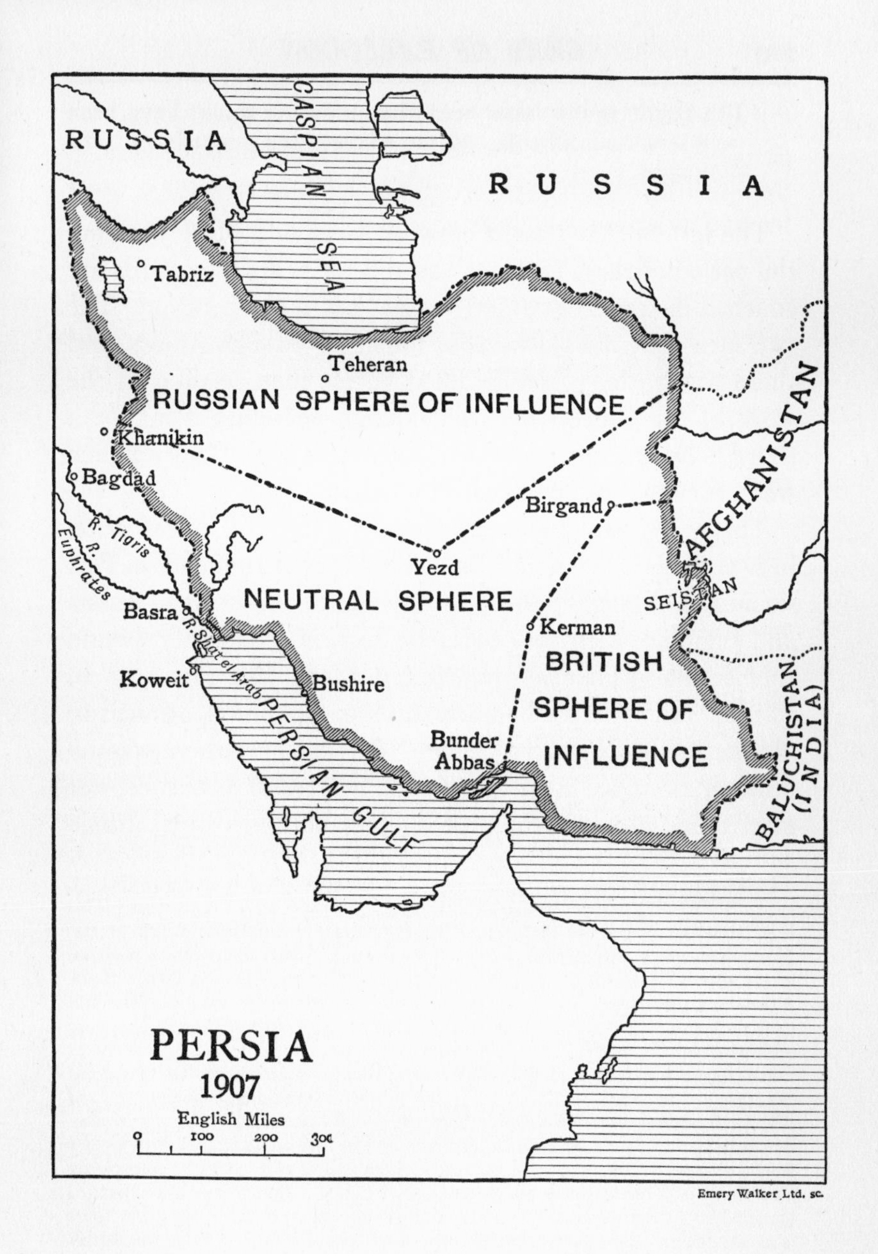

Emery Walker Ltd. sc.

not to penetrate into that region was kept, and was regarded as a sufficient security for our Indian frontier. But unless we intended to drive Russia out of North Persia by force of arms, we had no alternative but to acknowledge it as her Sphere of Influence, as it already was in fact before the Treaty was made. In the light of later events the agreement was attacked as an infringement of Persian independence. But Persian independence did not exist and could not at that time have been brought into being. The misfortune that Teheran, the Persian capital, lay far in the north, exposed to Russian invasion and necessarily in the Russian Sphere of Influence, was a fact of political geography for which Grey was not responsible. As he once said in the House of Commons (July 10, 1912), 'I sometimes wonder whether everybody who talks about Persia in this House, knows where Teheran is.'

The Agreement affected also Tibet and Afghanistan. Both Russia and England undertook to abstain from all interference with the internal administration of Tibet, and to send no representative there. Russia recognized Afghanistan as outside her orbit, and promised to conduct her future political relations with that country through the British Government, and to send there no agents of her own.

Taking the Agreement as a whole Grey considered it not only as good general policy but as a good bargain for England on the points alone: 'Anyone behind the scenes knows that what we have gained strategically is real, while the apparent sacrifices we have made commercially are not real.' In September 1907 he wrote to Runciman, as his friend and colleague:

> I expect that the comments of the newspapers will give you suggestions and material as to what to say on the Russian Agreement. The answer to the extremists who say that we

should not have any agreement with Russia is that without an agreement friction in Asia was sure to increase and would sooner or later have led to serious consequences, possibly to war, certainly to very much increased military expenditure. You might take your stand on the broad principle that to remove causes of quarrel between nations by mutual concessions and agreements is thoroughly in accord with Liberal principles; and that to neglect or refuse an opportunity of removing such causes is to perpetuate bad feeling between nations till it gets beyond control and leads to war.

The two alternatives to the policy of agreement were:

1. To exploit the present situation in Persia by a forward policy at the expense of Russia; or

2. To sit still while Russia did this at our expense. The critics on our own side do not advocate the first alternative; the consequences of the second would be beyond their control and would lead to increased military expenditure when public opinion here became indignant and alarmed.

As to critics on the other side, the answer to them is that their logical alternative to our agreement is a forward policy in the annexation of Seistan and a frontier protectorate over Southern Persia to be defended by force.

Our agreement secures the north of the Persian Gulf, the whole Southern coast ports, and Seistan from being exploited to our disadvantage. That is it secures all that is strategically vital to us. On the other hand it does secure Russia from any competition of ours in concessions, etc. in Northern Persia. But anyone who looks on the map at the situation of Northern Persia and Teheran must be aware that this must in the long run have been the consequence of geographical situation; and indeed Russian influence at Teheran had already been established.

The formal recognition of our position towards Afghanistan is a great point gained, and generally we now have a settled basis on which to discuss Asiatic questions with Russia when necessary.

The old guard of Gladstonian Liberalism, in the persons of Campbell-Bannerman the Prime Minister, and Lord Ripon, the former Viceroy once so bitterly attacked for his

Liberalism in that post, wrote to congratulate Grey upon the Treaty:

> *Campbell-Bannerman to Grey. September* 3, 1907. My hearty congratulations on the Russian agreement which is a great achievement. For a time at least it removes the danger of an Asiatic avalanche and will make things easier in Europe. Even if the respite prove comparatively brief, you have at least the honour of having secured it by your tact, patience and firmness. I will send a line of appreciation to Nicolson.
>
> *Lord Ripon to Grey. September* 6, 1907. I congratulate you very much on the Russian Convention. It is quite satisfactory to me and is a triumph of your patience. To my mind the great point is the Russian acknowledgment of an exceptional position in regard to Afghanistan. Of course the present or some future Amir may give us trouble; but we must face that as well as we can.

The Anglo-Russian Agreement was published at once, and, unlike Lansdowne's Agreement with France, had no secret clause.

Morley's account of the reception of the Treaty in Parliament in February 1908 is as follows:

> We had two first-rate speeches in the H. of C. from Percy and Grey. Percy is before all else a Turcophil and therefore he is hostile to all Russian accommodations. He really differs from Lansdowne's more experienced and responsible views of the Agreement, but of course he could not give full cry against the Convention when Lansdowne had blessed it. He is a singularly attractive speaker.... Grey followed Percy in that curiously high, simple, semi-detached style, which, combined, as it always is in him, with a clean-cut mastery of all the facts of his case, makes him one of the most impressive personalities in Parliament. Or must I qualify this immense panegyric of mine? He has got no great ample pinions like Mr. Gladstone; he hardly deserves what was said of Daniel Webster, that every word he used seemed to weigh a pound. Still he is a remarkable figure, wholly free from every trace of the theatre; and I confess it warms my heart to think that we have two men like

Grey and Percy to fill the seats of Power in our country, when the time comes.... When I wound up by claiming from Balfour a practical acceptance of the thing, as broad and unconditional as Lansdowne's, he confirmed my challenge by demonstrative assent.[1]

Campbell-Bannerman not only approved of the Agreement with Russia, but shared Grey's belief that demonstrations by English Liberals against the Czar's domestic government only injured the cause of Liberalism in Russia by driving the Czar into the arms of Germany. Indeed C.-B.'s breezy language on the subject was at least as strong as Grey's.

Campbell-Bannerman to Grey. October 8, 1906. I entirely enter into the view expressed by Nicolson and endorsed by H. M. as to the folly of the deputation to Russia. It is bad taste and ill timed and may be mischievous. I also was consulted by the same Donald Smeaton, M.P. who wrote to Nicolson, and I told him to have nothing to do with it, on two main grounds. (1) That the visit might offend the Russians, even the progressives, as an illbred interference; and thus (and as giving a flavour of foreign origin generally) set back the tide of reform and liberty. (2) That it enabled the Russian Government to say if this is the sort of friends you are going to be, we prefer the Kaiser. And where should we be then?

Grey to Katharine Lyttelton. June 28, 1909. I really haven't had time to read anything. *A Room with a View* was the last book: it is very good and so I hear is *The Longest Journey*, by the same man — Forster. I am amused by your asking my opinion on Budget, Duma, Czar and Turks, and then ending by saying you don't expect a long letter, only a note.

As to the Czar, the I.L.P. say there were some 800 executions in Russia last year. That is true, but they don't say that there were about 1500 murders and some thousands of terrorist outrages. The Czar is a kind, moral family man, who as an English squire, would be much respected in his parish. His direct control of the huge machine of Russian bureaucracy is

[1] *Recollections*, II, 245.

necessarily slight. He will be remembered as the Czar under whom Russia secured a Duma and a Constitution. But we have in this country a number of people who don't want to know the truth and to do good, but to express their own emotions. Dram-drinkers I call them, for they must be in a state of emotion and when you attempt to dilute their emotions with the truth they are as angry as the drunkard, whose whiskey you dilute with water.

For us to insult the Czar, when all the rest of Europe receives him, is to play straight into the hands of the reactionaries in Russia. The Russian revolutionaries, who wish to embroil their country with any foreign country in order to overthrow the Russian Government, come here and it is easy to play upon the emotions of our dram-drinkers, in fact supply them with the stimulant they crave for. Russia is slowly and with pain and throes working towards better things: she has progressed more in three years than seemed possible considering how slowly human affairs must move in such a vast country. Our attitude towards her internal affairs should be one of benevolent neutrality and hope.

I send you a caricature of myself which a private secretary has just sent in a box. I am always consoled for my nose by remembering that Hazlitt thought the smallness of Coleridge's nose was an indication of weakness and spoilt his appearance. 'The nose,' said Hazlitt, 'is the rudder of the face.'

To Katharine Lyttelton. Cottage, Itchen Abbas. July 25, 1909. This is to tell you that I know you were alive a few days ago, for I met your Talbot sister and she told me you had been heard of. I had another evening of her glorious music, an evening spent on the Delectable Mountains when the Pilgrim was at his weariest. Today I am at Cottage. There hasn't been one hot day this summer, and you can't have the full glory of Cottage, without hot sun and still weather to set off the moist coolness and fresh green of the water meadows. But Cottage can adapt itself to every mood and no complaint has been heard of it. I have had a mood this week of feeling the past very near to me, and when that comes I always feel as if I might die very soon, but I don't think it means anything.

I suppose you understand the position in Russia. The Revolutionaries are scattered and broken in Russia, and are

H. W. Barnett

AET. 48, 1910

trying to make trouble here. In Russia itself there is a struggle between the Reactionaries on one side and Stolypin (a really good man) and the Duma on the other. The Reactionaries wish to abolish the Duma; the Duma is intent on working out reforms by Constitutional means. The question for us is whether we will help Stolypin and the Duma by being civil to the Czar as long as he stands by them: or whether we will play straight into the hands of the Reactionaries by insulting the Czar as Keir Hardie and Co. want us to do. But for us to say this in public would be obviously fatal.

How awfully dull this is! It has bored me to write it. But perhaps it will help you to understand how odiously disinteresting political work is. Now if I tell you that one of my two bread-eating cottage robins, which comes into this room, has, after rearing two broods this year, fallen into a most deplorable moult and lost its tail, but that its manners are just as perky as ever and that it amuses me to see how very unconscious it is of its personal appearance — that is something pleasant and interesting.

Grey to Lord Knollys. July 25, 1909. I was exceedingly pleased and encouraged by your letter conveying the King's approval of what I said in the House of Commons on Thursday.

It is I fear impossible to make any impression upon the extreme men who oppose the Czar's visit. They want something about which to be violent and to force the more moderate Labour men to be violent too. They have chosen the Czar's visit for this purpose and they will not discuss it on its merits. They prefer to abuse the members of the Duma rather than to abandon their position.

It is also impossible from the Government bench to bring out the merits of the question. The King's influence with the Czar, and the friendship of the British Government are really a support to Stolypin (whose character even Russian revolutionaries respect) and to the Duma and all friends of constitutional progress in Russia. Discourtesy to the Czar on our part would be a blow to all this element in Russia. But for a British Minister to say this would naturally be resented in Russia and made a reproach to Stolypin and the Duma.

Grey to Munro Ferguson. January 19, 1912. *Fallodon.* Dear Ronald, I hear the *Daily News* has been attacking me; but

> even if they got rid of me they wouldn't get their policy adopted, because it is impossible. If we went in for the Asiatic policy that they advocate, we should soon have to enlarge our army expenditure to defend our Indian frontier; all the old alarms about that would be revived again and not without reason. In Europe we should be completely isolated and as their policy includes unbridled comment continuously upon the internal affairs of other countries, and attempts to interfere in everything, we should soon be on equally bad terms with everybody. In fact a policy composed of the maximum of interference and the minimum of friendship would be about as expensive and disastrous as could be contrived.

The Russian Agreement had been well received in England at first, but trouble began in Persia at once and went on to the end. The battle between a Reactionary and a Constitutional party among the Persians themselves complicated the relations with Russia, and gave her expansionists on the spot opportunities they were not slow to seize. English opinion became restive. When Doctor Hodgkin, the historian, Grey's friend and Northumbrian neighbour, wrote to him to expostulate against our compliance in the continued encroachments of Russia on the independence of North Persia, he replied (January 23, 1912):

> Of course I should not demur to your right to express an opinion on public affairs and I appreciate the courtesy of having written to tell me what your opinion is, but I hope you won't mind my saying that I think you approach the Anglo-Russian agreement from a wrong point of view. Previous to that agreement it was our policy to head back Russia in every direction. We did it in the Crimean War, we did it in the time of Lord Beaconsfield and we did it in recent years in the Far East. For years I have held that this was a mistaken policy, that it would be a better way to come to an agreement with Russia by which she should not acquire influence or use what influence she had to disturb our Indian frontier. That was the *fons et origo* of the Anglo-Russian agreement. At the time

when that agreement was made, Russian influence was already predominant in the north of Persia and the Shah was her creature. It was no part of the Anglo-Russian agreement to destroy Russian influence or to extend our responsibilities to protect Persia. I would never have been a party to committing this country to extension of responsibility in that direction. The Persians revolted against the Shah, and Russia, relying on the fact that we should not interfere in northern Persia and exploit the situation to her disadvantage, remained passive while the Shah, whom she had nursed, was driven out. A constitutional party succeeded to power, they set to work to destroy Russian influence in northern Persia and to worry the Russians out of it. The result was inevitable; they worried the Russians further in; but for us to have supported the Persians against the Russians in the North of Persia would have been contrary to the whole spirit of the Anglo-Russian agreement and would have been perfectly futile unless we had been prepared to make war upon Russia in Europe, for if you look at the map you will see how impossible it is that we could interfere by force at Tehran which is quite out of our reach. Had it not been for the Anglo-Russian agreement the Russians would either have interfered to keep the Shah on the throne or their troops would have been in Tehran long before this. I do not believe this country would have gone to war to prevent that and I should have thought it deplorable if it did. . . .

I ought to add that since the Anglo-Russian agreement was made (it does not apply only to Persia) the Russians have scrupulously abstained from doing anything prejudicial to the security of our Indian frontier. If the agreement is to be declared at an end we must prepare to put the defence of our Indian frontier on a war footing and sooner or later there must be war between Russia and ourselves over these Asiatic questions.

The ill conduct of the Russian consuls and colonels in Persia was connived at in some quarters of the amorphous Imperial bureaucracy, often against the wishes of the Foreign Office at St. Petersburg; for the so-called Russian Government was, as Grey called it, 'a despotism without discipline.'

He continued to remonstrate with very little effect, in such letters as the following to Sir George Buchanan, Nicolson's successor in the St. Petersburg Embassy (February 11, 1914):

> There is a great deal of discontent here about the working of the Anglo-Russian Agreement respecting Persia.
>
> The Agreement was based on the assumption of the independence and integrity of Persia. Since it was made, Russia has entered upon a military occupation of the north of Persia, and Russian Consuls have perpetually interfered in the internal administration of the provinces. I have not taken great offence at this, because long before the Anglo-Russian Agreement was made, and at the time it was made, Russia had a preponderating position in the north of Persia in practice, owing to the fact that the Shah and Tehran, the capital, were so much under her influence. Therefore, when the Shah was deposed and an anti-Russian Government succeeded him in Persia, I regarded it as not inconsistent with the spirit of the Anglo-Russian Agreement, whatever it might be with the letter of it, that Russia should take steps to prevent her losing in the north of Persia the position that she had occupied there before the Agreement was made. I never intended the Agreement to be construed so as to make Russia's position less favourable than it was before. But the fact that there is a Russian military occupation, that there are no signs of its diminution, that Russian trade has ousted British trade in the north of Persia, that owing to disturbances on the southern trade routes British trade is being so handicapped that Russian trade may displace it even outside Russian influence, in the neutral sphere: all this makes public opinion here sensitive.
>
> If the Russians would really make an enlarged Persian Cossack Force under Russian Officers an honest and efficient Force, would rely upon it to keep order in the north of Persia, would withdraw Russian troops, and would make Russian Consuls work loyally to support the Belgian Financial Administration, and would support the Persian Government instead of impeding and obstructing them, there would be more chance of making progress with public opinion here about the Trans-Persian Railway.

Grey had said all this and much more to Sazonov personally, during the Russian Foreign Minister's friendly visit to Balmoral in September 1912.[1] For years he kept on saying it to St. Petersburg through our Ambassador, and always in vain. The hug of the bear on North Persia was not to be loosed by words; with or without the Agreement with England, Russia would have kept her troops there, and only force could have dislodged them.

The Agreement of 1907 did not prove a settlement but only a valuable postponement of Anglo-Russian disputes in Asia. If the Balkan question had not existed to divide Russia from Germany, or if the Germans had been less fierce in their championship of the Austro-Hungarian cause against the Slavs, the Anglo-Russian Agreement might soon have broken down. But though its geographic scope was Asiatic only, it had paved the way for Anglo-Russian friendship in Europe. As an integral part of the Triple Entente the Agreement was successful, owing to the popular passion in Russia on behalf of the Slav race in the Balkans. On that question English policy in Grey's hands was merely that of a neutral peacemaker, but it was none the less the Balkan and Austro-Hungarian question, in which Grey took neither side, that attached Russia to the Entente and induced her government only partially to violate the Asiatic agreement with England.[2] That made the German people think themselves 'encircled.'

How far did Grey allow humanitarian considerations to interfere with the main outlines of his policy? Where, as in North Persia, we could do nothing for the Persians without fighting Russia, he held out no false hopes. But in dealing

[1] *G. and T.* IX, 750–53.

[2] This view is, I think, implied both by Sir George Buchanan (*My Mission to Russia*, I, 91), and in the brilliant biography of Nicolson by his son (*Lord Carnock*, page 261).

with Macedonia and the Congo he made sacrifices in the one case and in the other case ran risks, in order to uphold humanitarian interests for which no other great European Power cared a straw. In the case of Macedonian Reform, it was a policy which he inherited from Salisbury and Lansdowne, to see the less scrupulous Germans entrench themselves in the favour of the Sultan, and to sacrifice British influence and interests in Turkey, rather than connive at Armenian massacre and Macedonian misrule.

But in the case of the Congo, Grey had himself to break fresh ground, for the question only came to a head in his period of office. Here also, rather than let the Congo atrocities continue, he ran the risk of a serious, possibly a fatal, check to his general policy; it may even be said that he risked England's safety by the line he took. For Belgium might have been driven into the arms of Germany, if the matter had been conducted with less than his skill, tact and consideration, or by a British Minister whose character did not, like Grey's, half persuade the cynical Europeans that this Englishman was not a hypocrite but an honest man.

The Congo had long been, under an old international agreement, almost the private estate of King Leopold of Belgium. Through the agency of various companies, he had turned it into a vast slave-farm, contrary to the Treaties under which he held his powers. This state of things was exposed by the gallant and disinterested efforts of a private individual, E. D. Morel. The British public had taken fire, and the Foreign Secretary too. But the Foreign Secretary knew that fire was not enough. His plan was to encourage the Belgian State to take over the Congo from King Leopold; but he would only recognize the transfer on condition of wholesale reform, and in particular the abolition of forced labour. British rights in the Congo were in his hands the lever to secure our humanitarian demands. Neither Germany nor France nor any great Power save the distant United States cared about the matter. But thanks to Grey's firmness and tact, thanks also to the better elements in the Belgian people and Parliament, and to the high character of King Leopold's successor on the throne, Congo Reform was an accomplished fact before the War of 1914, and Belgium and England had not fallen out.

In the rather similar affair of the Putumayo atrocities in South America, Grey achieved a similar success. In that case United States humanitarian feeling was nearer to the scene and more potent as an ally. Grey's publication of the Putumayo Blue Book in July 1912, based on Sir Roger Casement's reports, was a personal act of the Foreign Secretary, not suggested by the custom of his office but by his own indignation.

In one other matter where humanitarian feeling was involved, the over-severe sentences passed on members of the mob that had murdered a British officer at Denshawi in Egypt, Grey had to defend in the House of Commons action which at heart he had come to disapprove. In July 1908 he wrote to Mrs. Francis Buxton:

> The Denshawi sentences erred grossly on the side of severity and the harm done by them here and in Egypt was many fold greater than any leniency. And I have had for two years to defend them in public!

If Grey had been able to come to this conclusion during the few days before the sentences were carried out, he would not have shrunk from the extremely strong step of overriding the advice of the authorities in Egypt, and of Lord Cromer, then on holiday in England. Unfortunately they declared that the severity of the sentences and their immediate execution alone could prevent serious danger to the peace of Egypt, and Grey did not come to the conclusion that the advice was wrong till after the executions and floggings had taken place. His lifelong belief in the wisdom and moderation of Cromer, so amply justified upon the whole, had made it impossible for Grey to think him wrong on an Egyptian question — until it was too late.

The following letters of Grey will help to reveal his policy on the Congo and Putumayo affairs and the feelings that prompted it:

> *To Henry Newbolt* (1908). As for the Congo, the only government that can take the country over is Belgium, and we must work to make it possible for them to do this — we should only give a handle to others by playing 'the interfering foreigner.'
>
> *To Sir A. Hardinge* (*British Minister at Brussels*). *February* 28, 1908. I wish to give you in the rough my ideas as to how we should proceed respecting the Congo State. Feeling in this country is exceedingly strong and unanimous. It is true that the people here have accepted my attitude of waiting till the Belgian proposals have actually been presented to the Belgian Parliament before we say anything official to Belgium. But when those proposals are made known, I must, with the United States if possible, point out to the Belgian Government that we consider the monopolies and commercial position generally in the Congo to be inconsistent with the free trade provisions of the Berlin Act, and that if necessary we might have to propose Arbitration with regard to them. . . .
>
> We should also tell the Belgian Government what the actual situation in the Congo is, as disclosed by our reports and by the report of the American Consul-General; and ask them whether they will be prepared to give an assurance that, when they take over the Congo, this system will be changed and brought into accordance with the Berlin Act and the Brussels Act regarding the treatment of natives. If the measure proposed to the Belgian Parliament is such as to leave the real

control of the Congo in the King's hands, while making Belgium nominally responsible, I think we should have to say at once that a transfer on these conditions would not be satisfactory, inasmuch as it would not place the Belgian Government in a position to be able to guarantee that the Treaty obligations, which the King has violated, will be fulfilled.

So much on the assumption that the Belgian Parliament is really to be asked to annex the Congo.

On the other hand, if the present Session of the Belgian Parliament closes without an arrangement being come to, then we shall have to take a new departure. In this case, I propose to act on the assumption that we shall have to deal, for an indefinite period, with the King and with the existing state of things in the Congo. I shall say to Belgium that she need be in no hurry, and that anything we may do before she makes up her mind to take over the Congo will be provisional, and subject to revision directly the Congo passes out of the King's hands into hers.

Here is a sketch of the action which I have in my mind:

I propose to demand at once that the King should consent to go to Arbitration as to whether the monopolies and concessions and the commercial side of his policy generally in the Congo are in accord with the Treaty obligations by which the Congo is bound. I should thus make it clear that, while we desire to uphold our commercial interests, we are prepared to submit to Arbitration everything in which it can be said that we have a selfish interest.

I should then go on to say that the state of things disclosed in the last reports of our Consuls and in the report of the American Consul General prove beyond dispute that the forced labour system of the Congo State virtually results in the slavery of a large part of the population. I should explain that this was such a flagrant violation of the conditions on which we had recognised the existence of the Congo State that if, in a year's time, that system had not been changed we should cease to recognise the existence of the State.

Then we should regard the Congo as territory without a Government and equally open to every one. But we should not ourselves attempt to exercise any jurisdiction over any but British subjects. We should maintain in the Congo the

Consuls, whom we now have there, in the capacity of British officials residing in the district for the purpose of protecting British subjects and exercising jurisdiction in case of need. As a consequence, we should of course refuse to allow any import duties to be levied upon any British goods. We should send a gun-boat to the lower part of the River, and also probably send one above the Falls, a thing which I believe can be done: but their use would be limited to preventing British subjects from being interfered with....

I know there may be some technical difficulties in the way of the course which I propose. But public opinion here will make light of technical difficulties, and I consider that the state of slavery disclosed by our last Consular reports is such as to transcend technical difficulties and the letter of Treaties. I am convinced that, probably during the year which would intervene before we took action after making our announcement, some arrangement would be made with the consent of the other Powers by which the Congo would be transferred from the hands of the King....

My own personal feeling is that we are justified in any measures which will result in taking the Congo out of the hands of the King. He has forfeited every claim to it he ever had; and to take the Congo away from him without compensation would be less than justice, for it would leave him still with all the gains he has made by his monstrous system.[1]

To C. P. Scott, July 25, 1912. I do not see any reason to deprecate the Meeting that it is proposed to hold with regard to the state of affairs in the Putumayo district. With regard to your other enquiry, I am confident that the fullest reliance may be placed on the statements in Sir Roger Casement's Report. The inaccessibility of the Putumayo region is one great difficulty, but a resident Mission there will make a great difference. The only thing I should deprecate would be any action on our part that would make us lose touch with the United States, or alienate their sympathy, as it is American public opinion that must be the most potent factor in either American Continent.

[1] See also his speeches on the Congo in the House of Commons, particularly on February 26, 1908.

On European and Persian policy C. P. Scott in his *Manchester Guardian* was the most well-informed and intelligent of Grey's critics, and his reasoned attacks on the entente policy rendered the division of opinion in the Liberal Party all the more difficult for the Foreign Secretary. But the two men respected each other personally, and their relations can be read in the following letter of Grey's (September 21, 1912):

> MY DEAR SCOTT:
>
> I do not anticipate a development such as you fear. If there is one thing more than another that I have striven to secure during the last seven years it is that we should not incur any increase of Imperial liabilities. It has not been easy to secure this: there have been difficulties in other places than Persia, though they have not all got into the press. I admit that it is not easy to put the Persian Government on its legs in Southern Persia but even so I do not regard British occupation as other than most undesirable.
>
> If you are to be in London in the week of October 7th I wish you would let me know and come to see me. I am seriously concerned at the trend of a certain section of Liberal opinion, which seems to set no store by the peace we have enjoyed on our Indian frontier, and seems to me to be quite reckless in attempting to make us take all Persia under our protection.

The other great Liberal journalist of that era was Mr. J. A. Spender, who on so many occasions over so many years did so much to reconcile the differences that divided Liberals. He was in agreement with the general lines of the Entente policy, and his *Westminster Gazette* was regarded in some quarters as 'the organ of Sir Edward Grey.' Mr. Spender, however, tells us that 'I cannot remember a single occasion on which Grey asked me to write an article or prompted me to say one thing and not another.' But the two men were friends and they were constantly discussing Foreign Affairs together, Grey with that detached and impersonal frankness which seemed to set him above the mêlée even while he was in the midst of it.

> Though always courteous and friendly to journalists [writes Mr. Spender] Grey had a real indifference to what was said about him which I have never seen equalled in a public man. Asquith met Press attacks with a stoicism which scarcely masked the fact that he felt their injustice; Lloyd George met them with a fiery determination to be even with the journalist; Grey neither met them nor seemed to feel them at all. His attitude was always that he was quite ready to go if people wanted him to go, and that he had no reputation to nurse in view of a future career. (*Life, Journalism and Politics*, I, 170.)

V

Japan — United States — The German Navy — Grey and Shipbuilding Questions — Cabinet Crisis of 1909 — The Naval Arrangements of 1912

IF HOLSTEIN and Bülow were fatal to Germany by raising up for her a host of enemies, Grey was correspondingly serviceable to England by preserving and increasing her friendships. Had it been otherwise we should have lost the war. Grey, it cannot be too often repeated, always kept two objects in view, with that simplicity of mind and purpose so often charged against him as a fault, a simplicity which never lost sight of the wood for the trees. One object was to preserve peace; the other was to be sure that if war came we should have a chance to win. It is difficult to see which of these two objects he could properly have neglected, though his critics often argue as if either the one or the other was of no account. The dread event proved that our margin of survival was small enough, so small indeed that we could not have won through if Grey had thrown either Russia or Italy into the arms of Germany, or terminated the Japanese Alliance, or alienated the statesmen and people of the United States. His steady, quiet pursuit of friendships for England, undeviating for years on end, so different from the giddy turns of opportunist diplomacy, achieved great results in spite of great obstacles.

The Japanese Alliance was the work of Lord Lansdowne, who had made it in 1902 and renewed and extended it in 1905. The question of its further renewal came up in 1911 and Grey had no doubt of its necessity. We were then less than ever in a position to dominate unaided the waters of the Pacific, when the strength of our fleet was needed for home defence against the dangerous rival in the North Sea. But the continuance of the Japanese Alliance was no simple matter. For it could not be allowed to impair our friendship with America, which Grey always regarded as the first of British interests. And moreover it might have been hard to prevent it from endangering the Anglo-Russian Agreement, had not Russia and Japan been completely reconciled in 1907 largely through the good offices of Great Britain.

The question of Japanese immigration to the Pacific coast of America might have caused our Japanese Alliance to stink in the nostrils of English-speaking folk on both sides of the Canadian border. Grey guarded against this danger; on March 30, 1908, he wrote to his friend Ambassador Bryce at Washington:

> It seems to me that the situation with regard to Japanese immigration is, from the political point of view, very critical. I do not believe that the Japanese will do anything, even if the United States or Canada pass an Exclusion Law, so I do not mean that there is likely to be war. But the Pacific slope is in a high state of fever, and what I fear is that a suspicion may arise among the people there that, when the pinch comes, we shall not support them in resisting Japanese immigration. Should such a suspicion get hold of them, there would be no limit to the untoward political consequences which might ensue. I therefore spoke very explicitly on this point to Mr. Mackenzie King, telling him there was no reason whatever for such a suspicion.

This was addressed to the door of United States opinion, as well as to Canada.

On January 27, 1911, when the Treaty with Japan was coming up for renewal, he wrote to his friend and kinsman Earl Grey, then Governor-General of Canada:

> My dear Albert,
>
> It would be better that we should not discuss the Japanese Alliance until we can do so privately when the Dominion Premiers are over this year. Laurier, I have no doubt, understands the different aspects of it. But one or two others, and certainly the Australians, require a good deal of education.
>
> They must realise that, if we denounce the Japanese Alliance, we can no longer rely on the assistance of the Japanese Fleet, and we must prepare for the possibility that Japan may enter into arrangements which may bring her into hostility with us. This would mean maintaining on the China Station a Fleet superior not only to the Japanese Fleet, but also to any probable combination of the Japanese Fleet with any other Fleet in those waters. This would, of course, be in addition to maintaining the two-Power standard in European waters, both in home waters and in the Mediterranean. The logical conclusion of denouncing the Japanese Alliance would be that Australia and New Zealand should undertake the burden of naval supremacy in China seas. This they are neither willing nor able to do.
>
> I do not believe that there is the least danger that Japan will ever attempt forcible measures on the American side of the Pacific. Such action is no part of her policy, and it is not within her power. But I agree with you that we ought not to treat her in the spirit of an attorney in Manchuria or other regions in which she is naturally interested.

Speaking in the House of Commons on July 10, 1912, Grey, in referring to the growth of the German fleet in the North Sea, declared that diplomacy could afford no substitute for a home fleet able to defend the island from invasion and blockade; but, he added, further afield diplomacy can afford a substitute for another immense naval armament in the Pacific — by the Japanese Alliance. And after the war he said, in retrospect over the whole period when he was in office, 'The Japanese were good Allies.'

Alike in peace and in war Grey pursued friendship with the Government and people of the United States as a primary object. Not only did he think it essential to our safety in the dangers that surrounded us, but he was idealist enough to hope that the two great sections of the English-speaking world would stand together for righteousness and peace. Both took, for instance, the same eccentric view that humanity mattered in Macedonia and the Congo. Moreover he had a natural affinity to the type of American statesman with whom he had to deal, due in part to the simplicity of his own life and thought, and his boyish delight in throwing off the trappings of ceremony and officialdom when it was possible to do so without misunderstanding. He would have got on well with Lincoln, and the democratic liberalism of his nature was akin to the American atmosphere in which Theodore Roosevelt, Colonel House and Ambassador Page had been brought up. The more easily did he make the conquest of their private affections, which proved of no small public importance. And many other leading Americans, not excluding the reserved and unapproachable Wilson, felt that in Edward Grey their country had to deal with an honest and friendly Englishman. We have already noted [1] his personal friendship with Theodore Roosevelt, begun by correspondence and cemented in the bird-haunted glades of the New Forest. And it proved of even greater consequence that Colonel House, the one man in whom Wilson for awhile con-

[1] See pages 181–83.

fided, fell no less completely under Grey's charm during his visit to England shortly before the war.[1]

Grey has been blamed for not putting himself in personal contact with European statesmen, other than the Ambassadors in London through whom he transacted affairs. Probably, however, it was a wise instinct that prevented him from seeking to make things better by personal conferences at Berlin with spirits so uncongenial as the Kaiser, Holstein, Bülow and Tirpitz. If they would not believe their Ambassador Metternich, they would not have believed Grey any the more for coming to tell them himself. Haldane, in 1912, and other British statesmen since, have found that visits to foreign capitals have their dangers! But where, as in the case of these Americans, personal contact could lead to understanding and mutual trust, Grey used it to better purpose than anyone else could have done.

The first matter in which he looked to the United States for co-operation was the cause of world disarmament. As early as July 1906 he wrote to Mr. Whitelaw Reid, the American Ambassador in London, about the coming Conference at The Hague:

> If, when the time comes, the United States proposes the reduction or limitation of Armaments as a subject for consideration, I am sure that our delegates will be instructed cordially to support the proposal. And the initiative of the United States in this matter would be very welcome to us.

In the following February he wrote to President Roosevelt, again urging that America should bring forward the question

[1] Seymour's *Intimate Papers of Colonel House*, I; *Life and Letters of Walter Hines Page*. Page (I, 263) records in March 1914 an amusing incident: 'Then Grey said (which is very true) that he was much criticized for *bowing low to Americans*. Then we each bowed to the other. Think what a photograph that would make for our crazy friends, he and I bowing to one another!'

of limitation of armaments: 'It will be a poor lame Conference if the Powers all meet there and shirk the question.' [1]

But Germany would not even discuss limitation. She regarded any such proposal as an insulting interference with her sovereign rights. There had been plenty of goodwill at Washington, but America could not turn the fixed purpose of the Kaiser and his advisers. Substantially therefore The Hague Conference of 1907 came to nothing and marked another milestone towards Armageddon.

In 1911, Grey and Bryce, on excellent terms with President Taft's Administration, negotiated a Treaty of General Arbitration of which both had the highest hopes as an influence to lead the whole world towards the path of peace. By the terms of this instrument the two great English-speaking democracies were to bind themselves to bring to arbitration every possible dispute, however vital, however closely affecting national honour or feeling. 'The example,' wrote Grey in March 1911, 'would spread, and I am not without hope that one or more great European Powers would eventually make a similar agreement with us and the United States. The effect of such agreements on disarmament and the *morale* of international politics would be considerable.' But in the following year the United States Senate tore the Arbitration Treaty to pieces.

The next round in the ceaseless struggle between executive and legislative which keeps American politics in eternal unrest took place over the Panama Tolls, during the first two years of Wilson's Administration. The United States had constructed the great Canal, and therefore desired to impose lower rates upon American ships. But the Government of Washington had bound itself by the Hay-Pauncefote Treaty

[1] *G. and T.* VIII, 203.

with England of 1901 to treat all foreign ships using the Canal as favourably as its own nationals. The Taft Administration, in its last year 1912, evaded this obligation and promoted a Bill to give lower dues to ships of the United States engaged in the coastwise trade between the Eastern and Western ports of the Republic. This Panama Act of 1912 passed into law, Congress and the outgoing President being for once agreed, at the expense of the Treaty rights of Britain. In these alarming circumstances Grey wrote to Bryce at Washington on September 8, 1912:

> I shall be glad to hear what you think about Panama Canal Tolls. My present intention is to submit the full text of the Bill and of Taft's official Memorandum thereon to the Law Officers and Lord Chancellor. The Cabinet should then draw up a State paper to be presented to the United States Government. But had we not better present this *after* the Presidential Election? If so, we shall take our time for consideration here.
>
> Taft's view that the Hay-Pauncefote Treaty meant that the United States were free to deal with their own Ships as they liked, and were only bound to treat us as well as other foreign Powers, seems to me quite outrageous.
>
> The coastwise trade is a more difficult matter; but the only conceivable exception that would not be a breach of the Treaty is that the United States should subsidize (not exempt from Tolls) to the amount of the Tolls United States shipping engaged exclusively in coastwise trade. And it is doubtful if that could be applied in practice so as not to violate the Treaty.
>
> In the long run if we can get no agreement with the United States Government, and if they adhere to Taft's view of the meaning of the Hay-Pauncefote Treaty, we must ask for Arbitration. If they refuse Arbitration on such a point, it will put back the cause of Arbitration a hundred years. That is why I do not want to precipitate a request for arbitration yet. It is a very serious prospect.

Then things took an unexpected turn for the good. Woodrow Wilson defeated Taft at the Presidential election, and the new President soon came to the conclusion that the Hay-Pauncefote Treaty was open to no interpretation but that set upon it by the British lawyers. On that issue his uncompromising rectitude fought its first and most successful battle with the Senate. In March 1914, after a long and bitter contest, Congress at the bidding of the President repealed the Panama Act of the Taft Administration. It was a great triumph of international good faith in face of very strong opposing forces, and it cleared the decks for friendly relations between England and America during the world war.

Grey's careful management of the Panama dispute, based on frank and friendly exchange of ideas with Page, House and Wilson, was aided at Washington by the sympathetic diplomacy and engaging personality of his private Secretary, Sir William Tyrrell, whom he sent over during the illness of Bryce's successor in the Embassy, his other friend Cecil Spring Rice. Wilson would not have won the battle of the Panama dues against the Senate if Grey had not aided him by concession on the other troublesome matter of Mexico. Wilson's inexperienced idealism led him to insist upon the overthrow of President Huerta in that lawless land. His policy embarrassed England, who had large commercial interests in Mexico, requiring to be protected by good relations with the Dictator for the time being. Grey was better aware than Wilson that there was little reason in Mexico to prefer one 'cutpurse of the Empire and the rule' to another. But in recognition of the Monroe Doctrine and in order to keep friends with America, he stopped English diplomatic and consular action from impeding Wilson's proceedings, although he thought his policy of interference unwise. Thus left unsupported by England, President Huerta fled in July 1914, though his flight did not bring the golden age in Mexico.

In the same summer the Panama Tolls Bill had been repealed: Grey felt gratitude to Wilson for having faced trouble and unpopularity which he might have avoided, in order to retrieve a point in his nation's honour. The Panama and Mexican affairs had brought Grey, Tyrrell and the British Foreign Office into close and friendly relation with Wilson, House and Page, and had taught them much about America on the very eve of the war. The opposition in Congress, which Wilson had with such difficulty overcome, revealed to Grey how strong were the elements in America hostile to Britain — strong but not the strongest if handled with incessant caution. These lessons were not forgotten in the terrible months and years that followed.[1]

Relations with Germany, from the beginning to the end of Grey's tenure of office, were largely determined by the building of the German fleet. Growing fear for our safety at sea, on which our existence was staked, affected not only Grey's diplomacy but the public opinion that lay behind his action. During the first two years of his Secretaryship, Campbell-Bannerman's plan was tried out, of reducing the pace of our ship construction in the hope of tempting Germany to do the same. It appeared to have precisely the opposite effect.[2]

[1] Seymour's *Intimate Papers of Colonel House*; Hendrick's *Life and Letters of Walter Hines Page*; Grey's *Twenty-five Years*.

[2] See the figures for 1906–07 given in Mr. Churchill's *World Crisis*, I, 39. See also *G. and T.* VI, 508, 581–82, 588, reports of Captains Heath and Watson, and Sir Edward Goschen's conclusions based on that and other information: 'I consider that there is but small doubt that up till now (February 1911) Germany has always taken advantage of any slackening in British Naval construction to increase her own activity in shipbuilding, and that *vice versa* her activity in this direction has slackened off when the British Naval Estimates increased.'

Germany treated the Prime Minister's friendly gesture as an opportunity to draw up into a serious rivalry of sea-power. His public proposal for an agreed mutual reduction of armaments was taken by the Kaiser as an insult and by his naval advisers as a trap, by which Germany might be persuaded to accept the existing condition of British superiority at sea.

The Kaiser had the artist's temperament, that would have flourished in the Quartier Latin, but was warped by Byzantine pomp and power. He dashed from mood to mood and from project to project; now like Napoleon he divided the world with the Czar in the imperial yacht at Björkö; now with 'English' humour he invited Haldane to 'be a member of my Cabinet for the evening.' Now he enjoyed like a sportsman and good companion the social life of his grandmother's pleasant realm; now he turned to vent in marginal expletives his irritation with the stubborn islanders who thought the size of his navy was any concern of theirs. Would that he had known less or more about England! His love-hate towards her and her fleet was a psychological tragedy that involved millions beside the leading actor. But in all his changes of mood and purpose he clung to two fatal misconceptions, that England's friendship could be won by frightening her, and that any agreement for mutual limitation of armaments would derogate from his dignity as the Sovereign of the most powerful State in the world.

About the time of Campbell-Bannerman's death (April 1908) and Asquith's succession as Prime Minister, it became apparent that we could no longer with safety go slow on shipbuilding while the Germans went fast. We had made the case worse for ourselves because, just before the Liberals came into office, we had laid down the original Dreadnought, and its prime author, Admiral Sir John Fisher, had in his usual breezy style boasted to the world that it could make an end of all other craft afloat. His challenge was overheard by the Germans, whom his policy enabled to compete with us 'from scratch,' by building rival Dreadnoughts, on the assumption, only partially true, that older and smaller types in which we had so great a start were out of date and more or less useless. So, too, Fisher's language, half earnest, half jest, threatening to 'Copenhagen' the German fleet, was regarded as a bad joke by his countrymen, but was not regarded as a joke at all by the serious Germans. It was natural for them to suppose, on the analogy of their own constitutional custom, that our naval and military authorities had an influence on policy which, in fact, they had not, outside their proper sphere of technical advice. Certainly Grey was not going to make an unprovoked attack on Germany; but Fisher's unruly tongue did harm oversea.

And so by 1908 German construction in Dreadnoughts was close on our heels. Grey's papers show that he had received many warnings from the Continent, some indirectly from Socialist leaders in Germany, of the ruthless power of the governing military caste, and its intention to use its might some day in a final war of conquest. How much was he to believe of this? In any case he thought that we should, in the interests alike of safety and of peace, have a margin of superiority over the German fleet. He strove in vain to make the Berlin Government believe that naval limitation was the key to good relations. But when their Ambassador Count Metternich sent on to them these warnings of Grey's backed by his own, the Kaiser would only fly into a rage. Metternich lost favour at home for his faithful advice.

To this period belongs an interesting family letter of Sir Austen Chamberlain, who throughout these years of hot party strife always retained a watchful eye for the interest of the country as a whole, and never lost personal touch with opponents who were jointly responsible for her welfare.

> *Austen Chamberlain to Mrs. Joseph Chamberlain, June* 23, 1908. I had some conversation with Edward Grey last night. He told me that he had pointed out to Metternich that as long as the German press pursued the line of hostile and menacing criticism which they had adopted, he must not be surprised at the attitude of some English writers. The whole trouble arose from their insisting on building ships which were not commerce-protectors and were not suitable for defensive action in their home waters. Impartial observers — Dutch naval officers for instance — all inferred that Germany meant to attack us, not now but about 1915. What other inference was possible? No neutral thought that we were preparing for aggression. He had sent for Metternich after the Reval meeting [of the Czar and King Edward] and had told him that no new Alliances were being formed and that the only subjects of a political nature discussed were Persian and Macedonian questions; so Metternich could not complain that Germany was again being kept in the dark.

It is quite likely that the German Atlantic fleet was intended not in the first instance to attack England, but to secure her neutrality while France was being crushed: but in fact it rendered such neutrality on our part impossible.

Under these conditions was waged the great battle in the Cabinet over the number of Dreadnoughts to be laid down and the pace at which construction was to proceed. It was an ugly situation, for admittedly the question turned on rival calculations as to the pace at which a foreign power was actually going to build. Mr. McKenna was convinced of the fact of German acceleration by a comparison of figures, noticing the discrepancy between the new German naval law and the much higher provisions for shipbuilding in the German estimates. The real difficulty in these calculations lay not so much in determining the date at which the keel of a ship was laid down, but the date at which work was begun on its component parts and the collection of material. During the winter of 1908–09 the Cabinet was in possession of evidence which showed that the Germans were accelerating this preliminary work. It followed that the Cabinet had to decide whether the Germans proposed to continue this acceleration and complete the ships in advance of the scheduled time. Grey was unable to obtain satisfactory explanations on this point through Metternich, so he decided that the British programme ought to be large enough to meet any possible completion of the German ships before time.

This nice question for experts, involving our relations with Germany, became in democratic England a political controversy, conducted with noisy shouts that carried far across the North Sea. If the proposals that Grey made to Metternich for an exchange of information between the experts had been accepted by Germany, the atmosphere of suspicion and the public agitation in England would have been avoided. But, as it was, the Conservative Opposition attacked Ministers for not building fast enough, and many of their own Liberal supporters and newspapers attacked them for building too fast. Inside the divided Cabinet Mr. Lloyd George, backed by Mr. Churchill, who was not yet at the Admiralty, espoused the cause of naval economy, and they were supported by Morley and Loulou Harcourt. Mr. McKenna for the Admiralty stood firm for rapid building and Grey's support enabled him to win a battle that at one moment seemed lost. Mr. McKenna writes to me, describing what occurred:

> After the discussion at which my proposals were rejected, I remained behind in the Cabinet room doing up my papers

> and reflecting on the terms in which I should send in my resignation. I suppose Grey discovered that I had not left the room with the other members of the Cabinet, for after a little while he came in again and said to me, 'You look very dejected.' I replied that I was and that I was sending in my resignation. He answered, 'Do you really mean that? Are you so certain that you are right?' I answered 'absolutely certain. I have no alternative but to go.' Grey replied, 'If you go, I shall go too. I shall see Asquith.' When the Cabinet next met, either Asquith or Grey opened the proceedings with the suggestion that the decision on the shipbuilding programme should be reconsidered. It was reconsidered, and the programme, with immaterial variations, was sanctioned.

The following letter of Asquith's marks the final stage:

> *March* 19, 1909. My dear Grey, Ll. G.'s remarks were, I believe, resented by the whole Cabinet, with the doubtful exception of Winston. Harcourt spoke to me about them afterwards with much indignation. The fact is that Ll. G. and Winston and J. M. feel that the course of things this week has been a complete *débâcle* for them and their ideas, and the two former cannot help reflecting how they would have looked at this moment if they had resigned, with (as Winston predicted) 'ninety per cent. of the Liberal Party behind them.'

During this decisive struggle, Grey, feeling that the safety of the country was at stake, had thrown in his whole mind, working for hours together at the technical details with Fisher and other admirals. The point at issue was whether or not we should trust the Germans not to continue to accelerate their programme. The decision to take no chances in the matter prevented the Germans from being subjected to any such temptation. If we had built more slowly in 1909–10, they might have continued as they had begun, and built ships faster than they actually did when they saw we were in earnest.[1] But how little our margin in the actual war ex-

[1] 'The German ships of the 1908–09 and 1909–10 programmes were not completed in advance of the "normal" time; but this is no evidence of German inten-

ceeded our necessity is now only too well known by proof.

The following are notes that Grey passed to Morley during one of these crucial Cabinets in February:

> I fear if we say 'we lay down six this year' the party will be split. But if we do *not* promise to lay down six, I think with the figures of German building disclosed the feeling of apprehension in the country will be such that the country will become ungovernable. There will not be only scare but *panic*. I am convinced that six must be laid for this year, but that by saying it as part of a *definite* programme you will diminish the fear of *indefinite* naval expansion....
>
> The Board of Admiralty will resign on four. The minimum on which they will remain is six. There is the difference between *scare* and *panic*.

And again on February 13 he wrote to Morley:

> As to Navy Estimates, do remember that the critical time must come about 1912. If we err at all we must err on the side of safety: we must be in advance rather than in arrears; for the former error is reparable, the latter is not.
>
> My own ambitions and interests in life are so dead that I am prepared to admit that these islands would be happier without an Empire and with ten millions only of population; at any rate they would be better adapted to the sort of life I like to lead. But the Cabinet would not thank me, if, when the Navy Estimates appeared, I justified my continued presence in the government by proclaiming this point of view. And being as I consider bound in honour till further notice to adjust policy to the other point of view, I cannot stay in the Cabinet if there are Navy Estimates which seem

tions in the winter of 1908 and the spring of 1909.' (E. L. Woodward, *Great Britain and the German Navy*, page 240.) This authoritative work should be studied on the whole question, particularly chapters X and XI on 1909. These chapters should be compared to Mr. Noel Baker's book, *Private Manufacture of Armaments* (1936). The British Government had other evidence of acceleration besides Mulliner's, on which Mr. Baker lays overmuch stress. See also the reports of Goschen and Captains Heath and Watson cited above (page 237, note), *G. and T.* VI, 508 (*sub* Shipbuilding), 581–82, 588, sec. 3. And see *Grosse Politik*, XXVIII, and *G. and T.* VI, for Grey's representations made through Metternich, on which see *Woodward*, chapter X.

to me not to provide a sufficient margin of safety against possible German strength in 1912–13.

His defence of the enlarged programme on which the Cabinet at length decided, made to the House of Commons on March 29, 1909, shows how fatal he thought the race in armaments would prove to Europe, how fatal also unilateral disarmament by Great Britain:

> The great countries of Europe are raising enormous revenues, and something like half of them is being spent on naval and military preparations. You may call it national insurance, that is perfectly true, but it is equally true that half the national revenue of the great countries in Europe is being spent on what is [*sic*], after all, preparations to kill each other. Surely the extent to which the expenditure has grown really becomes a satire, and a reflection on civilisation. Not in our generation, perhaps, but if it goes on at the rate at which it has recently increased, sooner or later I believe it will submerge that civilisation.... Is it to be wondered that the hopes and aspirations of the best men in the leading countries are devoted to trying to find some means of checking it?
>
> But, Sir,... if we alone, among the great Powers, gave up the competition and sank into a position of inferiority, what good should we do? None whatever, no good to ourselves because we cannot realize great ideals of social reform at home when we are holding our existence at the mercy, at the caprice if you like, of another nation.... We should cease to count for anything amongst the nations of Europe, and we should be fortunate if our liberty was left, and we did not become the conscript appendage of some stronger Power. That is a brutal way of stating the case, but it is the truth. It is disagreeable that it should be so, but in matters like this I know of no safe way except to look at what is disagreeable frankly in the face, and to state it, if necessary, in its crudest form.
>
> There is no comparison between the importance of the German Navy to Germany, and the importance of our Navy to us. Our Navy is to us what their Army is to them. To have a strong Navy would increase their prestige, their diplomatic

influence, their power of protecting their commerce; but it is not a matter of life and death to them as it is to us.

And he put the same idea in other words in a Foreign Office Note of January 1912:[1]

> There is no question of England aiming at the hegemony of the world. Her Army is far too small for any such ambition. All we desire is to be able to live on equal terms. But when we see Germany, having created already the largest Army in the world, proceeding apparently towards the creation of the largest Fleet also, we are naturally anxious as to whether it is equal terms or hegemony that Germany wants.

Then the Agadir storm came and passed. Crisis after crisis, each just averted, made war seem ever nearer. And the naval rivalry still darkly clouded the prospect. The outcome of Haldane's mission to Berlin in 1912 had been that Germany refused to slow down on shipbuilding unless we promised to remain neutral if France were attacked. That promise no member of the Cabinet, least of all Grey, would give.

And so, for all the growth in our Dreadnought programme, the German naval increase followed hard upon our heels, till in 1912 the Admiralty decided that it must move a portion of the Mediterranean fleet to home waters to meet the menace in the North Sea. This meant a partial abandonment of our old control of the Mediterranean; Grey and the Foreign Office deeply regretted it for a variety of reasons which they stated in vain; the Admiralty insisted on the change.[2]

At the same time France decided to concentrate in the Mediterranean and give up the attempt to match her weak

[1] *Grey Papers, F.O.*, volume 65, *sub* Ashley.

[2] There is a long correspondence on this subject in the Foreign Office papers.

GOSHEN COLLEGE LIBRARY GOSHEN, INDIANA

ships against the might of the German High-Seas Fleet. These simultaneous movements of the French fleet and of our own were taken, in either case, irrespective of the action of the other country. So at least Mr. Churchill, who had now been moved to the Admiralty, declared in his letter to Asquith and Grey in August 1912:

> If we did not exist, the French could not make better dispositions than at present. They are not strong enough to face Germany alone, still less to maintain themselves in two theatres. They therefore rightly concentrate their Navy in the Mediterranean where it can be safe and superior and can assure their African communications. Neither is it true that we are relying on France to maintain our position in the Mediterranean. . . . If France did not exist, we should make no other disposition of our forces.

Nevertheless, as Mr. Churchill pointed out forcibly in the same letter, the new distribution of French and British ships drew the Entente closer than before. It rendered it yet more unthinkable that we should stand neutral while France was attacked, since she would now plead that she had denuded her northern coasts relying upon our fleet to protect them. For this reason the fleet movements of 1912 committed us more than the Military Conversations of 1906. But in fact, as Grey realized better than many of his countrymen, we stood 'committed,' not by this or that word or act, but by the brute need of self-preservation: if we permitted France to be destroyed as a Power, her loss of independence would speedily be followed by our own downfall.

Yet the naval arrangements of 1912 seemed to 'commit' us more deeply and were useful in causing more Englishmen to realize the dread reality of the situation, which they disliked so much that many of them refused to face it. The formal protest, that we were still uncommitted even by the recent movements of the fleet, was duly made by Grey's letter to Cambon written at the behest of the Cabinet;[1] nevertheless, we stood committed not indeed by our pledged word, but by the march of German power towards hegemony by land and by sea.

In the letter to Grey quoted above, Mr. Churchill declared that the Entente now entailed 'the obligations of an Alliance without its advantages, and above all without its precise definitions.' The advantages of an Alliance were certainly wanting, but so also were its disadvantages; for an Alliance would have encouraged France and Russia to acts of intransigence against the Central Powers which they dared not perpetrate in face of the still remaining uncertainty as to British action. Meanwhile, opinion at home, both inside and outside the Cabinet, still steadily refused to promise to fight till the *casus belli* had emerged and been passed under moral judgment. Grey therefore could not have formed an Alliance, and he would not if he could. It was an evil situation, but no better alternative was possible.

Mr. Churchill was by this time in Mr. McKenna's place at the Admiralty. Chancellor Thomas à Becket had become Archbishop of Canterbury; the poacher had been taken on as gamekeeper. His energetic and fiery spirit, devoted in 1909 to naval economy, was now in the service of naval preparedness. It was a grave misfortune that we should have to clear decks for action in 1912–14, but, since it was so, it was well that the decks were in fact cleared.

Mr. Churchill's view of Grey's policy in broad historical retrospect is expressed in a letter he wrote to me in 1935:

> There is no doubt in my mind that Grey definitely accepted the task of resisting the German power, and of making

[1] See page 158 above for its text.

> England play a decisive part in that. This led to the Great War of 1914. Had he taken a different course, he would not have prevented war, but it would have been a different war, either a few years earlier or a few years later under conditions about which it is vain to speculate. If England had not resisted German militarism, in my view the German hegemony of Europe would have been established and our island would have had to face a united Continental block. It is the same old story from the days of Marlborough and Napoleon. I therefore consider as only minor questions whether Grey by doing this, that, or the other at a particular moment could have avoided a crisis. There may be much to be said on these points and whether his rigidity of character — he was a true Whig — always served the cause of temporary peace. His life's justification depends upon whether England ought to have done in 1914 what she did against Philip II of Spain, against Louis XIV and against Napoleon. I have no doubt what the answer should be.

The following letter of Grey's to his friend Sir Rennell Rodd, the British Ambassador at Rome, expresses his lines of policy as he saw them early in 1913 — to be friends with Germany if possible, not to resist her expansion in Asiatic Turkey, but not to become dependent on her by losing control of the sea. (Jagow, the German Ambassador at Rome, was at that moment being recalled to Berlin to succeed Kiderlen as Minister for Foreign Affairs.)

Private

LONDON,
13 *January*, 1913.

MY DEAR RODD,

Your letter with its account of your conversation with Jagow is very interesting and helpful.

You were quite right in saying that one of our difficulties in past years has been that we never know what Germany really wants. Metternich used to say to me with reproach that there was a time when we leant upon Germany. It is quite true that we used to do so: the French Press used even to talk at that time of the 'Quadruple Alliance,' so as to include us. During all that time, the attitude of Germany was never really that of a friend. The Germans used to give Lord Salisbury to understand that when Germany wanted some thing she must have it, because as we were on bad terms with France and Russia we could not afford to quarrel with Germany. Such an attitude would not do now that the days of isolation are over. We must have friendship if we are to give friendship.

The Press Bureau in Berlin has always been an obstacle to good relations between us. A Press Bureau is used to make mischief, and some German Diplomatists have done a good deal of mischief-making. That was the bad side of Bismarck's policy, or rather a bad method which he used in his policy.

If we could only have ten years of a man like Jagow to deal with, really controlling the policy of Germany, we should be on intimate terms with her at the end of the time, and on increasingly good terms all through it.

I quite agree that France, Russia, and ourselves cannot treat Asia Minor as Morocco. If there is to be a partition, Germany must be well in it, and I should not think of trying to exclude her. Indeed, we could truthfully say the same thing to Germany about Anatolia as we said to France about Syria: that we have no *political* designs there. Security as regards the Persian Gulf and its littoral is all that we want, and it can perfectly well be reconciled with the development of German interests.

As to the Navy, we must keep ahead of the German Navy: and every year the justification for our shipbuilding must be given openly to Parliament, which involves comparison with the German strength. Having but a small Army, we cannot rest the defence of Great Britain and the Capital of the Empire on diplomatic agreements or relations. If our Fleet was not superior to the German Fleet, our very independence would depend on Germany's goodwill; and even granting that people like Jagow would not take advantage of such a situation, there must be others who would take advantage of it, or be compelled by public opinion in Germany to do so. The Prussian mentality is such that to be on really good terms with it one must be able to deal with it as an equal.

Hence the persistent and inevitable comparison here of

German and British navies. These comparisons are resented in Germany as evidence of a gratuitous and unfriendly assumption on our part that Germany is hostile to us. But this is not their real motive. Germany has the biggest army in the world as well as her navy, but the navy is our one and only means of defence and our life depends on it and upon it alone.

I shall send to Goschen [at Berlin] a copy of your letter and of this letter of mine to you; so that if Jagow wants to continue conversation with him, he will know what to expect and on what lines to speak.

Yours sincerely,

E. Grey.

This letter, which was shown to the King, was minuted by him, 'An admirable reply to Sir R. Rodd's letter. — G.R.I.'

VI

The Annexation of Bosnia—Agadir—The Attempted Rapprochement with Germany—The Balkan Wars—Bagdad Railway and Portuguese Colonies

GREY, as we have seen, believed that England could not afford to lose control of the sea, and that she therefore could not permit a German hegemony in Europe. For if once the diplomatic independence of France were destroyed, Germany could array the Continent against Britain; and the days had gone by when our navy could protect us against such a Napoleonic combination. But Grey's policy was as far as possible from jealous antagonism to German expansion. As will be seen in this chapter, he negotiated with her an agreement to facilitate her future acquisition of more colonies in Africa. Still more important was his attitude to the Near Eastern question. If he had attempted to resist Germany's predominant influence in Constantinople and Asia Minor, or if he had encouraged the Slav powers of the Balkans against Germany's ally, then she might truly have talked of 'encirclement.' But Grey accepted Germany's ever-increasing hold on Constantinople and on the Bagdad Railway, although it was built up at the expense of Britain's former trade and influence, and was due in part to the Kaiser's easier attitude towards Turkish massacre and misrule.

And Grey acted, for some years successfully, as 'honest broker' to keep the peace between Austria-Hungary and the Slav interests in the Balkans.

If Germany had consistently supported him in the work of pacification in Eastern Europe, war would have been postponed, possibly averted. But the interpretation that she now felt obliged to put on her alliance with Austria-Hungary impelled her from time to time to clank the sabre in support of the most doubtful actions of Vienna, such as the annexation of Bosnia in 1908 and the final ultimatum to Serbia in 1914. If Germany had not allied herself to Austria-Hungary, she need never after 1870 have fought another war. But she had tied herself to the fatal chain of Balkan necessity, to take part in the 'irrepressible conflict' of nationality in South-Eastern Europe. From that issue Austria-Hungary could not escape participation in some form, for the Balkan and Austro-Hungarian questions were one. And in that question both Germany and Russia were now to be involved. Bismarck indeed had by various understandings with other powers prevented his Alliance with Vienna from implying the subordination of German policy. But now Germany had refused to come to terms with England about the fleet, was on ill terms with Russia and could not rely on Italy; therefore she must follow where Austria-Hungary led, or be left without a friend in the world. So at least argued both Aerenthal and Bülow. All Europe, therefore, was bound on the Balkan wheel of fire. For France, too, in reply to Bismarck's Triple Alliance, had bound herself to Russia. And in its turn Russian popular feeling supported the Czar's government in a passionate desire to help their Slav brothers in the Balkans. Russia's will to war was held in check by the fear of German arms, but it was growing in proportion as she year by year recovered from her Japanese *débâcle*. There were statesmen and soldiers in Austria-Hungary who did not wish to wait till Russia was again formidable, and who were determined to crush the Serbs whether the Czar came to their rescue or no.

There is no wonder, then, that Grey conceived a horror of the great European Alliances which would mechanically prevent the localization of a conflict in which any one of the Great Powers was involved. This thought led him to become during the war one of the chief originators of the League of Nations, as the only possible substitute for the Alliance system. And before the war he strove to mitigate the rival grouping of Powers by joint action through the 'Concert of Europe' to preserve peace. In particular his Balkan policy was based on the endeavour to settle differences by conferences of Ambassadors and agreements between all the Powers; and when Germany lent a hand, as in 1913, peace was in fact preserved.

On December 11, 1906, Grey wrote to Morley:

> Minto does not realize that this country could not have bid for the alliance of the present Sultan [the notorious Abdul Hamid] without losing its self-respect, which is a greater asset to it than any alliance. If the next Sultan rules 'for the public good' we may improve our relations with him. But I think a reformed Russia is more probable than a reformed Turkey.

However, in 1908 a Turkish revolution seemed to usher in a better age. Grey was warned by those who knew the men that Young Turk might prove Old Turk writ large, but so long as the appearance of a more liberal regime was kept up he thought it his duty to do nothing to render the path of the Turkish reformers more difficult, either as regards the opening of the Straits to Russia, or anything else. Austria-

Hungary, however, seized the opportunity to proclaim the annexation of Bosnia and Herzegovina, which she had been allowed to occupy under international agreement. To annex these territories without the leave of other parties to the Treaty under which occupation had been permitted, was a gross breach of international law; it was besides a challenge to Young Turkey and most of all a challenge to the patriotic passion of Serbia, that aspired some day to reclaim the million Serbs who inhabited Bosnia-Herzegovina. If they were finally annexed to the Croat provinces of Austria-Hungary, nothing could ever reunite them to Serbia but a war to destroy the Austro-Hungarian State.

Grey, in the name of international law and right, demanded that the matter should be brought before a Conference of the Powers. That a single Power should be allowed to tear up a Treaty as a scrap of paper, seemed to him a precedent too dangerous to pass unchallenged. But England's stand for the covenants that make for peace received as little support as his previous attempts to get the question of Macedonian Reform taken up by the Concert of Europe. He alone could not create a Concert of Europe, when every other Power preferred its own supposed interests to the common cause of law, harmony and peace. Germany supported Austria-Hungary; the Russian Minister, Isvolsky, gave away the case against the Bosnian annexation by secretly negotiating with Vienna for a deal at the expense of Turkey — Vienna to be allowed to keep Bosnia, and in return the Straits to be opened to Russia. Too late Isvolsky found that Vienna had tricked him, that Bosnia was annexed but the Straits could not be opened. This bred in the baffled intriguer a personal passion to be revenged on Austria-Hungary; he was succeeded at the Russian Foreign Office by the more level-headed Sazonov, but Isvolsky himself, transferred to the Paris Embassy, became there a focus of intrigue against the Central Powers.

So Bosnia was annexed by the fiat of Vienna, backed by Berlin. Then Serbia demanded compensation, and that again almost led to war. At first Russia supported Serbia's demand; then, when the Kaiser's mailed fist appeared behind the resistance of Vienna, Russia gave way because she was not ready for war, and France had no wish to fight in a Balkan cause. Austria-Hungary and Germany won a resounding diplomatic victory alike over Russian and Serbian interests and over British demands for international justice and the Concert of Europe. The Kaiser crowed aloud over the virtues of 'shining armour.' But it was a Pyrrhic victory, for the Russian people felt the sense of defeat and wrong, and were drawn together by the resolve never to suffer such another humiliation. And the Serbians, though they turned first against other foes, henceforth regarded the destruction of Austria-Hungary as the ultimate goal of their national ambition.

The rebuff to Grey's policy was most serious. He had tried to insist that the breach of treaty over Bosnia should be 'regulated' by an International Conference, and found himself practically alone in the demand. The French gave him no support, but lined up with Austria-Hungary and were annoyed because he would not console Russia and end the whole business by conceding the 'opening of the Straits' with equally little regard to Turkey's other Treaty rights. It was not the last time that English effort to stand up for international legality for its own sake has been interpreted by the European Powers as a Macchiavellian attempt to make trouble for some concealed but no doubt selfish end. That any country could honestly regard the defence of the Law of Nations as an end in itself, was inconceivable to the statesmen of Europe; but to Grey, as to other British Foreign Ministers, respect for international legality has seemed the only principle by which universal war could in the end be avoided. Thus 1908 held 1914 in its arms.

The next danger to European peace arose from Morocco, in the Agadir crisis of 1911. The Algeciras agreement of 1906 had proved only a temporary settlement; it had now been violated, as Germany claimed — or had proceeded to its inevitable and prearranged consequence, as France and England considered. In any case French influence and arms had penetrated into Morocco, to restore order in an oriental State falling into chaos and civil war. French action was not unreasonable, but neither was Germany's demand that she must receive compensation elsewhere in Africa, if she acquiesced in the absorption of Morocco by France. But the demand for practically all the French Congo was excessive, and above all Germany put herself in the wrong when she began the negotiations by the warlike gesture of sending the *Panther* to Agadir.

The initial pretence that there were German commercial interests to protect at Agadir was untrue and was not seriously urged. But though not a commercial port, Agadir might be made a naval base on the Atlantic, and therefore England was interested on her own account as well as on that of France. But above all, Grey could not allow the Germans to dictate to France by threat of war a humiliating colonial partition, for that would be the end of the entente, already strained by the diplomatic triumph of 'shining armour' in the Bosnian affair. M. Caillaux, then Prime Minister of France, would lead his countrymen into the arms of Germany if England now stood aside, and war when it came would see England without an ally.

This view of the situation seems to have been taken by the whole British Cabinet, which authorized Grey to represent to the German Ambassador on July 4, 1911,

> that I must tell him that our attitude could not be a disinterested one with regard to Morocco. We must take into consideration our treaty obligations to France and our own interests in Morocco. We were of opinion that a new situation had been created by the despatch of a German ship to Agadir. Future developments might affect British interests more directly than they had hitherto been affected, and therefore we could not recognize any new arrangement which was come to without us.

This was clear speaking, yet for close on three weeks Metternich could extract no reply from his Government, which continued to press the French and to treat England as if she did not exist or had not spoken. During this long and anxious period of waiting for a reply, Grey declined the dangerous suggestion of the French Foreign Minister that a French and an English warship should be sent to Agadir.

Then on July 21 Mr. Lloyd George came to the Foreign Office and asked Grey if there had been a reply from Germany. On hearing that the ominous silence was still maintained at Berlin, Grey's visitor suggested on his own account that he should, in the speech he was to make in the City that evening, warn Germany that England would fight sooner than be excluded from the 'Cabinet of Nations.' The Chancellor of the Exchequer showed the Foreign Secretary what he proposed to say, and Grey gladly agreed. 'The speech was entirely Lloyd George's own idea. I did nothing to instigate it, but I welcomed it.' The effect of this warning, coming from the leader of the Radicals and pacifists in Britain, had a tremendous effect in Europe. It caused wild indignation in Germany that almost led to war; but in fact it proved the road to peace. After several more weeks of anxiety an agreement was reached, by which France, in return for a free hand in Morocco, ceded two large strips of Congolese territory to the Germans.

The Moroccan question was at length removed from among the possible causes of war. But the crisis had left everyone more angry and more afraid. The pace of armaments was speeded up. And if Russia felt that she could not suffer a second diplomatic defeat after the Bosnian affair, Germany felt much the same after Agadir. In fact she had got good terms, but her original demands had been so high and she had sought to impose them by such haughty methods on France and England, that a fair agreement at the end seemed like a German defeat.

The situation was indeed alarming. The Great Powers of Europe were arranged in two armed camps, with Italy balancing between. But British-German antagonism had, owing to the building of the German fleet, come to the forefront of the picture. Even before Agadir, the *Round Table* had written in November 1910:

> The antagonism between England and Germany is the topic which dominates all others in the columns of the world press which are devoted to foreign affairs. An overwhelming majority of Germans regard war with England as inevitable. Germanism, they say, must and will prevail, for it is the most vital and self-sacrificing of the forces of the day. England, the colossus with feet of clay, lies across her path.

In this situation, made worse by Agadir, Grey could not possibly stand by and see France crushed by Germany, or drawn into her orbit, for either would be the doom of England. But he made unceasing and not wholly unsuccessful efforts to arrive at better terms with Germany in the interval after Agadir: first the Haldane mission that failed; then the pacification of the Near East in 1913 that succeeded for the moment; and lastly the agreements as to the Bagdad Railway and the future of the Portuguese Colonies, arrived at on the very eve of the war.

Haldane's mission to Berlin, in February 1912, originated from a suggestion conveyed through Sir Ernest Cassel and Herr Ballin that a British Minister should go over to pave the way to a *rapprochement.* Mr. Winston Churchill tells us that he and Mr. Lloyd George had helped to set the ball rolling; when it came back to Grey he understood that the invitation had the support of the Kaiser, and he therefore considered that it ought to be accepted, though he had no great hopes of success. He himself would not go, although that had been indicated: his going would frighten the French; and failure, which he regarded as too probable an outcome in any case, would have much graver consequences if it followed a visit of the British Foreign Secretary himself. But his friend Haldane, who was fully in his confidence, had personal contacts of his own with Germany and Germans, not excluding the Kaiser.

The story of the mission and its sequel has been told in full by Haldane, Grey, Bethmann-Hollweg, Tirpitz and other actors in the affair. The particular questions of the Bagdad Railway and the Portuguese Colonies, on which Grey two years later came to an agreement with Germany, were lightly touched upon; but on the more fundamental points, which were pressed to an issue, no agreement could be found.

For the British desired that the new German Naval Law should not be passed; and the Germans required a promise of British neutrality, in case of war between Germany and France, as a condition of any reduction in their own naval programme.[1]

The formula which Grey offered to the German Government on March 14, 1912, was as follows:

> England will make no unprovoked attack upon Germany and pursue no aggressive policy towards her. Aggression upon Germany is not the subject, and forms no part, of any Treaty understanding or combination to which England is now a party, nor will she become a party to anything that has such an object.

To which Metternich replied:

> I am afraid that the political formula you left with me today will not be found sufficient at home, as no mention is made of neutrality.[2]

Grey's formula was always the same for all parties, on every occasion from 1906 to the end; it was repeated by him to Sazonov when the Russian Minister visited Balmoral in the September following the Haldane mission.

> The question of whether we went to war [he told Sazonov] would depend upon how the war came about. No British government could go to war unless backed by public opinion. Public opinion would not support any aggressive war, for a revanche or to hem Germany in, and we desired to see diffi-

[1] *Twenty-five Years*, II, 74–84; *G. and T.* VI, 666–714; Churchill's *World Crisis*, I, 94–102; Bethmann-Hollweg's and Tirpitz' *Memoirs*; Huldermann's *Albert Ballin* (Cassell, 1922), 165 *et seq.*

[2] *G. and T.* VI, 713–14. It is no wonder Metternich wrote thus, for on February 28 the Kaiser had written to Kiderlen, the Foreign Secretary, saying that Metternich had 'aroused his displeasure' by transmitting the British proposals. 'He must avoid all discussion of naval matters, supplementary Bills, etc., until England has submitted to me, for my information the draft for the political Agreement including a neutrality clause! Until then I refuse to negotiate further.' (Dugdale, *German Diplomatic Documents*, IV, 78; *Gr. Pol.* XXXI, 141.)

culties between Germany and other powers smoothed over whenever they arose. If, however, Germany was led by her great, I might say unprecedented strength, to attempt to crush France, I do not think we should stand by and look on, but should do all we could to prevent France being crushed. That had been our feeling at the time of the Algeciras Conference, in 1906 and again last year.[1]

Both sides were warned beforehand: France and Russia knew that we should not support a war of aggression on their part; Germany had been told that we should actively resist aggression by her against our friends. If the Kaiser would not believe Grey, he might at least have believed the King. George V warned the Kaiser himself, as is shown in the following important letter:[2]

York Cottage,
Sandringham,
December 8, 1912.

My dear Grey,

Prince Henry of Prussia paid me a short visit here three days ago. In the course of a long conversation with regard to the present European situation, he asked me point blank, whether in the event of Germany and Austria going to war with Russia and France, England would come to the assistance of the two latter Powers. I answered undoubtedly yes under certain circumstances. He professed surprise and regret but did not ask what the certain circumstances were. He said he would tell the Emperor what I had told him. Of course Germany must know that we could not allow either of our friends to be crippled. I think it is only right that you should know what passed between me and the Emperor's brother on this point. I hope to see you when I come to London at the end of this week.

Believe me,
Very sincerely yours,
(Signed) George R.I.

[1] *G. and T.* ix, 761.

[2] Doctor Gooch and Professor Temperley had already found this letter of the King's, and decided on its publication, when I made my own search in the archives. It will be published in due course in *G. and T.* x (ii).

Two months after this interview, Nicolson, on February 18, 1913, wrote to Grey as to its sequel:

> His Majesty read to me a long letter from Prince Henry recording that he had communicated to the German Emperor the opinion which the King had expressed to Prince Henry at Sandringham in regard to our helping our friends — an opinion, the King said to me this morning which 'I as an honest man was bound to give.' I entirely agreed with him. Prince Henry said that the Emperor had been struck by what the King had said, but still more by the fact that Haldane on the same day had used practically precisely the same language to Prince Lichnowsky. The Emperor observed that he knew now where he stood: that he was always in favour of peace, but in view of the possible or probable attitude of Great Britain in future complications he could not be blamed if he were to make every preparation to meet every possible eventuality.

For years Count Metternich from the London Embassy had never ceased to warn Berlin of the inevitable consequences on English opinion and policy of the German shipbuilding programme. In Bethmann-Hollweg he had found a sympathetic hearer, but the Chancellor was not the ruler of Germany. Metternich in 1927 wrote to Maximilian von Hagen, as follows:

> About Christmas time [1911] I had the last interview with the Kaiser and Tirpitz in the Berlin Palace about our relations with England, and I laid emphasis on the favourable feeling in England. Tirpitz declared that he knew from a trustworthy source that at the time of the Morocco crisis, when the Kaiser was on his yacht in Norwegian waters, English torpedo boats had been ordered in the event of hostilities to sink the Imperial yacht. As the Grand Admiral gravely stroked his beard while telling this fairy tale, and the Kaiser turning to me cried: 'And you want me to come to an understanding with these people?' I realized that the Navy Bill had already been decided on by the two and further arguments were useless. . . . I was tired of the lonely struggle with Berlin, where I could find no support whatever.[1]

[1] *Times*, January 10, 1935.

In the following May, after the failure of the Haldane mission, Metternich was dismissed in disgrace from the London Embassy, from which indeed he himself was on the point of resigning since his advice had always been given in vain.

In 1912 the Balkan problem entered into a new phase with the alliance of Bulgaria, Serbia, Greece and Montenegro to liberate Macedonia and Thrace from the Turk by force of arms. This alliance and the war that crowned it with success had two distinct aspects. In the first place it was a war of liberation, necessitated by the persistent refusal of the Concert of Europe to compel the Turks to reform their administration of Macedonia. Under the Young Turks in 1911 things had only gone from bad to worse. For years England had urged the Great Powers to act about Macedonia; Grey, like his predecessors, had again and again warned Europe of the consequence of leaving that wound to fester. Now the inevitable had happened; the Balkan States made war to accomplish for themselves the task that the Great Powers had refused to perform by more pacific methods in the general interest. Grey's foresight in pressing for action by the Concert of Europe in Macedonia was sadly justified by the event. If the Great Powers had listened to the dictates of humanity, they would at the same time have subserved the cause of Peace.

But in its ultimate consequences the Balkan Alliance against Turkey in 1912 had another aspect besides that of liberation from Turkish misrule: it was necessarily a defiance of Austro-Hungarian and of German influence. Contrary to general expectation it led in October 1912 to the overthrow of the Turkish army, and the appearance of the

Balkan States, not least Serbia, as militarist Powers to be reckoned with in time of war. This was most unpleasant to Vienna and Berlin. But Grey was blameless in the matter: he had not either directly or indirectly instigated the Balkan Alliance. It had to some extent been fostered by Russia, as a set-off for her humiliation over the Bosnian affair four years back. Grey, on the other hand, had attempted to avert the need for such an Alliance by urging Macedonian Reform, and he all along worked to keep Austria and Russia in agreement on Balkan affairs. In October 1912 he wrote to Sir G. Buchanan at St. Petersburg: 'We must do all we can to keep Austria and Russia co-operating together in Balkan affairs: it is the only way to prevent them from falling out.' In the previous January he had expressed the same idea in a very interesting letter to our Ambassador in Paris.[1] From first to last it was his policy.

The immediate consequence of the defeat of Turkey by the Balkan Powers was a grave danger of general European war in 1913. Austria-Hungary, furious at the growth of Serbia's power, meditated an attack upon her, while the Russian government and people were determined not to allow her to be crushed. Grey strove for peace in a spirit of real neutrality, and France and Germany both backed him up. Consequently a general European war was just averted. But the price was the exclusion of Serbia and Montenegro from the outlet on the Adriatic which their arms had won from the Turk. An independent Albania was to hold all the Adriatic ports between Austro-Hungarian and Greek territory. This was a bitter pill for the Serbs and Russians to swallow, and it made further trouble certain, but for the time it prevented a European war.

[1] *G. and T.* IX, 527, 769.

The Balkan crisis [wrote Grey to Ella Pease on February 1, 1913] drags out its agony: the dreary part of Foreign Affairs is that nothing can be dealt with on its merits. Things have to be sacrificed to keep the peace between the Great Powers. If a good settlement of Albania would mean war between two or more Great Powers, and an inferior settlement would secure peace between them, the latter has to be preferred.

Indeed the fault in the arrangement was that neither Serbia nor Montenegro was allowed to reach the Adriatic. Grey had actively supported this 'inferior settlement,' as he himself called it, because the alternative was a general European war. How little then was there on his part a policy of 'encirclement' or rooted hostility to the policy of the Central Powers!

The instrument by which a Teuton-Slav conflict had been averted on this occasion was the Conference of Ambassadors suggested by Grey to carry out his ideal of action through the 'Concert of Europe.' Kaiser William refused to act through the Concert in 1908 and again in 1914, but on this occasion he agreed. France and Germany in 1913 both diligently sought to avert the conflict between Austria-Hungary and Russia. And so the Conference of Ambassadors, sitting in London under Grey's Chairmanship, just managed, by a series of compromises about Serbia's new frontiers, to avert the great conflagration. 'There were six of us,' he writes — the Ambassadors of Germany, Austria, Italy, France, Russia and himself for Great Britain. 'Such responsibility as there was of presiding fell to me, but we made the proceedings as informal as those of a committee of friends, as indeed we were.'[1]

In August 1913 they had done their work and separated, never, alas, to meet again. For when next year the Balkan

[1] *Twenty-five Years*, II, 95.

question blazed up again after Sarajevo, Germany refused a conference and reverted to her policy of 'shining armour' in support of her warlike ally.

At the end of the crisis King George wrote to Grey as follows:

BALMORAL,
18th August, 1913.

MY DEAR GREY,

Now that the Conference of Ambassadors is adjourned and its members have separated for their well-earned holiday, I wish to offer you my sincere congratulations on the results achieved and to express my high appreciation of the able manner in which you have presided over the Conference and steered its course through the many rocks and shoals among which it might have been at any time wrecked. You have by your patience, tact and statesmanship, secured Peace and gained the confidence of all the European Powers, while inspiring a similar confidence in the Parliamentary Opposition of this country.

I heartily share these feelings of absolute reliance in your management of our foreign policy, and join in the sentiments of gratitude so generally expressed towards you by your fellow-countrymen.

GEORGE R.I.

Yet the work done by the Conference of Ambassadors was negative and temporary only — it could have been no more in the then temper of Europe. The denial of Serbia's outlet to the Adriatic left Belgrade and Vienna on the worst possible terms. And the last months of the pacific Conference of Great Powers synchronized with a war between the Balkan States themselves (June–August 1913); they had fallen out in dividing the spoils of their late victory over the Turk. Bulgaria was the aggressor, and she was crushed by a combination of Serbia, Greece and Rumania. At the end Turkey joined in and recovered a part of Thrace. The Macedonian question was settled by force of arms in favour of Serbia and

Greece. The Great Powers, as Grey wrote, dared not interfere to impose a juster settlement, 'being too afraid of trouble between ourselves.'

And so the Balkan situation simmered on for another uneasy year. Bulgaria, sore and despoiled, inclined now to the German rather than the Russian side in order to wreak vengeance on Serbia; while Serbia, deprived of her window on the Adriatic at the orders of Vienna, waited eagerly for a general European war, for the chance to break up Austria-Hungary and attach all her Serb and Croat Provinces to a great Yugo-Slav Kingdom centred at Belgrade.

The partial revival of Turkish military power in the Balkan War of 1913 was followed by the appointment of the German General, Liman von Sanders, to a command in the Turkish armies. Russia appealed to France and England to resist this appointment. France was prepared to take up the cudgels, but Grey was pacific, and, as Lichnowsky testifies, 'His intervention contributed in no small degree to smooth the matter over.' The German officer remained, by a 'compromise,' as Turkish Inspector General and Field Marshal. So determined was Grey not to pursue a policy of 'encirclement,' that he made no effort to prevent the German influence from becoming paramount at Constantinople.

It was part and parcel of the same policy to accept German penetration into Asia Minor and down the valley of the Euphrates. But here it was necessary to negotiate a delimitation of areas between the old-established British interests at the head of the Persian Gulf, and the influence of Germany approaching the Gulf down the line of the Bagdad Railway.

The question was not new. Lord Lansdowne had hoped to come to terms with Germany over it in 1903, but had been prevented by an 'insensate outcry,' as he called it, of British public opinion against German development in those regions. The country rather than the Foreign Office was responsible for the failure of those negotiations, which may be regarded as one of the things that helped to increase bad relations and the German naval programme.[1]

Ten years later Grey had more success. The matter was in the highest degree complicated, for Turkey as well as Germany had to be brought to an agreement, and French, Russian and other interests were involved. One of the principal agents in this great negotiation, Mr. Alwyn Parker, writes to me:

> Russia reached an agreement with Germany in 1910, and it was embodied in the Potsdam Agreement of 1911, which bound Russia, *inter alia*, not to oppose the Bagdad Railway.[2]
>
> In March 1911 Sir E. Grey made an important speech defining the British position. He pointed out that the time to oppose the Bagdad Railway, if it was to be opposed in British interests, was before the concession was granted in 1903. It was within the right of the Germans and the Turkish Government to carry out the terms of that concession as they pleased on Turkish territory, but the railways were going to cost money, and the Turkish government had applied for an increase in customs duties which could not be levied without British consent. The British Government would agree to the desired increase in the customs duties if and when they were satisfied that British commercial interests would be safeguarded.
>
> Difficult and prolonged negotiations with Turkey took place

[1] Lord Newton's *Lord Lansdowne*, 254, and Mr. Gooch's *Europe before the War* (1936), I, 32.

[2] Apropos of this arrangement, Grey wrote to Buchanan at St. Petersburg on January 7, 1911: 'I am delighted that Russia should be on the best terms with Germany, so long as that is not allowed to make a breach between her and us.'

in 1913 and resulted in the settlement of a number of outstanding questions. They were of necessity followed by negotiations between London and Berlin, which took place at the Foreign Office. The substance of the arrangements arrived at was as follows. Great Britain undertook not to oppose the Bagdad Railway system, which was carefully defined. Germany undertook not to oppose British control of the navigation of Mesopotamian rivers. It was agreed that the terminus of the line should be at Basra, and the German Government bound themselves in no circumstances, except by agreement with Great Britain, to support the establishment of any port or railway terminus on the Persian Gulf. Both Governments undertook to prevent any discrimination in treatment on the railways or waterways. The German Government recognised the special position of Great Britain on the River Shatt-el-Arab. There were to be British directors on the Bagdad Railway board, and German directors on the River Companies under the chairmanship of Lord Inchcape. The British Government bound themselves not to support the establishment of any railway in direct competition with the Bagdad Railway.[1]

In this way a double object was achieved. Friendly relations with Germany were *pro tanto* secured, and so were our very ancient and very important commercial and political rights in the region of the Persian Gulf, which for centuries past our navy alone had policed and kept open to trade.

If Grey did not resist German expansion in Asia, neither did he resist it upon the African continent. For many years past it had been expected that the financial difficulties of Portugal would ere long force her to sell a part of her African Colonies: she was already seeking loans on the security of their customs. Arthur Balfour had, therefore, in August 1898, signed a Convention with Germany, to settle which of

[1] See also the article in the *Quarterly Review*, October 1917, 'The Bagdad Railway.' See map, page 211, above.

the Portuguese Colonies in Africa should be 'assigned to the British Loan,' and which 'assigned to the German Loan.' The possibility that this financial arrangement would some day lead to a change of political sovereignty on corresponding geographic lines was clearly envisaged in a Secret Convention, also signed by Balfour with Germany on the same day. According to Lord Sanderson, one motive for this Convention with the German Government was 'lest we should find them ranged against us in any questions which might ensue between us and the Boers.'[1]

Nevertheless, on the outbreak of the Boer War in the following year, the British Government reassured Portugal by a Secret Declaration, signed by Lord Salisbury on October 14, 1899, which renewed our ancient historic treaties, as guarantees of Portugal's colonial possessions against attack.[2] Balfour's Secret Convention with Germany agreeing on options for purchase, and Salisbury's Secret Declaration to Portugal against permitting forcible seizure, were not contradictory to one another. But the fact that they were both secret had an unfortunate air of stressing one aspect to Germany and another to Portugal.

Such was the situation that Grey inherited. In 1907, when the Kaiser was in England, a fresh agreement on the future of the Portuguese Colonies was adumbrated but dropped, and again during the Haldane mission of 1912. But in 1912–14 Grey renewed negotiations on a basis highly advantageous to Germany, leaving her wide options for purchase of certain of Portugal's African Colonies, particularly of Angola, the great district on the West Coast. But Grey

[1] *G. and T.* I, 71–73; III, 425.

[2] *G. and T.* I, 93–95. This Declaration is sometimes incorrectly called the 'Windsor Treaty.'

insisted that everything must be published, including the Salisbury Declaration of 1899. He would do nothing behind the back of Portugal, France or the world. The German Government disliked the idea of publication, and so, when war broke out in August 1914, although Grey had initialled this Agreement with Germany, he had not signed it, pending the consent of all parties to publication.

These are the facts. How then can Mr. Harold Nicolson, usually a well-informed writer, accuse Grey of 'negotiating with Germany a secret treaty providing for the partition of the Portuguese Colonies'?[1] On the contrary he was the first British Minister to insist that everything must be done in the open if it were to be done at all. The negotiations had of course been conducted in secret, as all difficult negotiations must be conducted if they are to have any chance of success. But the Treaty, if Grey was to sign it, was to be made known to Portugal and the world. It was only in war time that Grey consented to make secret treaties.

How genuine were these attempts to improve relations with Germany, we have the witness of the German Ambassador. Prince Lichnowsky was now in the place of Metternich and was carrying on his policy of reconciliation between the two countries, with equally little success at Berlin. He writes:[2]

> Sir Edward honestly tried to confirm this *rapprochement*, and his intentions were most apparent on two questions — the Colonial Treaty and the Bagdad Railway Treaty.... The object of the negotiations between us and England was to amend and improve our Agreement of 1898 [as to the Portuguese Colonies], as it had proved unsatisfactory on several points as regards geographical delimitation. Thanks to the accommodat-

[1] *Curzon, the Last Phase*, 40.

[2] *Heading for the Abyss* (Constable), 58–60.

> ing attitude of the British Government, I succeeded in making the new agreement fully accord with our wishes and interests. ... Sir Edward Grey intended to demonstrate his goodwill towards us, but he also wished to assist our colonial development as a whole, as England hoped to divert the German development of strength from the North Sea and Western Europe to the Ocean and to Africa.

Such is the testimony as to 'encirclement' borne by the representative of Germany who had the closest and most frequent dealings with Grey in the years that immediately preceded the war.

The following extracts from Grey's letters about the Portuguese Colonies show the bottom of his mind in the matter:

> *To Sir E. Goschen at Berlin. Fallodon, December* 29, 1911. As to the future it is clear from what Metternich has already said to me that the Germans would like the division of the Portuguese Colonies to take place as soon as possible. So should I.... On every ground material and moral and even Portuguese, it would be better that Portugal should sell her Colonies. *But* how can we of all people put pressure on Portugal to sell: we who are bound by an Alliance to protect and preserve her Colonies for Portugal — an Alliance renewed secretly for value received during the Boer War? And Portugal won't part with her Colonies — any regime in Portugal that did so would be overturned by a revolution — for when nations have gone down hill till they are at their last gasp their pride remains undiminished, if indeed it is not increased. It clings to them as Tacitus says the love of dissimulation clung to Tiberius at his last gasp. However, I am to meet Harcourt next month and study the map of Africa with him in a pro-German spirit: then the Cabinet will review the situation.

Early in 1914 Grey was informed by Bertie that the French were gravely alarmed at the Anglo-German *rapprochement* over the Portuguese Colonies. He replies to Bertie on February 8 that the present negotiations are merely a sequel to the Agreement of 1898, kept hitherto secret, and adds:

> The whole thing is an example of the inconvenience of secret treaties. If this agreement [of 1898] had been published at the time, all the fuss would have been over long ago. But it had been left secret, and subsequently our relations with France had changed; in fact they had been most happily reversed.
>
> *April* 7, 1914, *to Sir E. Goschen*. I cannot undo what was done with Portugal in 1899 and with Germany in 1898, and I must stand by both these agreements. But I will not do, nor if I can help it publish anything that is likely to embarrass Bethmann-Hollweg or Jagow in this matter, or to have an unfavourable effect on German public opinion. On the other hand, I cannot publish the Anglo-German Agreement, without publishing the Anglo-Portuguese Alliance as confirmed in 1899. And I cannot make any new secret Agreement.

In the spring of 1914 Grey committed what was probably, on the balance of considerations, a mistake in permitting the English and Russian naval attachés to 'converse' as to fleet movements in the Baltic in case of war. It is observable that this mistake was an outcome of one of his rare visits to the Continent, when he accompanied King George to Paris in April 1914. On the last day of that visit the French Minister for Foreign Affairs earnestly pressed him to sanction a naval conversation with Russia, because the Russians were asking for it as a guarantee that they were not being cold-shouldered by England.

The case was different from the military conversations with France, which had been imposed by military necessity, and without which the war would have been lost in 1914. The Russian naval conversations were, as Grey confessed in his *Twenty-five Years*, strategically a farce, because 'in a war with Germany, the Russian fleet would not get out of the Baltic and the British fleet would not get into it. But the difficulty of refusing was obvious. To refuse would offend Russia, by giving the impression that she was not treated on equal terms with France.' The British Cabinet agreed to the Russian naval conversations. There was never any 'naval convention,' or any talk of such on the British side.

But unfortunately the affair leaked out in the German press and bitter comments were made. Jagow, the German Foreign Minister, however, told Goschen that he was perfectly satisfied with Grey's explanations in the House of Commons. He declared that he had 'so much confidence in Grey's loyalty and straightforwardness that his mind was now completely at rest.' Grey's answer in the House had in fact been an evasion, though not an untruth. He had neither confessed nor denied that there had been naval conversations, but had repeated that there were no engagements with Russia 'to restrict or hamper the freedom of the Government or of Parliament, whether or not Great Britain should participate in a war,' and that 'no such negotiations were in progress.'

Grey's retrospective comment is as follows:

> The answer given is absolutely true. The criticism to which it is open is, that it does not answer the question put to me. That is undeniable. Parliament has an unqualified right to know of any agreements or arrangements that bind the country to action or restrain its freedom. But it cannot be told of military and naval measures to meet possible contingencies. So long as Governments are compelled to contemplate the possibility of war, they are under a necessity to take precautionary measures, the object of which would be defeated if they were made public.[1]

Nevertheless Grey had in this case been caught in a logical dilemma, for he confesses that his real reasons for consenting

[1] *Twenty-five Years*, II, 126.

to the naval conversations with Russia were political and not strategic. He had in fact been brought to see that military or naval conversations have a political as well as a technical aspect. He had not thought so in 1906 when Campbell-Bannerman and he had neglected to bring the French military conversations before the Cabinet.

In spite of this contretemps, Grey had, by the Bagdad and Colonial negotiations, removed all particular causes of quarrel between England and Germany and had produced a period of better relations by the early summer of 1914. The German Chancellor, Bethmann-Hollweg, writes in his *Reflections*, 'An agreement on Asia Minor questions was on the point of conclusion, and a Colonial agreement was already concluded, when War broke out. The policy of agreements on particular issues had proved itself practicable.' It was indeed not 'particular issues' between Germany and England that caused the war — all these Grey had removed — but the general issue of German conquest of Europe precipitated by German fears of Russia and the irrepressible conflict of Teuton and Slav in the Balkans. England could not, in the interest of her own survival, suffer the Continent to become Germany's vassal. That was the one and the sufficient cause of quarrel between the two nations.

VII

The Outbreak of War

THE assassination at Sarajevo of the Archduke Francis Ferdinand, heir to the Austro-Hungarian throne, took place on June 28, 1914. The crime was only too characteristic of the mentality and political methods of Eastern Europe, which have since the war spread westward apace. But this murder was neither the deed nor the desire of the Serbian Government of the day, which was not ready for another war, and did not wish to see it kindled for some years to come. Princip, the assassin, one of several Bosnian Serbs privy to the plot, was an unwilling subject of Austria-Hungary, but he had recently been in Belgrade, where he had been helped in his preparations by some army officers and some members of the 'Black Hand'; that famous patriot murder-gang was not, however, corporately involved. The assassin doubtless regarded his deed as revenge for the annexation of his own country in 1908, and a blow struck for the creation of the Yugoslavia to be. The news of the murder was greeted in Belgrade by the cruel rejoicings of a people race-mad, as all Europe was shortly to become.

In these circumstances it was inevitable that Austria-Hungary should exact from her neighbours severe guaranties for the cessation of Yugo-Slav agitation in Serbian territory.

Such demands in any compass of reason would have had the sympathy of England and of the world.

Indeed, as part of a settlement made in 1909, the Serbian Government had given pledges against the continuance of Yugo-Slav agitation, and these pledges had notoriously been broken. In 1914 the Viennese Government had already determined to put an end to this state of things. When therefore the murder occurred, Conrad the soldier and Berchtold the statesman seized the occasion to precipitate war with Serbia, by sending to Belgrade an Ultimatum such as no independent State could without qualification accept. And the authorities at Berlin, instead of cautioning their ally, gave her on July 5 what they themselves called a 'blank cheque' to send to Serbia whatever kind of note she wished.

This fatal error was in part the outcome of Kaiser William's first excitement of rage against the atrocity of the murder. Whatever others in Germany may have wished, it is probable that neither he nor Bethmann-Hollweg, on that fatal day, knew that they were unchaining universal war; they hoped that Russia would not dare to fight. It would be 1908 over again, another diplomatic victory of sabre-rattling by the Central Powers.

The authorities in Berlin and Vienna knew that Russian railways and Serbian reorganization would be more formidable in 1917 than in 1914. Russia, they thought, was less likely to march now than she might be in a few years' time. Better crush Serbia at once. Thus the armament race and the fear-struck calculations it everywhere engendered, helped to cause the actual outbreak of the war.

As Grey said in retrospect:

> Practically every nation in Europe was afraid of Germany, and the use which Germany might make of her armaments.

> Germany was not afraid, because she believed her army to be invincible, but she was afraid that a few years hence she might be afraid.... In 1914 Europe had arrived at a point in which every country except Germany was afraid of the present, and Germany was afraid of the future.[1]

Nothing was known of the 'blank cheque' given by the German to the Austro-Hungarian Government on July 5, and for nearly a month after the crime of Sarajevo things went on in very much their accustomed way in the world at large. On July 23, Mr. Lloyd George spoke in the House of Commons, again urging naval economy, the policy on which he had, ever since the New Year, been leading one-half of the Liberal Party, greatly to the embarrassment of the Prime Minister, Grey and Mr. Churchill. The author of the City speech on Agadir had varied his role once more, and was taking another turn among the prophets of pacifism, at a season that chance made peculiarly unfortunate. It was actually on July 23 that he told the House of Commons that our relations with Germany were better than they had been for years and that therefore the next budget ought to show an economy on armaments. That day Vienna sent the Ultimatum to Belgrade.

The long delay in the sending of this astounding document had rendered it impossible for Grey to take any action hitherto. Up till then Grey had had nothing but rumours, some optimistic from Belgrade, some the reverse from Vienna.[2] The least favourable rumour that he heard had only said that Austria-Hungary would probably demand of Serbia 'certain definite measures in restraint of nationalist and anarchist propaganda,' and would insist upon them,

[1] Speech in the House of Lords, July 24, 1924.

[2] On Mr. Fäy's criticisms (*Origins of World War*, II, 263–64) of Grey on this point, see Professor Temperley's reply in *Foreign Affairs, An American Quarterly Review* (January 1931), 319–20.

probably to the point of using force in case of refusal. That in any case was to be expected, but it was not expected that Vienna would claim, as she did claim in clauses 5 and 6 of the Ultimatum, that Austro-Hungarian authorities should collaborate with the Serbian authorities on Serbian territory and that the time-limit for acceptance would be forty-eight hours. The moment that Grey learnt of these terms, he saw that European peace was in the most terrible danger. He was convinced that 'a great European war under modern conditions would be a catastrophe for which previous wars afforded no precedent.' That conviction inspired his conduct during the week of agony that followed. He at once protested to the Austro-Hungarian Ambassador that the Ultimatum was 'the most formidable document I had ever seen addressed by one State to another that was independent'; and that clause 5 and the forty-eight hour time-limit gravely endangered the peace of all Europe. He warned the representative of the Hapsburgs that under modern conditions a great war 'would mean a state of things worse than in 1848, and irrespective of who were victors in the war, many things might be completely swept away.' [1]

The answer of Serbia to the Ultimatum was made within the forty-eight hours, and agreed to very much more than was expected, including even the collaboration of Austro-Hungarian authorities on Serbian territory, subject only to the 'principles of international law.' But every qualification was treated by Vienna as evasion. It was the conquest of Serbia, not her acceptance of the Ultimatum, that had been decided on. Submission was not enough.

Berlin demanded that the execution of Serbia by Austria-Hungary should be regarded as no business of any other

[1] *G. and T.* XI, 70, 73.

State: the war was to be 'localized.' But in fact nothing could prevent Russia from coming to the rescue of Serbia if she were invaded. No calculation as to present military inferiority could stem the surge of popular passion in Russia to save a Slav State from destruction. To permit the subjugation of Serbia would destroy Russia's influence outside her own territories, and lay the Balkan Peninsula at the feet of the Central Powers. To talk of 'localizing' a war to annihilate Serbia was absurd. Yet such was the attitude adopted by Berlin.

Grey set himself with speed and energy to save the situation. The semi-detached position of England gave her advantages as a mediator. Only the year before she had, with the goodwill of Germany, averted war over disputes between Vienna and Belgrade. He therefore proposed a revival of the Conference of Ambassadors in London, the men whose sessions had saved the peace of Europe in 1912–13. If their respective governments would again trust the same men to find a way out for this new dispute between the same two States, Grey was certain that a way would be found. It has been said that it was useless to propose such a Conference because it would have been packed to the disadvantage of the Central Powers. But they had not thought so or found it so in 1913. And the refusal of Germany was not merely a refusal of a Conference in that particular form but of any Conference at all.

For on July 28 Berlin turned down Grey's proposal for a Conference in London, and, so far from proposing a Conference elsewhere or under other conditions, roundly declared that 'Austria's quarrel with Serbia was a purely Austrian concern with which Russia had nothing to do.' Such a declaration meant war.

> The effect of these replies [writes Grey in his *Twenty-five Years*] was not only depressing, but exasperating. I really felt angry with von Bethmann-Hollweg and von Jagow. They had given us to understand that they had not seen the terms of the Austrian Ultimatum to Serbia before it was sent; they had been critical of it when they saw it. Von Jagow had said that, as a diplomatic document, it left something to be desired, and contained some demands that Serbia could not comply with. By their own admission they had allowed their weaker Ally to handle a situation on which the peace of Europe might depend, without asking beforehand what she was going to say and without apparently lifting a finger to moderate her, when she had delivered an ultimatum of the terms of which they did not entirely approve. Now they vetoed the only certain means of a peaceful settlement, without, so far as I knew, even referring it to Austria at all.

After this reply he had, in fact, little hope. The German Government, however, did not at the moment desire war, though it would not tread the sure road to peace. The Kaiser's first mood of unreflecting anger had cooled; he was surprised and impressed by the practical acceptance of the Ultimatum by Serbia and declared there was no longer any cause for war. At his orders the German Government advised her ally to halt in the course of violence on which she had been encouraged to embark. But it was too late. On July 28 Austria-Hungary declared war on Serbia, an act which could not fail to provoke Russian mobilization. Yet at this eleventh hour Germany first asked her to stay her hand, not to push her invasion far into the bowels of Serbia, to hold Belgrade as a pledge and to discuss the situation directly with Russia — after all.

This first and last conciliatory move on the part of Germany came too late. War was being waged on the Danube, and Russia therefore held herself bound to mobilize, if she was to save Serbia. She dared not wait, for mobilization was a slow process in her ill-organized mass, far slower than in the lands ruled by the Central Powers. Russia thought she could not afford to postpone mobilization while Serbia was actually being overrun, and that she must prepare for the hostility not only of Austria-Hungary but of Germany as well. And so, after some vacillations, the Czar on the afternoon of July 30 ordered a general mobilization. But before he had heard of this decision Moltke at Berlin wired to Conrad at Vienna recommending a general mobilization in Austria-Hungary, and adding that Germany would follow suit. In all Central and Eastern Europe the soldiers were in the saddle and rode mankind. At midnight on July 31 Germany sent an Ultimatum to Russia demanding the arrest of her mobilization, and to France demanding her neutrality. On August 1 Germany declared war on Russia. The Kaiser's effort for peace had been late and brief. Grey wrote to Spring Rice on September 18:

> In all the talk of who was responsible for the war, don't forget that Germany, who ostensibly went to war with Russia only because she was Austria's ally, was as a matter of fact at war with Russia on August 1, when Austria was still discussing with Russia in a friendly way. It was not till 5 days later that Russia and Austria were at war, and had they been left alone there would have been no war.

A year later Grey wrote to a friend:

> This war is one of the greatest catastrophes that has ever befallen the human race. The more I think of it, the more horrible it seems to me that Germany refused to agree to a Conference in July last year. Serbia had accepted nine-tenths of the Austrian ultimatum, and the outstanding points could have been settled easily and honourably, if they had been referred to an international Conference: it would not have taken a fortnight to dispose of them. The invasion of Belgium, in my

opinion, decided the overwhelming majority of our people to enter into the war; but the refusal of a Conference decided the fate of peace or war for Europe.

In April 1918 Grey wrote to Professor Gilbert Murray:

> I see Jagow says I could have prevented the war, but the German veto on a Conference struck out of my hand the only effective instrument I could use for peace. I thought the Germans might object to a Conference on the ground that Russia would use it to mobilize, and if Germany had made that her objection I could have protested against Russian mobilization or preparation for war pending a Conference. But Bethmann-Hollweg's objection to a Conference was absolute; and after he had refused and Russia had accepted a Conference I could not protest against Russian preparation for the event of war, especially as the German preparations were far ahead of the Russian, and I could not promise the armed support of this country to Russia.
>
> Von Jagow says Germany could not have accepted a Conference as she would have lost prestige, but he admits she lost no prestige in the London Conference of 1912–13, and the precedent of that was a guarantee that there would have been neither diplomatic defeat nor victory for anyone, but a fair conduct of another Conference composed of the same persons and conducted in the same way. And as Serbia had submitted to about nine-tenths of the Austrian Ultimatum there could have been no loss of prestige in submitting the one or two points outstanding to a fair Conference.

Nothing could now stop the avalanche; it had slipped over the edge. Could Grey have prevented it from being launched? During the rest of his life his sad mind perpetually reverted to the question, trying it again and again from every side, on sleepless nights and blind solitary days. To the end he could not think what more he could have done. Nor have his critics supplied any definite and convincing answer to that question — how could he have prevented the war?

In April 1915, in an unpublished Memorandum, he wrote:

> What Herr Ballin said was, apparently, that I was indirectly responsible for the war, because I had not pledged this country definitely either to support France and Russia, or not to support them. In the former event, Austria would have given way; in the latter, France and Russia would have given way. This was not true; but what it suggested to me was how far Herr Ballin was from understanding what democratic government meant. The idea that one individual, sitting in a room in the Foreign Office, could pledge a great democracy definitely by his word, in advance, either to take part in a great war or to abstain from taking part in it, is absurd.

Herr Ballin's remark was pardonable in a foreigner, but the argument is still repeated by some of Grey's own countrymen who should know more about England and her political institutions.

In April 1918, after the publication in Switzerland, contrary to the author's wishes, of Lichnowsky's memoir of his mission to London, which did full justice to Grey's efforts for peace, he wrote to Mrs. Creighton:

> I knew very well what Lichnowsky thought of me, but I did not suppose it would have become public. I never had any qualm of conscience as to my motives and intentions before the war. I used to torture myself by questioning whether by more foresight or wisdom I could have prevented the war, but I have come to think that no human individual could have prevented it. Nothing could have prevented it except a change of the Prussian nature.

One thing only he sometimes thought he ought to have tried — more direct English pressure on Austria-Hungary. His efforts were mainly directed to inducing Germany to restrain her 'weaker ally.' Would the Viennese soldiers and statesmen have listened to the direct representations of

England, if more strongly urged? It seems highly unlikely, in the light of everything we now know of their policies and temper during the crisis. Nothing but the knowledge that Germany would not support them would have stopped Conrad and Berchtold. Nevertheless Grey's assumption that Germany was the rider and Austria the horse was less true in 1914 than it had been in former years.

The most common line of facile criticism after the event is the assertion that if Grey had told Germany that we should take part in the war, peace would have been kept. This is still repeated, regardless of the fact that Grey could not pledge a country that had not yet come to any such decision. Until July 24, when the terms of the Ultimatum to Serbia became known, English sympathy was with the countrymen of the murdered Archduke; and English opinion takes more than a day to grasp new situations in Eastern Europe. Till the invasion of Belgium by Germany, half the country shrank from the idea of being involved in war over a Balkan question. If Grey, in the last week of July, had announced that we should join France in a European war if it broke out, most of the Cabinet with Mr. Lloyd George at its head would have repudiated him, most of the Liberals in the country and all the Labour Party, and a large section of opinion in the City and the Conservative business class. He could not speak that word for England.

> One danger [he writes], I saw so hideous that it must be avoided and guarded against at every word. It was that France and Russia might face the ordeal of war with Germany, relying upon our support; that this support might not be forthcoming, and that we might then, when too late, be held responsible by them for having let them in for a disastrous war.[1]

[1] *Twenty-five Years*, II, 158.

It is, moreover, overlooked by Grey's critics that in the last week of July he was taking advantage of the semi-detached position of England to negotiate a compromise and avert war, as in 1912–13. If he had declared England unequivocally bound to France and Russia in any event, he would have lost his bargaining power with Germany and Austria-Hungary. Moreover, if France and Russia had felt certain we should fight on their side, they would have been more inclined to take steps that might lead to war. This view was strongly felt and expressed in the Cabinet discussions, as I have been told by several who participated in them. And the view was shared by Sir Eyre Crowe himself, the Assistant Under-Secretary in the Foreign Office, a man who was usually regarded as too anti-German in his views and was certainly more anti-German than Grey. Yet as late as July 31 Eyre Crowe wrote in a minute: 'What must weigh with His Majesty's Government is the consideration that they should not by a declaration of unconditional solidarity with France and Russia *induce* and *determine* these two Powers to choose the path of war.'

Nevertheless, the German Government had ample warning. Time after time, ever since 1906, Grey had been telling them not to rely on our neutrality if they attacked France. In December 1912 the King himself had sent a similar message to the Kaiser through Prince Henry of Prussia, fortified by Haldane's simultaneous words to like effect.[1] Finally on July 29, 1914, Bethmann-Hollweg had the warning again straight, in Grey's indignant refusal of his bid for England's neutrality. The German Chancellor offered, if England kept out of the war, to annex only colonies of France and not any more provinces, after the German victory. The

[1] See page 262 above.

approach was refused in terms which showed the German Government the extreme probability that England would take part in war if war came.

> It would be a disgrace to us [was Sir Edward's reply] to make this bargain with Germany at the expense of France — a disgrace from which the good name of this country would never recover. The Chancellor also, in effect, asks us to bargain away whatever obligation or interest we have as regards the neutrality of Belgium. We could not entertain that bargain either.

Grey in fact could not have done more to warn and restrain Germany and her ally, without making formal declaration of our intention to fight, which public opinion in England would have repudiated and which would, moreover, have encouraged France and Russia to risk war.

For, after all, Russia as well as the Central Powers required restraint. And another charge against Grey is precisely that he did not restrain Russia from mobilization. His answer to this may be given in his own words:

> After Germany refused the Conference, I could not put pressure on Russia. She was far less prepared for war than Germany. If I had tried to hold back her military preparations, Sazonov would at once have said: Then will you help us if war comes? [1]

And, for the reasons given above, Grey could not in July pledge England to fight for Russia, less indeed than for France. When, after Germany's refusal of a Conference and the actual invasion of Serbia, Russia judged that her safety required the slow process of her mobilization to begin, Grey was in no position to interfere.

[1] Notes by Mr. G. P. Gooch of a conversation with Lord Grey on February 14, 1929.

War having been declared by Germany against Russia on August 1, and France being by her Alliance Treaty involved in the quarrel, the question remained, What would England do?

Grey believed that the conquest of France, to which Germany's first and greatest military effort was directed, would mean a German domination of Europe, as irresistible as the Roman Empire, with England for doomed Carthage. And the chances of instant French defeat were very great if we stood aside — they amounted as we now know to certainty. And he was sure that in the sequel we ourselves should be destroyed if we did not enter the war at once and as a united people. But such action on England's part was by no means certain. A false step might have ruined all. In the last days of July and the first three days of August, Grey's object was the same as Asquith's, to keep the Cabinet and the party together, not for party reasons, but because, if the Liberals split, the country would be divided and the result would be irreparable disaster. This fear inspired the anxious care with which he nursed opinion in the Cabinet, avoiding proposals which would have forced on a clash with Mr. Lloyd George and the neutralists, till the tide of events abroad should sweep away all doubts, and Britons had no choice but to say, 'We all are with you now, from shore to shore.' Grey once said to Lord Robert Cecil, 'I used to hope that I was meant to keep the country out of war. But perhaps my real business was to bring her into it unitedly.' [1]

[1] Lest I should seem to be claiming for the author of this biography a prescience he did not possess, I confess that I was a neutralist till the war had begun. Many of us did not realize how completely and how quickly France and Belgium would be defeated without our aid. We were wrong and Grey was right. But for anyone who was a neutralist at that time to blame Grey because he did not earlier declare that we should fight is the height of injustice.

In his speech in the House of Lords on the occasion of Asquith's death in 1928, Grey recalled the situation of that week:

> It is well known that in the early days of the last week of July 1914, the Government were so deeply divided that the division was apparently irreconcilable. The House of Commons was divided. The country was divided. It is my opinion that if there had been a precipitate attempt to force a decision it would not have helped these divisions of opinion, it would have brought them out and made them irreparable. It would be an error to suppose that Asquith in his own mind had not yet settled what the ultimate decision would be. But if the Prime Minister, as Asquith then was, had precipitated a decision, I believe the consequences would have been that at the moment of crisis we should have had a divided Government, a divided Parliament, a divided country.

The difficulty was the greater because Mr. Lloyd George himself was neutralist. Surely, therefore, he displays more than his usual temerity in the following passage in his *Memoirs*:

> Had he [Grey] warned Germany in time of the point at which Britain would declare war — and wage it with her whole strength — the issue would have been different. I know it is said that he was hampered by divisions in the Cabinet. On one question, however, there was no difference of opinion — the invasion of Belgium. He could at any stage of the negotiations have secured substantial unanimity amongst his colleagues on that point.

Mr. Lloyd George's great gifts are not strictly historical. He lives so keenly in the present that he cannot recall his own past, as in his attitude to this question of war in July 1914.

In the last week of July, Belgium had not yet declared that she would resist the passage of German troops, and many well-informed people thought she would come to terms with Germany rather than endure martyrdom. For some years past the British Government had had grave doubts as to what the attitude of Belgium would be, and we could not force her decision. So far, indeed, was she from appealing for our help that she deprecated any premature threat, made over her head to Berlin, that might seem to draw her in as a party to the disputes of the Great Powers. As late as August 2, two days after Grey had asked France and Germany whether they would respect the neutrality of Belgium, and only two days before the actual invasion, the Belgian Foreign Minister informed England that his Government 'have no reason whatever to suspect Germany of an intention to violate her neutrality' and 'have not considered [the] idea of appeal to other guarantee Powers, nor of intervention should a violation occur; they would rely upon their own armed force as sufficient to resist aggression, from whatever quarter it might come.' [1]

It was difficult to be more Belgian than the Belgians, and no one in the Cabinet, neither Mr. Lloyd George nor any other, proposed to raise the question with Germany either sooner or more strongly than Grey actually raised it.

Mr. Churchill bears him witness: he writes in his *World Crisis* (I, 200, 204):

> Every day there were long Cabinets from eleven onwards. Streams of telegrams poured in from every capital in Europe. Sir Edward Grey was plunged in his immense double struggle (*a*) to prevent war, (*b*) not to desert France should it come. I watched with admiration his activities at the Foreign Office and cool skill in Council. Both these tasks acted and reacted on one another from hour to hour. He had to try to make the Germans realize that we were to be reckoned with, without making the French or Russians feel they had us in their

[1] *G. and T.* XI, 271.

> pockets. He had to carry the Cabinet with him in all he did. ... Suppose again, that now after the Austrian ultimatum to Serbia, the Foreign Secretary had proposed to the Cabinet that if matters were so handled that Germany attacked France *or violated Belgian Territory*, Great Britain would declare war upon her. *Would the Cabinet have assented to such a communication? I cannot believe it.* [My italics.]

Several other surviving members of the Cabinet have given me accounts that fully bear out Mr. Churchill's as against Mr. Lloyd George's recollection. Mr. McKenna authorizes me to say that he firmly believes 'that the Cabinet would not have agreed to a threat about Belgium at any earlier stage of the negotiations.' And Lord Crewe has sent me the following statement:

> I did not keep any record of what passed at meetings of the Cabinet in July 1914, but I have a clear recollection of the most important issues that were raised. There was a general knowledge of the Treaties of 1839, and of the action taken by the Foreign Office in Mr. Gladstone's Government of 1870. But I am certain that if Grey or anybody else had suggested an announcement *urbi et orbi* that infringement of Belgian neutrality by anybody would be regarded as an act of war against us, it would have been promptly rejected by the Cabinet.
>
> All through the month, we attempted to exercise a mediating influence; probably the whole Government, including Grey, were a little over-flattered by the success of the Balkan Conference the year before. On this occasion such a spontaneous statement, almost a threat, would have been considered like the action of somebody sitting down to play a round game and saying to the party 'I suppose we may assume that nobody is going to cheat this evening.' On the other hand, Morley's statement in his *Memorandum on Resignation* (page 14), that Belgium 'played only a secondary part throughout our deliberations,' is coloured, as so many of these reminiscences are, by the personal prejudice of the writer. He seems to have thought that the Cabinet was divided between those

who, like himself, were determined to keep out of war at any price, and those who were only anxious to find an excuse for taking part in it. Whereas the great majority belonged to neither class. It has to be remembered, too, that though the invasion of Belgium was likely, and had been generally contemplated in the 'military conversations' that had taken place, it was by no means certain. Ten years later, when I was at the Paris Embassy, I was told on the highest authority that the French General Staff had foreseen the possibility of a German attack through Switzerland, and had made complete provision to meet it in concert with the Swiss General Staff.

I have never been one of those who are able to believe for a moment that the German attitude would have been modified by knowledge that we should resist the invasion of Belgium. Surely those who think so are confusing their knowledge of the power which we and the whole Empire were able to exert in the four years of war with the actual resources which everybody, including ourselves, knew to be available in August 1914.

CREWE

2 *May* 1936

The contemporary notes of the Prime Minister and his letters to the King[1] are positive evidence that the Cabinet discussed the Belgian question inconclusively as late as July 30 and 31, and considered that 'the matter if it arises will be rather one of policy, than of legal obligation.' It is clear from Asquith's notes, as well as from the evidence of other Cabinet Ministers that I have quoted above, that before August 2 the Cabinet would not have been agreed on the Belgian issue. Mr. Lloyd George, after opposing participation in the war, at the last moment became fired with a generous enthusiasm for Belgium. No one need blame him for being temperamental, for he has the qualities of his defects. But his retrospective creation of situations that never

[1] Quoted on pages 304–06 below.

existed, in order to cast blame on others, is unworthy of the great part he has played in the world's affairs.

Grey's own account of the situation is more generous and more true:

> In the Cabinet the two groups continued to work together for the one object on which both were heartily agreed, to prevent a European war; like two men who walk side by side on a straight road, but who see ahead a parting of the ways, and are determined, when they come to it, to go one to the right and the other to the left. Meanwhile, one side did not press the other to authorise a pledge to France; the other did not press for an intimation to France that we should stand aside. In that, at any rate, both were wise. Between the two groups were no doubt members of the Cabinet who reserved their decision. Their attitude also was to be respected. It was not opportunism; it was a tribute paid to the gravity of the situation. The Cabinet as a whole knew that it was not in a position to pledge the country.[1]

When on August 1, European war had broken out, the parting of the roads had come. But still for two or three days opinion in the Cabinet and country seemed to hang in the balance, though moving by rapid stages towards intervention. On July 31, when war was on the point of breaking out and Grey's peace efforts had clearly failed, he obtained the consent of the Cabinet to ask France and Germany simultaneously whether in the event of war they would respect the neutrality of Belgium. That at least he could do without waiting to know what would be the final attitude of Belgium to accepting our protection if offered, or that of the Cabinet and country to offering it. France replied that she would respect the neutrality of Belgium; Germany refused to reveal her war plans.

[1] *Twenty-five Years*, II, 193.

On the morning of August 2 (John Burns resigning), the Cabinet sanctioned yet another step; Grey was permitted to say to Cambon:

> I am authorized to give an assurance that if the German fleet comes up the Channel or through the North Sea to undertake hostile operations against French coasts or shipping, the British fleet will give all the protection in its power. This assurance is of course subject to the policy of His Majesty's Government receiving the support of Parliament and must not be taken as binding His Majesty's Government to any action until the above contingency of action by the German fleet takes place.... We thought it necessary to give them this assurance. It did not bind us to go to war with Germany unless the German fleet took the action indicated, but it did give a security to France that would enable her to settle the disposition of her own Mediterranean fleet.[1]

The British fleet, kept together after the recent manœuvres, was in effect already mobilized.

On the same day the leaders of the Conservative Opposition, hearing that the Cabinet was still divided, wrote to the Prime Minister that in their view 'any hesitation in now supporting France and Russia would be fatal to the honour and the future security of the United Kingdom.' Nothing was here said of Belgium. But in the course of the next two days (August 3–4) the violation of her territory, and her appeal for the help of Britain as one of the guarantors, swept

[1] *G. and T.* XI, 274. Mr. Churchill is, I think, not quite accurate in writing (*World Crisis*, I, 217) that Grey had given Cambon this assurance on August 1; he gave it on the afternoon of August 2, after the Cabinet authorization. What Grey really said to Cambon on August 1 will be found in *G. and T.* XI, 260. It was this: 'The French might be sure that the German fleet would not pass through the channel, for fear that we should take the opportunity of intervening, when the German fleet would be at our mercy. I promised, however, to see whether we could give any assurance that, in such circumstances, we would intervene.' And he duly consulted the Cabinet on that point next day and got the authorization. On this point see Professor Temperley's study of the question in *Foreign Affairs, an American Quarterly Review*, January 1931, pages 333–35.

round the hesitating opinion in the country and in the Cabinet to join in the war already raging in Europe.

By the Treaty of 1839, reaffirmed in 1870, England was 'liable for the maintenance of Belgian neutrality whenever either Belgium or any of the guaranteeing Powers are in need of and demand assistance in opposing its violation.' Such was our moral, and as some held our legal, obligation. Moreover it was the oldest and clearest of British interests to preserve the Netherlands from occupation by a great military and naval power, which modern weapons at land and sea would render a far more pressing danger to this island than in the days of Philip II, Louis XIV or Napoleon. Our moral and quasi-legal duty, and our interest in self-preservation, were therefore at one. The real danger to Belgian independence now lay all from the German side, but both Grey and our military authorities had been very insistent with France that her soldiers should not permit themselves to contemplate entry into Belgian territory in 'anticipation' of German invasion. This had been made a condition of the Military Conversations of 1906, and again, as Joffre's *Memoirs* testify, in 1912. French action in 1914 showed a scrupulous respect for this understanding. Moreover, in April 1913 Grey, in a conversation with the Belgian Minister, had given him the assurance that he asked, that Britain would on no account send troops into his country in anticipation of Germany or any other Power. But, Grey had then said to him, 'what we had to consider, and it was a somewhat embarrassing question, was what it would be desirable and necessary for us, as one of the guarantors of Belgian neutrality, to do if Belgian neutrality was violated by any other Power.' [1] In commenting on the record of this

[1] *G. and T.* IX, 787–88, Grey's letter to *The Times* of November 21, 1932, dealing with the Hardinge Minute of 1908.

conversation of 1913 in a letter to his friend Lady Selborne on December 15, 1914, Grey writes:

> I am glad that I did not say to the Belgian Minister that, if Germany violated the neutrality of Belgium, we would certainly assist Belgium: for then I should have been open to the charge that I had instigated Belgium to resist, and then had proved unable to save her from the immediate consequences of resistance, which she is now suffering so terribly. My reason for not giving, in the conversation, a pledge to take action if the neutrality of Belgium was violated was that such a pledge was not a thing that one could give without consulting the Cabinet. The pledge not to violate Belgian neutrality was, of course, a simple thing.

This letter illustrates one of the marked characteristics of Grey. He was always scrupulous not to lure other countries into false positions by promises of British support which he hoped and wished to give, but which he was not certain to be able to supply when the time came. Whether this scrupulosity sometimes hampered his policy may be argued, but at least it prevented him from landing his country, as she has sometimes been landed, in disgraceful situations due to arousing expectations not fulfilled in the event.

At the beginning of August the main German armies, far the most formidable array ever seen on this planet, were rolling westward, not against Russia, but against the French and Belgian frontiers. On the evening of Sunday, August 2, the German Ultimatum reached Brussels. Grey had been living for some days past with his best friend Haldane, with whom he had no shadow of difference, public or private.

> Under my roof [writes Haldane] he was sparing no effort to avoid the catastrophe. I was helping him with such counsel as I could give, but he was splendidly self-reliant. Telegrams and despatches were coming in at all hours of the night. In order

> that he might get sleep, I had a servant sitting up with instructions to bring them to my bedroom and waken me so that I might open the boxes with my Cabinet key and decide whether it was necessary to break in on Grey's rest. After dinner on Sunday, August 2, a despatch came saying Belgium was likely to be invaded. We talked it over and then walked across to No. 10 Downing Street to see the Prime Minister.

Asquith agreed that the army must be mobilized, and, as War Minister,[1] gave Haldane written authority to go next day to the War Office, where he was so well known and respected, and arrange for the mobilization to take place.

Next day, Monday, August 3, was the date of decision. The Cabinet met, in a different mood from the previous morning, when, in Mr. Churchill's opinion, it had 'looked as if the majority would resign.' Now they sanctioned the mobilization and all save a very few agreed that we had no option but to defend Belgium in arms. Mr. Lloyd George had at last come round, and his tardy enthusiasm launched itself in a crusade from which he was not again to turn back. That same morning the all-important news came through that Belgium had refused the German Ultimatum, and King George received from King Albert a 'supreme appeal to the diplomatic intervention of Your Majesty's Government to safeguard the integrity of Belgium.' 'Diplomatic intervention' had already been tried in vain on July 31; it could now only be repeated in the form of an ultimatum to Germany to keep her hands off Belgium or be at war with Britain. Such were the circumstances under which, early on Monday afternoon, Grey went down to the House of Commons to face the greatest and most tragic occasion of his life.

He came to give utterance to the opinion, as it had now

[1] After the Curragh crisis earlier in the year the Prime Minister was acting as War Minister also.

become, of the great majority of the Cabinet.[1] What the House and the country would think had still to be put to the test; that made his speech momentous.

In these circumstances it was very remarkable that he deliberately eschewed all appeal to passion, both in the tones of his voice, the choice of his words, and even in the facts that he selected for comment. A lesser man would have striven to snatch a verdict by the power of oratory, and by narrating and denouncing the crimes that Germany had committed against the cause of peace during the negotiations of the past weeks. But Grey wished England's great decision to be made in cool blood. He wanted a rational judgment of the situation as it was, and as it might be expected to become if we still clung to neutrality — or if we chose to fight. He feared also that if he appealed to passion on his side, he would provoke it on the other, and divide his colleagues and his countrymen more sharply into the partisans of peace and of war. Few would have used such restraint, but he had his reward both that day and in the memory of the world.

Gaunt from weeks of ceaseless toil and deepening misery, pressed every moment on every side by fresh imperious tasks, harrowed by those painful interviews with Cambon, whom he could not yet assure that we would stand by France, he had had no time to think what words he would use to the House; he had only, on Sunday evening, found time to arrange into notes the material of which his head was full, selecting the facts he would state, the arguments he would use, and the order in which they should come. The

[1] Apparently there never was a formal decision taken in the Cabinet to go to war or to send an ultimatum to Germany. But, Morley and Burns having resigned, the opposition in the Cabinet melted away and after Grey's speech in the Commons was no longer heard of.

words must look after themselves. About three on Monday afternoon he came into the House, crowded to the roof and tense with doubt and dreadful expectation, as seldom before in all its long and famous history. Years afterwards he told his friend Mildred Lady Buxton that, as he sat there waiting to speak, he remembered having seen the House similarly thronged and expectant when Gladstone was to introduce his first Home Rule Bill, and he himself had sat there obscure, a young bridegroom member from the North: on a wave of emotion he saw the sorrowful passage of time, all that had happened since then, hope doubly blasted, Dorothy's death and now this universal darkness of which he seemed the central point; he almost burst into tears. Yet, when the moment came for him to rise, he writes:

> I do not recall feeling nervous. At such a moment there could be neither hope of personal success nor fear of personal failure. In a great crisis, a man who has to act or speak stands bare and stripped of choice. He has to do what is in him to do: just this is what he will and must do, and he can do no other.[1]

And so he rose. A fairer speech was never made by a party to a quarrel, nor a more effective. He did not tell the story of his own recent efforts to preserve the peace of Europe and Germany's rejection of them. On that subject, when he might so easily have gained applause by rousing indignation against Germany, he simply referred the House to the papers about to be published.

> We worked for peace up to the last moment, and beyond the last moment. How hard, how persistently, and how earnestly we strove for peace last week, the House will see from the Papers that will be before it.

[1] *Twenty-five Years*, II, 215.

That famous 'White Paper,' indeed, which could not be brought out in time for the debate, proved his immediate justification and Germany's indictment, before his countrymen, America, and the world.

But the first part of his speech was not devoted to this easy theme, but to the necessary business of letting the House know, before it came to the decision of peace or war, how far if at all we were committed to France. 'It was essential to make clear to the House,' he wrote in his *Twenty-five Years*, 'that its liberty of decision was not hampered by any engagements entered into previously without its knowledge. Whatever obligation there was to France arose from what those must feel who had welcomed, approved, sustained the Anglo-French friendship, that was open and known to all.' The story of the Entente, the Military Conversations, the distribution of the two fleets since 1912, yesterday's pledge to France to hold the Channel, was fully told. To sum up, Were we committed to France? — technically not at all; whether morally, 'let every man look into his own heart, his own feelings and construe the extent of the obligation for himself.'

Then, for the last half of his speech he turned to Belgium, and here the sense that the House was with him began to prevail. He cited the commitments of 1839 and 1870, by which we had bound ourselves to guarantee Belgium, and he read to the House King Albert's appeal to King George received that morning. Then he added:

> If Belgium's independence goes, the independence of Holland will follow. I ask the House, from the point of view of British interests, to consider what is at stake. If France is beaten in a struggle of life and death, beaten to her knees, becomes subordinate to the will and power of one greater than

herself... I do not believe, for a moment, that at the end of this war, even if we stood aside and remained aside, we should be in a position, a material position, to use our force decisively to undo what had happened in the course of the war, to prevent the whole of Western Europe opposite to us — if that had been the result of the war — falling under the domination of a single Power, and I am quite sure that our moral position would be such as to have lost us all respect.

The main purport of his speech was to place our obligation to Belgium, which as a sentiment of pity and honour was more clearly felt in England than any other aspect of affairs, in its true and direct relation to the larger question of our duty to defend Western Europe from conquest by Central Europe, in order that our own independence and that of the small States of Europe might be prolonged into another age.

To the persuasiveness of the speech witness was borne by Lord Hugh Cecil, a detached intellect not easily satisfied, who had come down to the House in a critical mood. He wrote to his friend Wilfrid Ward:

Grey's speech was very wonderful — I think in the circumstances one may say the greatest speech delivered in our time or for a very long period, taking the importance of the occasion, the necessity of persuading many doubtful persons, the extraordinary success which it had in that direction, its great dignity, warm emotion and perfect taste.... I could deliver quite a lecture on the merits of the speech — its admirable arrangement, its perfect taste, and the extraordinary dexterity with which he dealt with the weak spot of his argument. This was the nature of our obligation to France, under the Entente. With wonderful skill he did not argue the point, but he changed to a note of appeal to the individual conscience, thereby disarming criticism in the one matter where he was weak, without any departure real or apparent from perfect sincerity. All these substantial merits set off by his wonderful manner go to make his speech the greatest example of the art of persuasion that I have ever listened to.

During the last part of his speech, when he came to deal with the Belgian question, it became apparent for the first time that almost the whole House approved. The news that 'they have cheered him' was carried to the Foreign Office, causing inexpressible relief to those who knew better than the public that if we stood arguing together on the verge of war the Germans would be in Paris in a few weeks and England left shamed, friendless and foredoomed.

Grey was briefly followed by Bonar Law and John Redmond, pledging the Conservatives and the Irish to the war, and by Mr. Ramsay MacDonald stating the position of the dissentients. Shortly afterwards Grey received and read to the House the official news of the German Ultimatum to Belgium and its rejection by King Albert's Government 'as a flagrant violation of the rights of nations.' The news, though merely confirming a situation known some hours before, had arrived too late to form a part of his speech, which would have been simplified and strengthened in its wording if he could have spoken of the Ultimatum and its rejection as facts already accomplished.

That night, as the lamps were being lit in the summer dusk, Grey, standing in the windows of his room in the Foreign Office overlooking St. James's Park, said to a friend: 'The lamps are going out all over Europe; we shall not see them lit again in our lifetime.'

On August 4 Grey telegraphed our Ultimatum to Berlin, protesting against the violation of Belgian territory and requiring a satisfactory reply by midnight. The hour arrived, eleven P.M. by our Greenwich time, while he was sitting with the Prime Minister in the Cabinet room at Downing Street. We were at war.

In his first great object, to preserve the peace of Europe, Grey had failed, in spite of all his efforts. And no man felt the failure more bitterly than he. 'I hate war, I hate war,' was his cry, when Nicolson came to his room in the Foreign Office to congratulate him on the speech with which he had convinced the House of England's duty. No pacifist realized more clearly than he the irreparable damage to civilization that must ensue from war under modern conditions. Nor would he get any compensatory thrill from its pomp and circumstance. It was all against the grain to him, sheer waste, contrary to the slow peace and growth of nature that was his soul's life. He would go out of his way to avoid a company of Kitchener's recruits marching down the cheering street; the sight merely cut him to the heart. Indeed his want of interest in the military side of things may be held a serious shortcoming in his equipment as Foreign Minister. For some days after the outbreak of war he was irritable to his assistants and secretaries, for the first and only time in his long years at the Foreign Office. Then his self-command and sweetness of temper returned; but not his happiness. His heart had been broken, for the second time in his life.

He had failed in his first object, to preserve peace. But he was destined to succeed in his second object, to prevent the establishment of German military rule over Europe. Thanks to him, Britain as a united country entered the war just in time to save France from immediate conquest, from which she could never have risen again, and which must have been speedily followed by our own ruin. In that autumn, when all round the globe men and peoples judged as spectators or took sides as actors in the most awful conflict in history, Grey stood in the world's mind as the representative of England's case. To him was largely due the impression that right was on our side. The idea that men had acquired of his character during the past nine years; his efforts for peace in the last crisis as shown in the documents published; and the great fact of the invasion of Belgium, gave us from the first that moral advantage which German methods of conducting war only increased as the struggle went on. So felt the Dominions and the whole Empire that marched at once. So felt many in the various neutral countries, some more friendly and some less, whose action or inaction helped to decide the event; till America, whose friendship Grey had always sought in peace and in war, saved the Allies in the end.

NOTE

The following quotations from Asquith's contemporary record of Cabinet proceedings bear out the evidence of other Cabinet Ministers, quoted in the text above, that Grey could not, as Mr. Lloyd George now says he should, have obtained Cabinet sanction at an earlier date to threaten Germany with war if Belgium were invaded.[1]

> Asquith to the King. July 30, 1914. The Cabinet carefully reviewed the obligations of this country in regard to the neutrality, arising out of the two Treaties of April 1839, and action which was taken by Mr. Gladstone's Government in August 1870. It is a doubtful point how far a single guaranteeing State is bound under the Treaty of 1839 to maintain Belgian neutrality if the remainder abstain or refuse. The Cabinet consider that the matter if it arises will be rather one of policy than of legal obligation. After much discussion it was agreed that Sir E. Grey should be authorized to inform the

[1] Spender and Cyril Asquith's *Life of Asquith* (Hutchinson), II, 81–85.

German and French Ambassadors that at this stage we are unable to pledge ourselves in advance, either under all conditions to stand aside, or in any conditions to join in.

. . . .

July 31 (*Asquith's Contemporary Notes*). We had a Cabinet at 11 and a very interesting discussion, especially about the neutrality of Belgium, and the point upon which everything will ultimately turn — are we to join or stand aside? Of course everybody longs to stand aside, but I need not say that France, through Cambon, is pressing strongly for a reassuring declaration. Edward Grey had an interview with him this afternoon, which he told me was rather painful. He had, of course, to tell Cambon, for we are under no obligation, that we could give no pledges and that our actions must depend upon the course of events, including the Belgian question and the course of public opinion here.

. . . .

August 1. There was no fresh news this morning. Lloyd George, all for peace, is more sensible and statesmanlike for keeping the position open. Grey declares that if an out-and-out and uncompromising policy of non-intervention is adopted, he will go. Winston very bellicose and demanding immediate mobilization. The main controversy pivots upon Belgium and its neutrality.

. . . .

If it comes to war I am sure we shall have a split in the Cabinet.

. . . .

August 2. We had a long Cabinet from 11 to 2, which very soon revealed we were on the brink of a split. There is a strong party against any kind of intervention in any event. Grey of course will never consent to this, and I shall not separate myself from him. Crewe, McKenna and Samuel are a moderating intermediate body.

But the second Cabinet held on August 2 seems to have

come nearer to agreement as regards Belgium, to judge by the following letter:

Lord Crewe to the King

August 2.

Lord Crewe presents his humble duty to Your Majesty, and has the honour on behalf of the Prime Minister to submit the report of the Cabinet held at 6.30 this evening....

As regards Belgium, it was agreed, without any attempts to state a formula, that it should be made evident that a substantial violation of the neutrality of that country would place us in a situation contemplated as possible by Mr. Gladstone in 1870, when interference with Belgian independence was held to compel us to take action.

VIII

Grey's Foreign Policy During the War—I: Eyesight—Haldane—The Expeditionary Force—Balkans—Italy

In time of peace the function of foreign policy is twofold: to avert war; and to secure that, if in spite of all war should come, the country shall not lack allies and friends. Grey had failed in the first and succeeded in the second. But when war has actually broken out, the issue is changed: the function of foreign policy is no longer to avert war, but to win it. In a desperate struggle for existence such as that in which England and the Empire were now involved, policy must adopt a technique and an ethical code somewhat different from those of normal times. For instance, Grey abandoned the principle which he had himself introduced into our peacetime policy, that there must be no secret treaties; under the duress of war he made secret treaties with Russia, Italy and Rumania.

But policy, even when it is the handmaid of war, must not be the slave of military and naval advisers, as it became in Germany with such fatal results. Grey saw that to throw to the winds all consideration for others is wrong even in wartime, and is not even the road to victory. In spite of much shrill advice he steadily refused to make mistakes corresponding to those of our antagonist, particularly in the matter of contraband. He thereby kept on terms with neutrals and prevented Sweden and the United States from passing into the ranks of our enemies. Moreover, he thought that he saw beyond the blackness a faint dawn of hope for mankind, in the idea of a League of Nations to maintain peace when it should return. From January 1915 onwards he worked for that end with the statesmen who then controlled American policy. His relations with Colonel House and thereby indirectly with Wilson were his greatest personal contribution to the policy that in the end won the war and founded the League of Nations.

In refusing to sacrifice prudence and humanity to the spirit of Mars, he was following his natural instincts. On October 14, 1914, he wrote to Sir Francis Blake:

> Have you read Bernhardi's and Treitschke's books? I really knew nothing of them before the war, but they reveal a deliberate purpose and an animosity that are appalling. Every ideal except that of force is abolished: and truth, honour, kindliness, uprightness are all to go by the board in the interest of Germany and force. War is deliberately to be made horrible and terrible, that people may fear to resist German domination.
>
> That is the sort of character that Prussian militarism has developed in its Officers: for it is the Prussian Junkers alone, I believe, who have created all this, and the rest of the Germans are people more akin to ourselves than any other race. It would be better that we should all perish than fall under the domination of the Junker spirit and people.

It was an irony of fate that the man who of all politicians had been the most anxious to retire into private life remained for eleven years at the Foreign Office, and sacrificed his eyesight in order to complete the term.

Sir William Lister has been good enough to write me the following letter about Grey's eyesight in 1914:

February 18, 1936.

I will of course with pleasure place any information I have at your disposal with regard to Lord Grey's sight.

Immediately before the War he was under the care of Mr. Angus McNab of Harley Street, and I was called into consultation with him on one occasion only in May or early June of 1914, just before the Serajevo murders; McNab was killed in France during the first few months of the War and I was in France throughout the War, and during this period he saw various doctors and unqualified practitioners. It was in October 1930 when he again consulted me, and by this time his sight was extremely limited.

McNab and I found in 1914 he had severe degeneration of the retina and choroid in each eye, which no doubt had started very gradually years before.

This was causing impairment of the sharpness of his sight necessitating stronger and stronger magnifying glasses for reading as time went on. It also caused both restriction of his field of vision and at the same time areas of blindness in the field, making the sight patchy and uncertain, so that at one moment he could see an object and at the next it was lost. It is a condition in which the delicate tissues of the retina and choroid are destroyed beyond repair and the tendency is for the process gradually to progress. It is therefore one which cannot be *cured.* All one can aim at is to endeavour to retard the degenerative process by keeping up the general health to the best possible standard and avoiding both bodily and ocular fatigue.

Knowing nothing of the brewing turmoil in the European situation, McNab and I strongly urged that he should take a prolonged holiday, so as to give his eyes every chance of stabilizing. To this he replied he was afraid such a course was quite impossible, but at the time he could naturally not divulge the reason.[1]

This answers your third question — 'Was he warned?' He was very definitely warned and urged to take a rest.

[1] The reason was at the moment the Irish crisis; a few weeks later the continental crisis and the War. — G. M. T.

> In your second question you ask whether continuance in office destroyed the chance of recovering his eyesight?
>
> As already stated, nothing known could have brought about a cure, but I have little doubt that the strain of his life and his work combined with constant reading had a definitely deleterious effect on his sight.
>
> The condition he had would inevitably have got worse, but he voluntarily gave up the chance of impeding the deterioration and in this way I feel he gave his sight in the service of his Country.

On April 22, 1915, Grey wrote to Sir Francis Blake, referring to these circumstances:

> In May last year two oculists, who had a consultation on my eyes advised me to give up work and go away for six months, and they said it would be imperative for me to do this if my eyes got worse. I could not well leave my colleagues in the Irish crisis and I postponed a decision till the end of the session. Before the session ended the war came: and I could not think of giving up work whatever the risk or cost to my eyes. But my eyes have got worse lately and a third independent opinion is positive that the trouble is serious and that to correct it I ought to undergo treatment and give up using my eyes for some time. I have decided therefore to withdraw from office as soon as I feel I can be spared.

But he could not be spared for another year and a half.

Some weeks' holiday in April and again in June 1915 were needed to stave off blindness. After that he was warned not to use his eyes for reading or writing more than two hours a day, but, as he wrote to a friend: 'I can't keep to that as far as reading is concerned when there is great pressure of work.' And so it went on till December 1916, when the reconstruction of the Ministry by Mr. Lloyd George released him, with ruined eyesight and by that time with gravely impaired health. He could scarcely have gone on working longer, even

Elliott & Fry

AET. 56, 1918

if political circumstances had not opened the way to his retreat.

The moment when he had most wished to resign, but was restrained by Asquith and the general voice, was on the formation of the Coalition Cabinet in May 1915, not because he objected to Coalition but because he deeply resented the exclusion of Haldane. He regarded the Lord Chancellor's dismissal as giving some apparent official sanction to the base yelping that had been raised against his friend ever since the war began, the flood of anonymous letters Haldane had received, and the lies that had been circulated about him. The bestiality that war lets loose, not least in a country like ours unaccustomed for a century past to any real sense of danger to itself, was vented on 'the traitor' Haldane, 'the friend of the Germans.'[1]

It was, as Haig and our soldiers have told us, due to Haldane more than to any other man that we had a formidable Expeditionary Force ready to go to France, and plans for sending it. Grey knew that well. The Military Conversations and the Haldane Reforms were the two parts of a scheme to save France from sudden overthrow that just, and only just, sufficed. But to a certain class of civilian journalist and stay-at-home all this was nothing. War mania required a series of victims, and Haldane was selected as the first.

On January 25, 1915, Grey wrote the following letter to Lord Derby:

> My dear Derby:
>
> Mrs. Asquith writes to me that you told her there was a story, universally believed on your side, which you would much like her to enquire into from me: the story being that

[1] It was a little later, in 1917, that an Italian friend of mine, who knew England well, said to me: 'England has made great sacrifices for the war: she has even sacrificed her respectability.'

there was a ship laden with copper, which I had held up at Gibraltar, and which Haldane instantly let go when I went for a short holiday, leaving him in charge in the Foreign Office. I would much rather deal with this sort of thing direct, and so I am writing to you.

There is not one word of truth in the story. The holding up and releasing of ships is dealt with by an Inter-departmental Committee on which the Admiralty, as well as the Foreign Office, is represented. The Admiralty representative is Leverton Harris, who has done real good service on the Committee. There were cases in which ships were released without consulting the Committee, but the last of these happened many weeks ago, long before Haldane set a foot in the Foreign Office, and he had nothing to do with them. For several weeks past, no ship has been released except through the Committee. If I intervene in the matter at all, I do so in what seems to be a special case, which I ask the Committee specially to consider. The machinery goes on automatically as a rule without reference to me. Haldane has never, whether in the Foreign Office or outside, intervened in the proceedings of the Committee; and, if any ships were released while he was temporarily in the Foreign Office, it was done automatically, not only without his intervention but without his knowledge.

That disposes of one particular lie; but I cannot express to you how indignant I feel about the attacks on Haldane. To him specially, more than to the whole of the rest of the Cabinet put together, it is due that, when the war broke out, we had the Territorials at home and an Expeditionary Force to send abroad. The actual decision of the Cabinet to send the Expeditionary Force to France when it was sent was, of course, one on which Kitchener, who was actually in the War Office at the time, had specially to advise the Cabinet, and the Prime Minister to guide it; but, apart from that, to Haldane's opinion as ex-Minister for War, under whom the Force had been created and organised, it was due — more than to any other individual member of the Cabinet — that the decision was taken to send the Force to the Continent on the outbreak of the War. To Haldane and those who worked under him in the War Office when he was there as Secretary of State for War, it was due not only that we had an Expeditionary Force to send abroad, but that we had artillery, ammunition, and other equipment for it, which enabled it to be the efficient Force it has proved itself to be, as well as to stand the strain of a continuous expenditure of artillery ammunition lasting over many weeks: an expenditure more continuous than had been anticipated even by any Continental Army.

The fact that we had not an equipment of artillery, rifles, and ammunition to enable us in a short time to send a Force of 1,000,000 men to the Continent is a thing for which Haldane is no more responsible than my one else: for no one ever intended, proposed, or suggested that this country should prepare such an equipment. If Haldane had proposed it, the Cabinet would not have agreed to it; and I believe that, if the Cabinet had proposed it, Parliament and the country would not have endorsed it during the time that Haldane was in the War Office, or indeed at any time before the War.

I hear you spoke to Mrs. Asquith in a friendly way of Haldane, so please do not take the somewhat downright tone of this letter as being intended to convey any reproach to you personally, though it is mild as moonshine compared to what would happen if I could get one of the real authors of the attacks upon Haldane alone in a room with me for ten minutes. There is a more than Prussian injustice in selecting him for attack. I have written very frankly to you, because I know you have a sense of fair play to which I can appeal with confidence.

To this Lord Derby sent the following straightforward reply, a generous letter considering the poisoned atmosphere of the time when it was written:

My dear Grey:

Very many thanks for taking the trouble to write to me with regard to the copper ship story about which I spoke to Mrs. Asquith. I shall be very glad to contradict the story. I can assure you that it had gained widespread credence.

May I say I entirely agree with what you say about Haldane and the Territorial Force? I have been a strong supporter of his scheme from the very beginning. I believe, as he did, in the Territorials and I am glad to think they have justified the confidence that was placed in them and their creation must always stand to his great credit.

You speak frankly in your letter to me. I equally will speak frankly to you. There are criticisms that can be made against Haldane's administration at the War Office some of which he may be able to answer, some he may not, but I entirely disagree with any criticism of any action of his being made a personal affair. I have never attacked him personally myself nor shall I do so. At the same time I cannot disguise from myself that quite apart from his administration at the War Office Haldane is very much disliked by my own political party. Although all hatchets are for the moment buried one cannot entirely forget all that went on before this War broke out. I think the chief reason for the attack on him at the present moment is due to this feeling of resentment against him.

Personally I like Haldane. There have been occasions when I have differed from him pretty strongly on military matters but I repeat that I have not and I will not be any party to the personal attack that is now being made on him.

When three months later the Coalition was formed, and one of the conditions of Conservative co-operation was that Haldane should go, the following correspondence passed on that occasion:

Grey to Asquith. May 26, 1915. My dear Asquith, It had, as you know, been my intention not to remain in the Government, unless Haldane were included in it. I need not enter into the reasons that have made it impossible for me to give effect to my personal preference at the moment.

I think, however, that it should be known how extraordinarily unjust are the attacks that have been made upon Haldane in certain quarters. I understand that he has been accused of intriguing with Germany behind the back of his colleagues; of weakening the Army, more particularly reducing the artillery; and of opposing or obstructing the sending of an Expeditionary Force to France. The true facts are that he has had no dealings with German authorities that were not undertaken either at the request or with the full knowledge and consent of his Colleagues, including particularly myself. It was due to the work done by him in the War Office that there was an Expeditionary Force of a certain strength and with a full equipment of artillery, ready to be sent abroad; but for his work, the Force would not have been available at a moment's notice. The effective artillery was strengthened, and not diminished, while he was in the War Office. Probably, inside the War Office, he laid it down that no orders were to be given for the despatch of the Expeditionary Force to the Continent without the authority of the Cabinet; but no doubt your recollection will confirm mine that, in council, he was one of those who most strongly advocated the despatch of the Expeditionary Force, when necessary, and no proposal to send it abroad met with opposition from him at any time. The Territorials and their organization, which has proved such an invaluable strength in this emergency, were created by him. He brought the Army to the very maximum strength, in numbers and equipment, which his colleagues were prepared to propose to Parliament, and which Parliament was prepared, as far as I can judge, to sanction before the war. Throughout the last ten years, there is no Colleague from whom I personally have, in policy, received more consistent encouragement and support. He possessed, and I believe possesses, in a peculiar degree, the confidence and goodwill of the soldiers who worked with him in the War Office: some of whom now hold the highest commands in the Field.

That, after this, Haldane of all people should have been singled out for the special sort of attack that has been made upon him, and accused of lack of patriotism or public spirit, is an intolerable instance of gross injustice, of malice, or of madness. His friends gratefully recognise that the larger part of the Press has never associated itself with these charges and has expressed due appreciation of his work. The authors of such attacks are perhaps incorrigible, and incapable either of fairness or knowledge; but I do not think that this moment should pass without the public — some of whom have been misled by the constant reiteration of the attacks, but who are fair-minded — knowing that Haldane's record of service in the last ten years, in the opinion of his Colleagues — and, I would speak again particularly for myself — is that of one of the most patriotic, public spirited and devoted Ministers and most loyal Colleagues who have ever sat in a Cabinet.

> *Asquith to Grey. May* 27, 1915. My dear Grey, I have received your letter of yesterday. Like you, I more than doubted whether I could find it possible to sit in a Cabinet in which Haldane was not to be included. He is the oldest personal and political friend that I have in the world, and, with him, you and I have stood together amidst all the turbulent vicissitudes of fortune for the best part of thirty years. Never at any time, or in any conjuncture, have the three of us seriously differed; and our old and well tried comradeship has been cemented during the last ten years, when we have sat and worked together in the Government.
>
> I agree with everything you say as to the injustice and malignity of the attacks to which, since the war began, he has been exposed. They are a disgraceful monument of the pettiest personal and political spite. I am certain that I am not using the language of exaggeration when I say — what can be said of no one else — that both as War Minister and as Lord Chancellor he has reached the highest standard that this country has known.
>
> He is far too big a man to care for the slings and arrows of the gutter-boys of politics. And he takes with him, in his retirement, the respect and gratitude of all whose good opinion is worth having, and the profound affection of those who, like you and me, know him best.

Asquith and Grey considered whether or not they should publish these two letters to vindicate their friend. They bear signs, indeed, of having been written for publication. They decided not to do so, probably for the very valid reasons suggested by a wise public servant in the following letter to Grey:

> The press seem to have entirely ceased their attacks and many of the papers have had articles thereon in the sense of your letter. I fear publication might only revive controversy, and would also lead to party recrimination. The obvious comment would be 'why knowing all these facts did the Prime Minister not insist on Lord Haldane remaining in the Cabinet?' And if the true answer is given [that the Conservatives would

> not come into a Cabinet in which Haldane sat] it must I am afraid lead to fresh friction between the two parties.[1]

The early arrival of the British army in France just saved Paris and the Channel ports from capture. But for the Haldane Reforms and the much-abused Military Conversations which Grey had sanctioned, the war would have been lost at the outset. For the Military Conversations had enabled the British and French authorities to lay plans together beforehand for the transport of our Expeditionary Force to France.

It was well that these preparations had been made. The rapidity of dreadful events in those early August days and the strength of the German invaders surpassed all expectation. Indeed it was not recognized until August 5 how urgent was the need to send across our army at once. On August 3, Bertie, our Ambassador in Paris, wrote to Grey:

> I am not surprised at His Majesty's Government declining to send a military force to France. I think that it would be of advantage to us to give naval aid in the war for it would bring it to an end sooner by starving Germany and it would give us a *locus standi* to determine the conditions of peace.

Thus even our Ambassador in Paris thought the French army would suffice to hold up the Germans at least for a while. It is not, therefore, surprising that on August 4 the Cabinet decided not to send the Expeditionary Force 'at the very outset,' though they 'still had in mind the possibility of despatching it.' [2] Indeed they had not yet had time to con-

[1] Lady Oxford has asked me to record how deeply Asquith felt Haldane's exclusion. She writes to me that when her husband told her that the Conservative leaders refused to join the Coalition if Haldane was a member of it, 'he had tears in his eyes; and you know he was not easily moved to emotion.'

[2] *Life of Lansdowne*, page 440, conversation with Haldane. Lansdowne's report does not show that Haldane on August 4 was himself against sending the Expeditionary Force at once, only that the Cabinet had for the present so decided. Con-

sult the soldiers and with due deliberation take the most vital decision of the war. But there was no real delay. For next day a special War Council was held of Asquith, Grey, Churchill and Haldane, with Kitchener, Roberts, Haig and other army chiefs, at which the immediate dispatch of the Expeditionary Force was fully considered; on the following morning (August 6) it was sanctioned by the Cabinet.[1]

The preparations for transport made by the military and naval authorities as a result of the Conversations that Grey had first authorized in 1906, worked to perfection in 1914. The army arrived in France just in time. As Mr. Churchill writes, 'Not a ship was sunk. Not a man was drowned: all arrangements worked with the utmost smoothness and punctuality.'

Grey's failure to unite the Balkan States was the greatest defeat of his diplomacy during the war. The Bulgarian attack on Serbia at the end of October 1915 was, when it occurred, an almost inevitable consequence of our military failure at the Dardanelles, for which he had no more responsibility than every member of the Cabinet. It is, indeed, probable that he should have given more attention at a much earlier date to the problem of bringing Bulgaria, Greece and Serbia to a settlement. But when all is said and done, the real reason why Bulgaria took the wrong side in November 1915 was that Russia was doing badly in the field, that we had been beaten in the Dardanelles, and had sent no troops into Serbia, and that for these reasons the realists at Sofia thought that the Germans would win the war.

sidering his own statements and those of Grey, it is natural to conclude that in the War Council of August 5 Haldane favoured dispatch of the Force. Grey says 'he never opposed it at any time.'

[1] Asquith, *Memories and Reflections*, II, 25.

I accompanied Mr. Seton Watson on a tour of the Balkan capitals. I mention this insignificant fact only because Mr. Lloyd George has printed in his *Memoirs* (1, 398–401) a letter that I wrote from Sofia on January 15, 1915, to my friend Francis Acland which Grey and other members of the Cabinet saw. The letter urged military action to save Serbia. And it urged the general principle that military success was essential to solve the diplomatic position in the Balkans; that principle answered exactly to what Grey said then and has repeated in his *Twenty-five Years*. But did he do all he could to bring about a military success in the Near East? He was not War Minister. Could he have done more to press this view on Kitchener? I do not know.

Mr. Lloyd George was that winter a strong advocate of earlier and more vigorous military action on our part to save the Serbs. But our military authorities regarded it as impossible to send an effective force into Serbia in 1915, because the railway up the Vardar valley from Salonica was only a single line,[1] and, moreover, the attitude of the Greek Royal Government, through whose Macedonian territory it would be necessary to pass, was by that time extremely doubtful. For these reasons it is very likely that the decision not to send direct aid to Serbia was right, and indirect aid would have been equally effective if the Dardanelles had been forced. The fall of Constantinople would have stopped Bulgaria from joining our enemies, and would probably have united all the Balkan States on our side. But Constantinople did not fall, and our failure there rendered Grey's Balkan diplomacy futile. He could not make bricks without straw.

Our naval and military failure at the Dardanelles, the ultimate consequences of which proved so destructive of all

[1] Ballard's *Kitchener*, pages 333–35.

for which Grey hoped not only in the Balkans but in the world at large, cannot be attributed to him. The man most responsible was Kitchener, and after him the Cabinet collectively. The worst that can be said of Grey in the matter is that if his great authority had been thrown on the side of more decisive military action at an earlier date, it is possible that the right steps would have been taken in time. His principal deficiency as a Foreign Minister was, in my view, that he took no interest in military operations. So little did he care about the problems of war that in 1906 he had not even been curious enough to enquire what had been decided at the Military Conversations which he had sanctioned. And therefore on the question of the Dardanelles in 1915 he took no decisive part. That is the sum of his misfeasance.

Grey's critics exaggerate his responsibility for our failure in the Balkans, through not understanding the position. Besides the fundamental difficulty arising from our delay to take military action and our subsequent defeat at the Dardanelles, he was hampered all along by Russia. One of his main preoccupations, too often forgotten in the retrospect, was the prime necessity of keeping Russia in the war. She was doing badly in the field, and Germany was always ready to buy her off in order to destroy us. The German party in Russia, always strong, was strongest of all at the court.

The rumour that England was intending to take Constantinople for herself caused alarm to our ally, and the Czar demanded a final settlement of the question. As soon therefore as an attack on the Dardanelles by the British fleet was contemplated, it became necessary to promise Constantinople to Russia. The Conservative leaders were consulted and they agreed to this reversal of the Disraelian policy. A secret treaty with Russia was drawn up based on that principle.[1] In a State paper of November 1916 Grey wrote: 'Russia would never have stood five months of reverses in 1915 but for the hope of Constantinople. Even now the assurance of it is absolutely essential to keep Russia up to the mark.' Grey's information from Russia was that a strong party there thought more of winning Constantinople than of beating the Central Powers, and that to alienate this middle party would give the political victory to the pro-Germans.

For this reason the Greeks could not be allowed to occupy Constantinople, or Russia would go out of the war. When Mr. Lloyd George writes,[2] 'For some inscrutable reason Sir Edward Grey rejected Greek overtures of help,' he has once more entirely forgotten the situation as it then was. There was nothing 'inscrutable' about Grey's reasons. Even the British attack on the Dardanelles was regarded with jealousy in Russia, and the Russian veto on a triumphant entry of the Greeks into that region was absolute. For it was well known that the Greeks aspired themselves to possess the city of Constantine.

Grey, indeed, had twice to decline Greek offers of assistance, and he was right on both occasions. First in September 1914 the generous offer of Venizelos to join the Allies would,

[1] In the Secret Treaty of March 1915 Russia, in return for Constantinople, was to allow the 'neutral zone' in Persia to come into the British sphere of influence. (See map, page 211.) The object was to prevent further Russian encroachment in Persia. Considering the fair way in which we had treated the Persians in our 'sphere of influence' hitherto, as compared to the conduct of the Russians in theirs, Grey was not hypocritical when he declared that this further extension of our zone was intended to 'secure the maintenance of Persian integrity.' The only way to preserve any Persian independence at all was to exclude the power of Czarist Russia from as much territory as possible, and the only way to do this effectually and finally was to put it into the British sphere of influence. (See on the Treaty, Buchanan, *My Mission in Russia*, I, 224–28. And see Note at the end of this chapter, *Conversation of Grey with Professor Gilbert Murray*, page 341 below.)

[2] *Memoirs*, I, 390.

if accepted, at once have brought both Turkey and Bulgaria into the field as enemies of the Entente, and Grey was officially informed from Petrograd that Sazonov 'was not going to allow Greece to drag Russia into a war with Turkey.' Grey could not alienate Russia and bring Turkey and Bulgaria into the war against us, merely for the Greek aid.

The second occasion was in March 1915, after Turkey's entry, when the Greek Government offered to send troops to help us take Constantinople. The Russian veto was repeated, and, though suicidal in its folly, it could not be disregarded then by Grey, as it can be disregarded now by those who refight the war according to their fancy. On March 3, Buchanan reported from Petrograd that the Czar could not allow the Greeks to attack the Dardanelles; and on the same day Elliot reported from Athens that the Russian attitude created a serious situation, as the idea of entering Constantinople as victor weighed seriously with the King, and the Greeks would not enter the war on any other terms. To tell the story without mention of the Russian veto is to leave out the essence of the affair. It is interesting to note that on March 14, Buchanan wired to Grey from Petrograd:

> Our conversations with M. Sazonof are of such an intimate character that we all express our views with great freedom, but on this particular occasion I was much annoyed that the French Ambassador should have opposed me when I was, by your orders, making urgent representations in favour of Greek co-operation.

It was Grey's task to suffer Allies as gladly as he could, while they threw away chance after chance of winning the war.[1]

[1] A very fair statement of the reasons for Grey's action in refusing the Greek aid in September 1914 and March 1915 will be found in Mr. Churchill's *Crisis*, I, 486, and II, 201–04.

The diplomatic catastrophe came at the end of October 1915, when Bulgaria attacked Serbia and aided the Austro-Hungarian army to conquer that little land of ferocious heroes. Could Grey's diplomacy have prevented Bulgar intervention, in face of the refusal of our military authorities to send an army into Serbia, and in face of their recent failure before the Dardanelles? It is just possible, perhaps, that Bulgaria, if she could have obtained delivery of Macedonia in the autumn of 1915, might have remained neutral, for the Bulgars had no love for the Germans and the Bulgar outlook was confined to the Balkans. But how was Grey to induce the Serbs to make actual surrender of their Macedonian prize to enemies whom they hated and feared, in return for mere promises of a great northward expansion after victory should be won? Victory to the north seemed most uncertain. And the new Italian claims in Dalmatia were a further complication. Serbia refused to make the necessary Macedonian concessions, Bulgaria attacked her, and she was conquered.

Some critics, not unfriendly to Grey, think he might have forced Serbia to make the concessions to Bulgaria, presumably by threats of withdrawal of aid. It is difficult to threaten to desert an ally; if our troops had been there we could have spoken with more authority, but except for some British naval guns she was defending herself. The dispatches printed below will at least illustrate how hard Grey strove to persuade the Serbians to consent.[1] But when all was over, the Serbian Minister said to him in London on November 5, 'even if the Serbs had let Bulgaria occupy the whole zone of Macedonia, she would still have made war upon them whenever there was an opportunity.' Nothing but the presence of

[1] See also *Twenty-five Years*, chapter XXVII.

British troops would have removed this rooted belief from the Serbian mind.

Grey to Sir C. des Graz (British Minister in Serbia), July 26, 1915. In conversation with me on the 21st instant, the Serbian Minister volunteered his willingness, if the concession of the line of the Vardar would secure Bulgarian support, to press this view on his Government.

I thanked him for his goodwill, but said I thought the offer of the line of the Vardar would not be sufficient to secure Bulgarian support, and that this could not be secured with a promise of less than the uncontested zone of Macedonia.

The Serbian Minister said that the uncontested zone, as interpreted by Bulgaria, was a thing that Serbia never could concede. Serbia would rather stand alone against the shock of an Austro-German offensive. She knew that she risked everything in this war, but her promise of such a concession would simply lead to war between herself and Bulgaria.

Grey to Sir C. des Graz, August 16, 1915. You should tell M. Pashitch that I am much disappointed at his reception of our proposals. I am at a loss to know what more he could reasonably have expected.

We offer him in effect Bosnia, Herzegovina, Slavonia and half Dalmatia with the ports of Spalato and Ragusa.

The future of Croatia must in great degree depend upon the wishes of the Croats, but we indicate the possibility of Croatia with the port of Fiume being free to join Serbia. And in any case we might stipulate that Fiume be a free port, and promise our influence to secure the union of Croatia and Serbia if the Croats desire it.

We ask in return the consent of Serbia to promise to Bulgaria the eventual cession of the territory that Serbia had herself agreed to give to Bulgaria in 1912, on the day when Serbia realises the above great acquisitions, and we ask Serbia to let troops of the Allies occupy up to the line of the Vardar when Bulgaria actually takes the field on the side of the Allies.

On Serbia's reply it depends whether there shall be Balkan unity or Balkan division.

With Balkan unity the hopes of Germany and Austria in the East disappear, and it will not be worth their while to attack

Serbia, and the future acquisitions of territory both to Greece and Serbia will be assured.

If, on the other hand, there is Balkan division, Austro-German troops will be diverted there, as being the part where success is most to be hoped for; Bulgaria will work independently to get Macedonia; Serbia will risk losing Macedonia and all prospect of gains in the West.

In short, Serbia has to choose between a brilliant future and the risk of losing everything. I understand the difficulties of M. Pashitch; but events make the choice inevitable and momentous, and there is little time in which to make it and none for bargaining further at Sophia, and I ask him to believe that it is in the plain interest of Serbia that I speak, and that I do so as a friend and an ally.

Sir Edward Grey to Sir C. des Graz, September 10, 1915. I do not expect Bulgaria to join the Allies at present, nor do I doubt that she would take any favourable opportunity to attack Serbia. [In fact Bulgaria had already made her Treaty with the Central Powers.] It is precisely for this reason that the Allies cannot now draw back from their offer to Bulgaria or accept the compromise offered by the Serbian Government. To do so, would be to force Bulgaria not only to wait for an opportunity to attack Serbia, but to do her best to make that opportunity, for what Serbia will not yield at a moment of German victories, she certainly will never yield when Germany is defeated. Bulgaria has only to remember the history of the last year. Serbian Government were ready to consider concessions in November, only to drop all idea of them as soon as victory was secured in December, and finally made the komitaji raids of last spring an excuse for withdrawing them *in toto*. It would be madness at this moment to convince Bulgaria that this procedure is about to be repeated.

The one way in which we may be able to assure the safety of Serbia from a flank attack in the immediate future is to confirm our promise of the uncontested zone to Bulgaria, and secure the consent of Serbia to the occupation of the Vardar line by Allied troops. Such a course will at least incline Bulgarian feeling so far towards us, as to make any attempt by Germany to force a way to Constantinople very hazardous. Bulgarian attack is the only thing Serbia has to fear at present.

She cannot fight on two fronts, but if danger of attack by Bulgaria is eliminated she may not have to fight on either.

It is on these considerations of defence, rather than on any hope of securing Bulgarian co-operation in the immediate future, that you should lay stress in speaking to Serbian Government; and you should do so, not as exerting pressure on a protégé for political ends, but as urging an ally to concert with us measures of military defence.

Grey to Sir Arthur Davidson, November 16, 1915. One misstatement ought, I think, to be corrected: I was so far from instigating a warning to Serbia not to attack Bulgaria before she had completed her mobilisation, that the British Minister was, I believe, the only one of the Allied Ministers in Nish who was not instructed to give this advice to Serbia. After the other Allies had warned Serbia in this sense, the Serbian Minister here was unwise enough to ask me my opinion. I told him that the political and diplomatic arguments were against making an attack upon Bulgaria, but I expressly declined to give an opinion whether strategic considerations might not override the other considerations.

If he hadn't asked me I should have said nothing, but I couldn't give him advice directly contrary to what others had given.

In October, Grey offered Cyprus to Greece if she would come to the rescue of Serbia, but the King of Greece refused to embroil himself with Bulgaria, though he would have been ready at an earlier date to take Constantinople if Russia had allowed it. On October 22 the Greek Government told Grey that 'military assistance to Serbia would involve the defeat of the Greek nation.'

After the conquest of Serbia in November 1915, military defeat engendered a complicated and disgraceful position for the Allies, turning on the question of an English and French occupation of Salonica, and the growing hostility between the Venizelist and Royal parties in Greece, which finally led to civil war and allied interference in Athens. The miserable story is well known. Some of the immense difficulties of the situation for the Allies, of which their own differences of opinion were no small part, is illustrated by the following dispatches of Grey:

> *Grey to Lord Bertie (Paris), December* 3, 1915. At the Cabinet this morning Lord Kitchener made a statement on the military situation which has led to a grave crisis. After a very careful review of the conduct and prospects of the war in the Eastern Theatre, he has come clearly to the conclusion that the continued employment of Allied troops at Salonica with the intention of retaining them there will lead to a military disaster which may be imminent.
>
> Unless therefore orders can be given without delay for the withdrawal of British troops he cannot remain responsible for the War Department and must resign.
>
> Lord Kitchener's view of the situation is shared by His Majesty's Government and all their military advisers.
>
> We are therefore confronted with a crisis of the first magnitude, which is so serious that, unless the French Government can accept this view, we desire to confer with authorised Ministers of the French Government in London tomorrow. If they cannot come to London, British Ministers are ready to meet them at Calais.
>
> Matter is very urgent. You should communicate at once with the Minister for Foreign Affairs and Minister for War.

The French, however, had their way, and the Allied troops remained at Salonica. Next year, Anglo-French relations were scarcely more harmonious. Our Allies were pressing for an offensive in that region to which our military authorities were strongly opposed.

> *Grey to Lord Bertie, June* 7, 1916. War Committee here believe that an offensive at Salonica must be detrimental to more important operations elsewhere and will be a failure and perhaps a disaster.
>
> It is said that if we oppose an offensive at Salonica Briand

will fall, all the blame for his fall will be laid upon us and alliance itself be damaged.

If so the situation is most intent [*sic*]. I shall be very glad if you can usefully send me any observations upon this, especially what the effect of our finally refusing to participate in an offensive at Salonica is likely to be.

In these disputes with France about operations from the Salonica base, Grey was acting merely as the mouthpiece of the military authorities on a purely military question. But the element of foreign policy entered more largely into our other dispute with France in that region, the question how much we should use force to coerce the Royalist party in Greece, which was growing openly hostile, while the rival party of Venizelos was on our side. The French were for earlier and more drastic interference than Grey and his colleagues approved.

Grey to Lord Bertie. August 30, 1916. The War Committee and ourselves are in doubt as to the precise purpose of the French Government in desiring to land a brigade at the Piraeus in order to take control of postal, telegraphic and railway communications and ports. It is not clear to us by what actual measures it is intended to carry out with so small a force what would be in effect a military occupation or at any rate the assumption of a number of Government functions. Whatever leakage of military or naval information may reach the enemy from the Court or General Staff is vexatious, but we cannot say that it has produced serious results or that it need be countered by such strong methods as the French Government desire. It will assist us if you can ascertain privately what they have in view after the landing of troops, and what they believe will be the effect on the Greek Government and on the position of the King. Is there any reason to believe that they contemplate the possibility of a revolutionary movement against the latter?

September 1, 1916. *For Lord Crewe and Lord Hardinge to consider.* (*Note in Grey's handwriting.*) I am disposed to think that the French should be told point blank that to encourage a revolutionary movement against the King of Greece would be

> much resented by the Emperor of Russia and might in consequence have unfavourable influence on Franco-British relations with Russia and be turned to serious account at Petrograd by Pro-German reactionaries.

The relations of the Greek Royalist party with the Allies went from bad to worse, till on December 9, 1916, two days before he handed over the seals of the Foreign Office, Grey was fain to telegraph to Elliot at Athens the decision to coerce the Greek Government:

> Recent events in Athens have proved conclusively that neither the King nor the Greek Government have sufficient control over the Greek Army to prevent Greek forces becoming a menace to peace and a danger to the Allied Armies in Macedonia.
>
> Under these circumstances the Governments of the Allied Powers are constrained to demand, for the security of their forces from attack, that the Greek troops now stationed in Northern Greece be immediately removed to the Morea, and that the evacuation commence within twenty-four hours and proceed as rapidly as possible. They further demand that any movements of Greek troops from the Morea to Northern Greece be immediately suspended. Failure to comply with these two demands will be regarded by the Allies as an act of hostility on the part of the Greek Government.
>
> The blockade of the Greek coast will be maintained until full reparation has been given for the recent unprovoked attack by the Greek forces upon the troops of the Allies at Athens, together with satisfactory guaranties for the future.
>
> You should make a formal communication to the Greek Government in the above terms as soon as your colleagues have received similar instructions.

Thus French policy, both in the matter of staying at Salonica and of coercing the Greek Royalist party, eventually carried the day. British policy, for which Kitchener, Grey and the Cabinet were all responsible, had not shown clarity or strength. We had never effectually resisted the

French purpose, or proposed a real alternative, yet we had hampered it and delayed it, and the disunion between France and England had prevented a firm hand in the Near East. The desire not to interfere with the internal affairs of Greece and not to violate her neutrality was a respectable motive, but was it a time and place to be respectable, and was our respectability saved in the end? These are difficult questions. They are made the more difficult because the French war policy in the Near East was mixed up with some very dirty home politics.

There was indeed no policy in the Near East that we could have adopted, after the autumn of 1915, that would not have been open to the gravest objections. The military and naval failure of the Dardanelles had rendered any satisfactory line of conduct impossible. There was only a choice of evils.

In November 1916 General Sir William Robertson, in an important official paper, wrote: 'Since the war began, diplomacy has seriously failed to assist us with regard to Bulgaria and Turkey.' To which Grey replied: 'Diplomacy in war is futile, without military success to back it.'

Italy declared her neutrality when the war broke out. She was nominally a member of the Triple Alliance, but she had for some time past been floating gracefully between the two European groups. Her adherence to the Triple Alliance had as early as 1887 been qualified by an agreement that Austria-Hungary should not occupy more territory in the Balkans except by previous agreement with Italy, a condition disregarded in 1908 and 1914. Moreover, a dozen years before the war, Italy had given France definite assurances that the obligations assumed under the Triple Alliance enabled her to pledge herself to remain neutral if Germany attacked her

Western neighbour. With Great Britain she was on even more friendly terms, though she had not positively stipulated in any treaty that she should not be called on to fight against England.

Italy had found her midway position advantageous. Neither side, for instance, interfered with her Tripoli adventure in 1911. Grey had then written to Nicolson:

> It will be tiresome if Italy embarks on an agressive policy and the Turks appeal to us. If the Turks do this I think we must refer them to Germany and Austria as being allies of Italy. It is most important that neither we nor France should side against Italy now.[1]

Her neutrality in August 1914 was from the first extremely 'benevolent' to our side, as the following correspondence shows:

> *Grey to Sir R. Rodd* (*Ambassador in Rome*), *August* 12, 1914. Today the Italian Ambassador, having impressed absolute secrecy on me, made a communication to me from the Italian Minister for Foreign Affairs [San Giuliano]. Italy desired to be neutral in the present war, but she felt the danger of a change of equilibrium being brought about, especially in the Adriatic and the Mediterranean; she felt the danger to herself from the animosity that Germany and Austria had towards her for having remained neutral, and she sympathised very much with the idea I had expressed the other day, that we were fighting to put an end to a military domination in the west of Europe. Italy might therefore be brought to side with us in this war. If so, certain conditions would be necessary. They were these:
>
> 1. The British, French, and Russian Governments to agree not to conclude peace separately from Italy.
>
> 2. The British and French fleets to unite at a given point with the Italian fleet in the Adriatic, and then together to destroy the Austrian fleet.
>
> 3. In the final victory, Italy to have the Trentino up to the

[1] *G. and T.* IX, 274.

Alpine watershed and Trieste; if Italy obtained this she would not object to a division of Albania between Greece and Servia, on the condition that the coast from Stylos to the mouth of the Boyana was neutralised.

4. Vallona, with the region near it, to be not only neutralised, but made autonomous and internationalised on the same basis as Tangier, with all Adriatic Powers, including Italy, taking part in its administration.

5. Italy not to keep any of the Aegean islands at present occupied by her, provided that Turkish integrity is preserved; but, if Turkish integrity is not preserved, Italy to have her part in the provinces on the Mediterranean.

6. The Italian concessions at Adalia to be maintained.

7. To give satisfaction to Italian public opinion, some functionaries, with some title or other, might be left by Italy on the Aegean islands at present occupied by her.

8. Italy to have a share of the war indemnity corresponding to her efforts and sacrifices.

9. The four Powers, Britain, France, Russia and Italy, to pledge themselves to maintain and defend the settlement and equilibrium resulting from the war; this agreement to have a pacific and defensive character, and not to pledge any Power to help the others in case of an aggressive policy and its consequences.

The Ambassador explained to me that these were only the views of the Italian Minister for Foreign Affairs, and did not pledge the Italian Government, as they must be submitted to the King of Italy. Also, the Italian Government must examine whether there was a probability of the dangers hinted at above; for, if these did not exist, it would not be possible for Italy to come into agreement with us.

I said that I could express only a first impression. It was that, if Italy became our ally and fought on the same side, we would, subject to the discussion of details, give a general assent to these conditions, and to some of them, such as the acquisition of the Trentino and Trieste by Italy, I had no doubt we would consent absolutely; but we could not pledge ourselves to any of these things till Italy stated definitely that she was prepared to join us.

The matter went no farther at the time. And when in the following March Italy resumed negotiations for her entry into the war, her terms had risen. San Giuliano had died and been succeeded as Foreign Minister by Sonnino, who increased the price demanded. In the previous August Sonnino had wished Italy to enter the war on the side of the Central Powers, but he now put up her alliance for sale to the highest bidder. In so doing he misrepresented the genuine idealism of much popular sentiment in Italy for the Allied cause. The need of the Allies for Italian assistance was by this time only too clear. Grey and Asquith were at one in believing that they had no alternative but to outbid the Central Powers, who were making offers to secure her neutrality. And if once she adopted neutrality as part of a bargain with our enemies, she must become more hostile to the Entente. So at least Grey believed, as is shown by this letter of his to Sir Rennell Rodd after the entry of Italy into the war:

> *May* 25, 1915. You have been through some very anxious moments lately, and I appreciate the steadiness and nerve that your telegrams show. I can assure you that the anxiety was shared here, and your coolness and courage were all the more appreciated, because we realised how much depended on the course events might take in Rome.
>
> Had Giolitti succeeded in forcing Italy on to the neutral track, and concluded a bargain with Germany and Austria in which Italy received certain advantages in return for neutrality, Italy would have been unable to maintain a real neutrality. She would have been told from day to day that her neutrality must be such as to satisfy German and Austrian needs, or else the advantages promised would be withdrawn; and Italy would have been forced into an attitude unfriendly to us and helpful to Germany and Austria. In the end, I think that Germany and Austria would probably have found some pretext for telling Italy that she had not observed proper neutrality, and they would have deprived her of all that they had promised.

That would have been bad for Italy in the long run; but meanwhile, during the war, we should have suffered very much by the attitude into which Germany and Austria would have forced Italy.

The Secret Treaty of London, which Asquith and Grey negotiated with Italy in March and April 1915, is indeed open to very grave objections, and it is fortunate for the peace of the Adriatic that the Slav population actually placed under Italy in 1919 was not so large as that which had been allotted in the Treaty.[1] Yet for Grey it had been a most desperate choice: to have refused a great part of Sonnino's demand in April 1915 would have kept Italy out of the war, with ever stronger tendencies towards the enemy's side. The war would then have been won by the Central Powers. That would hardly have helped Yugo-Slav aspirations. It is true that, as Mr. Seton Watson has so often and so ably contended, the terms on which Italy's adherence were purchased had considerable disadvantages even from the point of view of Allied success in the war; for the 'secret' treaty became known, and the Croats therefore fought better on the Isonzo front than they would have fought for the Dual Monarchy elsewhere. But to my thinking these disadvantages were far outweighed by the fact that so many Austro-Hungarian divisions were immobilized from service elsewhere for so many years of war by the Italian attacks. Grey has been much blamed for the Treaty of London; but if he had refused Sonnino's demands and the war had then been lost, what would men say of him now?

Whatever we may think of the Treaty we must at least see how it looked to the men of 1915. The idea of a great Yugo-

[1] The Italians on their part had not fulfilled the terms of the Treaty, for they did not declare war on Germany for a year afterwards, but only on Austria-Hungary.

Slavia was not so much to the fore as it was by 1919. Serbia was in the utmost peril, hemmed round by enemies. The complete break-up of Austria-Hungary was scarcely contemplated as possible. Yet, even subject to the terms of the Treaty of London, Serbia was promised, in case of victory resulting from the Italian Alliance, enormous accessions of territory, greater proportionately than those promised to any other of the Allies. And where would Serbia have been if she had been left alone to settle accounts with Austria-Hungary? That at least was how Grey saw the matter; and the military authorities urged upon him that Italy must be brought into the Alliance.

It was well, especially for the Serbs, that he saw it thus, for, as events proved, Italy's continued neutrality would have been fatal to the Allies, in the pass to which they were soon brought by the continued defeat and final collapse of Russia.

Russia, the weakest member of the Triple Entente, was the most difficult to persuade in this matter as in so many others. As early as March 3, 1915, Sazonov, even before he had heard the Italian terms, wrote to Grey that he was opposed to Italy's entry into the war. Naturally, therefore, when he heard Italy's claim on so large a part of Dalmatia, it was hard to obtain Russian consent. The Czar made himself the champion of the reversionary Slav claims on the Adriatic coast.

This arduous negotiation between grasping Italians and recalcitrant Russians was shared by Asquith and Grey. Neither of them knew much about the racial geography of the Adriatic coast, and the Treaty is not a masterpiece of accurate mapping. Throughout March Grey carried on the negotiation with zeal. Then his increasing blindness and insomnia made it necessary for him either to take a short holiday or resign for good. His enforced absence lasted only for the first two weeks of April, during which the Prime Minister continued the bargaining with Italy, precisely on the Foreign Secretary's lines, and helped the negotiations on almost to the point of agreement. On April 14 Grey returned and finished the task, including the extraction of Russia's consent.

The idea, which has found its way into print, that Grey ran away for a fortnight from his post out of disgust at the excessive Italian claims, to leave the onus of the Treaty on Asquith, is entirely disproved by the documents in the Foreign Office. For good or for evil he is responsible for the policy of the Treaty of London: he was not the man to shirk responsibility. Asquith and he were responsible together. Both thought that the Italian claims were most extortionate, but both held that the Treaty must be made or the war would be lost. It is a dreadful thing to be responsible for the survival of your country in war.

> *Grey to Sir Rennell Rodd, March* 8, 1915. The Italian Ambassador communicated to me last week very secretly, the conditions on which Italy would be prepared to enter the field on the side of the Allies, not later than the end of April.
>
> I told the Ambassador today that I must consult the French and Russian Governments before I could express any opinion on the conditions.
>
> The Ambassador pressed me very much for my personal view.
>
> I observed that the conditions went beyond those suggested last August[1] and that some of them seemed to me excessive from the general point of view; but, as there were none to which I need take objection purely from the point of view of British interests, it was unnecessary for me to say more till I had consulted the French and Russian Governments.

[1] See page 332 above.

The Ambassador agreed to my doing this.

The condition on which he expatiated most, and to which, therefore, I suppose he feared there would be most objection, was the claim to the coast of Dalmatia. He said it was absolutely necessary that, if Italy was to undertake so formidable a task as fighting Germany — for her entry into the field would mean this — there must be a great substantial advantage put before the Italian nation. He pointed out that we were now Allies with France and Russia; but time brought changes, and the securing of the substantial interests of Italy in Mediterranean questions might be desirable from our point of view. Also, it would not be to the advantage of Italy to get rid of Austrian domination on the Adriatic Sea, if the domination of Russia was to be substituted for it on the Dalmatian coast.

I said that all these questions must be approached from the general point of view, and not specially from the British point of view; and, as such, I must take them into consideration with our Allies: because, in questions approached from the general point of view, the decision of each nation must depend to some extent upon the views taken by other nations.

Grey to Buchanan and Bertie, March 22. His Majesty's Government have considered the Italian communication. We are of opinion that the real reason for the Italian demand is that the Italian coast between Venice and Brindisi could not be defended if the coast and island of Dalmatia became a base for submarines in the hands of another Power and that Italy will not be content with less than will give her effective control of the Adriatic.

We must therefore decide either to admit the Italian claim or forego the prospect of Italian co-operation.

Italian co-operation will decide that of Roumania and probably of some other neutral states. It will be the turning point of the war and will very greatly hasten a successful conclusion.

Grey to Buchanan, March 27. You should tell the Minister for Foreign Affairs [Sazonov] that I am in much need of some rest and intend if possible to go away on Wednesday for a week or so: this being Easter it is the best opportunity. One of my Colleagues will take the Foreign Office work in my absence, but I should have liked very much to get the Italian negotiations concluded before I go.

Unless the Russian 'aide-memoire' can be modified as I propose, I fear the negotiations may fail altogether.

Grey to Buchanan. March 31. There seems no chance now of coming to an agreement with Italy for some days and perhaps not at all if the Russian Minister for Foreign Affairs adheres to the line taken as reported in your telegram.

It is essential that I should have some rest and I am therefore going away for a few days. The Prime Minister meanwhile will personally take charge of the negotiations with Italy and other matters of importance and make whatever progress with Italy the Russian Minister for Foreign Affairs renders possible.

Grey returned on April 14, and finished the negotiations that Asquith had continued. On April 26 the Treaty of London was signed, and two days later Sazonov sent a handsome message to Grey after their tussle: 'à exprimer à Sir Edward Grey combien il apprécie que Sir Edward Grey ait prit sur lui la lourde et difficile tâche de diriger les négociations qui viennent d'aboutir.' Though they had frequent differences, Grey and Sazonov personally trusted one another, and Grey thoroughly understood the forces against which this faithful friend of the Allies had to contend in Russia.

Grey to Mr. Seton Watson. May 3, 1915.

DEAR MR. SETON WATSON:

I have received your letter and the telegram enclosed.

There seem to be very exaggerated ideas as to possible sacrifices of Slav interests. Apparently it is thought that Italy is to have the whole of the Adriatic coast, and the Slavs are to have no room at all on it. This never can be so.

If Russia, France, and Great Britain had not intervened last Summer, Serbia not only would not have acquired any new territory at all, but she would have been crushed and have lost her independence; and the rest of the Slavs in the neighbourhood of the Adriatic would all have remained subjugated to Austria. Instead of that, it is now assured that, if the Allies win, a union will be accomplished of Serbia and all the adjoining Serb territories that were previously under Austrian rule; wide access for Serbia to the Adriatic will also be acquired; and a greater and completely independent and sovereign Serbia will come into existence. The greater part, at any rate, of the Slav districts will become free and enabled to settle their own destiny. Whether, for instance, Croatia remains an independent State or wishes to unite with other Slavs, we presume to be for her to decide. In any case, Croatia, Serbia, and Montenegro will possess a very large share of the Adriatic coast.

I think that it is most unreasonable to say that, if Italy were to co-operate and help to achieve this result, she should be denied any footing whatever on the Adriatic coast. I had thought that it was admitted that there were Italian settlements on that coast even now;[1] and I understood that there were still more Italian settlements on that coast before they were crushed out by Austrian rule.

It would, I think, be most ungenerous if the Serbs and other Slavs were, in the final settlement, to refuse what reasonable concessions were found necessary to enable the Great Powers to secure for them the vast gains and advantages that are assured in the case of the victory of the Allies. There is not one of us engaged in this fight, whether it be Russia, France, or Great Britain, amongst whom there will not be people at the end of the war who will be disappointed at the gains acquired. We shall all have to make concessions to one another: not one of us can get one hundred per cent of the extreme national demands. The Serbs and other Slavs, who are really going to gain more than any one else, must not deny to those who are fighting for them the means of securing victory.

The Treaty of London of April 26, 1915, contained not all but a very great deal of the original demands of Salandra and Sonnino. It was well that they had been satisfied, for the King of Italy and his two chief Ministers had next month a

[1] Actually there were only a few thousand Italians in Croatia and Dalmatia apart from Fiume.

dangerous fence to take in their own country, which tested their determination to enter the war. In May, Giolitti's movement of neutralist opposition, backed by the Central Powers, had the Church and other potent forces behind it. It was defeated by the outburst of popular feeling in the Italian cities against vassalage to Germany and Austria, which just and only just sufficed to carry Italy into the war. It was a close run thing. So was the war itself, as events turned out; the participation of every one of the greater Allies proved essential to avert defeat.

The difficulties at Rome did not come to an end with the declaration of war. As Sir Rennell Rodd wrote to Grey in June 1916, 'A country governed with a minority in Parliament and most of the directing classes hostile to the Government is a nasty problem for diplomatists.' The following letter of Grey indicates the difficulties of the 'blockade' policy in Italy; the very high value Grey placed on the services of our Ambassador in Rome; and his gracious way of dealing with those who served under him abroad. A previous telegram on the 'blockade' question had a little hurt Sir Rennell's feelings. This made amends:

October 26, 1916.

MY DEAR RODD:

Very many thanks for your interesting letter of October 19. Perhaps my original telegram was somewhat unfortunately worded as I only meant to convey that we were not happy with regard to the question of Italian exports and were a little doubtful whether the Consulta really recognised the vital importance of the matter from the point of view of our blockade policy. All our information points to the fact that this policy is pressing more and more severely on German economic and industrial life every month and that its effect in the war is of the greatest importance, as it is sapping the internal moral of the enemy.

I need hardly assure you of my complete and continued confidence in you. The work that you did before the war was to my mind one of the greatest factors in inducing Italy to side with us and you seem to have acquired a position in Italy which an Ambassador seldom attains. The speeches made when Runciman visited Italy bear striking testimony to this fact, though none was needed. I quite realize the difficulties that you have to overcome in dealing with the Italian temperament and that it requires great patience and tact on your part to succeed.

(Signed) GREY OF F.

Please remember that we are very hard worked here: that telegrams have to be drafted in haste, so that they deal in one point without setting that in perspective to the whole: they explain curtly our difficulties here, without going on to explain that we do know and allow for the difficulties of the man at the other end.

And please never forget from sunrise to sunset and (unless in sleep) from sunset to sunrise that you are in my opinion quite invaluable and irreplaceable at Rome and that I never cease to be grateful that you are there.

G. OF F.

NOTE

CONVERSATION OF GREY WITH PROFESSOR GILBERT MURRAY, JANUARY 10, 1918

The following conversation, a year after Grey's retirement, noted down at the time by Professor Gilbert Murray, throws, I think, much light on Grey's views on the Secret Treaties and other matters arising out of the war.

January 10, 1918. Dined 8 with Glenconners to meet Grey.

After dinner I questioned him, first on the Treaties. The secrecy of course would be inexcusable in peace, unavoidable in war. First came our guaranteeing integrity of Turkey, if Allies won, in the peace treaty on condition of Turkey remaining neutral. The country and Grand Vizier wanted to be neutral, but Enver deliberately sent the fleet out and made them bombard Odessa and commit acts of war. This made war inevitable.

Hence second treaty — with Russia stipulating she should have Constantinople. Russia was suspicious that we were working at the Dardanelles and might get to Constantinople first. French disliked idea of Russia getting Constantinople, but hoped that we would take burden of opposing it. We on contrary agreed: but stipulated that Russia should *debar herself from all the neutral zone in Persia*. This is meaning of recognizing neutral zone as 'British sphere' — see treaty of 1907. It is merely the 'sphere' where Russia must not enter.

G. Murray. What about future of Persia?

Grey. Try to rebuild independence if possible, so as to have buffer state. But very difficult: cannot ring Persia round like Afghanistan. Too vast, and too tempting with oil and mines.

G. Murray. Have Shuster back?

Grey. Perhaps something of that sort. Shuster said to be 'a three-cornered man' in America.

G. Murray agreed, from his conduct in Persia.

G. Murray. Other treaties? Why was our bargaining power so weak?

Grey. Both France and Russia had constant offers of separate peace. He was told by leading French authority: 'You know, I could get a good peace for France tomorrow if I chose.' Same, but more so, with Russia.

G. Murray. Italy?

Grey. We did not tempt Italy. Never asked any country to join us in the war. Both Italy and Rumania came and offered themselves, demanding certain terms. Extortionate: and we beat them down as best we could, but *could not run risk of refusing an ally*. We never stipulated that Mesopotamia or Palestine should be ours: only that they should not go back to the Turk.

G. Murray. Is there any danger of the Germans coming down and taking Greece? Using coast for submarines?

Grey. Well, that leads to my reason for not deposing Constantine. Admired Venizelos more than any statesman in Europe. Could have deposed Constantine and forced Greece into war, but, before doing so, asked military experts if one could protect Greece against invasion. They said: No. Salonica not adequate. It would have been a real disgrace to us if we had forced Greece in and then let her be destroyed. This had not happened Rumania, nor Serbia nor Italy.

G. Murray. Salonica? You were against?

Grey. I merely acted as mouthpiece of military authorities.

Ld. Glenconner. Was it on that Carson resigned?

Grey. Well, it was said that he could not stand Kitchener. Carson used to murmur: 'That great stuffed oaf!' Carson wanted (1) an attack on Vienna from Salonica; (2) Establishment of a General Staff. (2) was established and immediately condemned Carson's project (1). Thereupon he resigned.

G. Murray reminded him of his word to the Austrian Ambassador in July 1914 about Revolution.

Grey. Was that in the Blue Book?[1] I remember I said to Imperiali and others, 'If there is war, there will be Labour Governments in every country and quite right too.' That was not put in the Blue Book.

G. Murray. How will peace come except by Revolution?

Grey. Might be Revolution, but also might come as soon as Government wishes for peace. Grey thinks that by changing tone of press German Government could change German opinion to peace in a fortnight. Thinks the central condition is Belgium. They should admit, as Bethmann-Hollweg did, the wrong done and offer amends for it. Possible, because a Chancellor has admitted it; and would mark the overthrow of the military party.

Sad story of the female versicolor teal lent to Kew by Grey and killed in air raid. No other female nearer than South America. Grey had bought this one from Antwerp Zoo just before war.

[1] Yes, see *G. and T.* XI, 70, quoted page 279 above.

IX

Grey's Foreign Policy During the War: II—The Neutrals—Propaganda—America—'Blockade'—Question of Peace Negotiations—Colonel House and President Wilson—Idea of League of Nations—Cabinet Crisis of December 1915—Peerage—Release at last, December 1916—First Thoughts in Retirement

I HAVE reserved for treatment in this chapter a group of war-time questions which it is impossible to separate one from another — Grey's dealings with neutrals; propaganda in foreign countries; contraband and the so-called 'blockade'; the question of peace negotiations; the idea of a League of Nations to preserve peace after the war; and his relations to Colonel House, President Wilson and opinion in the United States. In all this region of policy Grey's talents and instincts were at home and here he won his real success. The terrible demands made by a war for survival were most efficiently met, particularly in the matter of the 'blockade' of Germany, but not by neglect of all consideration for other countries and all thought for the future beyond the war. Grey never condescended to the so-called 'realism' which thinks only of advantage of the moment and only in military terms; that way of thinking, as the enemy found to his cost, is not the way to win a world war, which may ultimately be decided by the world's opinion.

The invasion of Belgium, and the publication of the White Paper, which had revealed Grey's efforts to prevent the outbreak of war, gave us a good start with neutrals. He refused to risk this impression by following it up with aggressive propaganda, in rivalry with the enemy's method. The great asset of Germany was the belief very prevalent in Europe that her armies were invincible, and on this she based her system of terrorising and bribing opinion in foreign lands. The method had some success in the Balkan capitals, but it recoiled on itself in great countries like Italy and the United States, where dictation was resented. Grey's personal friendship with American statesmen, and his recent experience of American politics and public opinion in the affairs of the Arbitration Treaty, Panama and Mexico, rendered him wary and wise at this greater crisis. And his friend Spring Rice, Ambassador at Washington, was equally persuaded of the need for caution. Our sympathizers in the United States were therefore left to conduct their own propaganda, with excellent results.

> *Spring Rice to Grey, Washington, September* 22, 1914. We have not asked for American help or sympathy, and we have been content to leave Bernstorff and his satellites unanswered. It is true that a deputation suddenly appeared, which, as was announced, was sent by our government to influence public opinion. But Sir James Barrie and his friends, as soon as the facts were made known to them, at once saw the necessities of the situation and if they stay here at all they will simply watch and not attempt to control the movement of public opinion. Americans like to do their thinking for themselves, and the less we try to help them the better. The determining factor is no doubt the attack on Belgium.

Opinion in other neutral countries was treated with similar self-restraint on our part.

> *Grey to the Prime Minister, December* 5, 1914. I have had evidence of the enormous harm that may be done by want of tact and blatancy in dealing with public opinion in neutral countries. It is difficult to overstate the importance of avoiding wrong methods of presenting our case and I would earnestly press it on your attention.

Grey's policy as regards Holland is laid down in his letter to Sir Alan Johnstone, our Minister at The Hague:

> *January* 20, 1915. I feel that the continuance of the independence and integrity of the Netherlands depends upon our success in this war. But, till we are in a position to assure the Netherlands that we can prevent their being invaded and devastated by German troops as Belgium has been, I do not think that it would be fair in their own interests to suggest that they should cease to be neutral. If Germany were to win in this war, she would doubtless retain Belgium, or at least Antwerp, and Dutch independence would be a thing of the past: it never could emerge from the German shadow, and would soon be absorbed. Our victory, on the other hand, would assure not only Dutch integrity, but Dutch independence and freedom.
>
> The time may come when we shall ask the Netherlands to recognise this: but that can only be when we are able to assure them, not only of future, but of immediate protection against German attack.

The organization of the vast business of controlling imports into neutral and allied countries that might pass thence into Germany, was carried on by the Contraband Department constituted in the Foreign Office. For the purpose of winning the war, this new department became one of the most important of the hastily contrived concerns which the adaptable genius of Englishmen cast up in those years of strain. 'The work of its organization,' writes Sir John Tilley,[1] 'was mainly done by Mr. Alwyn Parker, who was Head of the Department in its early history, and remained head when it was divided into seven or eight sections, each the size of an ordinary Foreign Office department.' Mr. Alwyn Parker has kindly sent me the following Memorandum:

The Conduct of the Blockade

When the Contraband Department of the Foreign Office was constituted, in the first week of November 1914, Sir E. Grey summoned to him the officials who had been placed in charge and indicated certain principles of policy whereof a record has been kept.

He said it was important that the Foreign Office, the Admiralty, the Board of Trade and the Procurator General should act in close consultation, and that it had accordingly been arranged that the Contraband Committee, on which each of these departments was represented, should meet daily at the Foreign Office, issue orders, in the light of all available information, regarding ships which had been detained and their cargoes, and keep official records of all their decisions.

Sir Edward Grey emphasised the vital importance of our relations with America. He recalled that in 1812 questions of neutrality had actually involved us in war with the United States, and that the surest way to lose this war would be to antagonise Washington, since, apart from all other considerations which he dwelt on, Lord Kitchener was dependent on munitions from America for his new Army. 'Mind, therefore, you keep a sense of proportion.'

He said that our position with Sweden was particularly delicate since, with Archangel closed by ice, the only means of getting munitions to Russia was in transit across Sweden, the Russian Government besides was very restive and apprehensive as to Swedish intentions, and we ourselves depended on Sweden, he was told by Mr. Runciman, for pit-props and iron-ore, and on Holland and Denmark for margarine and other supplies which had become very important. The object

[1] *The Foreign Office*, page 182.

of our policy must of course be to cripple the enemy; but if, by a cast-iron insistence on our maximum claims, we exasperated those neutrals on whose goodwill we and our Allies were dependent we should simply lose the war. He wished the department to seek to oil the wheels of diplomacy in every possible way and to try to establish friendly relations with neutral traders themselves.

'Many things combined to bring down the German people,' writes General von Kuhl, Chief of the Staff to Prince Rupprecht of Bavaria, 'but I consider the blockade the most important of them. It disheartened the nation.' Nothing can bring into clearer relief the wisdom, and the success of the course advocated by Sir Edward Grey than to contrast it with the ruthlessness, the resort to sudden changes and rash expedients, and the lack of a circumspect and directing policy, which marked the German submarine campaign and spoilt the German chance of victory

Sir Edward's position, more especially immediately before, and in the years following, the outbreak of the war, was beset with difficulties on every side; but he had the rare secret in times of high contention of singling out the central issues. During the earlier years of the Blockade it was due to his strong-handed grasp of shifting and dangerous positions, as well as to the co-operation of Dr. Page and the tact and address of Esme Howard, our Minister at Stockholm, that the priceless friendship of the United States on the one hand, and the neutrality of Sweden on the other, were preserved. Posterity sees as a whole, and no knowing and impartial man can deny now that both these conditions were essential to the final triumph of the Allied cause. A false step on our part in 1914 or 1915 and Sweden, the traditional foe of Russia, might have joined the Central Powers; another false step and public opinion in America might have compelled the placing of an embargo on the export of munitions upon which we were vitally dependent. The first aim of the Secretary of State was to soften, by negotiation and direct agreements with neutrals, the abrupt unilateral method of Orders in Council which had earned a bad name and provoked intense animosity in bygone centuries. Mistakes no doubt were made, but the War was won. A vast organisation was built up to impede

> enemy imports, it was constantly being checked and overhauled and supplemented; and of course, once the United States became a belligerent, complex problems became much more tractable. But it is not the least merit of Sir Edward Grey that, with a true statesman's eye to the demand of the instant, he recognised at early and decisive moments when essentials were in jeopardy. At such critical times he was vigorous and uncompromising in resisting sectional clamour at home, for it was not only strident but often based on distorted perspective and exaggerated proportions. Many of the authors of attacks on the conduct of the Blockade were incorrigible, and incapable either of fairness or knowledge.
>
> ALWYN PARKER

Grey, in his *Twenty-five Years*, has discussed several of the actions arising out of the 'blockade' for which he was responsible, particularly his fortunate refusal to make cotton contraband in the first year of the war. An opposite decision at that moment might well have provoked an embargo on the export of munitions from the United States. Grey did not go into the details of ordinary cases of ships and cargoes stopped, and his signature at the foot of innumerable telegrams on these subjects was usually a matter of routine. But he was consulted in critical cases, and he had laid down the lines of policy that were followed by the Contraband Department often against the wishes of the Admiralty and in face of much adverse criticism in the press and other influential quarters.

In February 1916 the Contraband Department had swelled to the size of a Department of State, and at Grey's request it was given this status in theory, though it was still housed under the Foreign Office roof and managed by Foreign Office officials. Lord Robert Cecil was placed at the head of the new Department of State, with a seat in the Cabinet.

Grey to Asquith. February 15, 1916. The confusion and want of guidance and policy in dealing with Contraband has reached a point at which I can no longer be responsible for the relations with neutral countries.

We are now threatened with the complete alienation of Denmark and Norway, who are both undoubtedly friendly by nature and I believe we are depriving both countries of things really necessary for their own use. The complaint outside in this country is that the Foreign Office interferes too much: the real fact is that there ought to be control by some Minister in touch with the Foreign Office, and there has been no such control.

I can't exercise the control without giving up the Foreign Office, but neither can I nor anyone else conduct Foreign Affairs unless the various Committees dealing with Contraband and export licences are under some judicious guidance. I should like to mention the matter at a Cabinet.

Next day the decision was taken.

Memorandum, February 16, 1916. Sir Edward Grey having represented the serious friction that was arising with Neutral Countries over commercial questions, and having stated that it was impossible to maintain with Neutral Countries the friendly relations that were desirable, and in some cases essential to the successful conduct of the war, unless there were some Cabinet Minister who could co-ordinate the work of the War Trade Department, the Contraband Department of the Foreign Office and of all the different Committees dealing with commercial questions, it was decided that Lord Robert Cecil should be asked to undertake this work and become a member of the Cabinet, retaining his office as Under-Secretary of State for Foreign Affairs.

H. H. A.

Lord [Robert] Cecil himself has sent me the following communication:

During the war, by almost an accident, I became Grey's Under-Secretary and, until his resignation, worked very closely with him. He was a most generous chief, always ready to make the best of any work done for him. From the outset

I was concerned with the so-called blockade — really, the organization of economic pressure of all kinds on the enemy. At the first, other Departments, like the Board of Trade and the Treasury and, of course, the Admiralty, had their say on different aspects of it, and I represented to Grey that it would be better to have a Cabinet Minister in charge. Accordingly, several people were asked to undertake it, including, if I remember right, Lord Curzon and Lord Milner. They refused, and Grey then went to the Prime Minister and asked that I should, as Under-Secretary, be put into the Cabinet, which was done. It was characteristic of him that the possibility of difficulty arising from two Cabinet Ministers in the same office — which to lesser men has seemed very formidable — never gave him any anxiety. He was indeed, more than almost any man I have known, free from petty jealousies and personal vanities. Indeed, partly owing to his dislike for urban life and his consequent perpetual wish to get out of office, he was politically completely disinterested. For all the years in which he was connected with the Foreign Office, I don't think there was a single day in which he would not have welcomed resignation. He held office because he thought it his duty to do so, and for no other reason. This conception that he was there to do a certain job which it would be cowardly for him to abandon was always present with him. Until he had been released by the action of others he could not go.

He did not interfere much in the 'blockade.' Occasionally he would suggest some small concession to a neutral. His main anxiety was to avoid a quarrel with the United States. He rightly judged that America had it in her power to do us fatal injury. If her citizens refused to supply us with arms and money we might well have been defeated. Indeed, it was her benevolent neutrality which probably caused the Germans to conduct their submarine warfare with such indifference to American interests as eventually brought the United States into the war. Then there was always the possibility that the war might end in a deadlock, and if that had happened the friendly mediation of America would have been priceless. Considerations of this kind were always in Grey's mind, and throughout the blockade controversies with America he never lost sight of them. To him, though it was very important to make our economic pressure as effective as possible, yet the continuance of American friendship was even more so. In keeping our policy on this line he was enormously helped by his friendship with House and Page and the complete trust both of them had in him. The value to the country of this element in Grey's character — the gift of inspiring confidence — cannot easily be over-estimated.

Was Grey a great Foreign Minister? I only worked with him for some eighteen months during the war, when the functions of diplomacy were, as he used to say, almost suspended. The Bulgarian question was a striking example of this truth. We failed to prevent Bulgaria from joining our enemies and it is possible to criticise some aspects of British diplomacy in this connection. But it is quite certain that the determining factor in Bulgarian action was the course of the war, which was altogether outside the sphere of the Foreign Office. Bulgaria waited to see what would happen in Gallipoli, and when we were defeated there she joined the Central Powers. On the other hand, Roumania was persuaded to join us and it would have perhaps been better if she had not done so. But the decision on the desirability of her assistance was not one for the Foreign Minister. A far more important matter was our relation to the United States. Here, as I have already said, Grey was convinced that continued American friendship was essential to us and in spite of his increasing blindness and other physical troubles, he never ceased in his efforts to secure it. In that negotiation, his great asset was his character. It was that, too, which at the beginning of the war gained favourable consideration of the World for our account of the causes which led to the outbreak of hostilities. Europe and the other civilised countries were *prima facie* disposed to accept as true anything that Grey said. Where he was in controversy with other countries as to facts, they preferred to believe him. They trusted his veracity and his fairness, and even when, later in the war, our blockade operations seemed inconsistent with neutral rights, foreign countries were ready to believe that our proceedings were really essential for our defence and were not the outcome of arrogant navalism. It was this impression which helped to keep such countries as Sweden and Holland neutral and, most important of all, prepared the way

H. Cecil

AET. 61, 1923

for that entry of America into the war without which we might never have attained victory.

It was a fact of great importance that before the war broke out Grey's relations to Ambassador Page and Colonel House were already based upon personal friendship and general agreement on international ideals. Page indeed became too open in his sympathy with the Allies to carry much weight with a President who hoped to preserve neutrality, but the detailed treatment of one dispute after another arising between England and America over contraband was greatly facilitated by the good understanding between Page and Grey at the London end of the cable. But even more important was Colonel House's belief in the British Foreign Secretary, and the similarity of their general attitude to questions of peace and war. Almost any other statesman would have treated House with rather more of correct politeness and less of that opening of the mind which proved the way to his confidence, and enabled Grey to throw a line over the President. When Colonel House went to Paris, our Ambassador there expressed scorn at the interference of the amateur diplomatist, till sharply called to order by Grey.

From first to last he held that we should need America, either to help us to win the war, or else to help Europe by her mediation to obtain a tolerable settlement if victory proved impossible to either side. From August 1914 till his resignation in December 1916 that was his standpoint from which he never moved. He hoped for the 'knock-out blow,' though he did not call victory by that name. He thought victory by far the best solution, provided it was followed by a reasonable peace, negotiated with the beaten enemy. Then and then only the German people would be freed from the Prussian military spirit and the nations would breathe an air less harsh. But he was by no means certain that complete victory was possible; he thought even defeat conceivable till the submarine menace had been got under control. Only American alliance would make victory swift and sure. Therefore, whether as ultimate mediator or as ultimate ally, America would be necessary to us before the end, and meanwhile she sold us munitions for which our need was absolute.

Because, then, America must not be alienated and because victory was not certain, the idea of peace negotiations must not be struck out from the possibilities of the future. To give America or her President the idea that we alone stood in the way of a negotiated peace would be to play the game of the German propaganda, and might also arouse the rebellion of our hard-pressed Allies. For in dealing with America and in dealing with the question of peace negotiations, Grey had to consider Russia, France, and Italy. He could not advise his colleagues to commit England to any declaration of policy, either pacific or bellicose, which would alienate any one of our great Allies; and he had to let the French Government know what Colonel House and he were doing. If we had been at war with Germany without Allies we could have dealt with the question of negotiations, to entertain or reject them, purely on their merits as regarded ourselves. But that was never the case. Germany was always offering our Allies terms for themselves if they would leave us to our fate. This complication, and the impossibility of foreseeing the course of the war, rendered it very necessary to be tentative and wait on events.

Grey's advocacy of a League of Nations to preserve peace after the war was over was not a mere bait to catch the Colonel and the President. His own heart and mind were in the scheme, and he regarded the participation of the

United States in such a League as essential to its success. He was prepared to work for this end with pacifists, not only with those who, like Professor Gilbert Murray, supported the lines of his policy all through, but with those who regarded the Foreign Office with suspicion. He saw Lowes Dickinson and encouraged him to go to America, to co-operate there with the eminent men of both parties who were already associated with the idea of a League to enforce peace, telling him that such a League would be welcomed by England, but that it should be initiated in the United States. Dickinson, who by no means took statesmen at their face value, came away from the interview much encouraged, and told his friends that he was impressed by Grey's earnestness in the matter and his deep feeling for peace. When Grey retired in December 1916, Lowes Dickinson wrote to him, 'I hope it is not impertinent for me to say with what profound regret, I may almost say with what despair for the future, I heard of your retirement from office.'

The gist of Grey's dealings with America has already been given to the world in his own *Twenty-five Years*, in the *Intimate Papers of Colonel House*, and in the *Life and Letters of Walter Page*. But I am here able to print a number of documents not yet published, which further explain Grey's policy and motives. They consist chiefly of secret cables to and from Spring Rice, and communications to Cabinet colleagues over here.

> *Spring Rice to Grey. September* 3, 1914. The President sent you warmest greeting and expresses his most sincere sympathy. He said: 'Every thing that I love most in the world is at stake,' and later: 'If they succeed, we shall be forced to take such measures of defence here as would be fatal to our form of Government and American ideals.' He spoke of the long

trial of the Civil War, and said with deep emotion that he was sure that our country would still show its powers of endurance for a high cause.

Officially, he would do all that he could to maintain absolute neutrality, and would bear in mind that a dispute between our two nations would be the crowning calamity.

Grey to Spring Rice. September 3, 1914. 7.20 *p.m.* I am most grateful for the President's message and his sympathy. If Prussian militarism succeeds the west of Europe will be no fit place for those of us who have been brought up to love liberty, humanity and good faith and I think the United States will feel the dark shadow of militarism nearer to them.

We wish in all our conduct of the war to do nothing which will be a cause of complaint or dispute as regards the United States Government; such a dispute would indeed be a crowning calamity as the President says and probably fatal to our chances of success.

Grey to Spring Rice. December 22, 1914. Your private and secret telegrams of December 18 and 20.

I can only give my personal view which is that there are two main objects to be secured:

(1) Evacuation of Belgium, compensation for the wrong done to her and re-establishment of her independence. If Germany agreed to this the barrier to peace discussions as far as we are concerned would be removed, for it is the one thing that is a point of absolute right and of honour for us to secure.

(2) A durable peace that will secure us and our Allies from future aggression.

German views aim at a durable peace by placing the west of Europe under German domination. Even a German pacifist professor said the other day that 'the principle of the absolute sovereignty of the individual nations must be given up.' We would rather perish than submit to that.

On the other hand the crushing of Germany is in the long run probably as impracticable as the domination of Germany, and secure peace is not to be obtained that way.

An internal change that made Germany a democratic State emancipated from the rule of the Prussian military party would be one solution of this problem, but it cannot be imposed directly from outside, though it might be the indirect result of defeat of Germany in war.

An agreement between the Great Powers at the end of this war with the object of mutual security and preservation of peace in future might have stability if the United States would become a party to it and were prepared to join in repressing by force whoever broke the Treaty. We should be quite willing that Germany should have future security by any condition that would also give it to us.

Such are my own personal views. Great Britain I consider is bound to fight on till the Belgian point is secured, even if we had to fight alone. That is an absolute minimum.

But there are also the views of the Allies to be considered. We have not yet discussed terms of peace with them and we are bound to do so when the time comes. Both will have to state their own conditions for themselves and what those will be will largely depend upon the progress of the war.

You can tell the President's friend [Col. House] the substance of this if you think it useful, but on condition that all knowledge of it is kept strictly to himself and the President only. It must on no account become known to the State Department.

It was at the request of Colonel House himself that arrangements were made for intimate and secret communication between Grey and the 'President's friend,' on account of 'the hopeless leakage of the State Department,' as House called it. Under Bryan that ill-organized office could not be trusted to keep a secret of state.

Grey to Spring Rice. January 2, 1915. Your private and personal and secret telegrams of December 24 and 30.

I gather that the President's friend considers there is no chance of the United States Government countersigning any agreement for preservation of future peace.

If this is so it is difficult to see how a durable peace can be secured without complete exhaustion of one side or the other.

German Government single us out for special animosity and work up hatred against us in Germany by the most unjust charge that we were responsible for this war and the aggressors in it. A peace made while this temper continues would leave us exposed to certain attack in future unless we spent even more largely than before on armaments.

Has President's friend any idea how in these circumstances durable peace making possible reduced expenditure on armaments can be obtained, unless there were some League for preservation of Peace to which the United States amongst others were a party and which would effectively discourage an aggressive policy or breach of treaties by anybody?

I cannot help feeling doubtful in absence of any confirmation from Berlin whether Germany is really prepared to concede restoration of Belgium. An American who has recently seen high officials in Berlin assured me yesterday that Germany was not disposed either for peace or mediation.

It is evident too from comments of German Press that summary published of American Note has led to expectations that there will be a breach between United States and England, and that United States sympathy will be with Germany. I hope full publication of American Note and the reception of our reply when we can complete it, which will be as conciliatory as possible, will remove this expectation. But for the moment I cannot help feeling from all indications that reach me that Germany is not prepared to make peace on terms that will concede what is just now and give us security for the future.

President's friend must not forget that France and Russia have to be consulted about European peace and that I could not open discussion with them unless very sure of the ground respecting Germany's real disposition.

Grey's Memorandum to the Prime Minister

February 24, 1915.

I have had several conversations with Colonel House since I made the last memorandum of a conversation with him on the 7th of this month.

He read me a few days ago a letter from Mr. Gerard, the American Ambassador in Berlin, saying that he was sure Germany would listen to peace proposals now, if they were made at once; but there was very little time; immediate action was necessary, otherwise the opportunity would have passed. Mr. Gerard states that Germany would not consent to an indemnity to Belgium, and expressed his own absolute conviction that Germany was sure to win on land.

Colonel House commented on this proposal as being impossible. He knew that we had to consult our Allies, and peace could not be brought about immediately.

I observed that the statement that Germany would not consent to pay an indemnity to Belgium provided no 'terrain' on which we could negotiate. German military operations were now having a success against Russia, and as long as Germany believed she could win on land, or greatly improve her position, she was not likely to listen to any terms of peace that we or the Allies could accept.

Colonel House discussed several times whether he should go to Berlin. I said that I should be very glad if he went: if only to satisfy my own curiosity as to what the German mind really was. But this was far too trivial a motive for a journey to Berlin; and unless Germany had really come to the opinion that she could not gain anything by prolonging the war, I did not believe that she would really desire peace.

We had much general discussion about the future, after this war: always on the same line, that the great object to be secured was the prevention of future wars and large expenditure on armaments. The ideals of the United States and Great Britain with regard to liberty and free government and democracy were the same. I expressed much appreciation of the work in the world of men like Mr. Nott, and of the sort of work that Mr. Hoover and the American Commission were doing for Belgium; and said that Great Britain was the only other country in the world that produced this type of man. Colonel House agreed cordially in all these views.

Colonel House repeated several times that he felt that the President and myself, and himself, were animated by a common purpose with regard to the objects to be secured in the terms of peace.

I agreed that this was so as regards the large lines; but I reminded him that, though this was absolutely true, and was the thing that I personally cared for most, yet I was also representative of the national point of view of a nation at war, and must take this into account as well.

Grey to Mrs. Creighton. September 9, 1915. Sometime the

war must end, but the end does not seem to come nearer, and I want a good peace. By this I mean a peace that will be made of a determination not to have this sort of war again. We cannot get this I fear unless the United States will take a hand in making the peace, and they have missed the opportunities of asserting themselves; or rather their public opinion not having chosen to assert itself by now is likely not to do so at all. Their best men are willing to see the true issues involved, but the bulk of the people do not.

Grey's Memorandum: The position of Great Britain with regard to her Allies

(Circulated to the War Committee)

February 18, 1916.

Sir William Robertson has circulated to the War Committee a Paper emphasising the influence that we ought to be able to exercise upon the diplomacy and general policy of our Allies.

It is quite true that, if we were to withhold the support that we give to our Allies, they could not continue the war. We could probably bring about this result even by withholding financial support alone, and it is therefore true to say that the power of the Allies to continue the war depends upon us.

But there is another aspect of the case, equally true, which is not taken into account by Sir William Robertson's Paper: Germany has taken care to make it known to our Allies that each one of them individually, or at any rate France and Russia, could have peace tomorrow on comparatively favourable terms, if they would separate themselves from us. Our Allies have, therefore, an alternative to continuing the war which is not open to us.

It is true that not one of our Allies has been so mean as to use this argument when contending for its own way in council; but it is also true that no consideration of Sir William Robertson's Paper will be just or adequate unless this feature of the situation is taken into account.

I would put the following propositions, which I believe to be all equally true:

(1) Our Allies are absolutely dependent upon us for any chance whatever of success in the war, and even for the power to continue it;

(2) We are dependent for our very existence upon success in the war, or at any rate upon continuing the war till Germany is comparatively exhausted, for in no other way can we get terms that will save us;

(3) Our Allies are not dependent upon the issue of the war to the same extent as we are, because they could get tolerable terms if the war was not continued;

(4) It is at best doubtful whether we could secure ourselves if the Allies abandoned us: we are therefore dependent upon the Allies for our safety to a greater extent than they are upon us.

My conclusion is not that we must therefore efface ourselves in the councils of the Allies: on the contrary, I think that we should urge strongly the advice and the policy that we think to be best. But, if we cannot make our views prevail by argument and influence, we must be very careful not to proceed to threats or pressure that might alienate our Allies.

In a number of documents printed below he explains his views on the vexed question of the 'Freedom of the Seas,' which he thought practicable only on conditions to be guaranteed by the United States, as part of a League of Peace; whether during the war it would be possible to let food into Germany in return for the cessation of the submarine campaign, was a question on which he felt at one moment, as will be seen, a certain suspense of opinion.

Grey to Spring Rice. June 1915. My personal view is that, if there were really a great League of Peace, which made aggression practically impossible, we might agree that, in time of war, all merchant shipping should be immune from capture, provided that other countries, such as the United States, would enter into an engagement that, if this immunity was violated by any Power they would go to war against that Power. We have long said that we might give up the right to interfere with merchant shipping if, by so doing, we could secure a great reduction in the expenditure on armaments, and diminish to vanishing point the risk of war. If such an arrangement were agreed to, it would be clear that the British Navy could not possibly be used as an aggressive force.

If, however, by freedom of the seas Germany means that her commerce is to go free upon the sea in time of war, while she remains free to make war upon other nations at will, it is not a fair proposition. If, on the other hand, Germany would enter after this war some League of Nations where she would give and accept the same security that other nations gave and accepted against war breaking out between them, then expenditure on armaments might be reduced and new rules to secure freedom of the seas made.

The sea is free in time of peace, anyhow.

I expressed these personal views to the President's friend, and there can be no objection to your making use of them as a personal expression of your own opinions.

Grey to Lord Crewe. Fallodon.[1] *June* 14, 1915. I think on the whole it is better when one is away to leave things wholly alone, and I am very doubtful of the advantage of making suggestions when I am only half in touch with what is going on. But I think the Government should make up its mind whether it will not be to our advantage in the future to agree to what is called the freedom of the seas. We are more dependent than any country has ever been upon having the sea free for our commerce. It is probable that the development of the submarine will a few years hence make it impossible for us ever again to close the sea to an enemy and keep it free for ourselves. If this be so we should make up our minds to agree in the final terms of peace at the end of this war to the immunity of commerce at sea in the future. If this premise and conclusion are right, then the practical question is to decide what concessions, conditions or guarantees we should demand in return for our consent to the future freedom of the seas if it is proposed to us either through or by the United States.

Another practical question is whether we should lose anything material by ceasing to prohibit the import of all food

[1] In June, as well as April 1915, Grey was forced to take a few weeks' holiday to save his eyes and enable him to continue in office at all.

> stuffs into Germany through neutral ports and by falling back as far as food stuffs are concerned upon the ordinary rules that apply to conditional contraband.
>
> If we decide that to change our policy and attitude on these two questions is desirable, we can I think, easily secure that the friction between Germany and the United States is not shifted to us and we shall retain and probably improve the good will and the advantageous position which we now hold in the United States. If on the other hand we decide that it is of paramount importance for us to maintain a rigid and inflexible attitude on these two questions we must face the consequence of possible trouble with the United States.
>
> It is important to decide without delay which of these two alternative policies the interests of the country require. We must avoid drifting into the position of incurring the disadvantage of the latter alternative and then discovering later on that the former alternative was the better policy. And if the former alternative is as I think, the better policy, the sooner that decision is taken the better, for we can then begin in our dealings with the United States to use it to great diplomatic advantage. I should like Asquith to see this letter.

The idea which we here find Grey seriously considering was the proposal put forward by Colonel House, that England should raise the embargo on foodstuffs entering Germany, in return for German abandonment of sinking merchantmen by submarines, and Grey added the abandonment of asphyxiating gas as a weapon in the field.[1] The British Cabinet, however, thought such an arrangement would be to Germany's advantage and Grey, as the next document shows, soon fell into line. Moreover, Germany turned the idea down, thinking that it would be to England's advantage. So the ruthless war on both sides went on. Grey may or may not have been mistaken even in considering this humane bargain, but he was very much afraid of the outcome of the submarine campaign. He did not foresee that that cam-

[1] *Intimate Papers of Colonel House*, I, 446–49.

paign which he so much dreaded would lead to the accomplishment of his desire, the entry of America into the war.

Grey's Memorandum to Cabinet

July 17, 1915.

In connection with Sir F. Hopwood's minute, which was recently circulated to the Cabinet by Mr. Balfour, I think it worth while to call the attention of my colleagues to a further argument by which we might justify the continuance of our blockade system in the event of the Germans offering to abandon the destruction of merchant vessels by submarines.

Our blockade, adopted as a measure of reprisal against the illegal warfare on merchant shipping pursued by German submarines, is a means of exerting pressure on the enemy of which the effect, comparatively small at first, gradually becomes greater. It has barely commenced as yet to be seriously inconvenient to Germany, whilst, on the other hand, the German submarine depredations have, from the start, been steadily destructive of British shipping, together with the lives of non-combatants, including women and children, and valuable cargoes, nearly 300,000 tons of British shipping, exclusive of fishing vessels, having been destroyed since the 18th February last. It is accordingly unreasonable to expect His Majesty's Government to acquiesce in this destruction of British life and wealth by discontinuing their means of retaliation almost before the enemy has commenced to feel its effects, and they could not contemplate such a relaxation of their policy unless the German Government first paid compensation for the consequences of their illegal submarine warfare.

Grey to Spring Rice. November 23, 1916. I presume that substance of my personal telegram of November 15th has already been communicated to Mr. Taft but in any case following should be forwarded at once to Taft, in reply to a telegram received by me from him today.

'I think public utterances must have already made it clear that I sincerely desire to see a League of Nations formed and made effective to secure the future peace of the world after

> this war is over. I regard this as the best if not the only prospect of preserving Treaties and saving the world from aggressive wars in years to come, and if there is any doubt about my sentiments in the matter I hope this telegram in reply to your own will remove it.'

Grey had a very strong feeling for Spring Rice. More than a dozen years after his friend's death, in the last year of his own life, he wrote: 'The things that stand out in my memory of Spring Rice are his patriotism and his humour. We are all "patriotic," but the welfare of his country was a matter of daily concern to him.'

In July 1916 the dismissal of the Allies' faithful friend Sazonov by the Czar gave warning that Russia might not much longer remain in the war.

> *Grey to Lord Crewe. July* 24, 1916. I am much concerned about the Russian upset. It looks as if the Reactionaries had carried everything with the Emperor. They will begin by working against us and France and will end with a revolution in Russia that will sweep away them and the Emperor; but that will be no compensation to us for what will have happened meanwhile. And if the Emperor would only trust moderate and capable men he would make his country great and have the adoration of his people. The contrast between what he might do and what he is doing is intolerable!

Things indeed were not looking cheery for the Allies, when in November 1916 Lord Lansdowne circulated to his Cabinet colleagues a Memorandum, very much on the lines of his public letter in the *Daily Telegraph* which a year later aroused so much comment. He raised certain questions without pretending to be able to answer them: what were the chances of winning the war outright? and whether, if the reply of the military authorities was unfavourable, an effort should be made to secure peace on negotiated terms? Sir William Robertson replied for the military authorities, and Grey circulated the following Memorandum from the Foreign Office, dated November 27:

> On the general question of peace, I will make the following reflections.
>
> It is a question, not of sentiment nor of rhetoric, but of cold, hard fact. It should be examined as far as possible, without emotion, certainly without sentiment, and without rhetoric. I think that everyone must feel that this is the temper in which Lord Lansdowne has examined it. I submit four observations as preliminary to a discussion:
>
> (1) As long as the naval and military authorities believe that Germany can be defeated and satisfactory terms of peace can eventually be dictated to her, peace is premature, and to contemplate it is to betray the interests of this country and of the Allies. I accept, and my own judgment, for what it is worth, agrees with the opinion of Sir William Robertson and Sir Douglas Haig on the military prospect, provided the Allies can continue the war with full vigour through next year, or even for the first eight months of next year. There have been but three factors, of unknown value at the beginning of the war, which have ever made me doubt of our power to outlast Germany: they were the Zeppelin, the mine, and the submarine. The Zeppelin I believe, for offensive purposes, to be a complete failure, and I have ceased to be anxious about it. The mine, though a great inconvenience, appears to be so controlled by the Admiralty that it cannot be a decisive factor in this war. There remains the submarine, which is not mastered, and for the present seems to be getting more and more beyond our control. The military authorities have expressed their opinion as to the prospect of defeating Germany. It remains for the naval authorities, with perhaps the Board of Trade and Lord Curzon's Committee, to estimate whether a breakdown in shipping, sufficient to paralyse ourselves or the Allies, is likely to bring us to our knees before military operations in the field can bring Germany to her knees. The future of this country depends upon our giving a correct answer to this question.

(2) As long as the military and naval authorities consider that the position of the Allies is likely to improve, even though it may not result in the ultimate and complete defeat of Germany, it is premature to make peace.

(3) If the military and naval authorities were of opinion that the position of the Allies was not likely to improve, that a year hence we should be able to secure terms of peace not more favourable than at present, it is obvious that it would be better to wind up the war on the best terms now obtainable, unless another year of war, while leaving Germany equally strong in the field, would have weakened her internally more than the Allies and made her recovery more difficult than theirs.

(4) If the time arrived when either the military or the naval authorities considered the chances to be that the situation would change in the course of the next few months to the disadvantage of the Allies and would progressively deteriorate, then it would be incumbent on the Government of the Allies to wind up the war at once on the best terms obtainable, presumably through the medium of not unsympathetic mediation; and, if they did not do so, they would be responsible for future disaster to their countries.

We have had a Paper from Sir William Robertson and from Sir Douglas Haig on the military situation. We ought to have one from the naval authorities on the naval, and more especially on the merchant shipping, situation. They alone can estimate what the losses of merchant shipping are likely to be during the next few months, and how far these losses can be relieved by releasing ships now requisitioned. On this latter point, of course, the opinion of the military, as well as of the naval authorities, must be obtained. The President of the Board of Trade and Lord Curzon have already given valuable contributions to the prospect. We have had from the War Office (I think) some figures of shipping required for Salonika.

Without drawing any conclusions of my own — which, indeed, I have not at present sufficient data to do — I would venture to say, with all respect both to Lord Lansdowne and to Sir William Robertson, that Lord Lansdowne has performed a faithful and courageous act in submitting a Paper that obliges these questions to be examined.

Grey to Spring Rice. November 26, 1916. I agree with view expressed in last sentences of your telegram and shall leave the peace articles and President of the United States alone. We cannot encourage his mediation without being prepared to accept it. On the other hand I see no reason why we should incur all the odium of refusing it in advance. If he made any proposal I should personally advise His Majesty's Government to suggest to the Allies that they should state the minimum conditions to be laid down on which they would accept mediation or begin discussion of peace terms.

When Grey left office in December 1916, his bequest of advice to the new Cabinet was given in the Memorandum that he afterwards printed in his *Twenty-five Years* (III, 68–71). In briefer form, he repeated that advice to Mr. Eric Drummond in a private letter on December 12, the day after he had given up the seals:

My dear Eric:

I hope our Government will:

1. Let the Allies be the first to suggest what answer should be given to the German peace proposal.

2. Give an answer in common and not separately.

3. Let the Allies know the exact prospect as regards shipping and finance before a final decision is taken, otherwise one or more of the Allies when they find the prospect out after having refused Germany's offer, will say they have been let in and will go for a separate peace.

4. The merchant shipping question should be thoroughly examined.

If we bear in mind the sea of troubles through which the Coalition Government of 1915–16 was heavily ploughing, and the differences that must inevitably divide any able set of men confronted every week with new problems of the utmost gravity, the wonder is that the Cabinet Ministers quarrelled as little as they did, and that Asquith succeeded in holding them together so long. Since Haldane's departure,

Grey was personally most in touch with his Northumbrian neighbour, Walter Runciman, President of the Board of Trade, and they were both usually in agreement with Reginald McKenna, who had become Chancellor of the Exchequer after Mr. Lloyd George went to Munitions. Owing to the offices they held, Runciman and McKenna were more concerned with our finances, shipping and industry, and were more feelingly aware than their colleagues of the parlous state of our sinews of war. Runciman was specially concerned with the consequences of the submarine. Their warnings were a useful corrective to the policies of colleagues whose thoughts ran too exclusively on the size of our armies in the field. Backed by Grey, this 'civilian' group helped the Cabinet to arrive at well-balanced decisions.

In December 1915 these questions came to an acute crisis, which almost broke up the Government, but under Asquith's healing hand led in fact to a compromise in which proportion was kept, so that our national resources and our manhood in the field were both maintained. The crisis arose because compulsory military service had at length become necessary, even in Kitchener's view. Sir John Simon resigned on the principle of conscription. Runciman and McKenna also intended to resign, not against the principle of compulsion, but because the form of conscription originally proposed would have withdrawn so many able-bodied men from mines, munitions and shipbuilding that we should have been in grave danger of losing the war behind the back of the army in France. Grey supported them with the threat of his own resignation.

The following correspondence passed:

Grey to Asquith. December 29, 1915. The main point on which McKenna and Runciman are resigning is one in which

I am in full agreement with them. Besides this, I have always felt that I ought to have left the Cabinet when Haldane went in May. His continued exclusion when the new vacancies occur will make the concession to ignorant and malignant clamour still more marked and injurious to the public service. The withdrawal from the Cabinet now of at least three important members with whose views I am in accord, with all of whom I am on terms of personal friendship, with one [Runciman] intimately so, and whom it will be difficult and I think in one or two cases impossible to replace in their respective offices without loss to the public service, makes me feel that I must ask you to accept my own resignation. I did not press this in May, because it was represented that my stay at the Foreign Office was then indispensable for public opinion both at home and abroad. For various reasons, in which I need not enter in a letter, that is no longer the case. There are even public reasons why there should now be a change at the Foreign Office. Under ordinary circumstances I should have given up the work more than a year ago to save my eyesight, but as long as it was thought and seemed to be essential that I should stay there, I put that consideration aside.

I shrink from adding to your difficulties, but with at least three members of the Cabinet resigning with whose views on the financial and economic needs I am in full accord, I have no confidence or expectation that this view will prevail in the Cabinet and it will in the long run be easier for you that I should go with them now rather than that I should resign separately at a later and probably a more inconvenient moment.

Please do not trouble to write. I can come to see you when necessary after you have definitely settled with McKenna, Runciman and Simon, who have been acting quite independently of me.

Asquith to Grey. December 29, 1915. I have just read your letter which fills me with despair. If I am to be deserted in this time of stress by all my oldest and best friends, it is clear that I must reconsider my own position. I have not as yet received any definite resignation from any colleague. Yours would, of course, be universally interpreted as a German triumph.

Grey to Asquith. December 30, 1915. I hear from McKenna and Runciman that the Cabinet tomorrow is to deal with the question of numbers of the army with reference to finance and trade. In my view this is the main and critical point, and I have urged McKenna and Runciman to come to the Cabinet and take part in the discussion, that if there is to be division in the Cabinet it should be on the big point on which we are I believe in agreement and not on the point of compulsion of unmarried men on which, subject to maintaining my view in the main point, I am prepared to support you and the decision of the majority at the last Cabinet. In any case I am ready to come to the Cabinet to discuss the main issue. I should like to see you before the Cabinet. I was much touched by your letter, and the situation is very critical and distressing.

The result was a compromise, in a case where compromise was the true policy. The needs of finance, shipping, mines and munitions were not fatally sacrificed to the man-power of armies, which were in fact dependent on those civilian interests of which Runciman and McKenna were the official guardians. Grey's intervention had had the happiest result.

Meanwhile Edward Grey's eyes grew steadily worse. In May 1915 he had written to his friend Sydney Buxton, then Governor of South Africa:

> My eyes are worse, and a third independent opinion forbids me to read or write at all for some months. I am told that if I do this and live mostly in the dark and always with dark glasses, the trouble may be stopped in a year or so and get no worse. Dark glasses I am wearing, but the rest of the prescription I cannot carry out properly unless I get out of office, and not even partially unless I get away for a month's holiday.

During his holiday in June, Lord Crewe, in whom he had complete confidence, was in charge of the Foreign Office.

Exactly a year later (May 15, 1916) Grey writes again to Buxton:

> The oculist assures me that if I could give up work for a year or more I might keep my sight for the rest of my life, but unless I can limit the use of my eyes I may lose the power of reading for good. I compromise by getting Crewe to come into the Foreign Office and taking some ten days leave once in every two months or six weeks, but it is a poor compromise.

In July 1916 a further lightening of the load was sought by his removal from the Commons, where he had to answer many questions, to the Lords, where he need seldom appear. But a few months later, after he had retired to private life, he confessed to a friend what had been his chief reason for moving to the Upper House:

> I took a Peerage that I might be free to go out of public life when I left office, and am now very glad that I did so. For one can do no good by talking now, and if I had still been in the H. of C. they would have made me go and sit on the bench and talk.

He did not wish to change his name by becoming a Peer, and hoped that if he was habitually called 'Earl Grey of Fallodon' it would sufficiently distinguish him from his cousin, Albert, who bore the famous hereditary title of Earl Grey of Howick. But Albert very naturally and rightly objected to the confusion likely to be caused by two Earls Grey. On learning of his objection, Edward at once solved the difficulty by asking for the lower title of Viscount instead; and so it was arranged. Viscount Grey of Fallodon was introduced into the Lords by his two oldest friends in the House, Haldane and Bryce.

BUCKINGHAM PALACE,
July 15, 1916.

MY DEAR GREY:

I have much pleasure in approving of your proposed title of Viscount Grey of Fallodon, and I fully appreciate your reasons for wishing to retain your family name.

I can quite understand your feelings of regret at parting from the constituency which you have represented with such distinction for upwards of 30 years and during parts of three successive reigns.

I trust however that in the Upper House you will have a more restful time.

Wherever you are you will always have my absolute confidence and regard.

Believe me,
very sincerely yours,
GEORGE R.I.

In December 1916 final release came by the break-up of Asquith's Government, and reconstruction under Mr. Lloyd George. In that complicated and embittered affair Grey took no such leading part as he had taken in the crisis exactly a year before. His general health had given way — he was living on 'spoonfuls of bread and milk' in July — and his eyes were quite unable to stand the necessary work. By no possibility could he stay in office for many months longer, and here was a chance of quitting it completely to his mind. His attitude towards Mr. Lloyd George's aspirations was not quite the same as that of the closer bodyguard of Asquith. As between the two men he greatly preferred his old friend the outgoing Prime Minister, but he had a suspicion that the country desired a change and that the fulfilment of its desire might perhaps help on the war. The way had indeed been prepared by a campaign of abuse of which he had his share, but which went off him like water from the back of one of his Fallodon ducks; he did not waste his small ration of eyesight in studying the amenities of the gutter press. He was much too glad of his release to quarrel with the method of his manumission.

One reason why he had no regrets was that he left Foreign Affairs in the hands of Arthur Balfour and Robert Cecil. He had been alarmed at Mr. Lloyd George's entirely bellicose method of brushing aside Wilson's feelers for peace, but he knew that Balfour and Cecil would never quarrel with America. He knew there would be no break in the continuity of his policies, nor was there till after the war had been won. Balfour's feelings about the importance of friendship with America coincided with those of Grey. Less than four months after he had retired, the harvest that he and Tirpitz had sown was reaped at length, and to his indescribable joy America entered the war.

The intense disapproval that he came to feel of Mr. Lloyd George's proceedings after the armistice was not felt so long as the war lasted. He had greatly admired his colleague's work as Minister of Munitions, and he saw the value of his restless energy and unconquerable courage. In war time there is much to be said for Danton's prescription of endless audacity, and the opportunist temper is then more in place. Be this as it may, the feeling of Edward Grey towards Mr. Lloyd George during the war was very much more friendly than it afterwards became. It is significant that he preserved, for his own amusement, a number of good-humoured notes that passed between them at War Cabinets. One of these, shoved across the Cabinet table during the period of negotiations with Italy in the spring of 1915, ran as follows:

> (In Grey's handwriting.) 'The daughter of the horse leech isn't in it with the Italians. What is the Welsh equivalent for this Biblical quotation?'

(Answer, in Mr. Lloyd George's hand.) '*Meibion y gele.* "Sons of the horse leech." We are too gallant a race to blame the other sex.' [1]

A number of letters illustrate Grey's feelings towards Mr. Lloyd George's Government at its formation. The first is addressed to Mr. Bell of the *Chicago Daily News*, who had wished to see a defence of the outgoing Government against the attacks of the Northcliffe press:

December 12, 1916.

MY DEAR BELL:

I am much obliged for your letter of the 9th and am very grateful to you for the personal thought that was the cause of your writing it. At the same time I feel that the new Government must have the best chance we can give it, and that a campaign of defence of past policy against the Northcliffe press or other critics cannot be inspired by the late colleagues of the present Government without dividing the nation and impairing the conduct of the war. It is true that we may be forced to speak out by circumstances or by continued attacks, especially if these are made in Parliament, but for the present so far as my own personal action is concerned I propose to retire to some of those innocent interests that you once spoke of so kindly. When I return to London I should like to renew our acquaintance.

Grey to Professor Gilbert Murray. December 23, 1916. *Fallodon.* The best chance of saving my eyesight is to stay at home and be in the open as much as I can. I didn't intend to seek the chance till after the war, but now it has come I can't help taking it. It is a great relief and an abiding satisfaction to me that Balfour and Cecil are at the F.O. and that Eric Drummond continues private secretary. With all this and with Hardinge still there I am sure all that the F.O. can do to keep things right with America will be done. I hope Balfour

[1] 'The horseleech hath two daughters, *crying*, Give, give.' Proverbs xxx, 15. I am obliged to Mr. Lloyd George for leave to print this, and for his explanation that, although the word is *daughters* in the Welsh translation of the scriptures, the masculine *Meibion y gele* is used in the pulpit and on the platform.

and Cecil, one or both, will see you sometimes. I would suggest your seeing E. Drummond when you are next in town and getting his advice.

As to the League to Enforce Peace. I doubt whether much can be done in public here as long as the war continues to be the subject not only of absorbing interest but of anxiety; till a safe end of the war is in sight people can't be expected whole-heartedly to promote what they hope to realize after the war.

To Haldane. March 25, 1917. *Gordonbush. Brora.*

My dear Richard:

No, indeed! I have not been in London or near it since I left Office in December — in fact, since then I have only once been in the train and that was to come here. It is a most beautiful and remote place, and I should be very happy if it were not for anxiety about the course of the war. I have for the time gone into the world that suits me. London and politics have always been really alien to me, and unless it seems that I am really wanted I shall not return to public life at all. Meanwhile, I am getting back strength of body and tone of mind, but my view of a civilisation that is based upon large cities is very pessimistic.

I rejoice at seeing Russia purge her Government and strike out for freedom, but revolution means confusion and violence for a time, and I am very apprehensive of the effect it may have on Russia's part in the War. France in revolution, however, became more, not less, powerful.

To Lord Buxton. May 29, 1917. *Itchen Abbas.* I have no knowledge, but I have a feeling that we are winning the war. If so, Lloyd George deserves great credit. I was told in London the other day that he really did push a lot of things through and get them done, and that the effect of his spending two days in the Admiralty was very great in speeding up the machine. There were certainly very many unpleasant circumstances in the way the Asquith Government was displaced, and many of us including myself had shamefully unfair things said about us; but then, so far as I am concerned, I was at one time very much overpraised, and I was really always miserable and out of place in public life. So long as I am let alone in private life, I have a feeling that it is sort of quits.

The Itchen trout are more fat than I have seen them for many years. I hooked a beauty of 2 lbs. 2 oz. near the top of the withy bed last Saturday and landed him just above the island, having to pass the rod over a large willow bush on the way down. I got about 5 fish today. I am much handicapped by my bad sight as I cannot see my fly on the water and if there is any wind which makes casting difficult I cannot tell where the fly is. The relief of being out of office continues to be unspeakable.

To Miss Haldane. September 18, 1917. *Fallodon.* Asquith is very easy-going and often does not realise the situation of other people. I hear he is in his own way sore about the way he has been treated by Ll. G. but Richard's case is far more unjust and exasperating than [that of] any of us.

To Lord Crewe (*Ambassador at Paris*). *February* 22, 1928. (*After Asquith's death.*) Your letter was very interesting. I was sure the French liked Asquith, because they were sure they could trust him; and they would appreciate his equanimity, courage and perfect temper and good will. He and Ll. G. would, as Briand says, have made a fine combination. There was no difficulty on Asquith's side, but Ll. G. was determined to oust Asquith and take his place. I have felt Asquith's death very much: it is true that his work was done, but we were very close together for so many years. I saw the beginning of his Parliamentary life; and to witness the close is the end of a long chapter of my own.

To Runciman. December 9, 1917. The real obstacles to peace seem to me to be the desire of the German people (it amounts to that) *not* to be masters in their own house and *not* to know anything except what their Government tells them; and their complete want of any sense of wrong done and need for reparation. To make peace with them still in this frame of mind would be at best a very regrettable necessity and not to be done except under pressure of utter necessity. But I think our officials and the French have not made nearly enough of the point that once the Germans will concede reparation and security, they will have nothing to fear for the future so long as they will live and let live on terms of peaceful development. This deficiency is not calculated to bring the German people to a reasonable frame of mind and plays into the hands of their militarist government. The need of correcting this is the justification of Lansdowne's letter.

Lansdowne's conditions of peace and Wilson's seem to be much the same, except that Wilson insists upon a change of form as well as of spirit in the German govt. This exception is I suppose the reason why the German papers abuse Wilson and praise Lansdowne and our papers do the reverse.

An American, Mr. W. K. Richardson, a frequent visitor at Fallodon, describes Edward Grey as 'a genial and merry host, particularly delighting to tell me American stories I had not heard.' On May 22, 1917, Grey wrote to this friend on the entry of the United States into the war:

Dear Richer: I have believed in Wilson throughout, on the ground that a man can be known through his friends. I got to know House and Page very well; they are both friends of Wilson, and House certainly a very intimate friend. I like both House and Page immensely, and found in both not only agreement in point of view but that sympathy of temperament and intimacy of spirit that beget friendship and confidence, and believed what they told me of Wilson.

I hope that in the long run your country will now become convinced that England is a free democracy with ideals and desires like those generally held in the U.S.A. Certainly your country is entering into the war in the same spirit as England did, the spirit of people who don't want war but feel that they are cornered and have no honourable way of avoiding it. We haven't all here been able to keep that spirit quite so pure as it was at the beginning; it can't be kept so when your people are engaged in the business of killing and being killed; and the awful brutalities of the Prussians could not but cause rage and hatred. But I do hope that if we win, the nobler spirit will get the upper hand. The letters from men at the front who are spending and risking their own lives are very fine; the absence of hatred is even more sublime than their self sacrifice and splendid courage.

Sometimes however I fear that in the civilian world, even if the Prussians are beaten in war, the Prussian spirit will have conquered the world.

Grey had two nephews to whom he was much attached — Cecil and Adrian Graves. Cecil, a soldier by profession, was captured during the first German onrush in September 1914 and had to endure the weariness of long prison life in Germany and later internment in Holland; he was much cheered by his uncle's letters.[1] Adrian was killed in the fighting of March 1918.

Grey to Captain Cecil Graves. October 2, 1916. Everyone belonging to you at home is well. After the war is over, if as I hope the war ends by getting it thoroughly into the heads and hearts of every nation in Europe that war is a bad thing, there will be a very interesting time. There must be great internal changes here and elsewhere. The old order of things may be dissolved in the consequences of the war. People's perspective is changed already in some things. Life is more serious and important, but death is less feared and more easily accepted. Suffering, if it be not embittered by injustice, is better borne because it is felt to be part of the common lot. I feel you have a terribly hard part in having to wait inactive and uncomforted for so long; it is harder than that of those who are still fighting, but we shall all honour you and welcome you when you come home with all your character and manhood upstanding in spite of the long trial.

Meanwhile the fine line

'They also serve who only stand and wait'

is not less true than when Milton wrote it.

March 28, 1918. It is very bitter and sad for you that Adrian is gone and you won't see him. I feel it very much, for the fine character that the war brought out in him and his attractive nature and cleverness made us all love and admire him. I had looked forward to seeing both of you and delighting in you as if you were sons. But it is of your mother that we have to think now. I do not feel that we ought to be sorry for Adrian: if the object of life is to live without reproach, to become a fine character and to act nobly, then Adrian's life has been a complete success.

[1] Captain Cecil Graves is now the owner of Fallodon, which his uncle left to him.

July 29, 1918. You write of pictures and of music. The great books, the great pictures and the great music of the world are tremendous and the longer one lives the more tremendous the really great things seem to be. It is well I think to consider what is great and always to keep it distinct in one's mind and to keep in touch with it. So many people as they go on in life seem to read nothing but new books and to go to the Academy to see the pictures of the year or even an Exhibition of modern freak pictures, but to cease to go to the National Gallery. I must go to the National Gallery with you when the war is over and the great pictures are all in their places. I can't see them properly now but I should enjoy hearing you see them. And I should like to talk to you about my favourite books and hear what you think of them.

My eyes have failed sadly, but my body is very fit again just now. I can eat anything and bicycle any distance though not fast. And I often think of bicycle rides that I may take you next summer, or even this autumn if the exchange of prisoners begins to work. The Germans have made a real mess of their last offensive and we are all in very good spirits. The crops are grand and we have had just enough rain.

BOOK III

FALLODON AGAIN

DECEMBER 1916 — SEPTEMBER 1933

I

Fallodon Again. December 1916 *to September* 1933

During the seventeen years that passed between Grey's resignation and his death, he was never again in the forefront of national or international affairs. The part he played in the League of Nations Union, in the Liberal Council and in the debates of the House of Lords was not unimportant, but he was always too blind and often too ill to lead a party, or to aspire to office. The amount of public work that he did corresponded to the amount for which he was fit. Whether he would have played a great part if his sight had grown better instead of worse, it is impossible to say. In such a case, the old struggle between his private desires and his sense of public duty might have been renewed. He was spared that, but he was spared little else.

His blindness steadily increased as the years went on, though he sought cures in many quarters but always in vain. To put it in terms of his favourite sport, first he had to give up the dry fly, then ordinary trout fishing, then salmon, till finally in 1932 he writes from Fallodon to Jack Tennant:

> I cannot see whether I put my worm into the water or on to the bank. With my ducks I can at any rate feel when they take it out of my hand, and distinguish some of them when they are very close.

It was an irony that tested the unconquerable sanity of his spirit, to be set free at last, too late; the leisure he had longed for was his, and the bounty of nature's loveliness was spread before him, invisible; every time he stepped from his library door into the garden, he was aware of the old familiar places undergoing the magic revolution of the seasons, but his eyes could scarcely mark the difference between December and May; he heard the birds in the pond that he had dug and in the bushes and trees that he had planted for them in years gone by, but they were voices of friends unseen; and as he sat on his favourite height at Ros Camp, though he could hear the curlews call as of old, he could see neither the purple of the heather close at hand nor the green of Cheviot far away.

He was equally cut off from books, of which as life advanced he had grown scarcely less fond. Fortunately he knew much of the best poetry by heart. Almost to the last he painfully read *The Times* political leaders held close up to his eyes, and occasionally wrote short letters by guesswork with his pen. But already by the time the war ended he had to dictate his longer letters, and depended on what was said or read aloud to him for the bulk of his political information. Such activities as he could still pursue were rendered possible largely by the devoted help of his friend, Mr. Henry Herbert, who had the cottage at Fallodon rent free, and in return did certain things he required: Mr. Herbert read to him and in his absence fed the ducks. He could read to himself continuously only in Braille. The advantage of blindness, he once said to me, was that one could keep one's hands warm while reading in bed, fingering the raised letters beneath the blankets! In the last months of his life he lost, by a final affliction, the sensitivity of his 'Braille finger.'

H. Cecil

AET. 61, 1923

The process of deterioration was continuous, but as early as May 1918 he wrote to Captain Barton:

> My sense of smell is nearly gone and my eyesight is very feeble and no use in watching birds. I classify the different parts of my body as being of different ages, as thus:
>
> | | | |
> |---|---|---|
> | Sense of smell . . . | aged 99 years | |
> | Eyes . . . . | " 95 " | |
> | Stomach . . . . | " 85 " | |
> | Sense of hearing . . . | " 56 " | (my age) |
> | Brain . . . . | " 56 " | |
> | Heart and lungs . . . | " 45 " | |
>
> It makes a very unequal team to get along with.

Other disasters fell thick upon him. Fallodon was burnt down in May 1917. Only the furniture, pictures and books on the ground floor were saved. After living in the kitchen wing till the war was over, he rebuilt the house, with the old bricks and in the same general style as before but with two storeys instead of three and with some change in the ground plan of the rooms. In February 1923 the Cottage on the Itchen was burnt, and was not rebuilt. How much these two breaches with the past meant to him, readers of this volume can by this time surmise. In 1922 his second marriage gave him a period of real happiness, but in 1928 Pamela, Lady Grey, died; and in the same year his brother Charles, of whom he had become almost as fond as formerly of George, was killed by a buffalo in Africa, as George a dozen years before had been killed by a lion. And besides these private strokes, Grey lived to see his hopes for the pacification of the world shattered, America withdrawn into herself, Europe armed to the teeth, and Germany under the Nazi regime. He foresaw a grim future for mankind, the more so as he had less than no sympathy with the increasing mechanisation of life.

But his private afflictions and public disappointments never broke his courage or soured his serene and constant spirit. Neither in his letters nor in his talk was there any cry of personal pain or even of impatience. He was unfailing in his quiet, humorous observation of life, and his determination to make the daily best of what was left. All who saw him went away cheered and elevated by the strong, even current of his talk, delightful, easy, humorous, sustained without effort high above the level of his griefs. Visitors to Fallodon were always made happy. The spring of fun in him was never dry. He loved to have P. G. Wodehouse read aloud, and to interrupt the reading with shouts of schoolboy laughter. He never showed depression in company, though he had some bad hours when alone. Yet solitude, which he had always loved, must to the end have seemed to him more good than bad, or he would have sought society more, especially after Pamela's death.

His principal achievement in these later years was the production of his books, a task which owed much to the encouragement of Pamela, his wife. In *Twenty-five Years* he told the story of his public career; blind as he was, he could not have searched the necessary documents without the devoted scholarly assistance of Mr. J. A. Spender. The publication of *The Charm of Birds* and *Fallodon Papers* put him in touch with a wide public on that side of thought and feeling for which he cared the most. They will live while there are song-birds left in England and people to care for them, be that time short or long.

As soon as Grey was out of office he went straight to Fallodon, where he arrived a few days before Christmas 1916. 'I had thought that when I was taken out of the shafts I should drop, and I did drop four days after I came here,' he wrote to a friend. He was ill with gastric haemorrhage, much pain and other serious symptoms. In a couple of months he was two stone lighter but was on the road of convalescence, enjoying life and liberty and not yet knowing how soon and how quickly his eyes were doomed to fail.

To Katharine Lyttelton, February 5, 1917. *Fallodon.* I got well enough, so my sisters are at their respective homes and I am alone. As I intended, I am now going through papers, and this first week of February I am looking through some of Dorothy's papers which are as she left them. It is poignant work. I untie knots which her fingers tied, and touch things that have never been touched since she touched them. There is so much to be done and enjoyed with a library inside and one's own house and home, and the country outside. It is a beautiful world outside of towns and much to be enjoyed, if the war were over, but what I care for most is on the other side, and I am ready to go there when I can honourably do so.

There is some snow, but not enough to make the fields pure white. The weather is an absorbing interest to me, to see the days lengthening and the great earth slowly but daily tilting England more towards the sun, the enormous process of the seasons. I believe men will never get right till they get united by some sort of admiration and reverence for the great elemental works of God and think less of their own artifices.

June 1, 1917. I have had wonderful days here: they make me long terribly to have Dorothy with me; but when I think of all the sad and awful things public and private I should have to tell her, if she came back, the war and all its horrors, and the grief it has brought to friends' homes, and then the other griefs. Think what a tale it would be as she asked how her various friends were — the Birrells, the Pauls, the Francis Buxtons. And now of course the burning of Fallodon would be added to the tale. Well, when I think of all this, I feel it selfish and cruel to wish Dorothy back, though I long for it so. It is better to wish that I should go to her.

No one can now live in the rooms she made at Fallodon or alter them or desecrate them after I am dead. That at any rate is safe, but I can never have a home that will be a home as Fallodon was. I can with the furniture that is saved make the inside of some of the rooms in a new house sufficiently like the old rooms to remind me perpetually that they are not the same. That is what I suppose I shall do after the war. Till then, there are 5 servants' bedrooms left in the kitchen wing. I shall live there in the shadow of the ruin, but the garden and familiar country will be there.

I am sure I can do no good by talking. I am disposed to think Lloyd George is doing well, considering all the difficulties he has to face.

January 16, 1918. It is fine but not comfortable to be looking on at the close of an epoch. I feel deep in me that the civilization of the Victorian epoch ought to disappear. I think I always knew this subconsciously, but I took things as I found them and for 30 years spoke of progress as an enlargement of the Victorian industrial age — as if anything could be good that led to telephones and cinematographs and large cities and the *Daily Mail*. I have nevertheless gone back on the N.E. Railway board which I like. I cannot bear the continuance of the war, but it has to be till the Germans cease to hope for victory.

To the Hon. Arthur Murray, *January* 21, 1918. As to sheep and shepherds and representing a point of view, many observations occur to me. Having had, for the first time for 30 years, leisure to think and even to speculate quite freely, alone, detached from political associates, with thoughts tied to no objective such as a speech, with sense of values changed by the greatest catastrophe in human affairs that has occurred within historical memory, it would be difficult to put a label on me that would be accurate. I think I tend towards the view of Western Civilization expressed in a book about China, by Lowes Dickinson [*Letters from John Chinaman*, Brimley Johnson, 1901], though it is many years since I read the book and my memory is vague. And this leads to the story of a Chinaman (from another book) who by being a recluse, living remote in the country, acquired such a reputation for wisdom that a deputation sought him out to offer him the throne. He made no reply, except to go away and wash his ears. I perceive that unless I send this letter at once it will not catch the post, and you being not yet detached from Western Civilization perhaps expect a reply to a letter in the same year or even month.

To Mrs. Creighton, May 30, 1917. *Itchen Abbas.* The beauty has been overwhelming; pear and apple blossom overlapped, and the profusion and splendour were more than human capacity could appreciate. I used to feel at this season of the year a sense of waste because I could not enjoy at once all that was spread abroad; till one day the overwhelming egotism of looking at it from this limited human point of view occurred to me, and I thought that God might be contemplating it all. Then I ceased to be oppressed by the sense of waste. The beauty of the season makes the contrast of man-made war more horrible and poignant; on the other hand it gives comfort and support. The sight of all this beauty and the feeling of response to it in oneself gives assurance that God rules in the Universe, and that evil cannot prevail. It is the same feeling expressed in the Bible and attributed to Noah when he saw the rainbow after the floods. Nevertheless in some of the most beautiful parts of the world man has for generations remained most cruel — the regions under the Turk are an instance.

To Mrs. Creighton, February 4, 1918. *Fallodon.* I think it is a good and wholesome check upon the horror caused by the war, to think of the things that even the war cannot shake or alter. Great music loses none of its power, but it must be great like the *Messiah* or a Beethoven Symphony. I am sure those things have the eternal in them. The wonder of the stars and the sense of the beauty of the world remain, too, undiminished, though I cannot enjoy looking at the sea here as I used to do, now that it is filled with mines and submarines.

The first thrush sang in the garden yesterday evening, and I had the same feeling of response to it. As long as we can still read those two lines of Wordsworth:

> 'My heart leaps up when I behold'

and

> 'The thought of my past years in me doth breed
> Perpetual benediction,'

and say definitely and decidedly 'yes' after each, we cannot be pessimists. But one may be very pessimistic about human affairs of a year or a generation or even an epoch, and yet be an optimist about the Universe. That is rather my feeling just now.

In October 1917 his old friend Doctor Pember lost his son Edward, killed as an airman in the war.

To Doctor Pember, October 6, 1917. I see the news in today's paper. I am full of deep sympathy for you and your wife and daughter and my heart goes out in the earnest hope that you may be able to endure, and that you may be able to support and comfort each other. I know very well that there is no escape from the suffering of grief. We cannot love much without suffering much, and the very pain of the suffering is an evidence of the strength of our love, so that we cannot even wish grief to be less than it is and must be. The best I can wish for you is that you may have courage and strength: you will yourself know just where to seek and find it. Some of it you will get I hope from the thought of all the pleasure you have had from Edward's life, and of his fine example. We who are left have to make our lives continue to be worthy of those from whom we are separated.

December 13, 1917. I am very glad to hear from you again after an interval and thus to know how you are. You are often in my thoughts. The occupation of work is the best thing for anyone who has to bear great sorrow; if they have work in hand and strength to do it and if they can sleep, the problem of how to endure life is solved for the present moment. Looking forward to the months and years that are to come is very dreary and depressing, but we do not live life in the lump but day by day, and each day brings its own work and some expedient to help us.

January 14, 1918. *Bowood.* I was glad to get your letter at Fallodon. We are all moved on with the world, moving in appearance away from the past, but taking it with us in our hearts and moving really towards a future that will reunite us with what we love.

For the present I have arranged an orderly life of unoffensive, congenial and gentle work. The N.E. Railway Committees and Board take me from Fallodon to York once a month and occupy me there Thursday and Friday; then I get to London on Friday evening and attend the British Museum [Trustees' Meeting] on Saturday morning. This has led to a Saturday to Monday here [with Lord Lansdowne] and I am now on the point of returning via London to Fallodon.

It is not surprising to find him at Bowood, for he had not been shocked by the much-abused 'Peace letter' which its owner had written to the *Daily Telegraph* in the previous November. Grey thought the outcry against it absurd; it was, he wrote, a wise discussion of possibilities in an uncertain situation, essentially the same as Lansdowne's Memorandum to the Cabinet of a year before, which had received serious attention in the most responsible quarters.[1]

In lighter and more academic vein is a letter of May 1917. The common room at All Souls, over which Doctor Pember so admirably presided as Warden, had good talk even during the war; and W. P. Ker was there to drop those rare, weighty words of his. One of these, reported by Pember to Grey, was that Shakespeare 'intended nonsense' in *The Phœnix and the Turtle*. Grey replies:

> MY DEAR FRANK: It is easy to say that Shakespeare intended nonsense and it may be true, for even more than Habakkuk he was *capable de tout*. But I think he had hold of some legend. What do you make of
>
> 'And thou treble dated crow,
> That thy sable gender makest
> With the breath thou givest and takest'? [2]
>
> I am very sorry for Bridges [who had told Pember that he had not read *The Phœnix and the Turtle*] because I don't believe anyone takes in new poetry after fifty, and the Threnos of the *Phœnix and the Turtle* is very delicate and beautiful. It is too late for Bridges to read it now.
>
> Your audit ale has made me more conscious of frailty than anything I ever drank. I can smile and scoff at the thought of going to the bad over wine or the finest liqueur, much as I

[1] See also his letter to Runciman of December 9, 1917, page 377, above.

[2] The author of *The Phœnix and the Turtle* perhaps referred to the 'legend' recorded in Pliny (*Nat. Hist.*, lib. x, c. 15): 'Ore eos parere aut coire vulgus arbitratur,' viz. the vulgar believe that the crow generates its progeny by the mouth. This was pointed out to Doctor Pember by Sir William Marris when Grey raised the question again.

appreciate and revere the best of these, but if I lived where I could have a jug of that ale at will I would not trust myself. I positively long to get drunk on it, and I have hitherto loathed the idea of being drunk.

To his friend Captain Barton he continued to write the chronicle of his non-human friends at Fallodon:

February 14, 1917. An absurd thing happened the other day; a robin entered the room at the same time as one of the squirrels. The latter came to the writing table as usual, but the robin not being used to the room flitted restlessly about, and the squirrel not being used to a bird in the room became very nervous and suspicious — paying no attention to me, indeed turning its back on me, but starting at every flit of the robin's wings, and looking all about the room to see what strange spirit was there.

October 24, 1917. The remarkable thing here at present is a great outbreak of tameness towards me personally; whether it is due to some improvement in my aura or to the approach of the Millennium (isn't the Millennium to follow Armageddon?) or to what I cannot say. In the first place the retriever dog, the relict of a keeper who left two years ago, has become absurdly attached to me; though I don't even feed it myself. A wild teal arrived in August and will now feed within a yard of my boots and is so tame that I never see it on the wing. Three waterhens also have become perfectly tame, which is not unprecedented but unusual. The dog being female might suggest that there was something sexual in the attachment, but the teal is a male; it arrived in 'eclipse' and has now 'assumed,' as the books say, its male 'nuptial dress.' The really happy life is to hit on one pleasant way of spending a day and to be able to repeat it day after day after day. These country pleasures never pall, and the sun never fails to rise and set, though it does it with variety.

November 22, 1917. Your motor car story is most valuable; it almost justifies the invention of motor cars, though they, like other means of easy locomotion, do really, under the specious guise of convenience, keep one in sedentary motion, whereas the pleasure of life is to be in exercise or at rest.

January 10, 1921. The ponds are over their banks and the

burn could hardly contain itself. Postmen on their bicycles found roads flooded and had to go by devious ways. My ducks enjoyed it and some flew about with excitement. I was excited. Only the waterhens remained calm and walked about in their usual places in the usual way.

His oldest friend, Sydney Buxton, in a privately printed memoir gives this account of Edward Grey and his Fallodon ducks:

He was successful in rearing no less than five-and-twenty species of duck, some of them very rare, and others which had not been bred elsewhere in England, or at all events under semi-wild conditions. His latest success was the rearing of broods of the American canvas-back. Amongst such a mixed community hybrids were not infrequent, and some of these were of distinguished parentage. These latter he occasionally described as 'High-Bred,' a term which, to his amusement, had been used by my typist in a letter of mine, in which I was referring to a rare hybrid that I had reared.

The water-hen, as he called it — known to most of us as the moor-hen — is one of the most difficult birds to tame, though they live all their lives cheek by jowl with human beings. He, however, by his patience and by his personality overcame their innate timidity, and latterly, a water-hen was one of the first to come to meet him when he arrived with his basket of bread; while another frequented the lawn and occasionally came into the 'Squirrel Room' in search of food.

In earlier days most of the ducks were pinioned; but for some years past they have been free to fly where they like, and to come and go as they will. Many of them fly away never to return, but a large proportion re-visit their home. Nothing delighted and heartened Edward Grey more than the return of a wanderer, especially if it had been absent for many months and become a wild bird, which yet immediately on arrival took its place in the dinner-queue and again fed from his hand as though it had never been away.

The evening feed — the duck dinner — was sacred, and the convenience of humans went to the wall. The duck is a sunset feeder, and so, of course, the Fallodon ducks must be fed at that particular time for half-an-hour or so; and, as there was no local Joshua, the house dinner in the summer was varied day by day.

Seated under a great larch tree at the head of the pond he distributed the bread and grain to his ducks crowding round, gobbling up their food, picking at his shoes or plucking at his sleeve to attract attention. He would check the greedy or the forward, encourage the shy or coax the timid bird, and even the wildest fed from his hand. Presently one of them, usually a Mandarin, would perch on his shoulder or on his hat, while others would flap on to the seat beside him.

We will leave him there.

Meanwhile his sight failed year by year. He saw ever less of the birds he fed, and his intimate letters to his friends gradually shrank to brief notes, bearing painful evidence that his guidance of the pen owed little to his eyes. Already in October 1921 he writes to Barton:

> I am in arrears with letters and can only say that I enjoyed your account of the pigeons. Oh! that I had eyes to see such small happenings, which like small jokes and many small things are more endearing than great mountains.
>
> *January* 2, 1930. As to Mandarin ducks, the Chinese have paid great attention to them. There is a pair on an old Oriental vase in this house. I think I must have told you that in China a pair are carried in a cage in marriage processions as 'emblems of conjugal fidelity.' What they do when the drake is in eclipse and practically indistinguishable from the duck, I do not know.
>
> *August* 26, 1932. Fallodon has escaped drought all this year. It has been served four times by bounteous rain. One of my favourite verses in the Bible is: 'Thou hast sent a gracious rain upon thine inheritance and refreshedst it when it was weary.' I like the epithets 'gracious' and 'weary.'

After he had left office, Grey took no part in politics so long as the war lasted.

> My peerage answers very well [he wrote to Munro Ferguson, Lord Novar, in July 1917]. It has made me quite free. But I

FEEDING THE DUCKS, 1931
Taken by Mr. Seton Gordon

never can remember that I am a peer, and I haven't been to the House of Lords this year. Nor do I go to ex-Cabinet meetings and I shan't go into public life again, unless it is for something that I really think I am specially wanted for.

As regards Parliament and party, he maintained this attitude of abstention till the end of the war, and was not personally involved in the bitter quarrel between Mr. Lloyd George and the Opposition under Asquith over the affair of Sir Frederic Maurice in 1918. His most important public correspondence during the last year of the war was with Professor Gilbert Murray about the formation of the League of Nations Union. That body arose by the merger of the League of Nations Society that had been founded in 1915, and the League of Free Nations Association founded early in 1918. These two bodies were ready to unite under Grey's leadership, and it was this fact that first brought him back into any connection with public life.

To Gilbert Murray, August 15, 1918. *Fallodon.* You write that you think that if I said I 'would become President if the two Societies were amalgamated, the difficulties would be overcome.' Well, I take the plunge and authorize you to say that. My failing eyesight hampers me very much, as it will take time for me to make the arrangements under which I can do work, and if I come to make speeches I shall probably have to do without notes. All this makes me very reluctant to take a position that may entail such things, but I will take the risk. I have received a letter from Dickinson, to which I have not time to reply before leaving home today, but I will tell him what I have told you.

After a meeting of the two Societies at the Central Hall on October 10, 1918, at which he spoke, the League of Nations Union was formed by their amalgamation in November 1918, with Grey as its first President. Thenceforth, in spite of his increasing blindness, he gave a good deal of his time to speaking and writing for the cause he had thus undertaken, and he occasionally spoke with effect in the House of Lords on Foreign Affairs.

The following letter, dated December 30, 1918, when Wilson was in England just before the opening of the Versailles Conference, is of interest:[1]

> DEAR COLONEL HOUSE:
>
> I sat next the President at dinner last Saturday, but it might be useful if I added to anything I said then one or two things about the League of Nations. They are, of course, my own personal opinion only.
>
> 1. There is an undercurrent of opposition in this country to the idea of a League of Nations, but if the project takes practical form, this opposition will be completely snowed under by an overwhelming mass of public opinion here, which is whole-hearted and resolute in favour of President Wilson's ideas. This opinion is so strong, that to disappoint it would be a great blow even to Lloyd George's Government. I cannot speak for the Government, but such things as Lloyd George has said to me about the League of Nations, and what I hear he has said to other people are very satisfactory, and the appointment of Lord Robert Cecil by the Government to take charge of the question inspires all of us who wish to see a League of Nations with complete confidence.
>
> 2. Our great fear is that a League of Nations Treaty might be wrecked by the Senate in the United States. We are afraid that for us to force the pace here might contribute to that result. It has happened before, that treaties have been opposed, or even wrecked in the Senate, when it was supposed that they were inspired by England, or that England had a special interest in them; and we see already, according to the newspapers, that such opposition is gathering. This makes some of us cautious in what we say, but President Wilson need, I believe, have no apprehension lest this country should not support the most concrete form of a League of Nations and the most far-reaching that can be produced at the Peace Conference.

[1] From a copy kindly lent me by Colonel House and Mr. Charles Seymour.

The latter part of this letter it might have seemed presumptuous for me to say to the President direct, and he may quite justly say that it is his province and not ours to be concerned with what the Senate of the United States is likely to do. The first part of this letter it would have been a little difficult for me to say quite openly to the President with Lloyd George sitting on the other side of him, though this difficulty was one only of form, the substance of what I have said being entirely favourable to Lloyd George himself.

Yours sincerely,

GREY OF F.

You can, of course, show this letter to the President if you think it seemly and suitable.

One of the last times I met Lord Grey [writes Mr. Alwyn Parker] was in November 1917. Conversation turned on the subject of peace, for I had just been appointed by Lord Hardinge to collate material and co-ordinate arrangements for the British delegation at an eventual Peace Conference. I remember, in fact I made a note of it at the time, that Lord Grey expressed an ardent hope that conditions of peace would be negotiated and not dictated. 'The end to be sought and worked for,' he said, 'is a just, fair, and reasonable peace, for only so can a settlement be enduring.' The next time I saw him was seven years later, and he recalled the conversation.

During the unhappy proceedings at Versailles from January to June 1919 Grey was wholly out of public life. His blindness was growing rapidly worse. 'I find having things read to me is very tedious and I am getting more and more outside current life and thought,' he wrote to Gilbert Murray in March 1919.

He had not had the least ambition to be sent to Versailles. The day after the Armistice he had written to Miss Constance Herbert, 'I hope not to be let in for these peace negotiations: even if asked I should refuse to take part unless it were for a whole-hearted co-operation with Wilson and League of Nations.'

On March 9, 1919, he wrote to Professor Gilbert Murray: 'During the war, so far as I know, though we signed some agreements with our Allies that can only be justified by the pressure of the war, we did not put into them exorbitant claims for ourselves. What we have done at the Peace Conference in this respect I do not know.' A little later, when he heard rumours how things were going at Versailles, he said to a friend, 'I am glad I am not there: they are out for loot.' But he made no public utterance, and so far as I know the only private interference he made with the negotiations was a letter to Balfour on June 3, 1919, suggesting that Heligoland should be made a bird sanctuary, under international protection against the slaughtering of the millions of birds that rested there on migration.

He was most unhappy about the Peace terms, particularly our retention of the whole of the German Colonies, and the extent of the Reparations — though some annexation of Colonies and some Reparations he considered just; and he thought the refusal to allow the Germans to be heard was an outrage without precedent. He was well pleased at the creation of the League of Nations, but felt that the treatment of Germany gravely compromised its future. The two aspects of the work at Versailles were clearly incompatible.

And already the value of the League was threatened by the danger that America would after all refuse to participate; this he had always thought would be fatal. In February 1917 he had written to a friend:

> Without the United States a League would be at best but a revived concert of the Great Powers of Europe, liable at any time to split into rival groups. With the United States it would have a stability and be on a high plane that has never been attained by anything of the kind before.

His intense anxiety on this point, on which he believed the future happiness of the world to depend, led him in August 1919 to accept the mission to America offered to him by the Government. His distrust of Mr. Lloyd George had been increased by his conduct of the Coupon Election of the previous winter and by the subsequent proceedings at Versailles, but had not yet reached the point it subsequently attained; and to help America into the League he was prepared to serve any government and to make any sacrifice of his own leisure.

So in September 1919 he sailed to America 'on a special mission to deal with questions arising out of the Peace pending the appointment of a Permanent Ambassador.' He knew the difficulties in the way: America's entry into the League had become a party question and a bone of contention between President and Senate. Wilson was behaving with great unwisdom in pursuit of his noble object; he was refusing to make any compromise with objectors who could thwart his whole plan. He no longer sought the prudent counsel of Colonel House. Grey hoped to induce the President to make the necessary concessions to American opinion, as he held the entry of the United States into the League to be more important than the precise terms of the Covenant. Whether if he had got into personal contact with Wilson the situation could even at that late hour have been saved, it is useless to speculate. For he was not permitted to try. The President, by a crowning calamity, became seriously ill and declined to see Grey at all during the months that he remained in the United States. In November 1919 Grey wrote home to Ella Pease:

> I was sent to discuss things with the President after Peace had been concluded. The Senate has declined to make any Peace and the President is too ill to discuss anything. I expect

> to be back by the end of January at latest. I get a nice walk occasionally and some good music, and sometimes bridge after dinner. I love the Americans. They seem to me more easy to get on with than English people, but they are very civilized and wear white waistcoats, and have not as a rule got any passion for country life; and I, being at bottom primitive and uncivilized, would have to go and live in the backwoods if I stayed in the country. Nevertheless life in Washington, if I was an Ambassador, would be far more tolerable than life in London.

This abortive visit to America was rendered pleasant by the warmth of his reception in unofficial circles. One incident in particular set him on the path of writing those essays on the life of birds and men which afterwards appeared in *Fallodon Papers* and *The Charm of Birds*.

> He was asked by Lawrence Lowell [writes Mr. Ferris Greenslet] to come up to Harvard to speak informally to the student body of the University. I happened to be with him in Washington at the time, and he asked me whether *Recreation, its place in a well-ordered life*, with special emphasis on birds and fishes would be suitable, and I naturally said it would. Well, without any other preparation than turning it over in his mind and perhaps taking a few notes, he got up at the Union before a thousand boys whom I suppose he couldn't see, and talked it off without a pause, with admirable balance and proportion of substance as well as felicity of phrase. We had a stenographer present who took him down verbatim. The copy so produced was sent to him for revision, but came back with hardly any changes. [It is now the third essay in *Fallodon Papers*.]

He returned to England, well knowing that the abstention of the United States from the League was a fatal blow. But it behoved him to make the best of a bad business, and he devoted the rest of his public life to the cause of European peace. His views on two important questions of League policy, the Geneva Protocol and League action to restrain Japan, can best be given in his own words.

> *Grey to Gilbert Murray. Fallodon. February* 1, 1925. The Geneva Protocol, like the Treaty of Mutual Assistance and Guarantee before it, is an attempt to solve the problem of security.
>
> The system of exclusive alliances and competition in armaments, that existed in Europe before 1914, proved a lamentable failure.
>
> The Protocol adopts another and more hopeful principle. From the British point of view there are objections to some parts of it. There is force in some of these objections, but we hope that after full examination and consultation with the Dominions, the Government will be able to propose some amendments, that will meet valid objections.
>
> It would be most unfortunate, if we were continually to reject what is proposed at Geneva, without giving any indication of something that the British Commonwealth of Nations is prepared to support.
>
> The problem of security lies at the very root of European difficulties. To solve it is the paramount need in international affairs. Our rejection or non-acceptance of what has hitherto been proposed or accepted by other nations makes the problem more than ever pressing and urgent.

On the other hand, he was anxious that the League should not undertake tasks which were beyond its actual strength, particularly outside Europe. Speaking at the Albert Hall on March 27, 1932, with regard to the question of restraining Japanese aggression, he said:

> I should like to say a word to those who regard the Far Eastern question as a test case, and say that by it the League of Nations will stand or fall. In my opinion, it is a matter peculiarly unfitted to be a test case....
>
> ... There are people who ask, could not the League of Nations have done more? I will ask — what more could it have done? The League of Nations is not a separate entity, but it is composed of the Governments of those countries who are

members of the League and it cannot act unless those Governments are all in agreement that action should be taken. Does anyone suppose that those Governments would be in favour of going to war in this case, or, if they had been in favour of going to war, that they would have been successful? I do not like the idea of resorting to war to prevent war. What we wish is to prevent war. War is a disagreeable thing, even if it is to be resorted to in order to prevent a war. It is too much like lighting a large fire in order to prevent a smaller one. Anyhow this instance seems to me peculiarly unsuitable for any action of that sort on the part of the League of Nations.

Then people say that economic pressure might have been used. There is provision in the Covenant of the League for economic pressure. This is quite true, but, again, look at the geographical circumstances. Economic pressure could not possibly have been applied unless it was done in co-operation with the Government of the United States. It would be mean, and I think not just, to say that the United States is responsible for the fact that no economic pressure has been applied, because I do not know that the Governments who are members of the League would have resorted to economic pressure without the United States. But I do say this, that in the peculiar circumstances of this dispute any action taken by the League which had not the co-operation of the United States would have been futile.

... So far from regarding this as a test case on which the future of the League of Nations depends, I say that whatever happens in the Far East, I shall feel that the League of Nations is as important as ever to the peace of the world. The real test of the success of the League is not to be found in what happens in the Far East. It is going to be found in the way nations, especially of Europe, succeeded in reducing their expenditure on armaments.

After the defection of America, Grey was more than ever persuaded that the only hope for ultimate European peace lay in our friendship with France for the purposes of the League, and as a means of drawing in Germany to enjoy common security. The sense of insecurity on the part of the French after we refused to guarantee their frontier was at the bottom of the Ruhr occupation and other mischiefs. In the debate on the Ruhr in the House of Lords on April 20, 1924, Grey said:

> I think it would be worth considering whether you cannot make some use of the instrument of the League of Nations to give security to France and to Germany also in the future. Our own security is bound up with French security, and I believe only by some big scheme that makes Germany feel secure as well as France will you bring about that feeling of security.

This idea was realized by Sir Austen Chamberlain's Locarno Treaty in December 1925, which rejoiced Grey's heart.

On November 5, 1928, at a Liberal luncheon, he made an important speech which diverted an attack then beginning against Sir Austen's policy of working with France for European peace — provided always, as Grey insisted, that it was not allowed to slide into an exclusive friendship, of which there was always danger:

> The wrong policy is the policy which Germany pursued after 1870. Germany made the Triple Alliance an exclusive Alliance, forced the pace in armaments, and that policy produced conditions in Europe which led to the war of 1914. I am convinced that is the true reading of history. Precisely because of that, I think it would be a grave blunder for the Allies to repeat the German policy of 1870, and so far they have not done so. On the contrary, they have pursued what seems to me the right policy — the League of Nations Policy and Locarno. That was the right policy. If the Government was about to go and make a separate political entente with France it would be a departure from the right policy.

One of the reasons why Grey came to disapprove so strongly of Mr. Lloyd George's Coalition Government in the years 1919–22 was that in his opinion the Prime Minister would not allow our Foreign Policy to take any stable form upon which anyone could rely. The regimen of quick change was exactly the wrong food for sick Europe. In the first years after the Peace there were many short-lived experiments: here is Grey's comment on one of them, made in a letter to Lord Novar of July 6, 1922:

> MY DEAR RONALD:
> As long as the leaders of the Conservative party swear by Ll. G. in public, however much they may swear *at* him in private, there is not much chance. I am told that Ll. G. now says that the Bolshevists are no good. It is a pity that it should have been necessary to have a huge European Conference, to strain the Entente with France and cold shoulder the U.S. Govt. in order to find this out. It is an expensive and cumbrous way of getting wisdom.

But Grey's objections to Mr. Lloyd George applied also to Ireland (prior to the Treaty) and to Home affairs. The Prime Minister's alliances with the magnates of the Press and his method of disposing of Honours and his 'political fund' won Grey's strong disapproval. He thought the standard of our political life was being lowered. He rejoiced therefore in the deliverance wrought in October 1922, when Mr. Baldwin's act of resistance overset the Coalition Government.

Edward Grey and Stanley Baldwin never saw much of one another, but they had much in common and if opportunity had offered might have become close friends. When Grey's second wife died, Mr. Baldwin wrote to him, and received the following letter in reply:

> *January* 6, 1929. *Fallodon*
>
> MY DEAR BALDWIN:
> It was good of you to write to me and I am very much touched by what you say.
> I have had much sorrow, but also very wonderful happiness

in my life. And is not the estimate of the sorrow also a measure of the greatness of the happiness? Both are agents in developing us, and I imagine that growth by experience and trial is the purpose of human life here.

But I have had so much of both happiness and sorrow that I feel exhausted and my mood is one of *nunc dimittis*.

I am sure you over-estimate my importance in public life, but now and then it comes to me to feel that I have something worth saying and that I want to say it and that will be so still. The difficulty is that to be a live person in politics one must take some hand in a party. I remain by conviction a Free Trader and that decides my party, but I do not feel zest for the old and eternal controversy, not from lack of conviction but from staleness and a feeling that there are plenty of others who can say what I think as well or better.

I am really echoing your own complaint that to be in public life one has to do much for which one has great distaste and no special qualification. One cannot pick and choose.

Every word, however, which you say about my importance to this country applies with more force to yourself. Personality is more than any special qualifications, more than all special qualifications put together. As long as you are at the head of a Government, it will stand for what is honourable.

The iron entered into my soul, when Ll. G.'s Govt. after the War let down public life at home and destroyed our credit abroad. Ever since it has been a relief to have public honour re-established and you will always stand for that. And besides there are those personal qualities which can be summed up as the gift for making troubles better and not worse. So I hope you will not be discouraged! Though I know only too well the sacrifice that office and House of Commons mean.

I seem to have been writing your own letter to me backwards, applying it to you as I did so.

Various efforts were made in these latter years to draw Grey into more definite leadership. Lord Cecil writes to me:

After the war was over, I had hoped to persuade him to come back to public life as the leader of a moderate progressive opinion. He hated the idea, and laid it down as a preliminary condition that he could in no case do anything without the consent of Asquith, which was not forthcoming. The more I urged him the less he liked it, and eventually I and others had to abandon the plan. Yet, looking back, I still regret that it failed. Grey had qualities so essential to our well-being, particularly in the after-war years, that the dream of a Centre Party led by him was one which still delights me.

In fact his blindness must have prevented him from leading a great party that aspired to office. The nearest approach to party leadership which he undertook was the Presidency of the Liberal Council, which marked the culmination of his quarrel with Mr. Lloyd George. One of its most active members, Mr. Vivian Phillipps, has sent me the following account of its inception:

Edward Grey's political activities during his later years were associated, in the main, with his work in connection with the Liberal Council, of which he was the President from its inception in December 1926 until his death.

The Council came into being, as a result of the disapproval with which large numbers of leading Liberals in the country regarded what appeared to them, at the time, to be an attempt by Lloyd George to control the policy of the Liberal Party, by the grant of subventions from his 'personal' political fund. In return for these subventions Lloyd George was stipulating for certain changes in the existing 'personnel' in charge of Liberal Headquarters, which would ensure a 'management' acceptable to him and sympathetic with his political outlook.

The acceptance of these stipulations by the National Liberal Federation gave rise to considerable unrest among Liberals in the constituencies, and there were threats of large secessions from the Party as a result of the National Liberal Federation's decision. Grey was in no doubt as to the right view of these transactions.

The idea that the Liberal Party should be under the financial control of any single individual, or of a group of rich men who could dictate its policy, was wholly repugnant to his conception of the right standards of British public life.

He invited a number of friends, who shared his views, to meet him for the purpose of considering what steps, if any, could be taken to preserve the independence of the Liberal Party, and to prevent the threatened disintegration in its ranks. The meeting took place on December 23, 1926, and among those who attended were Herbert Gladstone, his brother Henry Gladstone (afterwards Lord Gladstone of Hawarden), Walter Runciman, Donald Maclean, Gilbert Murray, Alfred Spender, J. M. Robertson, Lady Violet Bonham Carter, Earl Buxton, Vivian Phillipps, Geoffrey Howard and W. M. R. Pringle.

The following is an extract from the minutes of this meeting:

'A meeting was held at Lord Grey's house on Thursday, December 23, when there was a preliminary discussion as to what further steps should be taken in relation to the position within the Party. It was the general view that measures should be adopted in order to prevent those who disapprove of the contemplated sale of the Party machine to Mr. Lloyd George, from leaving the Party.

'It was agreed that an Association should be formed within the Party, to be called "The Liberal Council," and that its object should be stated to be "to enable Liberals who desire to uphold the independence of the Party to remain within it for the furtherance of the aims of Liberalism." Lord Grey was unanimously invited to become the President of the Council, and intimated his willingness to accept the position.'

Grey was deeply interested in the action of the Liberal Council, and though almost a dying man made great exertions in the cause. He believed that the good name of the Liberal Party and the honour and purity of English political life were at stake. As he said in his Presidential address they must 'stand before the country as a party against which no reproach can be brought.'

The Liberal Party was dying, and Grey died with it. He was too old, and he was too strong a Free Trader, ever to form other connections. He approved of a temporary coalition government to meet the nation's needs in 1931, but he had no thought of taking office himself, for his blindness alone now rendered that out of the question. He approved the action of the Free Trade Liberals in retiring from the National Government in protest against the Ottawa agreements in 1932. But his personal friendship with Mr. Runciman, who remained in the Cabinet, was in no way affected, and his attitude had become detached and philosophic.

His last speech was in April 1933, as President of the Liberal Council, when he said:

> I cannot provoke controversy by saying it is the Liberal Party, but it is Liberalism which has made England what it is today, and it will endure. As long as people are what they are in this country, they will be liberal, even if they do not belong to the Liberal Party. We have been attached to individual liberty and tolerance, but the British people have shown that, while they prized liberty above everything and would not tolerate the loss of liberty, they also have the conviction that order must be preserved in order that liberty may be enjoyed.

On June 4, 1922, Grey married Pamela, daughter of Percy Scawen Wyndham, and widow of Edward Tennant, first Lord Glenconner. The Glenconners had been his intimate friends for many years. He announced the marriage to Jack Tennant in the following letter from his wife's house, Wilsford Manor, near Salisbury:

> Pamela and I were married in the Church here by the Vicar this morning. We wanted to have it quietly. Christopher is here; and my sister, who lives about twenty miles off, came over in her car, but no one else except our two selves and the Vicar were in the Church. It is a great happiness to me that we have been able to marry as we had intended early in the summer. It will make a great and happy difference in my life and I like to think that it will be Pamela's happiness too, and will not make the home a less happy one for her sons. We shall

each continue to keep up our own homes as we have been doing. We have each a memory in the past to cherish.

These hopes were perfectly fulfilled. For six years an aftermath of domestic happiness based on mutual love and similarity of tastes smoothed Grey's rugged path. Pamela was devoted to birds and to books. She did much to prevent him from retreating too deeply into the seclusion of mind natural to a blind man living alone, and particularly natural to him. So far as she could, she stimulated his political activities; his political ambition nothing could galvanize into life. And, as he himself testified, it was due to her that he produced his books, for which many have cause to remember her with gratitude. He loved her home at Wilsford.

In November 1928 this interlude of quiet happiness came to an end. Pamela died. 'It is very hard,' he wrote to Mrs. Creighton, 'but I lived alone for more than 16 years and I can do it again, though I am very stricken.'

There had never been any contest in his mind between his memory of Dorothy and his affection for Pamela. They were different in kind and stood openly and simply side by side, as did the two gardens, named 'Dorothy's' and 'Pamela's,' into which he stepped from his library door so many times a day. But when in the last four years of his life he was left lonely again, his mind and heart, sustained by his wonderful memory, went back to dwell with Dorothy in the days of their youth and their love.

The veneration with which he was generally regarded in his old age took various pleasing forms, and none pleased him better than his unanimous election as Chancellor of his old University, where the great majority of the electors were more or less attached to the Conservative party, but on this occasion united with Liberals in the choice of Grey. His installation in the Sheldonian Theatre in 1928 was a memorable scene. Doctor Cyril Bailey of Balliol writes of it:

> He asked me to write his Latin speech for him, giving me in English what he wanted to say. He was by that time very blind and it would have been impossible for him to read it. So he suggested first that I should read it for him. A little later he wrote to me 'I have been looking at your speech and the roll of a Latin sentence is coming back to me. I might learn it by heart.' I shall never forget the magnificent dignity of his walk up the floor of the Sheldonian to his seat. When it came to the speech he delivered it just as if he were Cicero making it up as he went along, and there was never the faintest need for a prompt. When we met in the evening at the Balliol Gaudy he said to me 'I hear I used some words that were different from what you printed, and Pember said that mine were better,' and then went off into one of his glorious chuckles.

Grey was altogether happy in his relation to the three successive Vice-Chancellors with whom he was brought into official contact. The first of them was his old friend Doctor Pember. The University matters that chiefly interested him were the schemes for the Bodleian building, the foundation of the Oxford Society and the work of the Oxford Preservation Trust. 'Having regard to his grave physical disabilities,' writes Herbert Fisher, by that time Warden of New College, 'the measure of help which he was able to render in each of these three spheres of activity was a striking triumph of character over the tribulations of the flesh.' Indeed, he did not finally abandon the hope that he might give an address at the annual meeting of the Oxford Preservation Trust until the morning when he was stricken by the illness that proved to be fatal.

He was indeed deeply interested in the preservation of the beauty of Oxford and of its rural scenery that he had loved so well in his idle youth; and he had equally at heart the

AET. 70, 1932
Private photograph by Mr. Seton Gordon

rear-guard action waged on a wider front by the National Trust, in defence of the wounded beauty of all England. His connection with that body was so close that in 1924 a new post was specially created for him, that of Vice-President of the Trust, which has never been held except by him.[1]

His last speech in the House of Lords, on February 14, 1933, was not on politics, but was a plea for control of the emptying of ships' oil round our coasts, a practice most destructive of the birds that float on the waves. Previous speakers had spoken for the birds: he added a further argument:

> My Lords: I do not wish for a moment to minimize the terrible effect of oil pollution on bird life, which has been so forcibly put before your lordships. But there is one other aspect of the matter I would like to bring forward. One of the most famous tributes in our literature to our sea is that it performs its work of preventing the pollution of our shores.
>
> [The moving waters at their priestlike task
> Of pure ablution round earth's human shores.
> *Keats's Last Sonnet.*]
>
> Is all that to come to an end? Apart from what oil pollution does to birds, it is a horrible thought from our own point of view that our shores should be filthy. We are really proud of our sea, and rely upon the Government to take some action if possible to prevent it.

Another connection which he valued much in his last years was his part in the government of his old school. Doctor Williams, now Dean of Christ Church, was then Head Master of Winchester. He writes to me:

> Lord Grey was for some years a Fellow of Winchester College. He came pretty regularly to the meetings of the

[1] The President of the National Trust is Princess Louise, and there are a number of distinguished 'Honorary Vice-Presidents'; but there has never been, and perhaps never will be, any 'Vice-President' but Edward Grey.

Warden and Fellows, which were always on Saturdays, two or three times a term, and always at Winchester. He used to come generally on the Friday evening and travel North again on the Saturday night, staying for Friday night at the Warden's Lodgings.

I think he greatly enjoyed these meetings, and especially the opportunity they gave him of walking about Meads and the water-meadows and recalling old delights. He was a member of the trees sub-Committee and of course a valiant defender of our timber! He had much to do with the re-stocking and general improvement of the College fishing, and was once at least induced to talk to the College Fishing Club about his own fishing experiences: I remember how much he dwelt on the incidental joys they had brought him — the quiet watching of weather and water and all the creatures of the stream. I took him one morning to see a new plank bridge which we had thrown over the river to give quicker access to a new football ground, and he told me on the way home his regret that it had not been there in his own days: 'I should have had time for ten minutes more fishing every day'!

At the actual meetings of the Warden and Fellows he was always keen and interested about new projects: his judgment on these and all else was valued and enjoyed. It was clear to see that what he himself most enjoyed was anything that recalled his own experiences, and in details he was a great conservative. He was shocked, or pretended to be shocked, when he learned that Greek was no longer a compulsory subject, and one of his great desires was to restore the old names of the School Houses as he had known them: he had his way, and the names will gradually come back.

It needs no saying that Grey's visits brought happiness to all who met him. He was excellent company and often full of good stories. Two I remember: perhaps they are both old? One was of negotiations with Balkan statesmen, when after long and wearisome debates Grey at last made up his mind that he must show the iron hand: so next morning he came down to the conference room and said angrily: 'Ou signez ou allez!' (*sic*). The stupefied diplomats signed.

The other was of the Zoo (of which Grey often talked). An old lady watching a hippopotamus says to the keeper: 'Is it a male or a female?' 'I can't say that I know, ma'am: and perhaps it don't matter much to any but another hippopotamus.'

In the summer of 1933 his health, which had long been bad, gave way altogether, and those of us who saw him at his home that August felt him to be a dying man, though he could still stroll on the lawn and sit among the ducks. He had no long period of confinement indoors. On September 7 he died. His ashes were placed beside those of Dorothy under Fallodon trees.

The memorial service in Westminster Abbey, attended by a great crowd of rich and poor, all deeply moved, attested the sense of the nation's loss. In Embleton Church his Northumbrian neighbours gathered with a sense of sorrow yet more intimate; his friend Mr. Dawson preached:

> He meant far more to us than we can ever say, and to try to put into words what he was to us here is as impossible a task as it would be to a man to define the ties that bind him to his own stretch of countryside, its woodlands, its burns and its hills. This was his home. Here he was amongst his own people. We felt we understood him and he understood us. As one of our fishermen said to me lately, as together we discussed the bulletin on the gate, 'He belongs to us here.' For us who knew him and lived beside him and encountered him on our daily walks, he had the unmistakable qualities of greatness that a man, when he sees them, immediately recognizes and reveres.

What were those 'qualities of greatness' that men felt in his presence? I have heard more clever talkers, of more subtle mind, but never a more delightful stream of easy, masterly, humorous comment on the world and its odd ways. And the man was more than the words. Merely to be with him was a heartening experience, because there emanated from him a sense of power in repose, a strength of personality unequalled in any other man whom I have met: but it was quiet strength in unforced subjection to reason, formidable only to folly, and attuned to the kindly purposes of common life and welfare. His mind had high power of contemplation, in the poet's sense; but less of curiosity, except as a naturalist. Could this great reservoir of power, that seemed but half in use, have turned the mills of God with quicker pulse and to yet mightier purpose, if it had been impelled by a more inquisitive intellect or a more excitable temper? Or would that have been a mixture of incompatibles, fatal to the poised greatness of the man?

At the news of Edward Grey's death, men felt that something spacious and noble had gone out of life. He was not one of the world's supermen who initiate vast movements for good and as often for evil, and stamp their image on the time to come. The time that has come certainly does not bear his image. But it was not amiss to say, as many did say upon his death, that 'a great Englishman' was gone. For many troubled years, and at one terrible crisis, he had represented England at her best — her reasonableness, her justice, her desire for peace and friendship between all, and with that her determination not to be frightened into a submission or dazed into a tardiness that would allow one Power time to enslave the world. He was more complex in character than people knew, but in thought he was simple and in purpose direct and firm, and those are qualities which his countrymen usually understand better and value more than versatile cleverness and the artistry of change. They knew that he had served them for duty's sake, and that he had no personal motives and ambitions in politics, other than the sternly repressed desire to get out of them. For his heart was not in the streets or in the council-chambers but in the woods and beside the streams; and his books have taught many where and how the best joys of life in England are to be found. The two sides of his nature and of his achievement, the countryman-naturalist and the statesman, seemed separate and opposed, but they blended to make up Edward Grey; and in his last years the burden of blindness and personal sorrow, and of grief over the ways of the nations after the war, all of which he schooled himself to bear unembittered, perfected in gentleness his strong and patient spirit.

THE END

APPENDICES

I

Quotations from Grey's 'Fallodon Green Book'[1]

THE whole book of some one hundred and fifty large pages is in Grey's handwriting. The excerpts here given are typical of the whole. I have inserted a few explanatory words of my own in square brackets and italics. The first entry in the book was made in 1888, the last in 1906. It begins as follows:

The new pond was begun in the autumn of 1886 and filled early in the spring of 1887. Some yearling trout were put into it in May 1887, 200 into New Pond, 200 into Quarry [*a deserted quarry in a field near Fallodon full of clear water which Grey made a favourite fishing place*], and 50 into Old Pond.

List of ducks in 1888

One pair of Bean Geese.
" " " Ruddy Shieldrakes.
Two pairs Tufted Divers.
" " Pochards (Red Headed).
" " Wigeon.
" " Carolinas.
One pair of Mandarins.
" " " Pintails.
" " " Shovellers.
" " " Red billed Whistlers.
One White faced Whistler.
Three Teal (two drakes).
Three Spotted Bills (one drake bred in pond 1887 unpinioned, other two ducks one of them not quite pure).

[1] See pages 51 and 52 above.

1888. *March* 24 *to* 29. At Fallodon. Planted a number of trees in Old Wood and New Pond [*species given*].

April 2 *to* 7. At Fallodon. Wire fences [*fox-proof*] so as to include New Pond and shrubberies round it. A pair of Ruddy Shieldrakes were the first to go to it, and for a few days rigorously chased all the birds away. At last they got tired of mounting guard and Wigeon and other birds took advantage. This year several wild ducks have come to the pond. Dorothy and I watched a drake teal in full plumage one morning in April for some time. A golden eye, a pair of common Shieldrakes and a duck tufted diver have been seen by other people. The pintail laid a second time and reared two young ones, which died unaccountably when they were about three parts grown.

. . . .

1893. *April* 16. Yesterday the singing of birds was tremendous: the thrushes drown the blackbirds now: willow-wrens have come: there are several in the New Wood singing fairly well, but I have not heard or seen a blackcap.

May 28. Saturday and Sunday at home again — alone this time: D. stayed at Cottage. Hawthorn, lilac and laburnum in full flower; only one hawthorn in the Lands is a mass of it, but *it* is splendid; one can see nothing but flower on it. All the leaves are out and every tree is green except one or two old ashes, and even on them the green is showing at a distance. Over England generally there has been the greatest drought within living memory, lasting unbroken from beginning of March to middle of May; here there has been rain enough to start the grass, but people are complaining: the pond from heat and lack of fresh water has become foul and the trout have died in it. The young trees planted this season at the Quarry have suffered severely, but others planted a few years ago have made good growths already and look very well. Both my days here have been warm. I looked a little for nests and found, besides blackbirds and thrushes, one chaffinch, a willow-wren, a bullfinch and a wren: the wren has eggs in one of the nests which we found at Easter: I listened in vain in the favoured place for a wood wren; we haven't heard one on the Itchen either. Here there seem to be fewer chiff-chaffs and blackcaps than usual, though I have heard a few: willow wrens, on the other hand, seem even more numerous than ever; all day long their songs succeed each other. I came across more than one family of long tailed tits and one of golden crested wrens. Four great tits and one blue tit have nests in the boxes. A Gloire de Dijon on the porch is in full flower, some of its blooms even over. Already in the South the leaves are dull and it seems midsummer, strawberries, for instance, have been ripe and plentiful for a week; here the leaves are light and fresh, the days clearer and the smells sweeter: everything is more brisk and eager: as for garden produce, a fresh cauliflower, lettuces and radishes are the only things of the season. Now I go back to London, House of Commons and office, probably till the summer is over.

The unpinioned Carolina duck nested in a hole about the depth of a man's arm in an old broken elm nearly opposite the house on the Lands: it is about 30 feet from the ground: today I found her, outside the wire, with 6 birds about opposite the island of the old pond. I caught the young ones and put them over, the duck in great distress in the grass flapping round me: the next thing was to get her to join her brood over the fence, but she insisted on driving me away from the brood for about 150 yards before she would rise: then she flew to the new pond and then on to find them. Meanwhile, they scattered in the long grass: 4 of them she found and took over: the other two I rescued and carried in my hat and restored to her on the old pond. She had only six eggs, and hatched them all: I wish I had seen her bring the young ones down.

The Carolina paired with the Mandarin laid six eggs in a box under the deodar at the bottom of the garden and then deserted: they are under a hen, but I fear they will not hatch. The Chiloe Wigeon nested and her eggs are under a hen, but Henderson thinks they are bad.

The brood of Bahamas hatched by a hen died: the duck is sitting again.

There remain now one (or perhaps two) Carolinas, one wigeon, the Bahama, a Chili Pintail, the Chiloe wigeon, and hybrid Carolina-Mandarins to hatch or be hatched. I think our own Tufted will nest: her wing is clipped this year.

3 Japanese teal were bought in May: one is paired with my drake, but the other pair seem to have disappeared.

July 2. Came Saturday morning to go Sunday evening again. Rain wanted, but everything is green and refreshing after the brown burnt up grass of the South, where on the whole the drought has continued through June. We had our first basket of strawberries sent to London from here on June 22. They are at their best now. Raspberries just beginning: syringa passing away: honeysuckle coming in. D. is with me and we are both feeling the loss of a whole summer: it is expected that the Session will not end till the 3rd week of September. There are countless wasps' nests in the grass round the new pond and in the woods where the soil is loose. There are so many that it is difficult even to clear the grass away round the young trees. All but the quite newly planted trees are doing very well. Mr. Alcock's spruce in the old wood has a most astonishing leader. The old wood is a wonderful green tangle — full of willow wrens, which still sing, but very plaintively: we heard a garden warbler in it today: wrens sing from time to time, greenfinches twitter on, and just the note of a blackcap comes occasionally. Outside the wood the larks have it all their own way — the air is full of them.

. . . .

1894. *November* 4. After all the beeches have been a fine colour: they are very thin now: even most of the oaks have lost their green and the woods are in the very end of their autumn. The last ten days have been beech-mast time: numbers of squirrels are to be seen and some flocks of wood pigeons come every day to the beech clumps. But the most remarkable sight has been the bramble finches: all round the Lands from the cow-pasture gate to the bantam house there have been hundreds: it is splendid to have so many come to spend days here at this time, when there is no pressure of weather to force them, so that one can be sure that they come from choice and not from despair.

. . . .

1895. *January* 17. Bramble finches are still here in enormous quantities and at Howick it is the same. They swarmed into the ducks' feeding place in the hard weather and I caught one and could see clearly how the change to black in the head and neck may be caused simply by losing the edges of the feathers, not by changing the feathers themselves.

. . . .

February 1. I go to London tomorrow night for the session. For a week the ground has been covered with snow — about 6 inches fell and on Sat. and Sunday the trees were laden with it. . . . The birds have been very hard pressed: there were weak redwings a few days ago, but I see none now: weak fieldfares and a few exhausted missel thrushes are about. We have kept a constant supply of soaked dog biscuit and cocoa nuts in front of the library: more than twenty blackbirds, numbers of blue tits and some great tits have thriven well upon it and fed and quarrelled all day. There was one thrush, but he has gone; some starlings, chaffinches, a dunnock [*hedge sparrow*], about two sparrows, three robins and a few bramble finches are the only other birds that have come: except rooks, which we drove away for the sake of the others. There is no such thing as mercy in Nature, apart from Man: a well fed blackbird will drive away a starving new comer ruthlessly: distress may make birds too weak to fight, but there is no spark of pity or sympathy amongst them all. A sparrow hawk has made many attacks on this feeding place but they have been too quick for it.

. . . .

1896. *June* 2. D. found one golden crested wren's nest, but we could not get up to it: the birds were feeding. In one wren cock's nest, which I found at Easter, the bird was dead; it had apparently died quietly as it sat and looked quite undisturbed; this was simply touching, but there have been countless tragedies in other nests, whether it is weasels, or rats, or jackdaws hard pressed by the dry weather I cannot say, but countless young birds have been eaten out of nests. In one blackbird's nest close to the library the young birds I had been watching every day were eaten, and I found remains red and raw partly in the nest and partly hanging in the twigs: these have since been carried away, but today there is the clean picked body of a full grown thrush which has been taken to the nest and left in it after being picked. I think most of these things must happen in the early morning, for I neither see nor hear anything of the kind going on in the day nor late in the evening.

November 15. Yesterday there was a swallow over the kitchen garden: this is the latest that ever I saw. On the 3rd of November I saw a summer warbler in the creepers on the house and followed it to the bushes: it flitted about by fits and starts after the wailful autumn insects and in the intervals sat dozing in midday. The continuous bad weather of September and October may have prevented many of the summer birds from starting and have delayed them till they are too weak to travel.

December 30. It has been a broken autumn and winter for me, interrupted by many things and the seasons and days have passed by me little noticed. I have let myself be fretted and chafed always with little fragments of daily life and business and have been trivial unprofitable and internally blind and nearly dead. Now we are soon going to the West Indies.[1] We have had neither gales nor severe frost, nor snow here and today the temperature is 50°, with a warm wind and a low grey moving sky: and I see the winter outlook that is so well known, the pale green fields seen through bare brown trees. I love it all and wish I was going to stay in it quietly till the leaves come. A painless and sane old age in which to sit still and watch would be the greatest blessing of life: it seems too rare and great for me to hope for. I have seen little this winter: the two library window squirrels have become so tame that they will come into the room and take nuts and go about the floor close to us.

. . . .

1898. *December* 21. A very sad thing has happened. Our tame squirrel never came to be fed last Saturday, and we felt anxious about it: the next day it never came and we felt sure something was wrong and on Monday we found its mangled body on the garden path not far from the window. We think it has been killed by the others. It had been a daily pleasure to us for about two years and had become so tame that it would come right in to us to take its nuts, and the last time I saw it, it sat on my knee and eat its nuts one after the other. It was also very clever at opening the box in which we put nuts for it and went freely about the room. The male squirrel used to be kept away by this one, but he has known his way in for a long time and comes occasionally now: but he is a suspicious wild fellow, and hates us, and isn't clever with the box, like our dear dead one, though he can open it.

. . . .

1905. *April* 2. I had a good view of a woodcock one day in January, sitting at the foot of a larch in Ferny Hill; I watched it for some time within five yards before I put it up. Eight months are to pass now before we are here again; what changes will there be before then? I feel as if some were approaching.

1906. On the 1st of February Dorothy was thrown from her dogcart near Ellingham; she never was conscious afterwards and died in the schoolmaster's house between 3 and 4 on Sunday morning, two days and three nights afterwards. I am left alone, with no wish to live. Fallodon as it is today is what she made it; the planning and the taste is all hers. I cannot even keep it beautiful with-

[1] See pages 80 and 81 above.

out her. It is my wish presently to make a record of all that she did in the house and in the garden, in the hope that some day when I am gone the place may again belong to someone who will love it and be grateful to her. In the meantime I shall do what I can to keep it all as she left it and shall come here to rest and live in the happy past; if indeed I live 'for all my mind is clouded with a doubt.'

There is no further entry in the 'Fallodon Green Book.'

The duck breeding season, its successes and failures, was carefully recorded year after year. I append (on page 426) one of these lists for 1903 (not in Grey's handwriting).

Breeding Season, 1903

	Commenced	Eggs	Hatched	Date	Reared
Chili Pintail commenced sitting	March 21	5 Eggs	hatched 4 Birds	April 17	Reared 0
No I Red Crested Pochard commenced sitting	April 1	5 "	" 4 "	" 30	" 0
No II Red Crested " " "	" 5	6 "	" 2 "	May 4	Hybrid 1
Dusky Duck " "	" 10	9 "	" 8 "	" 8	Reared 6
No III Red Crested " "	" 11	8 "	" 1 "	" 10	" 0
No I Pintail, Eggs given to Mallard, commenced sitting	" 16	9 "	" 4 "	" 10	" 0
No I Red Headed Pochard	" 16	7 "	" 2 "	" 15	" 1
No II Red Headed Pochard	" 29	10 "	" 4 "	" 28	" 3
Wigeon	May 6	9 "	" 7 "	June 4	" 4
No I Carolina, No VI Barrell, commenced sitting	" 1	14 "	" 10 "	June 2 two of them Hybrids	" 10
No II Pintail, Eggs given to Chili Wigeon, commenced sitting	" 4	9 "	All bad		" 0
Rosey Bill, Eggs given to Hen, commenced sitting	" 9	9 "	hatched 8 Birds	June 5	" 4
No I Shoveller " "	" 10	10 "	" 10 "	" 2	" 4
No II Shoveller " "	" 11	11 "	" 6 "	" 5	" 1
No III Shoveller " "	" 13	8 "	" 5 "	" 6	" 0
Carolina, Eggs taken from Elm Tree, commenced sitting	" 13	8 "	" 5 "	" 12	" 4
Carolina in Middle Elm Tree	" 13	12 "	" 7 "	" 13	" 0
Carolina in No I Barrel	" 19	12 "	" 9 "	" 20	" 3
Bahama Eggs given to Hen	" 20	12 "	" 5 "	" 14	" 0
Brazilian Teal, Eggs given to Bantam	" 25	11 "	" 8 "	" 20	" 1
No I Pintail 2nd Brood, Eggs given to Mallard	" 25	8 "	" 7 "	" 18	" 2
No III Red Crested 2nd brood	" 30	7 "	left her Eggs		" 0
Tufted Pochard	June 15	7 "	hatched 6 Birds	July 13	" 2
Brazilian Teal 2nd brood	" 21	8 "	left her Eggs		" 0
Brazilian Teal (young Duck) Eggs given to Bantam	July 9	10 "	All bad		" 0
Carolina, 52 Eggs taken from Barrels and North Elm Tree and given to Hens			hatched 9 Birds	June 4	" 5
					Total 51

II

The 'Cottage Book'[1]

THESE are some entries taken from the Hampshire 'Cottage Book,' which was kept in MS. in a notebook from 1894 to 1905, and privately printed 1909. The printed volume has 137 pages.

Entries under E. are made by Edward Grey, under D. by Dorothy. The MS. notes in the margin, here reproduced as footnotes, were made at Grey's dictation in the last year of his life.

A friend wrote to Grey about the book, 'I love the way the book begins and ends. It's like a cloud which comes out of nothing in a summery hazy heaven and as softly disappears.' It begins as follows:

1894. *March* 3 *to* 5 (E.). A pair of long-tailed tits haunting the trees in front of the cottage.

March 17 *to* 19 (E.). The long-tailed tits busy building a nest high in the end lime tree.

April 7 *to* 9 (E.). Long-tailed tits look at their nest casually as if they partly wondered what it was. On Saturday I walked out from Winchester in the afternoon and saw wheatears, a redstart, a whinchat, and heard my first willow wren.

We heard two kingfishers making a great noise behind a willow blown up by the roots at the other side of the meadow opposite the cottage. On Monday, after I had gone to London, D. found the

[1] See page 55 above.

nest and saw small fish brought to the hole: she says that only one bird feeds and that the other watches. We found a thrush's nest with eggs and D. watched a chaffinch building by the Aquarium.[1] A hen chaffinch sings constantly in the poplars in front: its song begins like a chaffinch, but is quite distinct: less robust and finished and not the least like at the end: the bird is apparently paired and the cock seems to think that all is right. There is a great hum of bees in the willows. We saw and heard a cuckoo.

April 28 *to* 30 (E.). I came by the last train on Friday night the 27th, and walked out from Winchester, at midnight. It was warm and soft: I heard a nightingale, and one sedge warbler was singing within hearing of the road just where a piece of the river could be seen, light at the end of a little dark path. I walked with my hat off and once a little soft rain fell amongst my hair: there were great forms of leafy trees and a smell and spirit everywhere and I felt the soft country dust about my feet.

... A nightingale's song is the most wonderful, but the most imperfect, of songs. The long notes are divine, but they come seldom, and never go on long enough: the song continually breaks out with a burst, which promises a fine full spell, but it is always broken off in the most disappointing way. A blackcap's song, which comes next in quality, is short enough, but it seems finished in a way that no part of a nightingale's ever does, and one can't help thinking with some satisfaction of a good, steady old thrush singing right through from the beginning of February to the middle of June.

July 1 (E.). Two hot days. We have enjoyed both days immensely. When we arrived there was one wren singing most noticeably round the cottage; as I looked out it flew happily over the cottage from the poplars to the limes, singing as it passed over the roof: 'like a blessing' D. said when I told her. It sang nearly all day yesterday and today, always near us somewhere. Today as I was waking the first thing I was aware of was a blackcap's song: I knew of it for some time before I was properly awake: it too sang nearly all day close round us. Both these birds were still in full song, and it seemed as if they were a special gift to us — a parting one perhaps before all songs cease for the season. The woods are nearly silent, and it was very strange and sweet to have these two birds singing as loud and more constantly than any birds

[1] Name given to a part of the river where every trout was visible.

had been noticed to sing before. We sat out the whole day, till sunset, when we went for a walk in the meadows. D. planted some Test musk which F. Lubbock had sent her, and I bathed. The spotted flycatchers really have turned the old chaffinch nest into a spotted flycatcher's: there are four eggs and the bird is sitting, but flies off whenever we look round the corner.

1895. *May* 20 (D.). The same cold weather, 46. I lit the stove before lunch. Have not succeeded in finding a nightingale nest and felt very low about it. I was sitting on a tree root in a wet place watching wagtails when a stoat put its head out of a hole about two inches off my dress, hissed and made a noise like a loud harsh waterhen several times and then got quiet. I saw a blackbird chase a squirrel about twenty yards along the ground and then attack it as it corkscrewed up a large oak. It hit the squirrel several times. I could not see that the squirrel had an egg in its mouth. Three cuckoos flew about near me by the Aquarium; one of them I am nearly sure had an egg in its mouth and flew down in several places amongst the long grass, once close to the river. It was followed and worried by six little birds. I watched a robin fight. Two cocks kept at it for a long time and at last seemed to get their feet locked together. A very young thrush evidently thought that something was being fed, as it came rushing up to them and opened its mouth at them as they struggled. They went away laughing.

May 27 (D.). Splendid day, nice breeze, 70. I put a young whitethroat into the nest with the young cuckoo, which I think is about five days old. On Saturday it was white and red and today it is a sort of blue all over and looks horrid. I put the whitethroat onto its back and it at once stood up, leaning back with its wings spread and jerked slightly till it got the little bird onto the edge of the nest. I caught it and put it back at the bottom of the nest under the cuckoo who waited for a minute or two looking rather tired. Then it turned on its side and rubbed the little bird against the side of the nest till it got it squeezed onto its back, then it waited panting, then it straddled its legs out on each side, butted its head against the bottom of the nest, spread its wings backward and up and stood jerking for some time till it got the young bird over the edge, its head right down all the time. It stood in the same position for quite a long time to make sure that the bird was really out, and then fell down in a heap at the bottom of the nest quite exhausted. It could not have stood up without using its head as a lever.

June 9 (E.). The last day of our holiday: it has been bright and hot, up to 77, and nearly still. We went a walk to Ovington and above it by the river path in the still warm evening and fell in with a strange, but friendly, cat on the furthest bridge above Ovington. The last songs of birds are to be heard, but the blackbirds are failing fast and the thrushes sing humbly hidden amongst the dense leaves. All the vigour, almost the egotism of their spring manner is gone, when they sing by the hour from a foremost place on a bare tree. Another pair of spotted flycatchers have come to our garden railing and are doing up the old nest in which one brood of chaffinches and another of spotted flycatchers were reared last year. The first pair have three young birds, and the cock, who paid no attention when they were first hatched, now feeds them constantly. The hen bird often sits on them after feeding, to cherish them apparently, which seems very thoughtful and touching. Rain is badly wanted. The warm days and hot sun have made a clump of poppies in our garden come out passionately. Tonight it is so warm that we cannot give up going out and get to bed. While we were under the limes in the dark a beautiful little light glowed on Dorothy's arm. We brought it in and found a little black winged creature.

June 22 *and* 23 (E.). The Gov^{t} were beaten on Friday night, and we have spent these days in high hopes of an announcement on Monday, which will bring the end of this terrible time within sight.[1]

June 30 (*Sunday*) (E.). I came on Thursday afternoon: the Gov^{t} have resigned. I shall never be in office again and the days of my stay in the House of Commons are probably numbered.

1896. *March* 7 *to* 9 (E.). We came on Saturday morning: it is more than eight months since we were here, but hardly anything has changed: there is one new gate near us and a new fastening on another one and a new bridge in the water meadows: that is about all. But changes have happened to us: I am out of office, though not free of politics: and we have learnt to ride bicycles and brought them with us meaning to get out at Alton and ride them here: a

[1] During 1893–94–95 I had been in office as Under-Secretary for Foreign Affairs. During all this time our interest and pleasure in country things had been taking stronger and surer hold of us, I had become increasingly miserable at the tie to London and the curtailment of the time in the country, and the words 'terrible time' simply mean being in office.

reckless and hard-hearted innovation, which was stopped by the weather. We were prepared to rush into this dear place on bicycles for the first time in a way which I now see was inconsiderate and wanting in reverence to a place which has kept itself so unchanged for us. The rain obliged us to come by train in the usual way and to walk the bicycles humbly and thoughtfully down: they have remained unused since, and out of sight, and great as is the part they will play in our times here, they will begin slowly.

1897. *May* 23 (E.). I went in my waders to examine the kingfisher's place: one of them flew out close to me and I found one of the holes very dirty and could hear the young birds inside very distinctly. A pair of blue-tits are carrying the moss away from the blackbird's nest on the cottage to the top of one of the poplars. I watched them as I was sitting out, and saw the spotted flycatchers going to what I believe they have chosen for a nest, and a queen wasp getting wood off the trellis for her nest: it was the noise of the wasp sawing the wood that first made me notice her.

1899. *June* 25 (*Sunday*) (E.). I protest that D. might write more than she does in this book: I am sure Elizabeth [1] would.

Could anyone do a more summery thing than to lie in the middle of a mass of yellow ladies' slipper and listen to the bees in it? At any rate, that is what I did this afternoon. It wasn't quite perfect because the sun was not out, and the scent of ladies' slipper needs the sun to bring it out. For a moment I felt like a senseless field beast for lying down in such flowers and crushing them, but my doing so was a very proper tribute to the profusion of nature. In a garden where flowers are grown by the square foot it would have been a crime, but to the north of Itchen wood nature gives ladies' slipper by the acre. So I lay in it and put my eyes level with the flowers and listened to the bees.

1902. *May* 22 (*a Thursday*) (E.). I hardly dare to write anything about birds; I am so overshadowed by D. I went with her on Tuesday to be shown the stone curlew's eggs — we spied and stalked and crept and saw a stone curlew standing by a ragged lonely whin bush on the down, like a sentinel. As we got nearer it trotted off with the step of a ghost in the evening light, passed the nest and disappeared. In the nest we found one egg and one young bird hatched since the day before, which lay flat and uttered. Both the egg and the bird are coloured to match chalk flints that

[1] Probably a reference to 'Elizabeth and her German Garden.'

have been a long time amongst mole heaps. We daren't touch the bird or the egg and came away excited. After this how should the same book notice such things as that a pair of chaffinches come into our room for bread and that the hen feeds the young with it, or that there are robins' eggs in the alcove nest, of which the foundation and outside is blackbird — the middle wagtail — and the inside and top now robin-built; but these things are also true.

June 1 (*Sunday*) (E.). A warm day ending with rain, which stopped in time for us to have tea out; while we were at tea the white owl flew past hunting our side of cottage meadow and in a minute or two came back to the old walnut with an animal, which it eat on a branch; it took a long time to finish but we could not see its manners distinctly, because of the ivy, and we daren't move for fear of disturbing it. About nine o'clock in the evening we heard the Cathedral bells faintly in the distance, then presently a small cheer in Itchen Abbas, then the Itchen Abbas bells began and soon afterwards Avington bells; there were big guns in the direction of Portsmouth, and it is clear that some excitement is about. We suppose it to be the news of peace.[1]

1903. *November* 27 (E.). The water rail has shown itself to us at last, it made its noise and flew out from the reeds afterwards one day when we were on the bridge: it has been a great relief to us to know that this noise does belong to a water rail.

1904. *November* 23 (D.). Great sadness seems to have fallen over all this Itchen country since Lord Northbrook died last week. Nothing will ever be quite the same as it was. He was the reason of our having come here, and his kindness made a shelter for us.

1905. *November* 20 (E.). It is not known why our book has been so much neglected. I haven't had many days here, only week ends, but there have been a lot of these and D. has been here continually. Perhaps we are too well and strong to be properly grateful. The weather has been of all sorts and therefore good. The colour of beeches was destroyed by frost in October, but elms and oaks, especially the big elm road that crosses the big lime avenue have coloured well and the reeds are brown and feathery. Mice have worked horrors in the garden and there are rats, which we almost like for not being mice and being as we hope against mice. Our own spinks [*chaffinches*] are away, but our own thrush and dunnocks come to bread, and so do starlings, which we hope are the

[1] After the South African War.

ones reared every year in the poplar hole. Our own lime avenue has had a yaffle every day.

In August 1903 Grey wrote to Mrs. Creighton, who had the rare privilege of being sometimes the tenant (always solitary) of the Cottage:

> I never told you about the rent of the Itchen Cottage. It is paid to the birds in the form of bread, which is put on the grass in front of the glass door of the sitting room. There should be 2 blackbirds (a pair), 2 pair of chaffinches, a pair of pied wagtails (the male has an injured leg), one young robin and sometimes a pair of dunnocks, which are all more or less tame and need to be fed.

And in August 1906 he writes to her during another of her tenancies:

> Cottage book is put in the shelves next to [Hudson's] 'Hampshire Days.' There is very likely a bird's nest in the stove chimney which you must remove — you will find out when you light the stove!

The following letter to Dorothy, written on one of the rare occasions when he was down there without her, shows his peculiar feeling for the place:

> *August* 14, 1901. It's one o'clock and I have just got here and I feel as if my heart was too full and might burst; the place is so sacred. I move about it in the most touching way. I feel as if I must keep coming in every half hour to write to you. I have been on the bridge and eaten my figs on it and thrown the stalks into the river. I can hardly breathe for the sacredness of the place. It is very strange that you aren't here; stranger than I thought, but I suppose it wouldn't be so strange to you, as I am so often away. What wonderful days you must have here without me!

INDEX

GOSHEN COLLEGE LIBRARY GOSHEN, INDIANA

DA566.9.G8 T7
c.1
Trevelyan, George a
100105 000
Grey of Fallodon, life and
3 9310 00009895 2
GOSHEN COLLEGE-GOOD LIBRARY